DEVELOPING STRATEGIES FOR CHANGE

JOHN DARWIN

PHIL JOHNSON

JOHN McAULEY

FINANCIAL TIMES
Prentice Hall

An imprint of **Pearson Education**

Harlow, England · London · New York · Reading, Massachusetts · San Francisco · Toronto · Don Mills, Ontario · Sydney
Tokyo · Singapore · Hong Kong · Seoul · Taipei · Cape Town · Madrid · Mexico City · Amsterdam · Munich · Paris · Milan

Pearson Education Limited
Edinburgh Gate
Harlow
Essex CM20 2JE
England

and Associated Companies throughout the world

Visit us on the World Wide Web at:
www.pearsoneduc.com

First published 2002

© Pearson Education Limited 2002

ISBN 0 273 64675 3

British Library Cataloguing-in-Publication Data
A catalogue record for this book can be obtained from the British Library

Library of Congress Cataloging-in-Publication Data
A catalog record for this book can be obtained from the Library of Congress

10 9 8 7 6 5 4 3 2 1
06 05 04 03 02

Typeset by 3
Printed in Great Britain by Ashford Colour Press Ltd, Gosport

Contents

Acknowledgements

The three authors would like to thank our friends and colleagues who have consciously or inadvertently contributed to our understanding of strategy and change. We would particularly like to thank Paul Close, Paul Stokes, Ken Smith, Cathy Cassell, Joanne Duberley, Jim Bryant and Ruth Sacks, all of whom were kind enough to read early drafts, or shared in discussions, and gave much helpful feedback as the work developed. We would also like to thank students from the Doctor in Business Administration, the Masters in Business Administration and the Masters in Organisation Development programmes at Sheffield Hallam University for their many contributions to the development of our thinking.

PUBLISHER'S ACKNOWLEDGEMENTS

We are grateful to the following for permission to reproduce copyright material:

Figure 2.1 adapted with permission from The Open University and MESOL, from *Culture and Innovation. Book 5: Health and Social Services Management: Managing your Enterprise* by M.J. McAuley and P. Shanahan, copyright © 1994; Vignette 10.1, cited with permission of H.J. Heinz Company Limited, excerpt from statement to shareholders of H.J. Heinz Company for fiscal year ended 3 May 2000. Table 11.3 reproduced with permission from The Open University Press, from *Action Research for Health and Social Care: A Guide to Practice*, 1995.

While every effort has been made to trace the owners of copyright material, in a few cases this has proved impossible and we take this opportunity to offer apologies to any copyright holders whose rights we may have unwittingly infringed.

INTRODUCTION

The underlying rationale for this book is to develop a critical and radical under-standing of core debates in strategy and change. It is a central theme that this relationship is shaped by members' understanding of their organisations and such issues as strategy and change. This provides a rationale for our discussion of mindsets, subjectivity and the development of reflexivity as core issues. We shall explore the view that both strategy and attempts to manage change may be chimeras which present an illusion of control over a precarious world. This is a challenging, and ultimately satisfying, view of complexity, turbulence and the sorts of approach required of the manager that goes beyond rationalist recipes in developing strategy and managing change. These themes are expressed in the three parts that make up this volume. In the following sections we indicate how these themes are played out.

Part 1: Issues in strategy and change. In Chapter 1 we set the scene by explor-ing the rationalist approach to strategy and change. Writing about management and strategy has primarily been a twentieth-century phenomenon. The Modern Paradigm in management derives many of its elements directly from the Cartesian–Newtonian synthesis of which crisp logic and thinking based on 'either/or' is an essential element. This paradigm incorporates an epistemology and scientific method that are considered the basis of 'sound knowledge'. This provides a belief system which managers can adopt. The Modern Paradigm remains so strong that it continues to be a fundamental determinant of man-agement and organisational activity. Over the years partial alternatives to the rational approach have been offered. Perhaps the best known is the emergent process approach, advocated by Mintzberg. Another modification has been the 'human relations' perspective. Springing from this, Human Resource Management appears as another means of control, albeit more subtle and 'humanised' than the rational approach. Other added or altered dimensions include open systems theory and the contingency approach.

Relativity theory and quantum theory challenged the principal concepts of the Cartesian worldview and Newtonian mechanics. They do not negate the value and use of the Modern Paradigm. Rather, they help us to a richer way of thinking and acting in management, strategy and organisational development. They have implications also for management, since they challenge many of the approaches and ideas that rely on the belief that there can be a single perspective and a single concept of rationality. This theme informs many of the chapters of the book.

Some of these issues are taken up in Chapter 2. We explore the idea of organisational culture as it has been developed from a number of different perspectives. We start with the realist position. For most realists, culture is treated as functional and an organisational subsystem. This position is characteristically aligned to notions that culture change can be managed. Within the image of corporate culture there is an understanding that it is both possible and desirable to develop an overarching, unifying culture. The view that organisational culture may be seen as a form of domination points to core issues in the ways in which it can be seen as underpinning processes of strategic change.

There are, however, a number of ways in which understanding organisational culture may be seen as problematic. There is an emergent view that suggests that too much attention to the concept of corporate culture or organisational culture is dangerous. In this chapter we develop a more reflexive approach.

Issues of culture are linked with the issues we consider in Chapter 3 in which we explore the concept of the organisation mindset and the organisation paradigm. Mindsets seem to operate at two levels – a surface level in which the mindset can be easily accessed, and a deeper level that involves an understanding of unconscious and preconscious elements. It is the part of the mindset that operates at the preconscious and unconscious levels that is concerned with core issues of organisational fantasy, the sorts of inner meaning that members make of the organisation and their creation of organisational reality. At a deeper level what is at play are competing mindsets in relation to any major change process. In this chapter ideologies, archetypes and communities of practice are regarded as coterminous with the concept of the mindset.

We suggest two key themes that may (unless they become mere techniques) represent a radically new understanding of the management mindset. We look at the development of emotional and spiritual understanding in the management of change. In order to achieve integration of the personal mindset into engagement in the organisation attention must be paid to the emotional and spiritual elements. It is suggested that the development of emotional intelligence is related to the concept of emotional capability. These themes link with issues of reflexivity and Critical Theory, which are considered in later chapters.

Part 2: New approaches to change and power. In Chapter 4 we explore a core dynamic in the management of change. We look at conceptualisations of management power in strategies for change. Understanding this issue can be notoriously difficult, not least because many managers seem reluctant to admit to exercising power. Nevertheless it may be argued that managers need to understand how power operates in order to be able to intervene and change organisations. A common notion underlying much strategy writing is that the exercise of power is something that benefits the whole membership of an organisation. From this unitary perspective, power as a concept is rarely mentioned. Managerial ideology serves to obfuscate the exercise of power from those who suffer its consequences.

From a different perspective – the pluralist – power is the medium through which conflicts of interest are resolved as different groups and individuals secure and mobilise different power resources in their pursuit of sectional interests. Other pluralists concentrate on how the distribution of power resources within an organisation can vary over time. We then move onto a consideration of radical approaches to power. This perspective is grounded in the assumption that society and its institutions are in a state of confrontation between fundamentally opposed and irreconcilable, class-based vested interests. In this view power is an unequally distributed phenomenon. It is argued that the material and symbolic power of owners and management far outweighs that of labour.

In this chapter we show how the epistemological problems encountered by the radical perspectives on power have lent impetus to the development of a postmodern stance. This problematises radical concerns with emancipation of the oppressed. This has close links with the consideration of the significance of Critical Theory in understanding issues of change. Here, the development of reflexivity as part of organisational capability is seen as a crucial element in the management of change.

There has, in recent years, been a growing interest in Critical Theory as an approach to developing a new understanding of organisations. In Chapter 5 we look at the ways in which Critical Theory (CT) can help develop a new understanding of issues of change. By pursuing an ontologically realist version of social constructivism, CT undermines the epistemological authority of management and demands consideration of the social processes which underpin and legitimise any knowledge claim. A fundamental aspect of CT is the development of self-knowledge and understanding generated through self-reflection. Self-reflection demystifies previously unacknowledged distortions and enables awareness of the link between knowledge and interest.

The aim of CT is to understand how management practices, such as strategy and change, are developed and legitimised within the shifting terrain of asymmetrical power relations. It does this by exposing the creative role of underlying social values, partial interests and power relations in producing those practices. CT research attempts to provide an account of the socially constructed knowledge and meanings which actors deploy in making sense of organisational reality – whether they are management theorists, practitioners or employees. CT aims to be emancipatory by enabling the analysis of organisational communities' varying taken-for-granted social constructions of reality which express their different practices, interests and motives. However, CT's programme for strategy and change is not without its problems and contradictions.

In Chapter 6 we aim to establish the differences between Critical Theory and postmodernism. We also seek to illustrate the implications of postmodernism for our understanding of strategies for change in terms of the deconstruction of texts, genealogy and the powerful truth-effects of narratives/discourses. Rather than viewing strategy as a resource for analysing and changing organisations, postmodern analysis treats strategy as a phenomenon for critical examination by focusing attention on how it constitutes, and is constituted by, social relations. Any strategic knowledge as such is seen as the outcome of a distinct discourse with its own mode of engagement constituted by its own rules, structures and epistemic criteria: a social product that produces social relations.

Postmodernists do not claim to produce truths about strategy. They see truth as a subjective outcome or effect of the social relationships that underlie strategic discourses and narratives. The individual is thereby constituted through exposure to historically and socially contingent discourses: through learning to speak a discourse, the discourse speaks to the individual by structuring his/her experiences and definitions of who he/she is. People within organisations may be differentiated according to their participation in a discourse that shapes their subjectivity. For instance, those groups who accept and deploy strategic discourses enjoy an aura of expertise and material privilege within organisational hierarchies, while those who are unable, or unwilling, to deploy that discourse lose status. There may be a vertical power order within a discourse, but the point is that there are always multiple discourses at play.

When we teach strategic management and change, a frequent response from managers is that they are comfortable with the rational planning approach, which they find straightforward. What does complexity theory offer to take us beyond this? The ideas discussed in Chapter 7 provide a framework for a coherent and fruitful approach to strategic management, and can be used in discussion with people when advocating the value of this approach. We explore the contribution that complexity theory can make to the management of change. We aim to identify key principles emerging from complexity theory, and relate these to logic and language, leading in turn to consideration of the use of metaphor, paradox and dialogue in management. This debate links to discussions about the role of power in and between organisations, which we discussed in Chapter 4. This chapter also explores the ways in which complexity theory draws upon both Critical Theory and postmodernism to offer rich and useful approaches to change management and organisational development.

In part the interest in complexity theory in management has arisen from disillusion with planning systems that seek to predict the future. The argument in complexity theory that systems are never in equilibrium has been one that has attracted interest. In contrast to the reductive approach of traditional strategic planning, complexity theory takes emergence seriously. Complex adaptive systems are learning systems, and it may be argued that learning is more likely in Pluralist and Open arenas.

We also take the challenge to binary thinking a stage further, by considering crisp and fuzzy logic. Crisp, two-valued logic facilitates a rigid perspective – the crisp boundary between organisation and environment, the neat categorisation of events and circumstances. We can replace 'crisp' boundaries within and between organisations with fuzzy ones. There is an important link between fuzzy logic and complexity theory, in which the 'high tension' of the boundary between order and chaos is considered the most creative arena. To date there have been few attempts to employ this approach in management theory but we believe that there is considerable richness in it.

Part 3: Linking change to current themes. The discussion of complexity leads to a consideration of issues of change and the design of organisations in Chapter 8. In this chapter we explore the significance of debates about organisational design. With the growth of the concept of organisation knowledge producers, there has been a movement away from organisations designed as task-oriented to organisations that are process-oriented. In such a setting management decision-making becomes subjective; organisation design needs to acknowledge that decisions made by members are the best that can be done in the circumstances.

In order to set the context for this chapter we look at two key prescriptive approaches to design which have pervaded management thinking in recent years. There is an exploration of delayering as part of a design strategy used by many organisations as rhetoric to restructure or re-engineer in order to become more effective. The second approach to design is downsizing. We show how this prescriptive approach to design has moved from fashion to strategic imperative only to assume a problematic status.

In this chapter, we take a realist perspective on the modernist/postmodernist debate. We suggest that we can regard both modernism and postmodernism as practical narratives about particular forms of organisation and we show how appropriate mixes of these narratives can produce new and innovative organisational designs that are fitted to their purpose. A key issue in this chapter is that design issues require careful and reflective crafting rather than a reliance on straightforward recipes and prescriptions. This is related to an underpinning theme of this book, which is to develop an understanding of the mindset and the development of the habits of reflexivity as part and parcel of the stock of knowledge of organisational members.

If Chapter 8 is concerned with the essentially internal affairs of design, Chapter 9 is concerned with the exploration of the essentially fuzzy interrelationship between an organisation and its environment. We consider the way in which a significant part of the organisational environment is the presence of *other* organisations. We explore the use of ecological themes as metaphor, and relate these to wider ecological themes. This is a topic of importance in understanding issues of change since attention to the environment has become part of an overall approach to risk management that many organisations pursue.

In this chapter we also look at the relationship between the organisation and the natural environment. We suggest that the response to the environment (and, as symbol, national and international legislation) occurs at a number of different levels. At Level I, organisations are completely reactive. In this state they are absolutely unresponsive and reactive to environmental initiatives. Levels II and III are intermediary stages. Level IV is that of integration where the organisation's environmental values, attitudes, beliefs and culture exhibit total support for the environment. The movement from Level I to Level IV is essentially concerned with the shift from a mindset that looks at the world as an object out there for which the organisation has no responsibility. Indeed the pervading mindset in Level I is that the organisation is nothing but a cork tossed hither and thither by the vicissitudes of fate. This contrasts with the mindset at Level IV, which is holistic, where thinking about, and acting within, the environment and the ecology are tightly integrated with the organisation's very purpose. This links with the core themes of Critical Theory and the development of reflexivity in understanding the self and the organisation and the organisation's relationship to its environment.

Part 4: How does it all happen? A key feature of modernist approaches to the management of change is that there are varieties of strategic mixes that underpin the mindset of decision-makers and approaches to the management of change. The process by which these prescriptive approaches to change operate is considered in Chapter 10. We then develop an understanding of approaches to change that represent alternatives to the strategic recipe. We ask: can there be approaches to change that are recipe-free, or are all approaches some way or another a 'strategic recipe'? We then suggest that it is possible to develop subtlety in the use of strategic recipes, prescriptive approaches to change, through the processes of organisational reflexivity.

We look at four dominant approaches to the process whereby issues of change may be aligned to the dominant strategic mindset, or recipe, within the organisation. These range from an approach that is geared to the maximisation of shareholder interest to models of strategy that emanate from the subjective, local knowledge of organisational members. We suggest that all the approaches to strategy have their strengths and limitations.

We propose that whatever recipe is adopted, issues of implementation and change management hinge on the extent to which there is deep, reflexive understanding of the nature of the recipe, or approach, as well as of its implications.

In Chapter 11 we look at two philosophically interlinked approaches to change: Action Research and Whole Systems Events. These take us beyond many of the essentially recipe-driven approaches to change that were considered in Chapter 10 although these approaches represent a practical outcome of what we call the subjective approach to strategy and change.

We look at the various forms of Action Research, but in particular focus attention on ways in which it has embedded within it a scientific approach, systematic enquiry and processes that encourage self-reflection. We then turn to consider Action Learning, which has a different parentage from Action Research. As with Action Research, several approaches have been identified. The relationship between Action Research and Action Learning is not often discussed. We suggest that there is a clear distinction.

These two approaches are placed into the context of the Whole Systems Event.

Typically this event brings together a large number of people for two to three days. Together they undertake a series of structured cumulative tasks. There are a number of minimum requirements, linked to core values. We suggest that the Whole Systems Event offers a viable approach to change management. The event is not 'top-down' in the way that so much strategic planning is. Nor is it simply consultative in the way that logical incrementalism can be. Participation of a wide range of people is possible: the democratic ideals drawn from Critical Theory (as described in Chapter 5) are present. The link between thinking and doing is emphasised throughout. This encourages reflexivity. As far as possible existing power structures are 'suspended'. This means that members have the potential to speak with a notion of equality of discourse. Finally, there is the challenge to control. In the Whole Systems Event the structure provides an order within which there is chaos: what happens within the process, and what the outcome will be, are neither controlled nor predicted. This optimises the opportunities for creativity.

In the final chapter we explore a persistent theme, which has emerged during the writing of this book. This is the need for reflexivity on the part of management researchers and practitioners during their engagements with organisations and change-management processes. We bring together many of the themes of the book in an exploration of how they relate to different forms of reflexivity, as well as the need on the part of the change agent to develop a full understanding of situations, others and the self.

This book was a collaborative endeavour. However, John Darwin was primarily responsible for Chapters 1, 7, 9 and 11. Phil Johnson was primarily responsible for Chapters 4, 5 and 6. John McAuley was primarily responsible for Chapters 2, 3, 8 and 10.

Part 1

ISSUES IN STRATEGY AND CHANGE

Chapter 1

THE RATIONALIST APPROACH TO STRATEGY AND CHANGE

The aims of this chapter are to:

1 Explore the 'modernist approach' in management thinking and practice.

2 Explore the origin of this approach in scientific thinking.

3 Explore the way that scientific thinking has developed.

4 Explore the limits to management and organisational activity based on this approach.

INTRODUCTION

Writing about management and strategy has primarily been a twentieth-century phenomenon. But is it based on eighteenth-century thinking? Keynes once argued that:

> The ideas of economists and political philosophers, both when they are right and when they are wrong, are more powerful than is commonly understood. Indeed the world is ruled by little else. Practical men, who believe themselves to be quite exempt from any intellectual influences, are usually the slaves of some defunct economist. (1936: 383)

Are managers in practice the slaves, not only of defunct economists, but also of defunct scientists and philosophers? And now that we are in the twenty-first century, is it time to take a critical stance?

In a perceptive analysis of management thinking Eccles et al. (1992) identified many buzzwords in strategy. A brief, updated listing of those that have been significant over the past decade includes the following: Globalisation; Core competence; Dynamic capability; Strategic alliances; Joint ventures, partnerships and networks; Total quality management; Customer-focused; Customer-driven; Partnering and supply chain management; Knowledge management; the knowledge economy; Downsizing, Delayering, Rightsizing, Flattening; Business Process Re-engineering; Empowerment.

They also argue – and we shall return to this point – that most, if not all, currently fashionable ideas are reinventions: old wine in new bottles, with packaging and presentation the critical factors. Here we take the same starting point, but will reach a conclusion that deepens that of Eccles and colleagues, in part by exploring the implications of Keynes' proposition for management theory and practice. We wish to suggest that this theory and practice have been dominated by an amalgam of ideas taken primarily from economics and the philosophy of science. These constitute a sort of paradigm – here called the Modern Paradigm – which in turn has its roots in the Cartesian–Newtonian synthesis which came to prominence several centuries ago.

We shall argue that the pure form of the Modern Paradigm was shown long ago to be untenable (as indeed was the Cartesian–Newtonian), and it has been widely critiqued in the management literature. Over the years this pure form has been softened and extended; it has been interwoven with what Gergen (1992: 208–10) has described as the 'romantic dimensions of organisational life', and a modified version developed which can fairly be considered as dominant in current management thinking. The 'public performance' of this is to be found in plans and the analytical approach to strategy and change, in which managers identify concerns and, through a process of rational choice, develop solutions for implementation (usually by others). In addition to this public manifestation, there is also a covert element. This is the mindset that places a premium on rational, linear, logical, 'scientific' approaches to management, and this persists despite the frequent critiques levelled against 'strategic planning' (for example by Mintzberg 1994; Mintzberg et al. 1998; see also Eccles and Nohria 1992).

Underpinning the argument are four themes. First, managers share with many others the need to be – and be seen to be – rational. We are all aware of the 'back-stage activity' which plays a crucial role in the development and implementation of strategy – power, politics and organisational process. But the 'public perform-ance' is rational – the argument that takes place in meetings and committees, the documents that are proposed to justify positions. As Grint argues, a convention of Western thought since the Enlightenment has been that rationality is the means by which individuals are persuaded to execute decisions made by others, or to change their opinion, attitude or behaviour (1995: 114). However, our con-ventional concept of what it is to be rational is rather limited. This is not a plea for adding 'right brain' to 'left brain' thinking, or for the importance of 'intu-ition'; rather, the suggestion is that we rethink what it is to be rational.

Second, in recent years dynamic capability has become a central concern of strategy, and one of the most important capabilities is the way the organisation's management thinks. The individual mindset of the manager determines how she or he reacts to new issues, shapes and understands the environment, and acts. As information and knowledge become the most important assets an organisation has, outstretching the traditional resources of land, labour and cap-ital, the collective mindset – organisational intelligence – also becomes ever more important. If, therefore, management thinking is based on outdated con-cepts, it may itself be outdated and inadequate, with damaging implications for the success of the organisation. We explore the concepts of the individual and organisational mindset in more detail in Chapter 3.

This is one of the major current debates in strategic management: the contrast between the 'competitive forces' approach to strategy and the 'resource-based' and 'dynamic capability' approach. Here we lean towards the latter, but this is not a matter of accepting one and rejecting the other, which would be to accept a crisp divide between organisation and environment. Rather, the argument will be that the former is subsumed in the latter. We argue that the organisation's analysis of its environment is itself part of the organisation's core dynamic capability, which is its intelligence, and that managers need to take account of the way in which the organisation creates its environment, and the environment creates the organisation.

It is useful to begin by summarising the resource and capability approach. This involves:

- Identifying the resources the organisation has – both tangible and intangible.
- Ensuring that these resources are not wasted through inappropriate use.
- Identifying ways of improving the tangible resources.
- Turning the intangible resources into capabilities – the capacity to deliver.
- Developing and sustaining an integration between these capabilities so that they genuinely become organisationally based.

The distinction between this and the competitive forces approach has been summarised by Teece et al. (1992), who describe the latter approach as involving three stages. First, pick an industry (based on its 'structural attractiveness'); then choose an entry strategy based on conjectures about competitors' rational strategies; and finally, if not already possessed, acquire or otherwise obtain the requisite capabilities to compete in the market.

By contrast, they see the 'resources perspective' leading to this process of strategic formulation: first, identify your firm's unique resources; second, decide in which markets those resources can earn the highest rents; and third, decide whether the rents from those assets are most effectively utilised by (a) integrating into related market(s), (b) selling the relevant intermediate output to related firms, or (c) selling the assets themselves to a firm in related businesses. Teece et al. extend this to their concept of the dynamic capabilities approach, which is not dissimilar to the approach described above.

Resources are limited. Like the traditional resources of land, labour and capital, the intangible resources of knowledge and information can be expanded and enhanced through use; but they can be shared without losing them. More and more, these are the basis for capability in the organisation. The competencies include knowledge, skill, experience, organisation and culture, communication and work across boundaries. Normann and Ramfrez (1993) argue that successful companies do not just add value, they reinvent it.

The emphasis on knowledge as one of the central assets of an organisation is developed further below, since knowledge is viewed here as an element of the wider concept of intelligence. As the first step in this, we can relate the capability approach to the debate about 'management mindsets'. Prahalad and Bettis have set out an approach to the latter in two papers on 'The Dominant Logic'. In the first (1986), they argue that few organisational events are approached by managers as totally unique and requiring systematic study. Instead, they are processed through pre-existing knowledge systems. They define a dominant general management logic as the way in which managers conceptualise the business and make critical resource allocation decisions: this is stored via schemata and hence can be thought of as a structure. As part of their supporting evidence, they point to the work of Allison (1971) on the significance of alternative frameworks in the context of analysing government actions during the Cuban missile crisis.

In their second paper, Bettis and Prahalad (1995) extend their discussion. They relate it first to the vast quantity of information available to managers thanks to information technology. While these data should make the task of sensing change and responding to it effectively considerably easier, what is found instead are information-rich but interpretation-poor systems. Thus we have systems that seem to confuse raw information or data with appropriate actionable knowledge. (It is worth noting at this stage that part of the subsequent argument will be that it is important also to avoid conflating information with data.)

They conclude that the dominant logic can be seen as an information filter. Organisational attention is focused on data deemed relevant by the dominant logic, and is filtered by this logic, as well as by the analytic procedures managers use to aid strategy development. The 'filtered' data are then incorporated into the strategy, systems, values, expectations and reinforced behaviour of the organisation. The dominant logic thus puts constraints on the ability of the organisation to learn, and is a primary determinant of organisational intelligence.

Bettis and Prahalad also usefully link their concept of dominant logic to the concept of complex adaptive systems, which will be explored later. They see the dominant logic as an adaptive emergent property of complex organisation.

The third underpinning argument is that, despite the fact that management literature is young (relative at least to other disciplines), there is a remarkable amount of 'old wine in new bottles'. Eccles et al. (1992) trace the origins of many currently fashionable ideas in work stretching back to Mary Parker Follett in the 1920s. Table 1.1 extends this analysis. (Those who would like to join the enterprise might care to try the Management Fad Generator outlined in Figure 1.1, updated from Darwin 1996.)

Table 1.1 Old wine in new bottles

Horizontal authority	1926
Promoting organisational knowledge	1926
Network organisations	1931
Postindustrialism	1946
Decentralisation	1946
Continuous innovation	1956
Turbulent changes	1950s
Core competence	1957
Temporary task forces	1965
The new organisation	1965
Self-management	1965

Why leave it to the gurus? You too can create a new Management Fad.

First, think of a three-digit number and take the corresponding word from each column below. Thus 218 gives Networked Empowered Transformation; 894 gives Knowledge-based Quality Management; 052 gives Integrated Evolutionary Capability; and so on.

Second, develop the fad you have chosen. Feel free to incorporate:

- new words or buzzwords (LeaderShift, Underlearn)
- clever acronyms (for example, the SHOCK Programme – Strategic Harmonisation Of Company Knowledge)
- additional buzz-phrases to ensure the proper ring of decisive, progressive authority (Exocet Culture Change, Downsized Realignment)

Now you are ready – hit the lecture circuit!

Column 1	Column 2	Column 3
0 Integrated	0 Professional	0 Partnership
1 Adaptive	1 Empowered	1 Strategy
2 Networked	2 Incremental	2 Capability
3 Responsive	3 Competitive	3 Organisation
4 Complex	4 Intensive	4 Management
5 Postmodern	5 Evolutionary	5 Culture
6 Benchmarked	6 Differentiated	6 Performance
7 Corporate	7 Environmental	7 Reengineering
8 Knowledge-based	8 Innovative	8 Transformation
9 Visionary	9 Quality	9 Leadership

Figure 1.1 The management fad generator

Why is this? Eccles and colleagues give part of the answer – the importance of rhetoric in the work of management. By way of example, the past is often depicted in management discussion as a more placid age in which hierarchies were able to prosper; yet this stereotype may well be inaccurate. Language – and thus ideas and concepts – are indeed the life blood of managers – which is why it is so important to analyse their origins.

The fourth underpinning theme follows from this. Extending the metaphor (and with apologies to the squeamish) we need new blood – a transfusion of ideas into management from sources beyond those traditionally tapped. This is one of the purposes of the present book.

PARADIGMS

This discussion makes use of the idea of paradigms, and in particular the notion of 'paradigm level'. We will take as the definition of a paradigm that it is 'the totality of thoughts, perceptions, and values that forms a particular vision of reality, a vision that is the basis of the way a society organises itself' (Capra

1988). It is useful to distinguish three paradigm levels. The first is the paradigm ascribed to a single organisation. The second is the overall approach to management, strategy and organisation considered legitimate by theorists and practitioners. The third comprises the general set of beliefs, theories of knowledge and attitudes towards power on which that management approach is based.

This three-level approach partly parallels Schein's (1992) approach to culture, with his distinction between artefacts and creations, espoused values and basic underlying assumptions (such as beliefs about the nature of human nature). But it is used here to characterise much more than 'organisational culture'. The mindset of managers establishes what is and what is not legitimate in the fields of knowledge, belief and power (see below for discussion of this 'triple lens'). Significant advances can be made by an organisation that changes its first-level paradigm. However, one of the arguments in this book is that a change at the second level will be far more valuable, and that this can be achieved only by scrutiny and reappraisal of the third level.

This is the case for all organisations. But as information and knowledge become increasingly the most important assets an organisation has, outstripping the traditional resources of land, labour and capital, the individual mindset becomes more important, and so does the collective mindset – organisational intelligence.

THE MODERN PARADIGM

'Management science' has sought to be just that – a science. Theorists have, therefore, sought to analyse the nature of natural science, and in particular its method, to find parameters and principles for adoption in their own work. At the same time, the influence of the social science seen as closest to natural science – economics – has been substantial, and this has been reinforced by the influence over the last decade of the 'competitive positioning' approach to strategy.

There are seven supporting themes to this characterisation of the scientific approach. The first is **logic**. One is expected to be logical, although it is rarely explained what this means, and it often appears to be used as a synonym for 'rational'. If we take it, more precisely, as the theory of valid inference, then this would certainly be expected to apply in areas such as management decision-making. Closely related to this is the assumption of **linear thinking**, which is to be seen particularly in the models and schemata that characterise much of strategic thinking, from flow diagrams to 2×2 matrices.

Third there is **quantification**. A high premium is put on quantitative methods, especially in decision-making. Fourth is **cause and effect**: science involves the search to identify the time-order of events: establish causal links between variables. Fifth, there is **reductionism**, which involves the search for basic elements. Sixth, there is the **split between thinking and doing** – or mind and body – expressed by Frederick Taylor in his fourth principle of scientific management:

> An almost equal division of responsibility between the management and the workmen. . . . All of the planning which under the old system was done by the workman, as a result of his personal experience, must of necessity under the new system be done by the management in accordance with the laws of the science. . . . It is also clear that in most cases one type of man is needed to plan ahead and an entirely different type to execute the work. (1967: 37–8)

Finally, there is the concern for **control**, so evident in much management behaviour.

Vaill (1989) identifies similar characteristics, although in his case they constitute a reason for rejecting a scientific approach to management – a conclusion as questionable as the one that identifies all the above as best practice. Alvesson and Willmott (1996) link this concern for scientific respectability to power.

This characterisation of modernism may be compared with Gergen's (1992: 211–12). It embraces the four aspects that he identifies: a revival of Enlightenment beliefs in the powers of reason and observation; a search for fundamentals or essentials; a faith in progress and universal design; and absorption in the machine metaphor. As Gergen argues, from these premises come views including scientific management theory, general systems theory and theories of industrial society based on rational laws of economic organisation and development (within which we could include much of what is called competitive or positioning theory).

EXAMPLES

It is possible to give many examples of the way in which these assumptions have been played out in management thinking. In their purer forms, they underpin the whole movement of scientific management, including the work of Frederick Taylor and Frank Gilbreth. The latter's basic principles include 'the replacement of rule-of-thumb methods for determining each element of a worker's job with scientific determination', and 'the co-operation of management and labour to accomplish work objectives, in accordance with the scientific method'. Although few would claim to be Taylorists today, many practising managers can identify the features he presents in their own organisation. Indeed Pollitt (1993) has argued that 'neo-Taylorist managerialism' underpins many of the key aspects of the assault on the public sector we witnessed during the 1980s and 1990s. The assumptions are also pivotal to the classical theories of bureaucracy developed by Max Weber and Henri Fayol, and discussed earlier.

Henry Ford added to Taylor's principles his vision of 'a new kind of rationalised, modernist, and populist democratic society' (Harvey 1990: 126) in which there was the new politics of labour control and management. Both Taylorism and Fordism took time to spread: Harvey suggests that it was not until after 1945 that class relations and the deployment of state powers changed to allow Fordism to come to maturity.

Grint (1991) argues that Taylorism had only a limited influence in the United States, and its full impact was to be found elsewhere: one of its greatest advocates was Lenin. Certainly, the Modern Paradigm fits well with authoritarian regimes (ironic, given the emphasis in the Enlightenment project on toleration and freedom), and not only state communism. Thus Bauman (1989) has argued that it is almost impossible to conceive of the idea of the extermination of a whole people separately from the engineering approach to society and the practice of scientific management of human setting and interaction. He sees the exterminatory version of anti-Semitism as a thoroughly modern phenomenon, something that could occur only in an advanced state of modernity (although recent examples of genocide across the world suggest that there are additional factors at work).

Turning to a less horrifying example, consider the schemata beloved of the strategic planning approach, which emphasise two key themes:

1 Linearity and cause–effect, with each stage following from the previous one.
2 The separation of analysis/choice from implementation, which again flows from Taylor's fourth principle. It is this thinking that leads to the Analysis–Choice–Implementation division of strategic management, with the third element focusing on enabling – setting the structures and resource allocation within which the workers will faithfully execute the wishes of the managers.

The primary alternative to the rational approach offered in the textbook literature on strategic management is the emergent, process approach advocated by Mintzberg. Grant's treatment of this in the introduction to his textbook is illustrative, and worth quoting in full. He summarises Mintzberg's 'crafting', and then comments that the approach he will take

> is to follow a rationalist, analytical approach to strategy formulation in preference to the 'crafting' approach advocated by Mintzberg. This is not because I regard planning as necessarily superior to crafting – planning in any detailed sense is not what strategy is about. . . . Strategy development is a multidimensional process that must involve both rational analysis and intuition, experience, and emotion. However, whether strategy formulation is formal or informal, whether strategies are deliberate or emergent, there can be little doubt as to the importance of systematic analysis as a vital input in the strategy process. Without analysis, the process of strategy formulation, particularly at the senior management level, is likely to be chaotic, with no basis for the comparing and evaluating of alternatives. . . . The danger of the Mintzberg approach is that by downplaying the role of systematic analysis and emphasising the role of intuition and vision, we move into a Shirley MacLaine world of New Age mysticism in which rationality is devalued. (Grant 1995: 20–1)

The assumptions of the Modern Paradigm are also present in theories of management decision-making, when presented as a linear and logical process through the stages of option generation, analysis (against such criteria as suitability, feasibility and acceptability), and choice of the optimum option which results.

Indeed, we can bring together these approaches to management, strategy and decision-making in the overall concept of technocracy, which Fischer (1990) sees as originating in Enlightenment ideology, and involving a system of governance in which experts rule by virtue of their specialised knowledge and position. It is 'fundamentally founded on an unswerving belief in the power of the rational mind to control societal change in constructive directions' (Fischer 1990: 41–2). Technocracy is logical, instrumental and orderly, seeking 'true knowledge' through the neo-positivist method. All this gives 'technocratic man' 'legitimation for his own rapacious appropriation of the physical world' (Fischer 1990: 44). In other words, technocracy is the Modern Paradigm in action, weaving an integrated view of knowledge, belief and power, the latter involving an authoritarian perspective (the rule of the wise).

CONCERNS

It may be fair to argue that no one has adhered to the purest form of this thinking since Gilbreth and Taylor. Numerous limitations in applying it to the 'real world' have been recognised, including the lack of perfect competition, perfect knowledge and information, and the rarity of the conditions under which it might actually be possible for managers to operate in a rational and maximising way in their decision-making.

One key development has been the notion of limited rationality. A second key concept to emerge is that of satisficing. For Herbert Simon (1960) 'management' is equivalent to 'decision-making'. On what basis do administrators make decisions? In place of 'economic man' Simon proposes a model of 'administrative man', who satisfies. Another consequence of the limitations to the pure approach was the emergence of 'muddling through', Charles Lindblom's description of 'reality', and James Quinn's logical incrementalism.

The softening of the pure scientific method, with its strong mechanistic overtones, has led to the desire to include the 'human' element, through the human relations school. This movement has sought to humanise the machine and raise the profile of organisational culture as an element on which theory and practice should focus.

The limits of linearity have been recognised, and this has most characteristically resulted in a circular approach to decision-making and to strategy. The articulation of these, however, continues to follow the sequence Analysis–Choice–Implementation. The paradigm has also been modified through the recognition of what managers really do. One consequence of all this has been a sharper distinction between the positive/descriptive and the normative/prescriptive.

The pure paradigm, with its focus on the equilibrium state, had obvious difficulties in the face of the increasing recognition of the importance of the environment. One consequence has been open systems theory, based on characteristics including steady-state and the balance of maintenance and adaptive activities. The environment, however, continues to be 'out there', and to cope with this, static equilibrium is replaced by dynamic equilibrium (Hodgetts and Kuratko 1990).

The second major form of modification to the 'pure' form of scientific management has been the attention paid to the human factor, leading to the human relations perspective. This has been both a way of managing and a way of providing a richer account of what is happening in organisations. Thus Anthony (1986) refers to two principal accounts of management now available. 'Official theory' is the classic account of management as rational purposive activity directed at the efficient achievement of goals, usually determined in economic terms. 'Real theory' recognises the role of self-protective behaviour, of the way people construct their own priorities and agendas, spend their time in brief, unscheduled conversations, and develop and maintain wide personal networks.

The human relations perspective can also be seen as a more sophisticated form of management control than that offered by Taylorism and Fordism. Fischer (1990) points to a number of studies showing that the Hawthorne experiments were either unscientific or inconclusive, and asks why they nevertheless occupy such a hallowed position in management thinking. He quotes Rose to provide the answer: 'What, after all, could be more appealing than to be told that one's subordinates are nonlogical; that their uncooperativeness is a frustrated urge to collaborate; that their demands for cash mark a need for your approval; and that you have a historical destiny as a broker of social harmony?' (Rose, M., 1975, p. 124, quoted in Fischer 1990: 134).

OUTCOME

This gradual enrichment of the traditional paradigm has led to a debate on whether there is 'one best way' or whether a contingency approach is needed, and to the recognition of the legitimacy of multiple approaches. But underlying these themes are a number of shared values:

- They recognise the problematic nature of the pure scientific approach.
- They accept the importance of strategic planning/design, but recognise its cyclical nature.
- They take for granted the importance of competition, and accept the merits of extending this throughout the economy, through privatisation and internal markets.
- They accept the importance of organisational culture, most frequently through shared vision, common purpose, and mission statements.

- They desire humanised bureaucracies and organisations.
- Organisations are seen as open systems, interacting with and adapting to their environment.

By way of summary, Table 1.2 indicates the way the traditional paradigm has been developed on a number of dimensions into the paradigm currently accepted as the basis of management theory and practice. These added or altered dimensions reflect the human relations movement, open systems theory and the contingency approach. This is an important paradigm, not to be discarded easily. It provides a valuable structure within which management theory can be explored and explained. But ultimately, its propositions are best seen in the same way as Ludwig Wittgenstein characterised his arguments in *Tractatus Logico-Philosophicus*:

> My propositions serve as elucidations in the following way: anyone who understands me eventually recognizes them as nonsensical, when he has used them – as steps – to climb up beyond them. (He must, so to speak, throw away the ladder after he has climbed up it.) He must transcend these propositions, and then he will see the world aright. (1921: 151)

OLD WINE IN NEW BOTTLES

Thus far we have focused on adaptations to the Modern Paradigm. But interwoven with this has been the frequent espousal of principles and practices which are seen to reject it – the Romantic approach characterised by Gergen (1992), who argues that organisation theory has drawn from two hegemonic bodies of discourse. First, theories have been enriched and informed by romanticist discourse of the nineteenth century, and second, by the modernist understanding of the person dominant within the twentieth century. He identifies the former in the work of the Tavistock Institute, Elton Mayo, Abraham Maslow, Douglas McGregor and others. The 'dead hand' of bureaucracy, the limitations

Table 1.2 Changes in the Modern Paradigm

Original	Modified
Rationality	Bounded rationality
Maximisation	Optimisation or satisficing
Rational decision-making	Be as rational as possible, or use *post-hoc* rationalisation
Rational design	Logical incrementalism
Linear	Circular or cyclical
Linear design	Open systems
Static equilibrium	Dynamic equilibrium/homeostasis
Scientific method	'Art and science'
Logical	Logical and intuitive
Quantification	Quantification where possible
Hard	Soften

of hierarchy, the negative consequences of a Theory X view of people – all these are seen to be consequences of the slavish implementation of Taylorist or neo-Taylorist theory.

Alternatives (such as those listed by Eccles, Nohria and Berkley 1992) are proclaimed: for example, the distinction between the 'control' and the 'commitment' approach is one which a number of writers have delineated (Walton 1985). The seductive power of 'the new' is both strong and profitable – the degeneration of management theory into fads and hype may seem a small price to pay for the consultancies that flow from them.

But beneath the heady excitement of novelty comes the sobering recognition that there is little new. Thus Eccles et al. (1992) recall the work of Mary Parker Follett, suggesting that her discoveries in the 1920s are quite similar to the lessons that today are packaged as 'cutting edge'. They identify five clichés of the new organisation:

1 Smaller is better than larger.
2 Less diversification is better than more.
3 Competition must be replaced by collaboration.
4 Formal authority must be diminished.
5 Time cycles must become shorter.

They then give many examples of the long lineage of these ideas. Jun and Storm's *Tomorrow's Organizations* (1973) also offers some fascinating insights into the principle that packaging has become more important than content, with its emphasis on the importance of self-management. Forester (in Jun and Storm 1973) identifies these characteristics of the new organisation:

• Elimination of the superior–subordinate relationship.
• Individual profit centres.
• Objective determination of compensation.
• Policy-making separated from decision-making.
• Restructuring through electronic data processing.
• Freedom of access to information.
• Elimination of internal monopolies.
• Balancing rewards and risk.
• Mobility of the individual.
• Enhanced rights of the individual.
• Education within the corporation.

STRATEGIC PLANNING RULES, OK

Despite these many examples of 'new thinking', stretching over many years, the following comments are not untypical. 'Hierarchy still rules corporate life' (*Harvard Business Review*, survey of 12,000 managers, May 1991); 'Part of the problem is that [companies] still measure themselves by classical input–process–output methods, based on Frederick Taylor's ideas from a century ago' (*Economist* 1993).

One reason why the 'old habit' of 'scientifically-based' rational management retains its power is its educational value. Roberts (1996: 56) comments that there are practical interests at work for the teacher that tend to push him or her towards the transmission of knowledge as fact. But there is also the continued evidence of the Modern Paradigm in action. Ritzer (1996) has identified the late twentieth-century successor to Fordism: McDonaldisation. Ritzer identifies four alluring dimensions that lie at the heart of the success of the McDonald model: efficiency, calculability, predictability and control. Subtle control is exercised over the customers, while those who work in such organisations are also controlled to a high degree, often more directly than customers.

Vignette 1.1

Critical to the global sweep of McDonaldisation is the support it receives from the customer – people appear to want this predictability, and thereby promote the whole approach. Thus, one of the many examples Ritzer gives is higher education, and personal experience by one of the authors has reinforced this. Following the untimely death of a colleague, he found himself the leader of a final year undergraduate course that involved nearly 400 students and eight tutors. The pressures towards standardisation and predictability were very strong – students in one seminar group would check what their colleagues in other seminar groups had been told by their tutors, and express concern if they perceived any difference. The most graphic illustration came when one tutor warned him that when asked if a particular question would be appearing on the exam paper, she had blushed – and she was now concerned that students would take this as confirmation (as indeed it was) and that others might then object that they had not been privy to this 'information'.

This experience supports the findings of Levine (1993) that:

- Higher education is not the centre of most students' lives – it isn't necessarily their most important activity.
- Students generally want their universities to operate like their banks and fast-food restaurants.
- Students generally do not want frills and extras – they want the equivalent of a McDonald's 'value meal'.
- In sum, 'all they want of higher education is simple procedures, good service, quality courses, and low costs'.

The roots of McDonaldisation in the Modern Paradigm are unmistakable. As Ritzer recognises, his argument provides a healthy challenge to those who see us now within an entirely postmodern world. McDonaldism embraces both modern and postmodern elements: it adds to Taylorism customer focus and the provision of 'risk-free risk' – safe fun.

A further important manifestation of this paradigm, thoroughly embracing the fourth of his tenets of scientific management (involving the separation of thinkers from doers), is strategic planning, with its basis in rational design. One of the most persistent critics of this has been Mintzberg. He supports Dror (1968) in arguing that a central concern is the desire for control, which we can couple with concern about the consequences of dynamic environments which 'threaten to crush them at every turn' (Grint 1995: 66).

Why, Mintzberg (1994) asks, does the planning school make such a fuss about turbulence, the very thing it cannot handle? It would be possible, as Grint argues, to choose a different representation of the environment and the actions it implies of the manager. But the strategic planner takes a different course (hardly surprising, as she/he would eschew any suggestion that the environment has been created). Mintzberg suggests that planning is so oriented to stability, so obsessed with having everything under control, that any perturbation at all sets off a wave of panic and perceptions of turbulence. He identifies four assumptions behind strategic planning: formalisation, detachment, quantification and predetermination.

These, it will be noted, relate closely to the seven characteristics of the Modern Paradigm cited earlier. If people believe that strategic planning is the right way to do things, then it is hardly surprising that it remains so popular, whatever Mintzberg and others say. This is particularly notable in the public sector, where 'strategy' and 'strategic planning' are frequently used interchangeably in discussions, and where 'neo-Taylorist managerialism' (Pollitt 1993) has become an important factor.

More recently, as we have seen, the management 'gurus' have put considerable stress on the 'coming of the new organisation'. Although each may advocate this as a new idea, it is arguable that they have tended to be little more than a variation of Burns and Stalker's (1961) divide between the mechanistic and the organic (Table 1.3).

Table 1.3 The mechanistic and the organic

'Old'	'New'
Mechanistic	Organic
Hierarchy	Network
Modern	Postmodern
Entrepreneurial	Post-entrepreneurial
Fordist	Post-Fordist
Taylorist	Post-Taylorist

Earlier we identified the way that this, often cyclical practice of repackaging the old as 'brand new' extends throughout management. The great fashions (or fads) which periodically sweep management thinking have usually incorporated elements of a new approach – for example, Peters and Waterman's (1982) rejection of rational planning in favour of 'strong culture' organisations, the push for Total Quality Management, or the current pursuit of Business Process Re-engineering (on the latter, see Grint 1995: Chapter 5). The underlying prescription is that the world built on the beliefs of Taylor, Weber, Ford and Fayol – the Control and Command Economy – is dead. The mechanistic organisation must be superseded by one that is 'alive', adaptive, empowers its workforce, liberates its management, replaces control with commitment, is more democratic, is a learning organisation.

There are, of course, examples of organisations moving towards a different way of working and managers adopting new methods. But despite this many organisations remain mechanistic and bureaucratic, and many managers cling to traditional concepts of good management and planning. 'Liberation' finds its counter-position in the need for scrutiny. Freedom is contrasted with the need for accountability (especially in the public sector). Linear, rational planning remains strong, as does 'logical' decision-making based on ever-more powerful quantitative tools. Competitive/positioning strategy remains focused on the use of rational tools, often derived from neoclassical economics. Human Resource Management appears as another form of control, albeit more subtle and humanised.

The question that arises, therefore, is why this shift in thinking is so prominent in the literature, stretching back over 25 years, but so little evident in practice. There are many possible explanations, and we will focus here on four, each of which adds to the picture.

First, it can be argued that although these changes have been advocated for many years, it is only now that they are becoming possible. Information technology is seen as of particular importance here, and it is argued that technological development has at last reached the stage where it can and will have a substantial effect on organisations (this is the argument, for example, of Tapscott and Canton 1993). Linked to this is the view that change is happening, but it is not yet very evident. This explanation considerably overplays the role of technology: as we have seen, the developments advocated were seen to be quite feasible years ago, when information technology was of a much more primitive nature. It is the argument of 'technological fix', and in its technocratic aspects its lineage goes straight back to the Cartesian–Newtonian synthesis, which we shall explore below.

Second, there is the argument that much of the debate is rhetoric (the thesis of Eccles et al. 1992). Allied to this argument is the view that much of management thinking occurs in cyclical fads: swinging between centralisation and decentralisation, between single and multiple financial centres, between focus on the core and expansive organisational policies.

This argument takes no account of the role of the Modern Paradigm, although it undoubtedly helps to explain the role of management fads. It should be noted that Eccles et al.'s argument is subtle: they seek to move 'beyond the hype' by developing an action perspective on management underpinned by three key elements: rhetoric, action and identity.

Third, it can be seen as closely linked to resistance to change. Like any major change, there is resistance from those with most to lose – and in this case proposals have been put forward which have substantial implications for large swathes of managers, in particular middle managers. Delayering and management downsizing do not necessarily prove attractive to those who may thereby find themselves occupationally challenged.

Fourth, there is the argument that changes are being seriously attempted, but they are being done in organisations where the dominant paradigm remains based, ultimately, on the Cartesian–Newtonian synthesis (in line with the comment of Keynes at the start of this chapter). For example, if those who advocate empowerment nevertheless believe, fundamentally, that control is essential to prevent abuse, then the results may not be effective.

A variant of this fourth argument focuses on the role of management fads. Thus Gill and Whittle (1993) identify several themes. They discuss the role of consultants with 'cure-all' products. They point to the arguments put forward by Tichy (1983) that the prevailing belief system of American managers seems to be dominated by the grand strategy or bold vision, which is high on masculinity and status but perhaps low on reflection and learning. They point to the anti-intellectualism involving 'a regression to check lists and eight-point plans typified by Peters and Waterman's *In Search of Excellence*' (1982: 290). More fundamentally, they look to psychoanalytic factors, drawing on the work of Kets de Vries and Miller (1984). Thus the 'dramatic' organisation is characterised by boldness, risk-taking and a fascination for techniques and new methods. What emerges here is a picture of chaos very different from the one to be considered later – 'uncertainty, constant frenetic activity and unrelenting pace, fear of losing ground to competitors, the inability to reflect for more than a few minutes are the costs of a role interpretation which is coming to be increasingly valued in western, middle-class, managerial cultures' (Gill and Whittle 1993: 291–2).

TRIPLE ANALYSIS

The four arguments above are not mutually exclusive, and it is possible to develop a theory of change rooted in the fourth, but taking account of valid elements of the other three. There is, however, an added dimension to be considered before doing so, and this relates to the value of using a multiple-perspective approach, in part to escape the trap of relying on a single 'rational' approach to decision-making. This idea, introduced earlier, originates in

Graham Allison's study (1971) of the United States' response to the Cuban missile crisis. He considered it from three perspectives: the 'rational actor' model, an 'organisational process' model, and a 'bureaucratic politics' model. A number of writers have embellished this theme and modified the concepts, but the three-fold model has remained largely intact. As used here, the three 'lenses' are knowledge, belief and power.

Using this triple analysis we can recast the debate as follows. The Modern Paradigm (like the Cartesian–Newtonian synthesis) incorporates an epistemology and scientific method that are considered the basis of sound knowledge. This, therefore, provides a belief system, which managers can adopt. A crucial element of this is the view of power: power is seen as control – over nature, over machines, over systems, over people, over the future.

However, the belief system is not unproblematic. We have already seen the many modifications made to the original paradigm in the light of its failure to fit what is. But, it may be argued, it continues to reflect what should be. This distinction between the positive and the normative is a strong vein running through management theory, with rational planning modes tending to reflect the latter. A common practice in management is *post-hoc* rationalisation, as Mintzberg, Quinn, Eccles and Nohria have all identified.

Stacey (1991: 10–11, 19) argues that the following characterises what managers say about strategic choice:

- Leaders of organisations should set objectives, make statements of mission, and articulate vision, dreams or intents.
- The leaders should inspire all members of the organisation to believe in the vision.
- Strategic management requires action, embodied in a long-term plan, which sets out the route to the goal.
- The purpose of strategic management is to match the company's capabilities to the requirements of its customers in a more effective manner than the competition.
- Success flows from:
  - developing a clear vision of where and what we are to be as an organisation in the long-term future;
  - analysing information on how and why the environment is changing and will change in the future;
  - continuously matching our competitive capability to the change, maintaining a dynamic equilibrium so that we continue along our predetermined path to the future;
  - inspiring and enthusing everyone in the organisation to commit to the vision and work together as a closely knit team with strongly shared cultural norms.

But is this what managers actually believe? Consider Schwartz's (1990) experiment with a class of students. He described two types of organisations. One was a textbook organisation, operating like a clock: everybody knows what the organisation is about and is concerned solely with carrying out its mission; people are basically happy in their work; the level of anxiety is low; people interact with each other in frictionless, mutually supportive cooperation; and if there are any managerial problems at all, these are basically technical problems, easily solved by someone who has the proper skills and knows the correct techniques of management. The other type, the 'snakepit' organisation, is the opposite. Here, everything is always falling apart, and people's main activity is to see that it doesn't fall on them; nobody really knows what is going on, though everyone cares about what is going on because there is danger in not knowing; anxiety and stress are constant companions; and people take little pleasure in dealing with each other, doing so primarily to use others for their own purposes or because they cannot avoid being so used themselves. Managerial problems here are experienced as intractable, and managers feel that they have done well if they are able to make it through the day.

Schwartz outlined these alternatives to his students, and asked them to indicate which type of organisation more closely approximated the picture of the organisation they knew best. The results were dramatic. Approximately three-quarters of the students responded, and of those most indicated that the snakepit model was the better fit. (We have done the same experiment a number of times with MBA classes, getting very similar results.)

Schwartz's further comments are also relevant. He found that, irrespective of this result, his students wanted to know the techniques for managing clockworks. He concluded that the idea of the clockwork organisation had much more than pragmatic significance for them. It was rather an article of faith. We would put a different slant on this, based on our discussions with managers: the clockwork model is a form of security. Faced with uncertainty, and the need for 'proven tools and techniques with which to cope', they retreat to the Modern Paradigm.

The clockwork picture is, of course, derived from the Cartesian–Newtonian synthesis, and relates very closely to the Modern Paradigm as discussed here. It is part of a belief system about what should be, based on the beliefs held about that synthesis. This is strongly reinforced by the prescriptions on power which are integral to the synthesis, and give legitimacy to the use of power by managers. (Thus the divide is not as neat as Schwartz's metaphors would suggest – and it has proved important when discussing his approach to emphasise that it serves also as an illustration of the powerful hold which dichotomous thinking has on the Western mind.)

The knowledge base of the synthesis, and indeed the synthesis itself, were severely undermined in the twentieth century, although following Keynes we would argue that this does not imply a change in the belief system. We should bear in mind that many of the implications of modern science appear both counter-rational and counter-intuitive, while the Cartesian–Newtonian synthesis continues to explain perfectly adequately much that we see in everyday life. How many of us, for example, use non-Euclidean geometry, or find it easy to envisage the coastline of Britain as a fractal with a dimension of 1.25 – about a quarter of the way between a line and a plane?

Equally important, as we shall see, the most enthusiastic protagonists of the 'new science' in management adopt an apolitical approach, neglecting many of the implications of power. Extending the third of the arguments above to all in management, how realistic is it to expect them to abandon power bases because their scientific perspective is outdated?

The argument to be developed in this thesis seeks to provide an approach to strategic management that integrates new scientific insights. It would be naïve, however, to think that this will be adopted because it 'makes sense'. Part of our earlier argument about the weaknesses of the rational approach to management has been a critique of precisely this naïveté – the belief that good rational arguments will prevail, irrespective of people's belief systems and power relationships (a belief which incorporates the view that there is a single rationality).

Despite the partial development of alternatives put forward by a number of authors, the Modern Paradigm remains so strong that it acts as a fundamental determinant of management and organisational activity. It provides a strong underpinning to concerns about loss of control, about the consequences of 'letting go'. Management control systems are maintained and developed because there is fear of the alternative – of things 'getting out of control' and so leading to chaos – as well as a desire to maintain control. In the public sector the imperatives of expenditure restraint and public accountability provide powerful arguments for the maintenance of control. Distrust also has empirical support – the reality of abuse following relaxation of monitoring systems – and this again is a particular concern in public bodies (the 'sleaze factor' is only one manifestation of this).

The argument here is that these concerns are reinforced by a now outdated perception of science and rationality, which sees control as both possible and desirable. The extent to which this is rooted in human thought can be seen by considering the work of Argyris, and in particular his two works, co-authored with Schon, on *Organisational Learning*. In these they consider the 'theories of action with which most people are acculturated in modern industrial societies' (1978: 4). They find that 'when human beings deal with issues that are embarrassing or threatening, their reasoning and action conform to a particular model of theory-in-use which we call Model I' (Darwin 1996: 92). This model has four 'governing variables', or values, that actors strive to satisfy through their actions:

1 Define goals and try to achieve them.

2 Maximise winning and minimise losing.

3 Minimise generating or expressing negative feelings.

4 Be rational: 'This is the counterpart to value 3. It is an injunction to be objective, and intellectual, and to suppress feelings. Interactions should be construed as objective discussions of the issues, whatever feelings may underlie them' (1996: 93–4).

The action strategies adopted to satisfy these governing variables are:

1 Design and manage the environment unilaterally.
2 Own and control the task.
3 Unilaterally protect yourself.
4 Unilaterally protect others from being hurt.

In another work on the same subject Argyris states: 'Our hypothesis is that Model I has been learned through socialization. This hypothesis . . . has yet to be proven directly' (1992: 26). Argyris and Schon argue that the methods of organisational learning in most organisations are embedded in this model, with harmful consequences that reinforce single-loop learning and irrational behaviour. They then develop an alternative Model (O-II), which they acknowledge to be rare: 'Neither of the authors knows of an organisation that has a full developed Model O-II learning system' (1996: 112). We will return to this in a later chapter, but for the moment what is important to note is the relationship between the values underpinning Model I and the tenets of the Modern Paradigm. In each we see the imperative to control – self, others, the task, the environment – and to be rational. Model I, Argyris argues, 'is held by all of the individuals studied so far' (1992: 26). If we accept his hypothesis, then it is worth asking why this socialisation takes place. An important reason, argued here, is the web of ideas about what it is to be rational, reasonable and scientific – and thus, in the present context, an effective organisational worker.

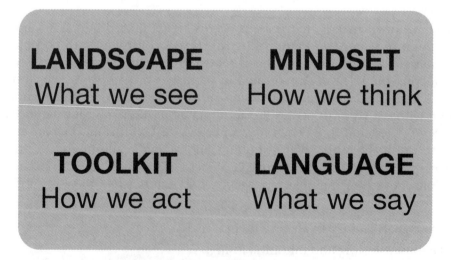

LANDSCAPE
What we see

MINDSET
How we think

TOOLKIT
How we act

LANGUAGE
What we say

Figure 1.2 Domains of the paradigm

FOUR ASPECTS OF THE PARADIGM

Before exploring the roots of the Modern Paradigm, it is worth extending the earlier discussion of mindsets, to suggest that any paradigm may usefully be considered as a pattern of four closely interrelated aspects, as shown in Figure 1.2.

If we consider the Modern Paradigm, the landscape is a route-map or plan, detailing as far as possible the past, present and future. It is a landscape of (clockwork) machines, and it has another important element – everything within it has solid foundations. The mindset has been summarised in the earlier discussion – rationality and analysis are dominant. The language used by managers includes the list shown in Table 1.4.

The toolkit of the Modern Paradigm includes many of the concepts, frameworks and tools that have been developed in management over the past half century, for example:

- SWOT
- PEST(EC)
- Five force analysis
- Value chain
- Generic strategy
- Ashridge Mission Models
- Critical success factors
- Balanced scorecard
- Plan
- Cultural web
- Stakeholder analysis
- Levering and stretching resources
- Force field analysis
- Organisation life cycle
- Structure: forms and forces
- Product portfolio mix
- Dynamics of globalisation

Table 1.4 The language of the Modern Paradigm

Control	Analytical	Predictable
Order	Safe	One best way
Modern	Logical	Structured
Objective	Certain	Planned
Realist	Foundations	Competitive

- Alliance development and maintenance
- Scenario planning
- Knowledge management

The snakepit is in many ways the obverse of the Modern Paradigm – it is one of the reasons managers cling to the clockwork, because the consequence of not having control is feared to be chaos. The landscape is evoked by its name – a hostile place where few wish to be. The mindset was described earlier in Schwartz's words. The language is in large part the opposite of the Modern (Table 1.5).

Note that only one word remains the same: 'competitive'. But whereas in the Modern Paradigm this is related to competitive markets and competition between organisations, in the snakepit it is much more likely to be about competition within organisations, between those struggling for power (or just for survival).

What of the snakepit toolkit? Survival makes it important to understand the levers of power, and stakeholders' interests and influence. An understanding of defensive routines will help, as will the ability to thrive in conflict. Ideas, like people, struggle to survive in the snakepit, as the following vignette illustrates. Another useful source of ideas on how to survive in the snakepit comes from literature, as the vignette on Richard III suggests.

Table 1.5 Clockwork and snakepit states in the Modern Paradigm

Modern	Snakepit
Control	Chaos
Order	Disorder
Modern	Postmodern
Objective	Subjective
Realist	Non-realist
Analytical	Instinctive
Safe	Unsafe
Logical	Illogical
Certain	Uncertain
Foundations	No foundations
Predictable	Unpredictable
One best way	Any way
Structured	Unstructured
Planned	Unplanned
Competitive	Competitive

Vignette 1.2

24 ways in which to kill an idea

Early in his management career one of the authors was given a list of '22 ways in which to kill an idea' – not, of course, to use himself, but to provide a reference table when it was being done unto him. Over the years this has proved a useful comfort factor in the Snakepit, although it has developed into 24 ways. Not long after joining the senior management team of an organisation he suggested some specific work to be done on income-generation. The Director of Finance offered to take the lead in pursuing this idea – which seemed at the time a good idea, given his seniority (Way 22). He also suggested that it would be useful to extend the remit to cover all aspects of income generation (Way 23). The promised working group never met. On a later occasion a committee reached an impasse in restructuring the senior management team. The author, with two colleagues, put forward a short paper suggesting a way forward. At the first discussion nine Ways were employed; at the second, three days later, another five Ways were brought into the discussion; at the third meeting, three days thereafter, the proposals were agreed.

1 **Ignore it:** Silence will intimidate all but the most enthusiastic proposers of ideas.

2 **See it coming and dodge:** You can recognise the imminent arrival of an idea by a growing unease and anxiety in the would-be originator. Change the subject, or – better still – end the meeting.

3 **Scorn it:** The gently raised eyebrow and a softly spoken 'You aren't really serious, are you?' work wonders. In severe cases make the audible comment, 'Utterly impracticable'. Get your thrust home before the idea is fully explained, otherwise it might prove practicable after all.

4 **Laugh it off:** 'Ha, ha – that's a good one, Chris. You must have sat up all night thinking it up!' If she has, this makes it even funnier.

5 **Praise it to death:** By the time you have expounded its merit for five minutes everyone else will hate it. The proposer will be wondering what is wrong with it himself.

6 **Mention that it has never been tried:** If it is new this will be true.

7 **Prove that it isn't new:** If you can make it look similar to a known idea, the fact that this one is better may not emerge.

8 **Observe that it doesn't fit with organisation policy:** Since nobody knows what the policy is you are probably right.

9 **Mention what it will cost:** The fact that the expected saving is six times as much will then pale into insignificance. That is imaginary money; what we spend is real. Beware of ideas that cost nothing though, and point out, 'If it doesn't cost anything, it can't be worth anything'.

10 **Oh, we've tried that before:** Particularly effective if the originator is a newcomer. It makes her or him realise what an outsider she is.

11 **Cast the right aspersion:** 'Isn't it a bit too trendy?' or 'Do we want this clever academic stuff?' or 'Let's be careful we don't outsmart ourselves'. Such comments will draw ready applause and few ideas will survive collective disapproval.

12 **Find a competitive idea:** This is a dangerous one unless you are experienced. You might still get left with an idea.

13 **Produce twenty good reasons why it won't work:** The one good reason why it will work then gets lost.

14 **Modify it out of existence:** This is elegant. You seem to be helping the idea along, just changing it a little here and there. By the time the originator realises what is happening, the idea is dead.

15 **Encourage doubt about ownership:** 'Didn't you suggest something like Chris is saying last year, Pat?' While everyone is wondering, the idea may wither and die quietly.

16 **Damn it by association of ideas:** Connect it with someone's pet hate. Remark casually to Al: 'Why, that is just the sort of idea that Jo might have thought up'. Al hates Jo. The originator doesn't, and will wonder for weeks what hit him.

17 **Try to chip bits off it:** If you fiddle with an idea long enough it may come to pieces.

18 **Make a personal attack on the originator:** By the time she has recovered, she will have forgotten that she had an idea.

19 **Score a technical knockout:** For instance, refer to some obscure regulation it may infringe. Use technology as a weapon: 'But if we do that we will need to provide everyone with networked software to replace their current packages, and they would resent having to learn new systems – you wouldn't want to put us all to that expense and trouble, would you?'

20 **Postpone it:** By the time it's been postponed a few times, it will look like a rather old idea.

21 **Let a committee sit on the idea.**

22 **Offer to take lead responsibility for developing the idea.** Establish a working party, and then simply avoid calling any meetings.

23 **Generalise:** Suggest that this idea needs to be considered in a much wider context – so wide that it becomes impossible to handle.

24 **Encourage the author to look for a better idea.** Usually a discouraging quest. If he finds one, start him looking for a better job.

Vignette 1.3

Richard III: Change agent *extraordinaire*!!!

At one level Richard III was a very successful change agent. In the course of Shakespeare's play he:

- seduces and marries the widow of a man he has killed;
- has his elder brother murdered, leading in turn to the death of his other brother, the King;
- has the person who then assumes power, the Queen's brother, murdered;
- locks up, and later murders, his final rivals for the throne, the King's two sons;
- eliminates the chief minister;
- and thus becomes King against all the odds.

In the course of the progression to the throne, as Judy Weinsoft (http://www.r3.org/struttxt.html) says, Richard takes such diverse roles as:

• Devoted brother	• Pious convert	• Cornered, sweating rat
• Stalwart friend	• Benevolent uncle	• Bluff soldier
• Witty wooer	• Good protector	• Innocent

- Loyal subject
- Plain blunt fellow
- Reluctant prince
- Political manipulator
- ?? (Insert your
- ?? own ideas!)

But look at the cost! Not only are people sacrificed to his ambition, Richard himself pays a high price. At the start of the play Richard has friends and allies; by the end he is alone, and his reign as King lasts a mere two years before he is overthrown.

He persuades his supporters to do some terrible things: What does this say about leadership – and about those who follow?

What does the story tell us about the power of language and the way that language can be used to manipulate people and events?

What does the story tell us about the need for change agents to keep the trust of their allies, and the consequences of betrayal?

Shakespeare is giving us a lesson in change management – and in the appalling consequences of not thinking through the implications of change. He does this by showing us both the public performance and the backstage activity. Shakespeare often shows the backstage activities in his plays – the private discussion, the secret deals, the shifting alliances. But in this play we get more – the private thoughts of the 'chief conspirator'.

Richard III is almost the only major character in Shakespeare's plays who talks so directly to the audience – he is almost inviting us to join his conspiracy! As Ian McKellen, who plays Richard III in the film which he also directed, says: 'Richard needs to talk to us. He needs to share his secrets – and Richard, my God, has he got some secrets!'

This is just one example of the lessons we can learn from Shakespeare – his histories and tragedies all offer something of interest, and not just in terms of leadership. The Fool in King Lear, for example, tells us much about the potential of, and the dangers of being, a devil's advocate.

See also P. Corrigan (1999) *Shakespeare on Management* (Kogan Page: London).

THE ROOTS OF THE MODERN PARADIGM

We dig now for the roots of this management thinking and find these in the Cartesian–Newtonian synthesis. It is important to emphasise three points. First, scientific method is only one element of the 'Enlightenment Project' – there is much else in that which is not explored here. Thus Hamilton (1992) suggests that the 'paradigm' of the Enlightenment would, at minimum, include the following ten ideas:

1 the primacy of reason and rationality;

2 empiricism;

3 scientific knowledge based upon the experimental method;

4 universalism;

5 progress;

6 individualism;

7 toleration;

8 freedom;

9 uniformity of human nature;

10 secularism.

Of these, the first six are important in the Cartesian–Newtonian synthesis.

Second, the critique below is not intended to belittle the achievements of the Cartesian–Newtonian synthesis; rather, it is concerned with identifying its limitations. Third, it is not suggested that science has now abandoned that synthesis: much current work (for example, in evolutionary theory) continues to have this method as its centrepiece.

The Modern Paradigm is underpinned by a deeper synthesis – a worldview perspective which explains much of what Argyris and Schon have characterised as 'Theory in Use'. In characterising this, we can usefully begin by a fuller consideration of the notion of paradigm. Popularised by Thomas Kuhn, paradigms are seen as important to understanding how people work and act, and how fundamental changes in perspective can occur. The underlying concept, however, has a longer lineage: it is that of the worldview perspective. There are three important elements here. First, while the world perspective affects – indeed, determines the boundaries of – behaviour, it is fundamentally based in language. Second, changes in the perspective can be hard to identify because the language may not change substantially, while the concepts within it do. Third, even between different conceptual structures, there is partial commensurability.

Ajdukiewicz (1973) also considered the relationship between different categories of statement. A demarcation has frequently been sought between empirical and interpretative statements, especially by those who seek to maintain the notion of 'value-free' statements. Ajdukiewicz holds that the decision to accept or reject empirical statements on the basis of the evidence is as arbitrary as the decision whether to accept interpreting statements. For by choosing a particular conceptual apparatus we may make it impossible for these empirical statements to be even formulated. The decisive factor in determining our world perspective, therefore, is not empirical evidence, but the conceptual apparatus in which we choose to work; in other words, the language we use.

This theory implies that it may be possible to choose two different types of conceptual apparatus in such a way that, from the same evidence, two radically different world perspectives may be formulated, both fully compatible with that evidence because that is how it is interpreted. This, of course, relates to the discussion on rationality, for it implies that there will be different interpretations of what is rational depending on how that and related concepts are formulated within each world perspective. It has implications also for management, since it challenges many of the approaches and ideas which rely on the belief that there can be a single perspective and a single concept of rationality: these include notions of common culture, common values and the management of resistance to change. In this sense culture is part of a shared world perspective, and will therefore be shared only in so far as the latter is.

While there have been attempts to define what we mean by a paradigm, few are as rich as the approach taken by Ajdukiewicz, who recognises the central role of language and the extent to which the world perspective embraces method and conscious thinking. Indeed, one could go further: the closely related Sapir–Whorf (Whorf 1956) hypothesis argues that each language has its own metaphysics (see also the definition by Capra given earlier, p. 15).

SCIENTIFIC RESEARCH PROGRAMMES

Lakatos has provided some useful additional conceptual tools in his delineation of scientific research programmes. He distinguishes two types of methodological rule:

1 **Negative heuristic**: tell us what paths of research to avoid. It 'forbids us to direct the [modus tollens] at the "hard core". Instead, we must use our ingenuity to articulate or even invent "auxiliary hypotheses", which form a protective belt around this core, and we must redirect the modus tollens to this' (1978: 48).

2 **Positive heuristic**: tell us what paths to pursue. It 'sets out a programme which lists a chain of ever more complicated models simulating reality: the scientist's attention is riveted on building his [sic] models following instructions which are laid down in the positive part of his programme' (1978: 50).

In effect, this thesis may be seen as a scientific research programme exploring the potential of an interlinked set of ideas for strategic management.

THE CARTESIAN–NEWTONIAN SYNTHESIS

The Modern Paradigm relies on a view of science and scientific method born of the stunning success of the Cartesian–Newtonian synthesis. After decades of uncertainty, as Western science moved painfully towards a heliocentric picture of the Universe, with all its profound metaphysical implications, it seemed that a basis for 'certain knowledge' had been achieved. For several centuries the implications of the 'mechanical universe' were to be explored, developed and refined. To understand the Modern Paradigm, we therefore need to understand the nature of this synthesis, and the method and epistemology it embraced.

Many philosophers, scientists and thinkers contributed to the synthesis. We will select five here. The first is Francis Bacon. In discussion with Capra, Carolyn Merchant argues that Bacon connected two principal strands of what was to become the Cartesian–Newtonian synthesis: the mechanistic conception of reality and the male obsession with domination and control in patriarchal culture.[1] Tarnas comments that the argument for the subjection of nature to human dominion was reinforced by the biblical support as found in Genesis – subduing nature could be seen as a religious duty (1991: 241–2). A third important strand in Bacon's thinking was the argument for a technocratic society, founded on scientific rationality and technological progress (Fischer 1990: 67).

The second is Galileo, who emphasised the overriding importance of mathematics: 'The book of nature is written in the mathematical language ... without its help it is impossible to comprehend a single word of it' (*Il Saggiatore, Opere,* VI, 232: quoted in Koestler 1959: 535). Galileo separated what could be measured or quantified, which he considered real, from what could not, which exist only in the observer's mind.

The third is Descartes, for whom mathematics provided the certainty that could underpin knowledge:

> Above all I enjoyed mathematics, because of the certainty and self-evidence of its reasonings, but I did not yet see its true use and, thinking that it was useful only for the mechanical arts, I was astonished that on such firm and solid foundations nothing more exalted had been built, while on the other hand I compared the moral writings of the ancient pagans to the most proud and magnificent palaces built on nothing but sand and mud. (1968: 31)

> In our search for the direct road towards truth we should busy ourselves with no object about which we cannot attain a certitude equal to that of the demonstrations of Arithmetic and Geometry. (1967: 5)

For Descartes, the machine is the dominant image; this extends to living beings, which are seen as machines, albeit very special ones. One of the dominant themes in management stemming from the Modern Paradigm has been the clockwork organisation, and the notion that all phenomena can be reduced to machine characteristics has its origin in Descartes: 'We see clocks, artificial fountains, mills and other similar machines which, though merely man-made, have nonetheless the power to move by themselves in several different ways ... I do not recognise any difference between the machines made by craftsmen and the various bodies that nature alone composes' (quoted in Capra 1982: 47).

The third important element which Descartes brought to the synthesis was the mind–body split: 'I am not this assemblage of things called the human body .... But what, then, am I? A thing that thinks' (1968: 105–6).

We now come to Newton himself, who synthesised Descartes' mechanistic philosophy, Kepler's laws of planetary motion and Galileo's laws of terrestrial motion in one comprehensive theory. Capra (1982) comments that before Newton there were two opposing trends in seventeenth-century science, which we have identified above: the empirical, inductive method represented by Bacon and the rational, deductive method represented by Descartes. Newton, in his *Principia*, brought them together, emphasising that neither experiments without systematic interpretation nor deduction from first principles without experimental evidence will lead to a reliable theory. Thus he went beyond Bacon in his systematic experimentation and beyond Descartes in his mathematical analysis, thereby developing the full methodology of the Cartesian–Newtonian synthesis.

The profound impact Newton had is well illustrated by Alexander Pope:

> Nature and Nature's laws,
> lay hid in night:
> God said, Let Newton be!
> And all was light.

The fifth thinker to be mentioned here is Locke, who began the task of translating the Cartesian–Newtonian synthesis to the human sciences. 'Following Newtonian physics, Locke developed an atomistic view of society, describing it in terms of its basic building block, the human being. As physicists reduced the properties of gases to the motion of their atoms, or molecules, so Locke attempted to reduce the patterns observed in society to the behaviour of its individuals' (Capra 1982: 55).

THE KEY ELEMENTS OF CARTESIAN–NEWTONIAN METHOD

Capra identifies four sets of concepts that form the basis of Newtonian mechanics:

1 The concepts of absolute space and time, and of separate material objects moving in this space and interacting mechanically with one another.
2 The concept of fundamental forces, essentially different from matter.
3 The concept of fundamental laws describing the motion and mutual interactions of the material objects in terms of quantitative relations.
4 The concept of rigorous determinism, and the notion of an objective description of nature based on the Cartesian division between mind and matter.

From these we can identify the following themes. It should be apparent how these have been retained in the perceptions outlined earlier.

Atomism and reductionism

As Harré (1984: 128, 144) has described, atomism invites us to explain the properties and powers of individual things and of materials as due to their fine structure, that is as due to the dispositions and interactions of their parts. The properties of individual things and of materials, he argues, should be redefined for scientific purposes as structural relations among standard elementary individuals. In addition, in an ideal form of description, quantitative items replace qualitative items.

We may illustrate this by returning to the management literature. Hosking and Morley (1991) argue that the 'entitative concept of organisation' dominates the literature in organisational behaviour and human resource management. Following Meyer et al. (1985), they identify five elements to this perspective, including membership and organisational boundaries; the whole having an identity recognised by its members and by others; the entity having relatively well-defined purpose(s); the entity having a formally prescribed structure; and the distinction between the organisation and its environment(s). We can see here also the interlinking between atomism and crisp logic.

Reinforcing our earlier argument, Hosking and Morley (1991) find this entitative approach not only in scientific management, but also in human relations and organic systems approaches.

Quantification

The importance of quantification to Newtonian science is apparent in the comments of Harré above. It has been reflected in the paramount role given to mathematics in any discipline wishing to be worthy of the name 'science'. This was the particular contribution of Galileo, with both its positive aspects, providing a powerful analytical methodology, and its negative, excluding that which cannot be expressed in numbers from the domain of science.

Determinism and prediction

Determinism flows naturally from reductionism. Hawking (1988) refers to the French scientist the Marquis de Laplace, who at the beginning of the nineteenth century argued that the Universe was completely deterministic. He suggested that there should be a set of scientific laws that would make it possible to predict everything that would happen in the Universe, if only we knew the complete state of the Universe at one time. A key element of determinism is the nature of cause–effect relationships. If these can be shown to be direct and predictable, then the case for strategic planning has strength; without this foundation, there are serious questions to be raised.

Crisp logic

Crisp logic – the thinking based on 'either/or' – is an essential element of the Cartesian–Newtonian synthesis. It is two-valued logic: propositions take one of two unique values, true or false. Composite propositions, and those constructed within predicate calculus, take their truth-values on the basis of rules defining logical connectors and valid inference.

The economic and evolutionary dimensions

The Modern Paradigm in management derives many of its elements directly from the Cartesian–Newtonian synthesis. It has additionally inherited a number through its acquisition of themes from other disciplines. Two in particular are worth noting. The first is economics, whose extended influence was magnified in the 1980s by the development of competitive strategy. The second, touched on briefly in the previous section, is evolutionary theory (which, of course, has close connections with competitive strategy in the descriptions of organisations competing in hostile environments). Articulations of Darwinian theory frequently stress Cartesian–Newtonian thinking.

In defence of Darwin, however, we should recognise that he developed his theory within a dynamic tension between the Cartesian–Newtonian synthesis and an alternative view, which is illustrated in the following letter home on Darwin's impressions of the Brazilian rain forest: 'If the eye attempts to follow the flight of a gaudy butterfly, it is arrested by some strange tree or fruit; if watching an insect, one forgets it in the strange flower it is crawling over; if turning to admire the splendour of the scenery, the individual character of the foreground fixes the attention. The mind is a chaos of delight.'

Howard Gruber has examined Darwin's development of his theory:

> The meaning of his whole creative life work is saturated with ... duality.... On the one hand, he wanted to face squarely the entire panorama of changeful organic nature in its amazing variety, its numberless and beautiful contrivances, and its disturbing irregularity and imperfections. On the other hand, he was imbued with the spirit of Newtonian science and hoped to find in this shimmering network a few simple laws that might explain the whole movement of nature. (quoted in Briggs 1992: 37–8)

And Briggs comments: 'Darwin's admiration for complexity and his belief in the Newtonian model of simple natural laws brought him an important step toward the artist's aesthetic (sense of harmony and dissonance), but in the end the emphasis of evolutionary theory fell on the simplicity side of the equation – on scientific law' (1992: 39). One cannot help wondering what Darwin would have made of complexity theory!

THE CRACKS IN THE CARTESIAN–NEWTONIAN SYNTHESIS

The success of the synthesis was dramatic for many years: so much so that it still dominates thinking by lay people when they consider science. But in the nineteenth century cracks began to appear. Three of these cracks are briefly described below to illustrate the theme.

Non-Euclidean geometry

Formulation in mathematics began with Euclid, who set out five axioms, and rules in inference, through which all geometrical propositions could be proved. This axiomatisation was of course 'true', since it was a statement of the geometry of the real world. Or was it? There were always doubts about Euclid's fifth axiom (which stated that through a point outside a given line one and only one parallel to the line could be drawn). Many attempts to derive it from the other four axioms were unsuccessful, and finally in the nineteenth century it was shown that this was impossible, since these four were in fact consistent with two other, very different, parallel axioms. One of these, developed by Lobachevski, states that an infinite number of parallels can be drawn through a point outside a given line (see Norden and Shirokov 1993; Perminov 1997); the other, developed by Riemann, states that no parallels can be drawn. The significance of these discoveries lay in the way they undermined an area of apparent 'certain knowledge', giving weight to the view that no such thing is possible. This is reinforced by the argument that Lobachevskian geometry may provide the better account of our world on a cosmological scale (see, for example, Penrose 1990).

Gödel and Hilbert's formalism

The divorce between the axioms of geometry and the real world meant that new ways of showing the consistency of this axiomatisation were needed, since it was no longer possible to view its realisation through the real world as 'taken for granted'. And the problem was not confined to geometry. Arithmetic and logic were being translated into formalised theories, and the consistency of these needed to be established. This need was increased by the discovery of a number of disturbing paradoxes.

Mathematicians hoped that a rigorous formalisation of mathematics would overcome these problems. To do so, the formalisation would need to satisfy two conditions – consistency and completeness. This was the goal of the formalist school, led by David Hilbert, who sought a secure foundation for mathematics, and hence for sciences which employed mathematical principles. But in 1931 Kurt Gödel destroyed these hopes with his theorem 'On Formally Undecidable Propositions in Principia Mathematica'. In one of the most brilliant and elegant proofs in mathematics Gödel showed that any such precise ('formal') mathematical system of axioms and rules of procedure whatever, provided that it is broad enough to contain descriptions of simple arithmetical propositions, and provided that it is free from contradiction, must contain some statements which are neither provable nor disprovable by the means allowed within the system. In summary, if any formalisable system of arithmetic is complete, it is inconsistent; if it is consistent, it is incomplete.

Quantum mechanics

We now know that Laplace's hopes of determinism cannot be realized, at least in the terms he had in mind. The uncertainty principle of quantum mechanics implies that certain pairs of quantities, such as the position and velocity of a particle, cannot both be predicted with complete accuracy. . . . The uncertainty principle had profound implications for the way in which we view the world. Even after more than fifty years they have not been fully appreciated by many philosophers, and are still the subject of much controversy. (Hawking 1988: 172, 55)

Quantum mechanics represents an important challenge to crisp logic. Thus, Wheatley (1992) has provided the following description of the double-slit experiment. Most simply, this experiment involves electrons that must pass through one of two openings (slits) in a surface. After passing through one of these slits, each electron lands on a second surface, where its landing is recorded. A single electron will pass through only one of the openings, but its behaviour will be affected by whether one or both slits is open at the time it passes through either one of them.

The electron, like all quantum entities, has two identities, that of a wave and that of a particle. If both slits are open, the electron acts as a wave, creating a pattern on the recording screen typical of the diffusion caused by a wave. If only one slit is open, the resulting pattern is that associated with separate, particle behaviour. On its way through one slit, the electron acts in a way that indicates that it 'knows' whether the second hole is open. It knows what the scientist is testing for, and adjusts its behaviour accordingly. If the observer tries to 'fool' the subject by opening and shutting slits as the electron approaches the wall, the electron behaves in the manner appropriate for the state of the holes at the moment it passes through one. The electron also knows if the observer is watching. If the recording apparatus is not on, the electron behaves differently. When the electron is not being observed, it exists only as a wave of probabilities; unless someone is watching, 'nature herself does not know which hole the electron is going through' (John Gribbin, quoted in Wheatley 1992: 61–2).

CONCLUSION

Capra (1982) has conveniently summarised the cumulative impact of several of these developments (excluding the mathematical). He argues that by the end of the nineteenth century Newtonian mechanics had lost its role as the fundamental theory of natural phenomena. Maxwell's electrodynamics and Darwin's theory of evolution involved concepts that went beyond the Newtonian model and indicated that the universe was far more complex than Descartes and Newton had imagined. Despite this the basic ideas underlying Newtonian physics, though insufficient to explain all natural phenomena, were still believed to be correct.

However, the first thirty years of the twentieth century were to change this situation radically. Relativity theory and quantum theory challenged all the principal concepts of the Cartesian worldview and Newtonian mechanics. The notion of absolute space and time, the elementary solid particles, the fundamental material substance, the strictly causal nature of physical phenomena, and the objective description of nature – none of these concepts could be extended to the new domains into which physics was now penetrating.

There is an important additional consideration: the negative consequences of the instrumental rationality that is so much a feature of the Cartesian–Newtonian synthesis.[2]

The Cartesian–Newtonian view is not so much wrong as it is limited. In many situations of everyday life Newton's mechanics are all we need; in almost every situation where we encounter Euclid's geometry it works fine. But as this view has been pressed into service in other areas of life it has proved much less successful (see, for example, Schaef (1992) on the implications in psychiatry and psychotherapy). Science and logic in the twentieth century have brought many new ideas and theories – and it is of value to consider the implications of these for our working lives.

We are not faced with choices between 'rational planning' and other modes, such as intuitive, incremental, adaptive, visionary or interpretative. Instead, we have three options, which have been well summarised by Willmott (1994), who suggests three possible paths of development in responding to the crisis of (hyper-)modernity, where all forms of meaning and authority become problematised and parodied:

1 A conservative path, which reasserts the value (or at least the functional necessity) of modernity's certainties and virtues.

2 A path that celebrates the crisis through a full embrace of hyper-modernity, making a virtue of contingency and impermanence by constructing a sense of self-identity through the incessant undermining of all divisions and barriers – e.g. Peters' (1989) incitement to thrive on chaos.

3 A path to seek the development of a radically postmodern mode of being in which dualistic theory and practice is challenged: sharing the scepticism about all authority and divisions, but equally sceptical about the taken-for-granted influence of a dualistic mode of being in which, for example, the mind is assumed to act independently of the body (Willmott 1994: 118–19).

Recasting this within the present argument, the first response would be to persist with the Modern Paradigm, and when it clashes with what actually happens, cloak the latter in the words of the former. This can be achieved, for example, through *post-hoc* rationalisation, where we construct rational explanations of what happened after the event, or say 'so much the worse for theory', or blame the environment for its excessive turbulence.

The second would be to reject any coherent theory – still more any grand narrative – perhaps instead following Peters' line, where the search for excellence is rejected in favour of thriving upon chaos, which in turn is replaced by liberation management and the pursuit of Wow! The Management Fad Generator would thus acquire an additional rule – ensure that your fad has built-in obsolescence.

The third option is to develop a framework with the following characteristics:

- It does not negate the value and use of the Modern Paradigm.
- Rather, it helps us to a richer way of thinking and acting in management, strategy, and organisational development.
- It provides the 'legitimacy' which is currently to be found only in the Modern Paradigm, not by seeking firm foundations, but through negotiated bases for thinking and activity.

Many of the chapters in this book develop and illustrate such a framework.

NOTES

1 'Bacon was the first to formulate a clear theory of the empirical approach of science, and he advocated his new method of investigation in passionate and often downright vicious terms. I was shocked by the extremely violent language, which Merchant exposed in her papers in quotation after quotation. Nature has to be "hounded in her wanderings" wrote Bacon, "bound into service" and made a "slave". She was to be "put in constraint" and the aim of the scientist was to "torture nature's secrets from her"' (Capra 1988: 238).

2 Thus Alvesson and Willmott comment: 'The rosy, positivist view of science, pictured as the benevolent agent of enlightenment, was forcefully challenged by Horkheimer and Adorno . . . in *Dialectic of Enlightenment*. Modern civilization, they argue, has become progressively mesmerized by the power of a one-sided, instrumental conception of reason. Beguiled by successes in conquering and harnessing nature, people in modern societies are seen to be trapped in a scientistic nexus. This nexus, Horkheimer and Adorno contend, is no less constraining, and is in many ways much more destructive, than the myopia of pre-modern traditions which the enlightening advance of science has aspired to replace: "In the most general sense of progressive thought, the Enlightenment has always aimed at liberating men from fear and establishing their sovereignty. Yet the fully enlightened earth radiates disaster triumphant" (ibid.: 3). Perhaps the most obvious symptom of this disaster is the relentless effort to dominate nature, associated with the ruthless exploitation of scarce natural resources and widespread environmental destruction and pollution. Although Horkheimer and Adorno do not refer directly to ecological crisis as a force of negation, their analysis certainly points in this direction. For them, civilization is doomed by the inescapable instrumentalism of our relationship to nature' (1996: 75).

REFERENCES

Ajdukiewicz, K. (1973) *Problems and Theories of Philosophy*, Cambridge: Cambridge University Press.

Allison, G.T. (1971) *Essence of Decision*, Boston, MA: Little, Brown.

Anthony, P.D. (1986) *The Foundation of Management*, London: Tavistock.

Argyris, C. (1992) *On Organizational Learning*, Oxford: Basil Blackwell.

Argyris, C. and D. Schon (1978) *Organizational Learning: A Theory of Action Perspective*, Reading, MA: Addison-Wesley.

Argyris, C. and D. Schon (1996) *Organizational Learning II: Theory, Method and Practice*, Reading, MA: Addison-Wesley.

Bauman, Z. (1989) *Modernity and the Holocaust*, Oxford: Polity Press.

Bettis, R.A. and P.K. Prahalad (1995) 'The Dominant Logic: Retrospective and Extension', *Strategic Management Journal*, 16.

Briggs, J. (1992) *Fractals: The Patterns of Chaos*, London: Thames and Hudson.

Bryson, J.M. (1987) *Strategic Planning and Non Profit Organisations*, San Francisco: Jossey Bass.

Burns, T. and G.M. Stalker (1961) *The Management of Innovation*, London: Tavistock.

Capra, F. (1982) *The Turning Point*, London: Flamingo.

Capra, F. (1988) *Uncommon Wisdom*, London: Flamingo.

Darwin, J. (1996) 'Dynamic Poise: Toward a New Style of Management – Part One', *Career Development International*, 1:5.

Descartes, R. (1967) *Philosophical Works, Volume 1*, Cambridge: Cambridge University Press.

Descartes, R. (1968) *Discourse on Method and the Meditations*, Harmondsworth: Penguin.

Dror, Y. (1968) *Public Policy Re-examined*, San Francisco: Chandler Publishing Co.

Eccles, R.G., N. Nohria and J.D. Berkley (1992) *Beyond the Hype*, Cambridge, MA: Harvard Business School.

Fischer, F. (1990) *Technocracy and the Politics of Expertise*, Newbury Park, CA: Sage.

Galileo (1623) *The Assayer*, in S. Drake (trans.) (1957) *Discoveries and Opinions of Galileo*, New York: Doubleday.

Gergen, K. (1992) 'Organization Theory in the Postmodern Era', in M. Reed and M. Hughes (eds) *Rethinking Organization: New Directions in Organization Theory and Analysis*, London: Sage.

Gill, J. and S. Whittle (1993) 'Management by Panacea', *Journal of Management Studies*, 30 (2): 281–95.

Grant, R.M. (1995) *Contemporary Strategic Analysis*, Oxford: Basil Blackwell.

Grint, K. (1991) *The Sociology of Work*, Cambridge: Polity Press.

Grint, K. (1995) *Management: A Sociological Introduction*, Cambridge: Polity Press.

Hamilton, P. (1992) 'The Enlightenment and the Birth of Social Science', in S. Hall and B. Gieben (eds) *Formations of Modernity*, Cambridge: Polity Press, in association with the Open University.

Harré, R. (1984) *The Philosophies of Science*, Oxford: Oxford University Press.

Hawking, S. (1988) *A Brief History of Time*, London: Bantam.

Hodgetts, R. and D. Kuratko (1990) *Management*, Orlando, FL: Harcourt Brace Jovanovich.

Hosking, D.-M. and I.E. Morley (1991) *A Social Psychology of Organizing*, London: Prentice Hall/Harvester Wheatsheaf.

Jun, J.S. and W.B. Storm (eds) (1973) *Tomorrow's Organizations: Challenges and Strategies*, Scott, Foreman and Company.

Kets de Vries, M.F.R. and D. Miller (1984) *The Neurotic Organization*, San Francisco: Jossey Bass.

Keynes, J.M. (1936) *The General Theory of Employment, Interest and Money 'Concluding Notes'*, London: Macmillan.

Koestler, A. (1959) *The Sleepwalkers*, Harmondsworth: Penguin.

Lakatos, I. (1978) *The Methodology of Scientific Research Programmes Volume 1*, Cambridge: Cambridge University Press.

Levin, A. (1993) 'Student Expectations of College', *Change*, Sept.–Oct.: 4.

Meyer, M., W. Stevenson and S. Webster (1985) *Limits to Bureaucratic Growth*, New York: Walter de Gruyter.

Mintzberg, H. (1994) *The Rise and Fall of Strategic Planning*, London: Prentice Hall.

Mintzberg, H., B. Ahlstrand and J. Lampel (1998) *Strategy Safari*, Hemel Hempstead: Prentice Hall.

Norden, A.P. and A.P. Shirokov (1993) 'The Heritage of N.I. Lobachevskii and the Activity of Kazan Geometers', *Russian Mathematical Surveys*, 48(2): 47–74.

Normann, R. and R. Ramrfez (1993) 'From Value Chain to Value Constellation: Designing Interactive Strategy', *Harvard Business Review* (July).

Penrose, R. (1990) *The Emperor's New Mind*, London: Vintage Books.

Perminov, V.Ya. (1997) 'The Philosophical and Methodological Thought of N.I. Lobachevsky', *Philosophia Mathematica: Series III*, 5(1): 3–20.

Peters, T. (1989) *Thriving on Chaos*, London: Pan Books.

Peters, T. and Waterman, R. (1982) *In Search of Excellence*, New York: Harper and Row.

Pollitt, C. (1993) *Managerialism and the Public Services*, Oxford: Basil Blackwell.

Prahalad, C.K. and R.A. Bettis (1986) 'The Dominant Logic: A New Linkage between Diversity and Performance', *Strategic Management Journal*, 7.

Ritzer, G. (1996) *The McDonaldization of Society*, London: Pine Forge Press, Sage Publications.

Roberts, J. (1996) 'Management Education and the Limits of Technical Rationality', in R. French and C. Grey (eds) *Rethinking Management Education*, London: Sage.

Rose, M. (1975) *Industrial Behaviour: Theoretical Development since Taylor*, London: Allen Lane.

Schaef, A.W. (1992) *Beyond Therapy, Beyond Science*, San Francisco: HarperCollins.

Schein, E.H. (1992) *Organizational Culture and Leadership*, San Francisco: Jossey Bass.

Schwartz, H.S. (1990) *Narcissistic Process and Corporate Decay*, New York: New York University Press.

Simon, H.A. (1960) *The New Science of Management Decision*, New York: Harper and Row.

Stacey, R.D. (1991) *The Chaos Frontier*, London: Butterworth-Heinemann.

Tapscott, D. and A. Canton (1993) *Paradigm Shift*, New York: McGraw-Hill.

Tarnas, R. (1991) *The Passion of the Western Mind*, London: Pimlico (1996 edition cited).

Taylor, F.W. (1967) *The Principles of Scientific Management*, New York: W.W. Norton and Co. (first published 1911).

Teece, D.J., G. Pisano and A. Shuen (1992) *Dynamic Capabilities and Strategic Management*, Mimeo.

Tichy, N.M. (1983) *Managing Strategic Change*, New York: Wiley.

Walton, R.E. (1985) 'From Control to Commitment in the Workplace', *Harvard Business Review*, March–April: 77–84.

Wheatley, M. (1992) *Leadership and the New Science*, San Francisco: Berrett Koehler.

Whorf, B.L. (1956) *Language, Thought and Reality* (ed. J.B. Carroll), Cambridge, MA: MIT Press.

Willmott, H. (1994) 'Bringing Agency (back) into Organizational Analysis: Responding to the Crisis of (post)Modernity', in J. Hassard and M. Parker (eds) *Towards a New Theory of Organizations*, London: Routledge.

Wittgenstein, L. (1961) *Tractatus Logico-Philosophicus*, London: Routledge and Kegan Paul.

Chapter 2

CULTURE AND CHANGE MANAGEMENT: ESSENTIAL DEBATE OR ESSENTIALLY A DIGRESSION?

The aims of this chapter are to:

1 Explore the implications of some of the ways in which organisational culture is portrayed in the literature from a realist perspective and the implications of these portrayals for managers.

2 Come to an understanding of some of the ways in which consultants and managers understand organisational culture as a 'practical' approach to the management of situations that confront them.

3 Explore the proposition that, rather than presenting managers with easy recipes for the management of change, realist theory sets up challenges of a high order.

4 Develop a critique of the realist position – explore the idea of organisational culture as a chimera – a metaphor that has reached its 'sell-by' date.

5 Synthesise this debate through the development of an understanding of the metaphor of organisation culture as essentially a practical metaphor with an understanding of its complexity and ambiguity – the realist position in postmodern guise.

INTRODUCTION

In this section we explore the different views of culture which engage, one way or another, with the idea that culture can be explored from a realist perspective. Underpinning this understanding of culture is the claim that there is a discrete phenomenon that can be identified as organisational and that culture is an aspect of organisational life that binds members together. It provides normative control within the organisation, provides a bulwark against uncertainty and doubt in relation to both the present and the future, and a sense of collectivity which also (arguably) permits a degree of autonomy. There are, however, different approaches that realists take in understanding organisational culture, for within the realist arena there are fundamental differences of opinion about the very essence of culture. These reflect fundamentally opposed ontological stances and differences with regard to issues of change and strategy. We shall discuss these differences in later sections; what is common ground between the various schools is that there are different elements of culture which can be identified with greater or lesser degrees of refinement.

Although, as many (e.g. Brown 1998) assert, there is a diversity of definition of organisation culture, there is an inner core of understanding. Culture is concerned with the meanings that members give to past, present and anticipated future experience and the ways in which these meanings are shared. The anthropologist Clifford Geertz suggested, in a wonderfully cavalier manner, that 'the culture concept to which I adhere has neither multiple referents nor, so far as I can see, any unusual ambiguity: it denotes an historically transmitted pattern of meaning as embodied in symbols, a system of inherited conceptions expressed in symbolic forms by means of which men [sic] communicate, perpetuate, and develop their knowledge about and attitudes toward life' (1973: 89).

THE IDEA OF ORGANISATIONAL CULTURE AS REALITY

For the cultural realist there is a convention that culture is presented as a layered model. Schein has probably been a leading proponent of this approach. Since his seminal article (1981) he has refined his understanding of the concept although his versions of the model have a consistency of analysis. He analyses culture in terms of the linkages between three levels of culture. At the heart are the basic assumptions which are in his terms deeply seated, taken for granted and therefore not open for inspection. According to Stacey these assumptions are such that people simply accept them 'without question as they interact with each other' (2000: 48). *Contra* this sense of mystery, Trice and Beyer (1993) suggest that basic assumptions cannot be altogether unconscious because, if they were, members would not be aware of cultural violations when they occur. At the second level in Schein's model are the core values, which he identifies with 'strategies goals and philosophies' (1992: 17). At the third, surface, level are the artefacts of organisational life associated with 'visible organizational structures and processes' (Schein 1993: 17). In an earlier discussion of culture Schein (1985) emphasises the interrelatedness of the elements through the use of the analogy of cultural forms as the water lily. At the surface, floating on the water, are the floral manifestations of the culture – the artefacts – and at the roots are the deeper fundamental aspects of the culture.

Another model, developed by the Bath Consulting Group (Hawkins 1997), depicts culture as three building blocks – closely integrated aspects of culture. These are what they call the 'Espoused Culture'. This surface block is the public presentation of the culture. They also refer to the 'Enacted Conscious Culture', what they think of as 'the lived culture that is noticed and can be verbalised'. At the deepest level there is the 'Unconscious Culture' which is the 'unthought known that is collectively experienced but not unnoticed by conscious reflection and not able to be verbalized' (Hawkins 1997: 428). Their model appears to have a *prima facie* resemblance to the Johari Window (Hall 1973; Schneider and Barsoux 1997) model of individual behaviour. There is a preoccupation with the relationship between the unknown and, to all intents and purposes, unanalysable (apart from the rigours of the psychoanalytic couch) with the observable and public areas of access to the self. In another representation (Harrison and Shirom 1999: 260) the layers of culture are represented as geological seams as from the surface (high visibility) to the depths (low visibility). This seam model suits the purposes of these authors in that they claim that there is no necessary connection between the elements of the different seams. Three separated but interlinked blocks, six seams of culture, a waterlily, three pyramidal blocks of culture – and now an interrelated ovular representation of culture. Each representation is a metaphor for capturing, in the realist tradition, the idea of culture.

A SYNTHESISING REALIST MODEL

In the representation of culture in Figure 2.1 what has been attempted is to show that although there are indeed layers of culture that are inextricably intertwined, the boundaries between the elements are permeable. The form of the model is also designed to suggest that although there are deeper elements to culture they are more amenable to discovery than some writers suggest. However, this model has the same problem, as do other representations of organisational culture – it takes as a starting point a monolithic version of the culture. Thus, even if one were to use the model as a diagnostic device to explore the relationship to the culture from the perspective of a counter-culture within the organisation, that very act presupposes a dominating discourse about the culture. There are, however, quantitative devices by which – and this is reported without irony – 'culture-conscious management' can develop maps of the organisation's subcultures which 'will lead to discussions how much cultural variety is present and how much is desirable' (Hofstede 1998: 11).

A travelling fortune-teller once visited the author of this chapter. She artfully inveigled herself into his house. To the astonishment of all she began to unfold the story of the members of the household and this gave her a remit to foretell our futures that was full of a misplaced confidence and optimism. She was able to tell that story, to capture the culture, because she had a keen sense of observation – she understood at least some of the vehicles of culture, the artefacts, and heard some of the processes of cultural communication as they took place between the members.

Schein (1992) is more cautious on this matter. He suggests that the more superficial aspects of culture may be amenable to the senses, but difficult to interpret. He suggests that interpretation of culture is uncertain because when organisations are observed either as outsiders or as insiders the observer brings into the situation projections and meanings that are based on the observer's

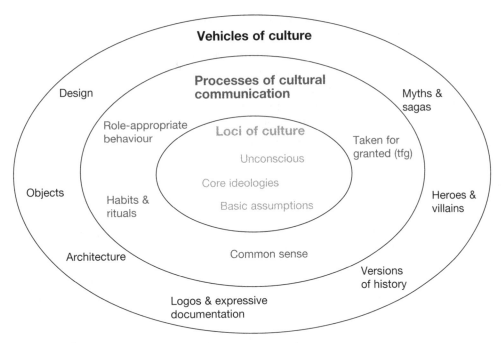

Figure 2.1 A realist concept of culture
Source: Adapted from McAuley and Shanahan (1994). Acknowledgements to the Open University and MESOL for permission to reproduce this figure.

reality. But this is to assume that there can be in any case an objective assessment of the culture. This is a theme to which we shall return.

The outer layer represents, or captures, 'the most faithful depiction of the cultural identity of an organization, of its material culture, of its symbolic landscape, of its forms of control' (Strati 1999: 159). However, there is a delicious complexity in this, which may be illustrated if we take one of the vehicles of culture as an example. The architecture of a building is a cultural statement that is made by key stakeholders as to what they want themselves and others to understand is the essence of their organisational aspiration. But at the very moment when these key stakeholders are looking at their building with pride and joy as a cultural icon, it may just be the case that others are looking at it with a sneer and derision; notions of fitness for purpose are differentially distributed. In this sense the artefact is *designed to* represent a particular set of cultural values but may be *oriented to* as representing diversity of cultural principles and aspirations. Architecture is located in a particular time, it is associated with a particular cultural milieu, and with the passage of time that architecture may be regarded as an icon or anachronism of present cultural ambition. What counts here in understanding the culture is not only the cultural intent of the designer, the architect and other key stakeholders who sponsor the architecture, but also the interpretations and the projections and the meanings of the phenomenon to others.

Similarly, in the central layer, we would suggest that none of the processes of communication is a static given, although there may well be some members who wish for the simple certainty of their particular version of organisational common sense, or role-appropriate behaviour, or whatever to prevail. Where there are relatively rigid requirements about role-appropriate behaviour, there is at play the requirement for strong relational institutions, just as where the habits and rituals within the organisation (such matters as the conduct of meetings) there is the strong hand of a regulatory framework (Parsons 1951).

Vignette 2.1

Culture change in a major consulting organisation: from button down collar to deconstruction

In 1999 there was a move towards open-plan office working within the company. Symbolically the transition from closed office space towards a concept that teams of people should engage in networking activities represents a change in the surface symbolism of the organisation – at the level of it is good to talk. However, we can also interpret in this surface culture change a deeper level of symbolism at play in the sense that at a deeper level sometimes these symbols can provide 'a camouflaged expression to repressed ideas and desires' (Gabriel 2000: 92) in some of the core values of the organisation. There has been a change in the dress code within the organisation so that members are encouraged to wear informal clothing. This artefact change symbolises a relaxation of habits and rituals and presages changes in the understandings of role-appropriate behaviour. There is also a shift here in the common-sense assumptions about the nature of what it is to be an employee in Arthur Andersen Consulting. And then, maybe, there is also a hint of deeper symbolism as well in relation to the very core of what it is to *be*, at the level of basic assumptions, in the consulting business.

Source: based loosely on Jones (1998).

In the centre, the heart of culture, there are four elements. In the conceptualisation of core ideology as a combination of core values and core purpose we were deeply influenced by Collins and Porras (1996). In their study of highly successful surviving organisations they suggest that at their heart these companies have a strong core ideology. This is the sum (not to be conceptualised too mechanistically) of the core values which are 'the organizations' essential and enduring tenets' (Collins and Porras 1996: 73) and the core purpose which is the 'organization's fundamental reasons for existence beyond just making money' (Collins and Porras 1996: 73). It is acknowledged, at the same time, that by no means all organisations have either as well articulated, or as noble visionary values and purposes as do the companies in their study. For example, there are many companies whose core purpose may well be, primarily, just to make money and whose core values are purely instrumental to this end. Indeed, the very term 'core ideology' can cause discomfort – Trice and Beyer point to the ways in which a strong ideology can induce organisational ethnocentrism and 'interfere with co-operation and co-ordination . . . and lead to such phenomena as passing the buck or blaming the victim' (1993: 11). This insight leads to a proposition that both the core ideology and the core values can have dysfunctional as well as functional elements within them. This will be discussed in a later section.

Vignette 2.2

The levels of culture at Hewlett-Packard

For Hewlett-Packard, the garage in which the business was founded and which features in advertisements is, at least at the level of espoused culture for public consumption, an icon, an attachment of sentiment that is deeply embedded in the culture. The garage symbolises core values espoused by the company in relation to its approach to undertaking business. In this sense one particular artefact, architecture, is linked with the myths and sagas, the heroic, utterly enthusiastic and visionary but socially aware nature of the founding fathers. This heroic aspect is part of the pattern of cultural transmission. It is a taken for granted that 'if you're not willing to enthusiastically adopt the HP Way, then you simply don't belong at HP' (Collins and Porras 1996: 121).

It is also linked with deeper aspects of the culture. At the level of core values it is asserted that Packard and Hewlett 'simply held deep convictions about the way a business *should* be built and took tangible steps to articulate and disseminate those convictions'. This core value is linked with another core value – that, in order to exercise this responsibility, the company needs to maintain control over its own destiny in order to ensure its long-term survival. One way of doing this is to follow a conservative financial strategy 'as a governor to keep the speed of the company's evolution at an appropriate scale' (De Geus 1997: 175). This core value pervades the organisation; it is organisational common sense, a taken for granted. Role-appropriate behaviour is towards demonstrable capability (McAuley 1994) in membership of a 'company of incredibly disciplined managers operating with a level of leanness and efficiency usually only found in small, cash-constrained companies' (Collins and Porras 1996: 189). At the level of basic assumption, it is a fundamental axiom that the company had responsibilities to employees, to customers and to the community (Collins and Porras 1996: 75). The organisation, at the level of basic assumption, 'embraces the tension between profit and purpose beyond profit. . . . Packard made it crystal clear that the Hewlett-Packard Company should be managed "first and foremost to make a contribution . . . to the advancement of science and the welfare of humanity." Yet "anyone who cannot accept (profit) as one of the most important (objectives) of the company has no place . . . on the management team . . ."' (Collins and Porras 2000: 57). As organisational ideology it is axiomatic that 'there is promotion from within the company and that first line managers are indoctrinated [sic] towards the company; there is constant discussion of the HP core values' (Collins and Porras 2000: 211). The emphasis on the company as collective entity is expressed through the establishment of 'learning communities' in which members deal with critical business issues (Sieloff 1999).

CULTURE AS FUNCTIONAL – TOWARDS THE CULTURAL RECIPE

Pervading the argument we have pursued so far, in a particular realist tradition, is a notion that culture is purposive, that it is not just a component of organisational life, but is one of the engines for organisational effectiveness. The intellectual lineage for this view emanates from the functionalist tradition. This perspective views culture as a phenomenon that is purposive and provides a meaning structure around which members can arrange their lives. For reasons that will unfold as the chapter develops, this model has particular appeal for those within the modernist tradition that would wish 'to interpret knowledge about culture as a tool of management, and culture itself as a variable to be manipulated' (Hatch 1997: 231). In this view, culture is seen by most writers to be concerned with an inner core of meaning, the core values that members hold, which in some sense or another binds them together. Essentially, this understanding of culture is ostensive in the sense that a claim is made that, in principle, culture can be discovered and identified, and its evolution can be explained through 'scientific' investigation. It is something that an organisation 'has' rather than 'is' (Mumby 1988; Hawkins 1997).

Organisations have culture because it is part of the human condition that there is a 'need for order and consistency (such that) assumptions become patterned into what may be termed cultural paradigms' (Schein 1981: 6). Within this definition members 'live in the culture' such that 'even if they are active, their actions are restricted because they only form a part of a larger pattern' (Czarniawska-Joerges 1991: 286). Schein illustrates this passivity in the face of culture in a more recent definition of culture when he suggests that culture is best viewed as 'the accumulated learning of a given group.... Given ... stability and a shared history, the human need for parsimony, consistency and meaning will cause the various shared elements to form into patterns that eventually can be called a culture' (1992: 10). Although he does argue that such a settled culture may fail to thrive within particular organisations, he attributes such disability to structural matters rather than the shaping of human will and intent.

This functionalist view may be illustrated through the work of Talcott Parsons whose writings on the nature of culture in society in general come from a tradition that has influenced later generations of organisational theorists. Parsons was a sociologist, but the functionalist trend in his writings can also be discerned in anthropologists' writing in that tradition. Lying at the heart of the functionalist paradigm is a notion of culture as a balance between the individual and the group and the organisation, and a preoccupation with the role of value-systems in the shaping of our experience. It is a view of culture that stresses the idea that culture, as with all social phenomena, has a function. The pervasiveness of culture lies in the ways in which culture as a concrete phenomenon provides an answer to the problem of order. It is an utterly mundane fact, according to writers in this tradition, 'that there is a certain order which persists below all the causes of disorganization in individual and collective action' (Rocher 1974).

The institutionalisation of culture is the means by which a reconciliation is achieved between 'personal motivations' (Parsons 1951: 51) and the more general patterns of what Parsons calls the social system. This insight can also be used to look at culture in organisations. Parsons suggested that, in a general way, there are three strands within which culture operates. He suggests that the social system is 'a network of social relationships' (Parsons 1951: 51). At the heart of creating order within this complexity there is a need for '*relational* institutions' (Parsons 1951: 51) – the pattern of relationships through the 'statuses and roles of the parties to the interactive process'. In the realist model of culture (Figure 2.1) the areas of organisational life in which the preconditions for the operation of the network in any particular organisation are manifested lie in the central layer. The culture of networking is expressed through the symbolism, the metaphors in use, what happens when the taken-for-granted aspects of organisational life are disrupted and in the issues of role-appropriate behaviour. To give an example. Generally speaking, within professional organisations, the taken-for-granted mode of address between colleagues is as peers, and at the different levels of hierarchy there is characteristically an avoidance of *overt* conflict through the expression of direct hostility or aggression. The relational institution is that, embedded in the culture, where there is hostility, this is expressed indirectly – through memos or e-mails, through ironic or sardonic comments, through pointed jokes or through subversive political action.

At another level, Parsons suggests, 'particular actors, individual or collective, act in terms which may, to a greater or lesser degree, be independent of the moral-integrative patterning of the social system ie the overall collectivity itself' (1951: 51). In order to avoid the risk of this independent action overwhelming the organisation there is, he suggests, an aspect of culture that needs to be *regulatory*. There can be independence of thought and action, on the one hand, without the need for a formal framework of rules and regulations, but on the other, in order not to impair the integrity of the system, there will be agreed values that control the extent of independence. Schein suggests that what he called the basic assumptions are shared by members of the organisation 'as it solved its problems of external adaptation and internal integration, that has worked well enough to be considered valid and, therefore to be taught to new members as the *correct way to perceive, think and feel*' (1992: 12; our emphasis). In this sense the rituals that are part and parcel of organisational culture, from a realist perspective, 'are forms of presentations orientated toward an ordered and organized social behavior and toward a common world view' (Blau 1998: 564). However, the organisation does not necessarily have it all its own way: from a realist perspective there are anti-rituals which 'help to sustain a matrix of collective understanding in terms of which unique, spontaneous and authentic action is also possible and interpretable' (Blau 1998: 564).

Parsons suggests that there is a third element to culture 'where the content of the institutions concerned consists only of patterns of cultural orientation as such. It is a question of beliefs, of particular systems of expressive symbols, or even of patterns of moral value-orientation when only "acceptance" rather than commitment to action are involved. These will be called *cultural* institutions' (Parsons 1951: 52). In organisational terms what Parsons is referring to are those aspects of organisational life that might, for example, be seen as ideals to which members would wish to aspire but which, in the everyday conduct of affairs, are not felt to be attainable or conflict with other ideals. This feature is transcendent as an aspect of organisational life in those organisations that may be characterised as occupying the missionary (Mintzberg 1989) position. He suggests that there are business organisations such as religious groups or charities that can be absolutely pervaded by the regulatory culture; he also suggests that there are organisations in which ideology is a key control component. This is an issue to which we shall return. Argyris and Schon's (1978) distinction between espoused theory and theories in use may illustrate this aspect of culture. In another sense these cultural institutions may be aspects of organisational life that some members may baulk at but live with as the preconditions of everyday life in the organisation.

Crucially, in the work of functionalist sociologists and anthropologists, there is an emphasis on systems in states of quasi-equilibrium, of their operating in harmony and in balance. Thus, for example, Parsons suggests that where freedom in issues of status and role exists (i.e. higher levels of autonomy), the system develops compensating adjustments through a greater tightness in the regulatory framework. The very basis of this continuing balance within the cultural system comes through the convergence of individual and collective perspectives – 'the basis of order is the structure of systems of action in the fact that they are internalized in the personality and at the same time institutionalised in society and culture' (Rocher 1974: 35) – and in organisations. An implication of this is that a functionalist view cannot 'come to grips with the hurdle of illegitimate social order and intended manipulation' (Czarniawska-Joerges 1992: 38). Another implication of this is that functionalist models of organisational culture cannot readily deal with disequilibria that are caused by major disruptions; on the issue of cultural change writers in this tradition are relatively silent.

There is a tendency, not only in Parsons but also in others in this tradition, to ignore the ways in which culture is dysfunctional, and has consequences that do not contribute to organisational well-being. Areas of dysfunction include such matters as the ways in which culture legitimates the continuation of present organisational practices, or can be seen to take the side of management in any discussion of cultural effectiveness, or can take an unduly optimistic stance with regard to issues of the management of culture (Trice and Beyer 1993: 12). There is also a stress within the perspective, on understanding culture to be a component of the whole social system.

However, this paradigm provides managers with great consolation because it legitimates management attempts either to manage the culture or, paradoxically, to provide a defence against the anxiety of such an arduous endeavour, to hand the task over to others. By looking at culture as a subsystem of the organisation, numerous models have been generated that can be used as a vehicle by which managers can explore issues of culture and reach delicious conclusions about culture change and the ways in which modifications of the culture fit into other sub-systems. Perhaps the most famous of these models is the 7S (and the various adaptations of it) that consultants and academics have introduced over the years. Interestingly, within this model in their discussion of culture (subsumed under the term 'Style') the authors suggest that 'not words, but *patterns of action* are decisive. The power of style, then, *is essentially manageable....* Another aspect of style is *symbolic behaviour*' (Waterman, Peters and Philips 1980: 17; our emphases). A more recent model – the cultural web – assumes the possibility that a 'representation of the taken-for-granted assumptions, or paradigm, of an organisation and the physical manifestations of organisation culture' are achievable. They also suggest that cultures, as sub-system, are 'not easy to change and that therefore they can impair the development of organisational strategies' (Johnson and Scholes 1999: 73).

TOWARDS A MORE COMPLEX UNDERSTANDING OF CULTURE

In the previous section it was suggested that an understanding of culture is not value-neutral – but then little in social science is. Mumby (1988) distinguishes two broad approaches to organisational culture. In one, as we have seen, there is an understanding in which the adherents 'espouse and actively promote the management and change of organizational culture'. This explicitly managerial orientation 'views culture as an organizational variable (something the organization has) which can be manipulated to best suit the needs of the organization – normally the rationale for change lies with efficiency, productivity, and worker morale' (Mumby 1988: 7). In the second, there is a plurality of cultures within the organisation, such that 'an organization does not *have* a culture, it *is* a culture. The socially constructed nature of organizational reality is just that – *socially* constructed. Organizations are not deemed to have any existence independent of the shared values and meaning systems that are generated by organization members' (Mumby 1988: 8). We would add that there is an emergent view that suggests that too much attention to the concept of corporate culture or organisational culture is dangerous (Trice and Beyer 1983).

Something of this complexity is captured in Figure 2.2. As a metaphor, Figure 2.2 suggests that views of organisational culture can be multi-perspectival from the point of view of both the researcher and the organisational member. At the heart of this model is the suggestion that understandings of organisational culture are rooted in considerations of the cultural milieu in which the member customarily exists; in a perfectly banal way, members (and researchers for that

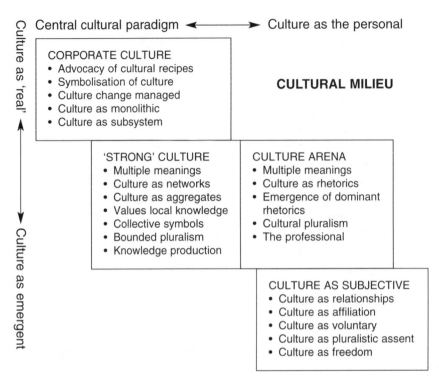

Figure 2.2 Different dimensions of the cultural domain

matter) tend to understand the culture in which they normally live to be the template for organisational cultures. In this sense they contain moral tales of organisational life, they provide accounts for the relationship between personal autonomy and organisational control. That is not to say that they do so uncritically. As models, or ideal types, we suggest that there are four distinctive cultural milieux:

1 Within the image of corporate culture there is an understanding that it is possible, and desirable, to develop an overarching unifying culture. This culture is one that can enrapture all employees of the organisation, although there may be some ambivalence about the relationship between autonomy and socialisation into the organisation (e.g. Pascale 1985). The corporate culture model is derived from functionalist understanding of the nature of life and it provides members with particular modes of solace and discomfort. The role of the manager in the organisation is, with regard to cultural understanding, primarily concerned with ensuring that the sense of cultural uniformity is maintained.

2 The idea of the 'strong' culture (Jelinek and Schoonhaven 1990) respects the notion of very high levels of cultural diversity in the organisation. This diversity comes through a deep respect for members' local knowledge, but suggests

that people are bound together through the common core of the passionately shared sense of organisational purpose. The role of the manager is to ensure that the diverse sources of local knowledge are shared and that there is a level of consensus about organisational purpose.

3 In the cultural arena (Strauss et al. 1964; McAuley 1994) there is a concern with cultural diversity, but this time located around the concept of professional and occupational identity. In this diversity the concept of organisational culture *per se* becomes less real. The role of the manager is to ensure that the rhetoric of management is well heard in the organisation. Part of that rhetoric is an assurance that the concept of unifying organisational culture (analogous to the concept of corporate culture) is of the greatest significance.

4 Finally, there is a culture of not having a culture, an environment in which 'the definite individual in his/her real relation to other individuals and groups' can come to find identity 'in the resultant web of relationships with the social totality and with nature' (Horkheimer 1937: 220). Through this notion of free association, so it is asserted, an understanding of the sort of culture that might meet human requisites is developed. In this sense, culture is the product of individual will and reason. Within this subjective culture there is a stress on characteristics of human autonomy and responsibility. On the other, there is a stress on consensus (Alvesson and Willmott 1996: 116) in collective decision making. The culture is the process that provides the bases from which the ideology of consensus is established, by which that ideology is communicated and the vehicles by which the cultural ideology is transmitted.

In a strange and paradoxical way these four versions of culture move us, in corporate culture, from a unitary view of culture through to a highly bounded, pluralist view of culture in the Strong Culture, through to a highly pluralist version of culture in the arena and back again to a unitary view of culture in the subjective view. It is argued, however, that the unitary bases of the first and the last rest on entirely different premises.

Corporate culture, so it is argued, is quintessentially management-driven, it is a culture of regulation driven by a managerialist agenda with the purpose of advancing organisational purposes whilst acknowledging the needs for a degree (but constrained within the organisational paradigm) of personal autonomy. In modern organisations, it is claimed, cultural regulation comes from the fostering of a limited degree of self-actualisation or personal development in order to engage members' commitment. It is a trade-off between the maintenance of personal identity and belonging to the organisation.

The subjective culture is also unitary, but this sense of oneness in the culture arises primarily as avoidance of domination. If there *were* to be the emergence of dominating discourses from individuals or groups, there would be 'tensions associated with denial of autonomy and responsibility' (Alvesson and Willmott 1996: 115). This would lead to unbearable conflict in which the cultural form could no longer hold or those very tensions 'would provide the basis of personal and collective resistance to forms of domination' (Alvesson and Willmott 1996: 115).

These are issues to be discussed later. We shall suggest the possibility of a synthesis as between corporate culture and subjective culture in processes of change.

ORGANISATION CULTURE AS THE GHOST IN THE MACHINE OF THE PROCESSES OF CHANGE

The view that organisational culture may be seen as a form of domination points to core issues in the ways in which it can be seen as underpinning processes of strategic change. There are two ways in which understanding organisation culture may be seen as problematic. On the one hand, there is a view that an understanding of culture gives opportunities to management to exploit and develop, with greater or lesser subtlety, vehicles for the oppression of organisational members. Their motivation would be to promote a particular view of strategic change and the management of the sort of organisational setting in which members are supposed to enact their everyday lives. On the other hand, organisational culture may be seen as a means by which members themselves come to understand the processes of oppression in which they are located.

From the perspective of some, but not all, writers who support the proposition that managers are legitimated agents of change, active culture management (e.g. Lundberg 1990; Pascale 1985) can provide a vehicle for change. The appropriate employment of culture as technology may lead to the development of alignment with organisational, managerially-determined purposes. A view such as this would sit comfortably, for example, with the rise and rise of the managerialist agenda. Underpinning the managerialist discourse are claims that it is only by developing clear patterns of managerial authority that organisations can 'replace difficulty and diffuseness by the order and control given by clear management' (McAuley, Duberley and Cohen 2000: 95). This constructed world of management is a manifestation of what has been characterised as the 'managerial metamyth which is based on the omnipotent dream of an ideal machine' (Sievers 1994: 88). A key aspect of the 'increasingly unrestrained managerial power in the private and public sectors' (Fournier and Grey 2000: 11) has been the view that issues of change may be seen as technical problems which can be resolved through technical means such as 'restructuring, downsizing, cultural re-engineering' (Fournier and Grey 2000: 11).

Within this view an understanding of culture may be seen as an invitation to manipulate, or as a mechanism by which members become disempowered whilst feeling empowered (the experience of 'false consciousness'). In this sense 'managerial interest in Human Relations and Corporate Culture can be interpreted as moves to exploit employee anxiety by contriving to provide a corporate antidote to it' (Alvesson and Willmott 1996: 114). This tendency may be seen in at least some versions of the learning organisation where the 'essence of the discipline of the shared vision ... lies in bringing individual visions into harmony with a larger vision.... The combination of mission, vision and values creates the common identity that can connect thousands of people within a large organization. One of the chief tasks of leaders, at both the corporate and local level, is fostering this common identity' (Senge 1993: 293). It is suggested that 'managerial attempts to employ corporate culture strategies' of self-fulfilment as a means of engendering commitment contribute to 'the very implosion of image and reality, truth and falsity which underpins the dissolution of the very mode of subjectivity upon which such managerial ambitions rest' (Hancock 1999: 171).

Issues of stability and change in the management of culture may be illustrated by reference to what have been characterised as 'visionary companies' (Collins and Porras 1996). These are the quintessence of what we have characterised as Corporate Culture. They are companies which are regarded, in the United States, as premier organisations, widely admired by their peers in the business world, which have been influential in the world, have shown an ability to change and have been around for a good number of years. A clear characteristic of these organisations is the adherence of members to the tenets of the organisational ideology so that ideological control preserves the core, the very heart, of the organisation, 'while *operational* autonomy stimulates progress' (Collins and Porras 1996: 136). Collins and Porras suggest that membership of these organisations involves acceptance of indoctrination processes, and through this fervent acceptance of the ideology. Allegiance to the organisation has an air of totality. There is also acceptance of the meritocratic elitism that pervades the organisation culture, in relation to both its external and internal environment. The role of management and leadership within this sort of organisation is to preserve the ideological core.

A different gloss on this is that the culture of ideology-led organisations is essentially regressive in that it emphasises dependency on the organisation rather than the development of autonomous self-determination. Schwartz (1990) suggests that the emphasis on ideology means that, even in very successful companies, increasingly, members become seduced by an organisational fantasy through the loss of autonomous will and consciousness. He suggests that members come to accept an organisational ideal, a Utopia in which there is a magical synthesis between 'individual happiness and spontaneity, on the one hand, and maximal performance and productivity, on the other' (Schwartz 1990: 125). This emphasis on symbolic management leads to a situation in which members no longer make choices through informed consent, but rather through cultural conformity. Although members may well put up interesting resistance through their practice of symbolisation into these incursions into the self and the group (Gabriel 1991), the possibility of culture conformity may well persist. Although members may put up resistance to attempts to manage culture through the process of giving 'new' symbols meanings different from those intended by management (Gabriel 1991), the process of culture management may be seen as essentially alienating.

There will inevitably, however, be culture change at other levels in order that the organisation can undertake internal adjustments, align to new forces and features in the environment, and anticipate the future (Lundberg 1990). An example of this may be illustrated in improvements in performance of Anglo-Dutch Shell (Trapp 2000). It would appear that the company has engaged in preservation of core ideology through a process of what is characterised as internal merger. In this context it is interesting that the person identified as the key change agent is an organisational insider, apparently deeply aware of the essence of the organisation. This may be seen as a process of culture shift where growth of investment (the metaphor of 'size matters' as a process of cultural communication) within a highly bureaucratic setting (organisational design as a vehicle of culture) has been replaced by a metaphor of the company as sceptical and learning in relation to investment decisions within an organisational design that is an 'efficient group'. However – and this is an issue to which we shall return – in relation to issues of change there has clearly been a complex inter-play between culture and structure (Hendry 1999); that is, although there has been culture change, it has not essentially been culture-led.

There is another view, however. It is that in this discussion of managing culture, of clustering around the vision, of the dysfunctional aspects of organis-ational culture as an engine for change, the debate is becoming somewhat inward-looking; there has been a fatal seduction in the concept of the culture metaphor as an agent of change in playing with the organisational mind. In this sense suggestions that culture is the key variable and that an understanding of culture *per se* necessarily gives rise to change (e.g. Lundberg 1990) may be seen as problematic.

CULTURE CHANGE AS ONE ASPECT OF A COMPLEX REPERTOIRE

When the formidable and highly influential Geertz was reconceptualising cul-ture he found that within the discipline the concept suffered a degree of 'ill repute ... because of the multiplicity of its referents and the studied vagueness with which it has been invoked' (1973: 89). In this section it will be suggested that the idea of an organisation culture is a sort of nonsense, that it is a metaphor taken too far, that it is an attempt by social scientists and consultants to explore little understood phenomena in order to give themselves a spurious sense of order. This critique is analogous to those perspectives on psychoanaly-sis (e.g. Gellner 1985) which suggest that such explorations of phenomena are pseudo-scientific movements, that its explanations fit experience only because adherents want there to be a fit – it is a feat of imagination. In this sense, accounts of organisational culture are tales told round the campfire and their provenance lies in the response of the reader as to the extent to which the account resembles, or fails to resemble, his or her own understanding of life.

This notion of culture as fashionable industry is taken up by writers such as Bate, who suggests that 'the 1980s are likely to go down in history as the "decade of culture". Since the late 1970's "organizational culture" has been a conceptual focus of organizational research and dialogue, shaped up by everyone, widely exploited, and expected to resolve or clarify a multitude of fundamental problems and issues. Now, however, signs indicate the popularity of this concept may be starting to wane' (1990: 84), although this decline might well be located in the attempts of cultural engineers to over-simplify the issues rather than in the concept itself (Bate 1994). It might be suggested – and there are interesting parallels – that the replacement paradigm, the postmodernist and the chaos debate are coming to be used to explore organisational life during this period. Thus in the case of organisational culture one writer suggests that it continues to be 'the newest perspective in organisational theory. It is at the same time both a radical departure from the mainstream of contemporary organisational behaviour studies and elaboration of long-established traditions ...' (Brown 1998: 5). Other claimants to be the new kid on the block suggest that Chaos Theory is 'a new scientific way of explaining the creative behaviour of dynamic systems, one of which is the successful business organisation' (Stacey 1991: ix–x). What seems to happen is that writers generate a 'good idea' about ways of understanding organisational life – for that is the mystery that is a critical part of our lives – and then turn it into a paradigm.

In the case of the concept of culture the development of the culture paradigm – particularly in the understanding of issues of change – has important consequences. Once managers get through the illusion that beauty parlour approaches to culture change – superficial modification of vehicles of culture – will produce anything other than the most superficial change they need to confront the suggestion that 'changes in corporate culture should be considered only after other, less difficult and less costly solutions have either been applied or ruled out' (Cummings and Worley 2001: 509). Given that some writers suggest that deep culture change can take five to ten years to achieve, it may be asserted that members are entering an illusory world of 'now you see it, now you don't'. At a more radical level, there are those who would argue that actively working on culture change is to engage in a dangerous illusion that you are engaged in a valid form of work. In this view it is much more important to focus on issues of innovation and development in encountering the marketplace. The necessary culture change will then follow (Newman and Chaharbaghi 1998).

At the same time we could assert that an understanding of organisational culture that goes beyond the mechanistic and its place in the processes of change corresponds to our experience of organisational life as process. It could be asserted that however uncomfortable the development of understanding of culture, understanding the implications of the ideology is in itself an important act of enlightenment that is essentially if uncomfortably liberating. Take the example of British Rail (discussed by Bate 1990). Although the organisation had gone through a process of major structural change, it remained stuck in the sense that there had been no improvement in performance. It was only through a detailed cultural understanding on the part of Board members of the dysfunctional aspects of the key metaphors that pervaded the thinking of senior management in the organisation that there was a shift towards greater effectiveness in the overall performance of the organisation. It enables us to understand issues of change as being about the relationships between members and as something that members construct (Gephart 1996) with greater or lesser autonomy. Members are enabled to understand the essentially human aspects of organisational life and from this the ways in which human will and agency engage in organisational change. In terms of the postmodern agenda, the development of capability to achieve a cultural critique within organisations allows actors to access their own capability in 'radical reflexivity'. This enables them 'to appreciate the limits and implications of their views ... a process of effectiveness theorizing' (Boje, Gephart and Thatchenkery 1996), which leads to effective action in an uncertain world. In this sense understanding culture as metaphor rather than as reality can help members engage in that type of serious intellectual and action-oriented flirtation that 'keeps things in play, and in doing so lets us get to know them in different ways' (Phillips 1994: xii).

REFERENCES

Alvesson, M. and H. Willmott (1996) *Making Sense of Management: A Critical Introduction*, London: Sage.

Argyris, C. and D.A. Schon (1978) *Theory in Practice*, San Francisco: Jossey Bass.

Bate, P. (1990) 'Using the Culture Concept in an Organization Development Setting', *Journal of Applied Behavioural Sciences*, 26(1): 83–106.

Bate, P. (1994) *Strategies for Cultural Change*, Oxford: Butterworth-Heinemann.

Blau, J.R. (1998) Book review: 'The Order of Rituals: The Interpretation of Everyday Life', *Human Relations*, 51(4): 563–7.

Boje, D.M., R.P. Gephart, Jr. and T.J. Thatchenkery (1996) Conclusion, in D.M. Boje, R.P. Gephart, Jr. and T.J. Thatchenkery (eds) *Postmodern Management and Organization Theory*, Thousand Oaks, CA: Sage.

Brown, A. (1998, 2nd edition) *Organisational Culture*, London: Financial Times/Pitman Publishing.

Collins, J.C. and J.I. Porras (1996; 3rd edition 2000) *Built to Last: Successful Habits of Visionary Companies*, London: Century Business.

Cummings, T.G. and C.G. Worley (2001, 7th edition) *Organization Development and Change*, Cincinnati, OH: South-Western College Publishing.

Czarniawska-Joerges, B. (1991) 'Culture is the Medium of Life', in P.J. Frost, L.F. Moore, M.R. Louis, C.C. Lundberg and J. Martin (eds) *Reframing Organizational Culture*, Newbury Park, CA: Sage.

Czarniawska-Joerges, B. (1992) *Exploring Complex Organizations: A Cultural Perspective*, Newbury Park, CA: Sage.

De Geus, A. (1997) *The Living Company: Habits for Survival in a Turbulent Business Environment*, Boston, MA: Harvard Business School Press.

Fournier, V. and C. Grey (2000) 'At the Critical Moment: Conditions and Prospects for Critical Management Studies', *Human Relations*, 53(1): 7–33.

Gabriel, Y. (1991) 'Turning Facts into Stories and Stories into Facts: A Hermeneutic Exploration of Organizational Folklore', *Human Relations*, 44(8): 857–75.

Gabriel, Y. (2000) *Storytelling in Organizations: Facts, Fictions and Fantasies*, London: Sage.

Geertz, C. (1973) *The Interpretation of Cultures*, New York: Basic Books Inc.

Gellner, E. (1985) *The Psychoanalytic Movement or The Cunning of Unreason*, London: Paladin Grafton Books.

Gephart, R.P. (1996) 'Management, Social Issues, and the Postmodern Era', in D.M. Boje, R.P. Gephart, Jr. and T.J. Thatchenkery (eds) *Postmodern Management and Organization Theory*, Thousand Oaks, CA: Sage.

Hall, J. (1973) 'Communication Revisited', *California Management Review*, XV(3): 58.

Hancock, P. (1999) 'Baudrillard and the Metaphysics of Motivation: A Reappraisal of Corporate Culturalism in the Light of the Work and Ideas of Jean Baudrillard', *Journal of Management Studies*, 36(2): 156–75.

Harrison, M.I. and A. Shirom (1999) *Organizational Diagnosis and Assessment: Bridging Theory and Practice*, Thousand Oaks, CA: Sage.

Hatch, M.J. (1997) *Organization Theory: Modern Symbolic and Postmodern Perspectives*, Oxford: Oxford University Press.

Hawkins, P. (1997) 'Organizational Culture: Sailing between Evangelism and Complexity', *Human Relations*, 50(4): 417–41.

Hendry, J. (1999) 'Cultural Theory and Contemporary Management Organization', *Human Relations*, 52(5): 557–78.

Hofstede, G. (1998) 'Identifying Organizational Subcultures: An Empirical Approach', *Journal of Management Studies*, 35(1): 1–12.

Horkheimer, M. (1937) 'Traditional and Critical Theory', in P. Connerton (ed.) (1976) *Critical Sociology*, Harmondsworth: Penguin.

Jelinek, M. and C.B. Schoonhaven (1990) 'Strong Culture and its Consequences', in J. Henry and D. Walker (eds) *Managing Innovation*, London: Sage.

Johnson, G. and K. Scholes (1999, 5th edition) *Exploring Corporate Strategy*, London: Prentice Hall Europe.

Jones, T. (1998) 'Working Life: Brave New Workplace: The deconstructed office may be the last word in trendy, but does it really work better?', *The Independent on Sunday – Business Section*, 11 October.

Lundberg, C.C. (1990) 'Surfacing Organizational Culture', *Journal of Managerial Psychology*, 5(4): 19–26.

Martin, J. (1992) *Cultures in Organizations: Three Perspectives*, New York: Oxford University Press.

McAuley, M.J. (1994) 'Exploring Issues in Culture and Competence', *Human Relations*, 47(4): 417–30.

McAuley, M.J. (1996) 'Ethical Issues in the Management of Change', in K. Smith and P. Johnson, *Business Ethics and Business Behaviour*, London: Thomson Business Press.

McAuley, M.J. and P. Shanahan (1994) *Culture and Innovation. Book 5: Health and Social Services Management: Managing your Enterprise*, Milton Keynes: Open University Press.

McAuley, J., J. Duberley and L. Cohen (2000) 'The Meaning Professionals Give to Management . . . and Strategy', *Human Relations,* 53(1): 87–117.

Mintzberg, H. (1989) *Mintzberg on Management: Inside the Strange World of Organizations,* New York: The Free Press.

Mumby, D.K. (1988) *Communication and Power in Organizations: Discourse, Ideology, and Domination,* Norwood, NJ: Ablex Publishing Corporation.

Newman, V. and K. Chaharbaghi (1998) 'The Corporate Culture Myth', *Long Range Planning,* 31(4): 514–23.

Parsons, T. (1951) *The Social System,* London: Routledge and Kegan Paul.

Pascale, R. (1985) 'The Paradox of "Corporate Culture": Reconciling Ourselves to Socialization', *California Management Review,* 27(2): 26–41.

Phillips, A. (1994) *On Flirtation,* London: Faber and Faber.

Rocher, G. (1974) *Talcott Parsons and American Sociology,* London: Nelson.

Schein, E.H. (1981) 'Coming to a New Awareness of Organizational Culture', *Sloan Management Review,* (Winter): 3–16.

Schein, E.H. (1985, 1st edition) *Organizational Culture and Leadership,* San Francisco: Jossey Bass.

Schein, E.H. (1992, 2nd edition) *Organizational Culture and Leadership,* San Francisco: Jossey Bass.

Schneider, S.C. and J.L. Barsoux (1997) *Managing across Cultures,* London: Prentice Hall.

Schwartz, H.S. (1990) *Narcissistic Process and Corporate Decay: The Theory of the Organizational Ideal,* New York: New York University Press.

Senge, P.M. (1993) *The Fifth Discipline: The Art and Practice of the Learning Organization,* London: Century Business.

Sieloff, C.G. (1999) '"If only HP knew what HP knows"; The Roots of Knowledge Management at Hewlett-Packard', *Journal of Knowledge Management,* 3(1): 47–53.

Sievers, B. (1994) *Work, Death, and Life Itself: Essays on Management and Organization,* Berlin: Walter de Gruyter.

Stacey, R.D. (1991) *The Chaos Frontier: Creative Strategic Control for Business,* Oxford: Butterworth-Heinemann.

Stacey, R.D. (2000, 3rd edition) *Strategic Management and Organisational Dynamics: The Challenge of Complexity,* Harlow: Financial Times/Prentice Hall.

Strati, A. (1999) *Organization and Aesthetics,* London: Sage.

Strauss, A. (1991) 'Paradigm and Prospects for a General Theory of Negotiation', in A. Strauss (ed.) *Creating Sociological Awareness: Collective Images and Symbolic Representations,* New Brunswick: Transaction Press.

Strauss, A., R. Bucher, D. Ehrlich, M. Sabshin and L. Schatzman (1964) *Psychiatric Ideologies and Institutions,* Glencoe, IL: Free Press.

Trapp, R. (2000) 'The Man Who Was Sure of Shell', *The Independent,* 4207, 12 April.

Trice, H.M. and J.M. Beyer (1993) *The Cultures of Work Organizations,* Englewood Cliffs, NJ: Prentice Hall.

Waterman, R.H., T.J. Peters and J.R. Phillips (1980) 'Structure is not Organization', *Business Horizons,* (June).

Chapter 3

MINDSETS AND PARADIGMS: THE INDIVIDUAL AND THE ORGANISATION IN TIMES OF CHANGE

The aims of this chapter are to:

1 Explore the concept of the organisation mindset and the organisation paradigm.

2 Develop an understanding of the rational approaches to the mindset and the prescriptive approaches to mindset change that have been promulgated.

3 Discuss the idea of the 'mindset' in the light of psychoanalytic thought to bring out the theme that the management of change needs this awareness of deeper elements in the response of the individual to change.

4 Develop understanding of the implications of multiple mindsets within the organisational arena and as discourses within organisational life.

5 Show how Critical Theory and the concepts of emotional intelligence, emotional capability and spiritual intelligence can lead to the development of the capability for mindset change.

6 Develop an understanding of the ways in which changing mindsets represent an interplay between the individual, groups and the organisation.

INTRODUCTION

The purpose of this chapter is to explore some of the issues that underlie the relationship between the individual and the organisation, particularly in a period of change. This theme will be explored through a discussion of the concept of the mindset as a concept that captures members' understanding of the nature of the reality that confronts them. In Chapter 2 there was reference to the concept of culture as the metaphor by which anthropologically- or sociologically-oriented understandings of organisation try to get to grips with the meaning structures that members create. The concept of the mindset is a convenient device for a more social psychological look at the organisation, although that will not prevent the incursion, from time to time, of sociological perspectives into the chapter. There will be an attempt to explore the contribution of the psychoanalytic approach in getting behind the rational aspects of the mindset. This will focus on a discussion of the appropriateness of this view in creating a rich and useful understanding of organisational life and the ways in which it illuminates key issues in the management of change. This has a relationship with the ideas of emotional intelligence in which it is suggested that there is a neat linkage between psychoanalysis and sociology. These themes suggest that the level of human action (as with strategic or technical action) in change needs to be radical rather than ameliorative. The chapter is concerned, then, with an exploration of the rich interplay between the conscious and the unconscious, the individual and the organisation, during periods of change.

MINDSETS, PARADIGMS AND OTHER SUCH MATTERS

There is a diversity of definitions of the idea of the mindset as it relates to personal and organisational life. For some (e.g. Kaiser 1986) it is defined as a collective awareness which is shared by key internal stakeholders. In this view it is a concrete phenomenon and can be subjected to a force-field analysis (Lewin 1951) of helping and hindering forces. This level of reality is such that members can freely choose new and better mindsets, and go through processes of unfreezing, movement and refreezing so that they can move onto an improved mindset. A related view is that the mindset is comprised of sets of mental models arranged in a series where a mental model is a basic unit of understanding. In this sense a mindset is the 'direction of one's thinking' (Mak 1999: 623). Another view is that mindsets are 'patterns of sense-making and behavior' that capture the ways in which members frame situations, evaluate the alternatives and then select responsive behaviours (Liedtka 1991: 544). Liedtka suggests a certain concreteness in the claim that there are four categories of mindset – managerial, political, bureaucratic and value-driven – to which managers adhere in order to develop behavioural responses.

The concept has also been characterised as 'a predisposition to see the world in a particular way that sets boundaries and provides explanations for why things are the way they are ... a filter through which we look at the world' (Rhinesmith 1992: 63). This is aligned to Weick's suggestion that 'sensemaking is a process of committed interpretation' (1993: 19) – the interplay of two quite distinctive mindsets. What he characterises as the 'interpretation mindset' is that aspect of the total mindset which members construct in order to interpret their external world. The 'commitment mindset' is the way in which members become committed to courses of action through driving 'interaction patterns by tying behaviors, explanations, social support and expectations together in a causal design. ... It is these patterns that people come to label as organizational designs' (1993: 19). What Weick suggests is that these two mindsets combine so that although members have the freedom to undertake interpretation and attribute meanings to the situations they encounter, they do so in the context of the stability and predictability given by their commitment. Of course, these two mindsets interplay in different ways in different situations. In some organisations where there is high bureaucratisation of the spirit, the control of the commitment mindset is very high, and the 'freedom' to interpret what is going on tends to be low. Where the commitment mindset is low interpretations through rumour and myth prevail and there is a lack of the sort of boundary management given by the commitment mindset.

Generally, the literature seems to treat the concept of mindset as attributable to individuals and groups within the organisation. Thus, in accord with claims that organisations have a mind and can be attributed, albeit in a limited sense, with consciousness (Broekstra 1996) there are writers who either explicitly or implicitly suggest that organisations (or indeed nations) can have a mindset. There is, however, evidence of mindset differentiation within Western cultures. For example, Weiss (1996) suggests that the pinnacle of human achievement would appear to possess a global mindset. Examination of the descriptor for this character suggests a true Renaissance person – they search for opportunities, can see the wood for the trees, value diversity, are sensitive to the needs of others, but are organisationally focused, they get on with life and accept uncertainty, they flow with the change. They are completely different from the much more restricted parochial or ethnocentric mindset. Limited research seems to suggest that Anglo-American managers tend to be more ethnocentric than European or Australian managers (Weiss 1996). As far as the authors of the present volume are concerned, to suggest that organisations are pervaded by a unifying mindset would be to stretch the idea of the corporate culture too far, although there may be dominating discourses which emanate from the mindsets of particularly powerful groups.

There is, however, a deeper level at which some writers have explored the concept of the mindset. In this view the mindset is composed of the relatively conscious elements mentioned above, but is also permeated by emotional material that shapes the paradigm within which the person and the peer group live. There are, in the inner life, a number of ways in which members repress what is uncomfortable or difficult to absorb into the understanding of the self (Fineman 1993). These repressions and conflicts form part of the mindset. There is also, however, according to Gear, Liendo and Scott (1989), the organising principle of the preconscious mind. This may be conceived as a psychic 'space' in which two key aspects of our response to the world are organised. The first is what they call the metaconscious. This is a device that enables members to inspect on a daily basis their assumptions about the nature of life, their paradigm. The other aspect is what they characterise as the 'potential unconscious'. This is a space in which we carry understandings of life that are 'dissonant to these assumptions and are actively excluded from incorporation' (1989: 2) into either the conscious or unconscious frameworks. The elements locked within the potential unconscious *could be* potentially beneficial in moving the person on if they are released. In order to explore this matter Gear et al. use the metaphor of the obsessive scientist who becomes so locked in to a particular theory or paradigm that his or her observations are profoundly limited by the narrow focus of the theory so that they can no longer see any other possibilities. This narrowing of the evidence reinforces the focus of the theorising. What is particularly important here is that the scientist may well be aware, in the preconscious, that there are indeed alternatives. However, these are denied, or seen as spurious or distracting, or as evidence of particular pressure groups. Gear et al. add that where there is a community of members with an overwhelming adherence to the mindset, 'social resistance is brought to bear on attempts to change a shared paradigm' (1989: 2).

The conceptualisation of the term mindset in this chapter is to see it as a combination of affectual (conscious, unconscious and preconscious) and intellectual components, whereas the paradigm is an expression of the intellectual position. As such it will generally be expressed in accordance with the scientific rationalities, unless the individual or group deliberately, as postmodern or New Age expressiveness, decides that it is better delivered in deliberately non-rational form.

Vignette 3.1

Scientists, for example, show flexibility in the mindset

The relevance of these comments may be illustrated by the ways in which research scientists as practitioners in practical and everyday ways resist movement, but are also capable of movement out of their particular mindset. For the majority of scientists the scientific paradigm is 'used to denote a provisional consensus among the relevant set of practitioners. It is the result of a particular mode of organisation, and it denotes a way of seeing things, of giving priority to certain problem sets' (Gibbons et al. 1994: 22). Gibbons et al. suggest that there are some scientists whose mindset is to develop strong adherence to conventional scientific practices. This becomes increasingly rigid such that they draw tight boundaries between what is and what is not science. These conservative scientists are in a situation where their mindset is confronting a considerable divergence between two contradictory forces. On the one hand is what they perceive to be the goals of science as conceived through their training and development in the community of science. In this view science is essentially curiosity-driven and focuses on the unknown to make it knowable; it is essentially speculative. On the other are what appear to be the new goals of science, a milieu in which the scope of science becomes strategic, purposive and outcome-driven. (See, for example, Rassam 1993; Cohen, Duberley and McAuley 1999.) As a response to the unbearable tension between their traditional socialisation into science and the 'new', they stick with those traditional behaviours which continue to be institutionally permitted (Merton 1968: 238). In other words, as a response to the anomic pressures produced by a clear dichotomy between different understandings of the goals of science they stick with what Merton characterised as a ritualistic response. They get on with the job of producing science according to the organisational rules as formally described. As Merton observed in a general way and Gibbons et al. point out in relation to the practical exigencies of scientific life, people like this are left behind, they are denied promotion and generally suffer the fate of members assigned to the role of the mediocre.

The other approach that can be taken by scientists is to admit into the mindset that the world of science is changing. Scientists undertaking this perspective move towards a paradigm in which they adopt a much more strategic approach to their careers, they become entrepreneurial, they learn new modes of discourse in order to influence stakeholders, and they move into new arenas of knowledge management (Gibbons et al. 1994). Within the schema suggested by Merton, these scientists are innovators in the sense that they have accepted the new cultural goals – in this case of science – and have rejected the 'institutional practices' (Merton 1968: 230) that characterise the practice of normal science. Of course, given the dynamic of the situation, it is likely that the institutional practices in which these organisationally entrepreneurial scientists engage become the settled organisational routines of the next scientific epoch. However, the movement from one mindset to another should not be seen as merely progressive, in a Darwinian sense. It might be suggested that entering the mindset of the possibility of a strategic and entrepreneurial approach to science is offset by repression (into the preconscious, and therefore no longer admissible evidence) of the advantageous aspects of the more traditional approaches to science.

THREE PRESCRIPTIVE APPROACHES TO THE USE OF THE MINDSET CONCEPT IN THE MANAGEMENT OF CHANGE

It was suggested in the introduction that definitions of mindsets seem to operate at two levels: a surface level in which the mindset can be easily accessed and a deeper level that involves an understanding of the unconscious and preconscious elements. At the surface level the relationship between the issues of mindset and change is enshrined in such pronouncements as moving the mindset through the implementation of new mission statements and declarations of intent, such as, for example, the need to move from dependency on material resources to human capital (Johnston 1997). One of the most powerful ways in which this process is undertaken is through declarations of the way in which organisational members are 'supposed' to relate to change issues and their effect on them.

An example of the way in which this is done is by contrasting the existing, unsatisfactory mindset with a different, much more refreshing example. Ryan (1999), for example, explores, in the context of the United States, the incursion into the arenas of work formerly occupied by not-for-profit organisations (e.g. in the social welfare area) by business organisations. He identifies four key mindset challenges – the economies brought by size of the business enterprise, increased levels of capital funding related to capability in delivery, mobility in terms of ability to move into and out of markets, and responsiveness to new needs – that characterise the business mindset. He suggests that although the business mindset has not yet demonstrated that it is more effective than the traditional not-for-profit organisations, funding will go to the former because they appear to be more sophisticated in technological and business terms. The mindset of government agencies aligns itself to the mindset of those who appear to be technologically smart and who are able to respond to the accountability rigours of the managerialist agenda. In this case the contrast is between the traditional mindset of those engaged in social welfare, which is found wanting, and the corporate mindset.

A different but related approach to the use of the mindset concept in the management of change is to draw a contrast between what is imagined to be the mindset of a nation under scrutiny and the mindset of a different nation. As a contrastive device the mindset of the latter is claimed to be much more satisfactorily aligned to the development of improved practices than the former. As an example, Mak (1999) contrasts what he takes to be the different mindsets of the West and the Japanese in relation to the issue of quality. He suggests that for the former there are profound differences in mindsets as between manager and worker, differences between supplier and customer, and so on. In Japan, by contrast, there is an emphasis on harmony, synthesis and trust. In the West there is an emphasis on systems, whereas in Japan the priority is given to a culture. If the 'West wants to catch up with the Japanese in the quality movement it has to cultivate a quality mind-set and bridge the gap between theory and practice' (Mak 1999: 625) . . . just like that.

However, it cannot be that easy. Locke (1996) has pointed out that there are three elements to understanding any management milieu at the national level. These are, at the fundamental level, the rudiments that are deeply lodged in the mindset, core aspects that are unchanging over long periods. The other two levels – the basic structures and the methods of management – are, however, amenable to change within the boundaries set by the rudiments. He suggests that the rudiments of the Japanese managerial mindset and the West's are very different. The Japanese tends towards group consciousness, whereas the Western is individualised. This leads to interesting consequences, he suggests, such as the elimination of the 'I' as anything other than a loose contextual source of identification in Japanese society as opposed to the 'apparently irreducible I of the West' (1996: 116). This appreciation of the contextual and of the social leads the characteristic Japanese into appreciation of contradiction and non-linear logic in serious business conversations rather than the characteristically Western need for order, logic and rationality in the conduct of business. It is because the social is so valued that Japanese behaviour is characterised by artful role-play, a preference for flight (a propensity for leaving difficult decisions until they sort themselves out rather than confronting them directly) (Takahashi 1997), and a clear distinction between frontstage and the backstage performance (Goffman 1956). This contrasts with the Western management preference for performances that claim to reflect integrity, even down to the value placed on the ability to be 'in your face'. What Locke is implicitly suggesting is the pointlessness of any superficial comparison of mindsets and then assuming that the 'inferior mindset' can take on unproblematically anything but the more superficial elements of that taken to be 'superior'.

A third approach to using the mindset concept in order to achieve change is to adopt the rhetoric of transformation in relation to change. Within this rhetoric, it is claimed, when 'a company reinvents itself it must alter the underlying assumptions and invisible premises on which its decisions and actions are based. To reinvent itself, an organization must first uncover its hidden context' (Goss, Pascale and Athos 1996). This emphasis on transformation is captured in the various change movements that come along from time to time that claim to develop new mindsets (e.g. Mak 1999; Dale, Cooper and Wilkinson 1997) as a means of changing the culture. However, behind the public rhetorics of the claims of the change movements to move mindsets there are likely to be political and other shifts in the backstage areas that will modify or subvert the overt claims to transformation. When McCabe et al. researched Total Quality Management in a major financial organisation they speculated on the extent to which 'managers at all levels use the discourse of quality to rationalise its actions. The extent to which a quality discourse constitutes the problems for which it purports to offer a solution' (1998: 407). In a political sense what is being suggested here is that managers may well be using the quality initiative to reinforce a fondly held mindset rather than engage in transformational activities. These reformulations of the transformational activity take place backstage. This is where the dialectical processes of doubt and promise, of risk and certainty, of collusion and transparency, of desire for control and desire for autonomy in change are enacted.

Vignette 3.2

Conflicting mindsets generate paradoxical outcomes

When the author read the exploration of a Business Process Re-engineering (BPR) programme in a financial institution (Knights and McCabe 1998) it occurred to him that there were a number of paradoxes rendered in the apparently straightforward agenda of the BPR initiative complex. These paradoxes were generated as the mindsets of the managers impacted on the discourse of the proponents of the change agents who initiated the re-engineering process.

The first paradox lies in the discourse that claims that the initiative will lead to major change. This claim for instant change from one state of being to a better state through communications and leadership does not take account of the tensions, resistance and political intrigue that exist between the different groups and their mindsets. Paradoxically, the more managers claim drama the less there is likely to be.

The second paradox is that of prescription. The language in which the prescriptions for leadership in BPR is expressed is 'explicitly masculine' in tone, 'evangelical' (Knights and McCabe 1998: 791) and brooks no resistance. The paradox is that the initiative is seen by members to be deeply manipulative so that it generates further resistance, and so reinforces of the existing mindset.

The third paradox is that the initiative makes major claims to humanise the organisation. Whilst there may be claims that the prescription is designed to improve the relationship between customer and staff, members are deeply aware that other agendas (e.g. downsizing, financial efficiency) may well be at play. The rhetoric of BPR indicates, for example, that there is a need to transform the mindset of people who regard themselves as 'workers' into the much more sophisticated mindset of those who regard themselves as professionals. This is achieved through a balance of gains and losses so that 'many changes, from empowerment gained to security lost, from alienation overcome to an encounter with the danger of burn-out, satisfaction bought at the price of high anxiety' (Hammer 1996: 51). However, it would appear that in many circumstances the losses prevail largely because BPR substitutes technical for human solutions in understanding the deeper processes of the work environment (Oram and Wellins 1995).

The fourth paradox is that of focus. Whilst BPR claims to be customer-driven, the paradoxical experience of customers may be that the service offered has become more impersonal through, for example, the centralisation of customer–staff interactions. Members of the organisation may well be deeply aware of the paradox and its impact on the overall understanding of the meaning of their work.

The final paradox is that of process. Most consultants and managers with responsibility for the implementation of the BPR initiative are ignorant of the 'reality' of political processes that occur between different mindsets of the organisation and therefore they ignore them. However, these political processes are at the centre of members' preoccupations. The paradox is that the more management wish to preserve a picture of competent management of the technical processes the more members will see the re-engineering as problematic in relation to the ways in which they conduct their political and relational affairs.

MINDSETS AS ARENAS AND COMMUNITIES OF PRACTICE

At one level these paradoxes arise, at least in part, because there is confusion about the very essence of the Business Process Re-engineering endeavour itself. The very language in which it is presented is vulnerable to misconception and misunderstanding such that members of organisations, the original authors of texts on BPR and (it might be added) consultants who work with organisations in the area are operating from different mindsets in conceptualising it (Belmiro, Gardiner and Simmons 1997). In a similar vein, in their critiques of Total Quality Management, Smith, Tranfield and Whittle (1994) suggest that one way through the disparity of definition is to understand the organisation archetypes, the mindsets, that underpin the approach of what they characterise as acknowledged quality leaders. They suggest that there are in all four key mindset conditions (planning, visionary, learning and transformational which interconnects the archetypes) and suggest that, by using these criteria in an instrumental manner, there can be a process of auditing and refocusing for companies which have lost the plot.

At a deeper level what is at play are competing mindsets in relation to any major change process. This may be explored through reference to the arena concept, a perspective which counters any temptation to regard organisations as 'the happy, harmonious, collaborative communities that many management texts imply' (Buchanan and Badham 1999: 41). The original study was based on research into psychiatric hospitals in the United States (Strauss et al. 1964), but there are ways in which all organisational life has the dynamics of that sort of institution. What they suggest is that as a result of training, socialisation, the ways in which members shape their organisational lives, and so on, they bring to the organisational feast different ideologies. In the terms of this chapter these ideologies may be regarded as coterminous with the concept of the mindset. The ideology is expressed through the occupational rhetoric – the distinctive language, or discourse, that members of the organisation will use in order to negotiate their organisational fate. They suggest that the basic structure of the organisation is determined, not by hierarchies, but by the mix of different ideologies in the organisation, by their very understanding of the nature of the work and by the relationship of the different mindset groupings to external stakeholders. In this situation power comes from the ability of one rhetoric (the expression of the mindset) to dominate another. It is not an absolute matter. In these terms what really counts is the ability of one mindset to assert control through definition of the situation, and then the capacity to regulate the ways in which interaction takes place within the organisation (Reed 1985).

There is more of an echo of this conceptualisation of mindsets in the work of writers such as Brown and Duguid (1998). Their perspective, derived from Nonaka and Takeuchi (1995), is that organisations are loci of knowledge. They argue that effective organisations are those in which the organisation of knowledge provides synergistic advantage over those in which the knowledge is located in disparate individuals or in disconnected groups. However, paradoxes of control and freedom can be found in managing the mindsets that constitute the active ingredients of knowledge production. Brown and Duguid suggest that 'institutional constraints help channel self-organizing behavior and knowledge production in productive rather than destructive directions' (1998: 93). They explore organisations as communities of practice (Lave and Wenger 1991) in which members develop 'a shared understanding of what it does, of how to do it, and how it relates to other communities and practices' (Brown and Duguid 1998: 96). Brown and Duguid suggest, however, that the mindsets (what they call 'world view') of the communities can become narrowly focused and engage in denial behaviours, self-delusion, self-fulfilling prophecies (Merton 1968) and other dysfunctional behaviours. It might be suggested that a core characteristic of the management mindset is the capability to 'understand and act on the rules-in-use in dynamic and in what are seen by others to be interesting but non-invasive ways, to negotiate and co-ordinate realities' (McAuley 1994: 425). In this way the management mindset is geared towards setting the processes by which the knowledge production context can be understood. This is easier said than done.

THE ROLE OF THE UNCONSCIOUS IN THE DEVELOPMENT OF THE MINDSET

It was suggested above that beyond the conscious understanding of the mindset there is a deeper significance to the concept. It is that part of the mindset, operating at the preconscious and unconscious levels, that is concerned with core issues of organisational fantasy, the sorts of inner meaning that members make of the organisation and their creation of organisational reality. This unconsciously created world feeds back into the meaning, the 'interpreted world' (Spinelli 1989) that members give to the situation that they encounter. At its most extreme it is a position where members 'are limited in the dimensions of their understanding by the narrowness of their experience. What is pathological, however, is not the narrowness represented in this limitation, but the dogmatic constricting reinforcement of this narrowness. Idealisation of what is valuatively consonant and denigration of what is valuatively dissonant are the frame mechanisms through which change is resisted' (Gear, Liendo and Scott 1989: 121). This is a situation, then, in which members reinforce, because of their anxiety, their negative impression of anything with which they disagree, and fervently build into their understanding of the situation any evidence that confirms their previously held mindset.

The underlying feature here is that at an unconscious level (although it does on occasion creep into consciousness) organisational members create the 'organisation [held] in the mind' (Stokes 1994; Stapley 1996). According to Stapley, this fantasy of the organisation comes through the need members have to conceive of the place in which they work as a holding environment. This term refers to the organisation as a place that helps people to manage (however inadequately) anxieties, gives members a sense of identity and being, and provides members with both physical and emotional nourishment. Of course, for some the organisation is 'not good enough' at doing this; for others it is just about 'good enough' in meeting members' needs for a holding environment. For some, in the narcissistic mindset (Schwartz 1990; Sievers 1994) the organisation is 'just perfect' so that there is a total feeling of symbiosis between member and organisation. The key shapers of the organisational mind can shape it to be a poor (this place is not about enjoyment or fulfilment) or mediocre (this place makes no big claims but tries to be a reasonable employer) or a good (this company aspires to treat its employees well) holding environment. Its members, in interaction with the organisation, can regard it with absolute love (a wonderful holding environment), conditional love mingled with hate (it's OK), or with hate (this organisation just does not care). As a product of activity of shapers, and not so influential members, the organisation is essentially a product of the mindset. In this sense members act 'as if' the organisation really exists and really is associated with human activity. 'The result is that we therefore attach to this object the same attributes as other influential objects' (Stapley 1996) even to the extent of regarding the organisation as a loving (or rejecting) parent.

This attachment to the organisation has a number of very important consequences. A core issue for members is the notion of the primary purpose of the organisation in which they work. Notions of primary focus come not only from socialisation into the organisation but also from moral and affectual understandings of purpose. Stokes (1994) suggests that there may well be issues of purpose, which affect members at an unconscious level and which result in denial of evidence. This suggests that attachment to the version of primary purpose held in the mindset is at variance with the existential actuality. Disappointments over the primary purpose can give rise to various forms of denial which then become fundamental, if unconscious, aspects of the mindset. One form of denial is where there is a collective agreement, collusion, to share and identify with an overriding, mythic mindset. He gives the powerful example of hospitals in which the unconscious sense of primary purpose is the heroic fantasy that death can be prevented. This means that 'the drive to preserve life as an organisational imperative can then become dominant, often irrespective of the quality of life the patient will have' (Stokes 1994: 122). There can be denial in the form of overwhelming conflict between the different ideologies within the organisation so that the organisation becomes split. Examples that can occur of this sort are, for example, when the debate between the production and marketing divisions threatens to destroy the very fabric of the organisation. Stokes suggests that this aggressive encounter is often caused by the experience of powerlessness (at an unconscious level) that is assailing both parties. They believe that they are engaged in a power struggle, but at a deeper level are (as through a glass darkly) dimly aware that the power in the situation rests elsewhere. The third form of denial that can rest in the mindset is that concerned with, on the one hand, idealisation of the purposes of the organisation (this organisation *ought* to be able to meet its targets and achieve quality outputs) and, on the other, an inability to meet the ideal. A consequence of this is that members are likely to experience guilt and anxiety and this is likely to be passed on to others in the form of persecutory behaviours realised as poor service or products.

It would be incorrect, however, to suggest that these unconscious aspects are invariably of a negative, problematic character. A useful approach to exploration of this matter of functional and dysfunctional aspects of the mindset is the distinction between what have been called 'W' and 'S' activities (Reed and Palmer 1975). Reed and Palmer suggest that W activity is mental activity (aspects of the mindset) characterised by attention to task, role and achieving objectives in realistic time spans. In this case members see the holding environment as reasonably reliable – it is 'good enough' – and the mindset is one that is driven by the possibility of a positive, useful outcome. 'S' activity occurs when external circumstances stimulate an unconscious internal mindset threat, which arouses anxieties about the individual's ability to respond adequately to the external demand. The resulting anxiety causes the individual to redirect his or her energies from the long-term 'W' task to the task of defending the self. When people are in 'S' activity the mindset is geared to defensive, denial activities so that when there is a concern to defend the current position it can be difficult to communicate with them about a task linked to 'W' activity. It may be necessary to resolve the presenting problem relating to 'S' activity before communicating the 'real' problem or issue relating to 'W' activity. If an individual or organisation is to maximise effectiveness it is necessary for there to be a predominance of 'W' activity over 'S' activity. Reed and Palmer (1975) suggest that seeking ways of alleviating or reducing 'S' activity in the mindset enhances the effectiveness of the organisation.

In the discussion of the unconscious elements one of the issues that seems to be important is that there can be a prevalence of what might be termed negative emotional states in relation to the world of work residing in the mindset of many organisational members. Schwartz (1990) has this moment of epiphany (both for himself as teacher and for his students as managers) when he is discussing with them his concept of the 'clockwork' and the 'snakepit' organisation. His idea is that we can look at the ways in which organisations handle issues of change, for example, as, well engineered, moving on in interesting ways, being an experience rich in positive incident and reward; or as chaotic, difficult, an experience of high anxiety but with an accompanying sense of *ennui*, an essentially destructive event. At first, he writes, managers spoke of their experience in the bright glow of the clockwork, but then began to reflect that much of their organisational life was actually experienced as in the snakepit. Although, clearly, there cannot be a generalisation of Schwartz's work to cover all managers in all organisations, there is enough evidence of 'S' activity as a feature of organisational life to suggest that there is something in the mindset that is alienated, at one level or another, from the organisation.

RADICAL MINDSETS THAT HELP EXPLORE ISSUES OF DEEP CHANGE

Although there is an extended discussion of the contribution of Critical Theory to an understanding of issues of change in Chapter 7 there are some facets of it that warrant mention here. As a mindset (at least at the conscious level) one of the aims of Critical Theory to explore the contrast between the 'subjective' world of self-determination and self-consciousness and the 'objective' world that creates consciousness for members. There is a preference in Critical Theory for the emergence of the former.

A pervasive feature of this volume is the dialectic between the conditions of modernism and postmodernism. An underpinning aspect of this discussion is the extent to which the shadow of the modernist organisation is the propensity to over-control organisational members, that the very mindset of modernism, with its concerns for rationality and efficiency given to a *milieu*, preconditions members to 'compliant efficiency' (Marcuse 1941). What Marcuse is suggesting is that key features of the mindset at the conscious level (e.g. rationality, autonomy and reason) are, within the logics of efficiency, effectively subverted to fit the prerequisites of the *organisational* structures, systems and control mechanisms. Essentially, they have become dehumanised, detached from human will, intent and agency. In this sense prescriptive approaches place a strong preference on technical solutions to problems, which is on the whole contemptuous of human values and represents a denial of meaning for the majority of members in the workplace (Sievers 1994).

The portrait of the subjective self has a certain Rousseauesque romanticism, and is captured well by Jean-Paul Sartre's suggestion that 'there is at least one being whose existence comes before its essence. [M]an first of all exists, encounters himself, surges up in the world – and defines himself afterwards. . . . Man is nothing else but what he makes of himself. Man is, indeed a project which possesses a subjective life' (Sartre 1948: 28). Critical theorists would suggest that left to itself, 'in the relationship of one self-consciousness to another does the individual, a new self-consciousness, come to be' (Frankfurt Institute for Social Research 1973: 45). In their occupation of the subjective world, members create amongst themselves a world in which there would be a 'natural' order which is, according to Horkheimer (1937: 218), the 'product of human work and organisation' and based on rationality and consciousness. It should perhaps be mentioned, *inter alia,* that this is 'unashamedly utopian thinking in management . . . offering concepts and ideas that challenge current management practice' (Alvesson and Willmott 1992: 16).

Horkheimer further suggests that if people are enabled to explore their society – and in terms of this chapter in relation to organisational life specifically – there would be an understanding of the implications of the 'two-sided character of the social totality in its present form'. This becomes 'a conscious opposition' to that side of the social totality which 'is comparable to non-human natural processes' (1937: 218). What this implies is that members would not accept as inevitable some of the ideologies, beliefs and practices that are presented to them as laws of nature, and hence beyond the capability of human will and reason. There is a view, for example, that global capitalism is an inexorable force, which it is beyond the ability of anybody (whether governments or global organisations) to manage in any way at all. That claim is a mindset position just as the position that suggests that, for example, 'the concept of *voluntarisme,* or active state . . . is particularly necessary in the conduct of economic policy' (Jospin 1999) is a mindset.

What critical theorists point to is the need to take a thoroughly sceptical gaze at taken-for-granted elements within the mindset. There is a special requirement to expose to the gaze those elements of the mindset that suggest that there is nothing to be done to reduce what are essentially repressive elements in political, social, economic, organisational or technological life. In what follows two key themes represent a radical representation, an epistemological transformation (Locke 1996), of the management mindset, which are geared towards the human aspect of organisations. Whilst not necessarily directly drawn from Critical Theory there is, if the concepts to be discussed are taken seriously, an interplay between them. Underpinning these ideas is an emancipatory mindset with an emphasis on releasing members from the restraining mindset that is created out of the repressions that underlie organisation and society.

FROM SERIOUSNESS TO HAPPINESS IN ORGANISATIONAL LIFE?

In April 2000 the newly appointed Director General of the British Broadcasting Corporation appeared before his 23,000 staff. According to one account 'he stood in front of a huge picture of a daisy-like flower and declared it to be his new management structure'. He told them 'of his plans to make the Beeb [BBC] "happier and more inclusive". Then he indicated that the days of his predecessor hierarchical directorates and departments were over' (Robins 2000: 4). His predecessor, John Birt, with his deep affection for structures and deep bureaucracies was the quintessential modernist working in a management-driven environment. Modernism is essentially a serious enterprise (Csikszentmihalyi 1975). As it has been played out, particularly in Anglophone societies, the rules of the game have been established by such features as the Protestant work ethic (Csikszentmihalyi 1975), and by particular understandings of the nature of capitalism and the imperatives that need to drive capitalist organisations (Locke 1996). According to Locke, other ways of driving capitalism are much more effective than that advocated by what he calls the American management mystique. And, in the Anglophone world there has been the inexorable rise and rise of the managerial mindset.

According to Reed and Watson (1999), managers have come to represent a core stabilising group in organisational life. They suggest that because of the death of distinctive ideologies such as socialism and communism, capitalism, whilst triumphant, has no more to say, with the result that managerialism has become the replacement dominating mindset. As management has become a universal practice managers have become specialists in control through knowledge and skill. In this sense they can claim to exercise their craft as a culture-free phenomenon. They also claim to be free from the impact of particular interest groups – management can make claims to be neutral. Although the claims of managerialism in relation to its claims to dominance are highly contestable (e.g. Sievers 1994; Locke 1996; McAuley, Duberley and Cohen 2000), there is little doubt that it has achieved dominance as discourse. Underpinning the managerial mindset is an understanding that organisational life is lived within the modernist gaze, that life is *for* the organisation, that personal fulfilment comes about through serious practical endeavour giving its members 'an alluring sense of authority in conditions that are uncertain and threatening' (Alvesson and Willmott 1996: 36).

There is, however, an alternative to this essentially authoritarian management mindset. Stacey, for example, discusses the concept of extraordinary management. What he means by this is the development of managers to undertake paradigmatic change and to deal with uncertainty and deeply innovative processes. As a practical accomplishment this calls for, among other characteristics, a mindset that can accommodate spontaneity in the development of ideas, and in which relationships are political, rather than hierarchical, in order to negotiate with members the best solutions. The management mindset is one which sees the organisation as a network of alliances with an emphasis on informal relationships, accessing deep local knowledge, rather than neatly ordered systems and structures. The manager's authority is gained through the quality of interpersonal relationships and through reciprocities of trust and respect rather than through formal authority. Because innovation and complexity are themselves, by definition, undefined in terms of start or end points, 'uncertainty, ambiguity, disagreement ... all make it impossible to start with intentional policy. ... No attempt is made to predict outcome. Outcome is articulated and interpreted ...' (Stacey 1996: 510). This ability to make things up spontaneously as one goes along and yet retain some sense of the structure of organisational life, to provide a holding environment which is 'good enough' but not oppressive, is a formidable feat. Stacey suggests that movement from a world of safety in ordinary managerialism to exigencies of extraordinary management should be undertaken only when there is some degree of security 'that the boundaries around any consequent instability are manageable' (1996: 512).

Self-organisation 'occurs when people form a group that produces patterns of behaviour, despite the absence of formal hierarchy within that group or authority imposed from outside it. Such groups could behave in what could be described as a completely uncontrolled way, for example a mob, but such groups may also behave in a way that we would have to describe as self-controlled' (Stacey 1996: 332). When Stacey conceptualises the principle in relation to organisational life there is a high degree of endogenous control. This comes about in a variety of ways. He suggests that when the mindset of members is geared towards self-organisation, they are aware that the micro-activities they undertake 'ha[ve] potential consequences', the outcome of their activities 'is the co-creation of all interacting agents' (Stacey 2000: 334). In this situation there are, he suggests, a number of constraints that prevent the situation becoming anarchic. These include the activities of other agents. He adds that power dynamics are of great significance in this situation, that 'some [actors] are pursuing more powerful strategies than others, in terms of survival. There is certainly no requirement for consensus but, rather the tension between competition and co-operation' (Stacey 2000: 334). In this sense self-organisation as a principle does not seem too far removed from the negotiated arena concept discussed earlier. He adds that the model of self-organisation posits neither the necessary empowerment of the disempowered nor the disempowerment of the empowered – the model is neutral in this respect. It might be observed that he is, in this respect, having his cake of preserving the status quo whilst indulging in the luxury of suggesting the delights of uncertainty and radical change.

There is, however, a linkage with the work of Csikszentmihalyi (1975, 1997) and his research on what he characterises as 'flow' activities. The active ingredients of flow are, in terms of this chapter, the constituents of a mindset in the sense that they represent an awareness of the world, a created relationship with external events. What can be an intense flow experience (a sense of harmony with the self, a sense of time passing very quickly) for some can be tedium and dullness for others – it is what the actor makes of it that counts. The key characteristic of a flow experience is that it is an activity that the person feels to be worthwhile for its own sake. It is autotelic in the sense that the activity itself gives the person pleasure, happiness and satisfaction.

In terms of challenge the 'person should perceive that there is something for him, or her, to do and that he or she is capable of doing it' (Csikszentmihalyi 1988: 30). The essence of this is that what confronts the person in flow is a situation that is challenging, that engages optimal skills in which the actor understands that there is the possibility to develop of further skills. He further suggests that flow takes place within 'clearly structured activities in which the level of skills can be varied and controlled'. The person understands that there is the possibility of relative autonomy (although flow activities may well involve working with others) and the activity has boundaries to it. Furthermore, he suggests that flow activities have relatively clear goals (it is difficult to experience flow when the actor has no idea why he or she is undertaking what is perceived to be a meaningless task). Flow activities also provide the person with 'rather quick and unambiguous feedback' (Csikszentmihalyi 1988: 30) so that the actor knows how well or badly he or she is performing (in order to make corrections, to restore the balance). Also – and this is very important – flow activities may be quite stressful, pushing at the boundaries of capability, but they do not provoke anxiety. Nor do they topple the person into 'S' activity: they enable the person to stay within the boundaries of 'W' activity. In essence, flow experience is an interaction between the personal (and group) mindset and the mindset that prevails within the organisation. If the mindset of management within the organisation is such that there are high levels of control and oppression, then it is difficult to engage in a flow experience. Though it is not impossible. Csikszentmihalyi (1975) points out that people in even the most oppressive situations can, with difficulty, carve out some sort of flow. They may, for example, play a different game from the official one.

What he argues is that essentially within the Western mindset, and in Anglophone societies more particularly, there has been a separation between the world of work and the world of leisure. The former is regarded by many as quintessentially serious, disconnected and meaningless (unless one has a naturally developed or learned autotelic personality), and that the latter is regarded as the place where pleasure is to be found. Of course – and he is clear about this – for some the world of work, traditionally, is a place of intense pleasure, where flow is experienced. Thus for some in business, capitalism 'developed its own rules, its own "irrational" rewards: the "irresistible appeal" of quantification, the possibility of lawful competition, and of getting immediate feedback on one's decisions ... the dramatic combination of skill and chance that is involved in business decisions' (1975: 188). This is a view of business as a game that satisfies and nourishes: a flow activity. However, at the heart of his argument is that the flow experience, which is restricted to the few in work organisations, can be part of the mindset of the many. The core precondition for this is that the person, or group, feels that they have a sense of control over their environment. However, he is not looking towards a complete, heroic, Nietzschean dominance of the environment. Rather, it is very much a mindset: 'to feel in control of the environment one must be able to define what the environment *is*. No one can feel in control of the total environment, the totality of forces and processes that may impinge on the state of human beings' (1975: 188). He is not saying that a flow experience will render everything in life perfect. What he is claiming is that building flow into consciousness of the world (which means creating in work environments the possibility of flow, the possibility of meaning) will make that situation better than a situation without the possibility of flow.

That is why, when Greg Dyke was appointed Director General of the British Broadcasting Corporation, he declared that he wanted the place to be a happy one in which to work. This came through his realisation that it is through enjoyment that people can be creative, innovative and reach their potential. However, the development of this sort of emancipation cannot take place unless the organisational and the social preconditions are right. Thus Senge suggests that 'To empower people in an unaligned organization can be unproductive ... empowering people will only increase organizational stress and the burden of management to maintain coherence and direction' (Senge 1993: 146). In terms of this chapter the word 'empower' could stand for a number of other enabling expressions, for example, the creation of enjoyment in the workplace.

THE DEVELOPMENT OF EMOTIONAL AND SPIRITUAL UNDERSTANDING IN THE MANAGEMENT OF CHANGE

The formidable sociologist Georg Simmel, writing in 1909, had a number of profound messages for those managing changes in the first decade of the twenty-first century. He wrote: 'the apparent pessimism of the majority of philosophical minds regarding the present state of culture is the widening gulf between the culture of things and personal culture' (in Frisby and Featherstone 1997: 101). Simmel's theme (and we can discuss it as an aspect of mindset influenced by cultural phenomena) is that as 'a result of the division of labour ... the technology at our service, and the knowledge, arts, lifestyles and interests at our disposal have expanded to an unprecedented variety' (in Frisby and

Featherstone 1997: 101). However, this growth of the external, the objective world, has been such that it can no longer be absorbed into the personal but is still part of the life of the person. It is experienced as out there, however. The totality of experience lacks flow. Paradoxically, people are drawn back into 'the subjectivism of modern personal life, its rootless, arbitrary character ... the vast, intricate, sophisticated culture of things, institutions, of objectified ideas, robs the individual of any consistent inner relationship to culture as a whole and casts him back again on his *own* resources' (Frisby and Featherstone 1997: 102). One response to this situation, in organisational terms, is a mindset of anomic dissatisfaction with the organisation, coupled with a desire to ameliorate conditions for the self and others but, crucially, without the faintest idea how to do it (Johnson and Smith 1999). The other response is the narcissistic mindset to which reference was made earlier – a recognition that since personal resources are not enough it is better to identify completely with the organisation or the benevolent transformational leader. Simmel argues that moving towards a more integrated world lies 'in the relationship of the subjective spiritual energies concentrated and unified in the self to the realm of objective, historical or abstract values' (Frisby and Featherstone 1997: 102). Recent times have witnessed the development of interest in spiritual intelligence, that is, work as a source of spiritual growth and connection to others (Mirvis 1997). This movement is interested in the very core characteristics of what it is to be human in terms of wholeness, flexibility, self-awareness, compassion, creativity and the questioning spirit (Zohar and Marshall 2000) and so provides a link with Simmel's preoccupations. On the other hand, this movement has within it the possibility to be a management fad, another technique geared to (albeit gentle) oppression. Mitroff and Denton (1999) argue that it may well have been a characteristic of the Enlightenment period that different elements (art, science, religion and organisational life) needed to separate in order to achieve maturity, but there is now a need 'to integrate spirituality into management. No organization can survive for long without spirituality and soul. We must examine ways of managing spirituality without separating it from the other elements of management' (1999: 88).

It is tempting to portray Simmel's great insight about the separation between the subjective and the objective as the first mention of information overload, which is characterised as a feature of the age of information technology (e.g. Collingwood 1997) but is really a pervasive feature of complex organisational life. There are two major themes in this that are relevant to the development of a creative mindset and the organisational preconditions for it. In order to achieve integration of the personal mindset into engagement into the organisation attention needs to be paid to the emotional and spiritual elements to create the possibility that organisational life can have flow, can have the possibility of integration between the self and the organisation. The term 'possibility' is stressed because, if there is to be respect for human will and intent, there is also the right to see the organisation as other, whilst maintaining a sense of sceptical, critical engagement with the organisation. There is an appreciable difference between the position taken here and the high degree of ideological and emotional commitment displayed in the so-called visionary company (Collins and Porras 1996).

At a very practical level, for example, there is an argument that, given the radical changes to the nature of the organisation and the globalisation of business, the dominant style of managing, at the senior levels, should be via the integrationalist generalist rather than the functional (Warner and Witzel 1998). In their discussion of the concept of the evolutionary organisation, Smith and Saint-Onge (1996) discuss the disequilibrium that can occur between the stage of development (where there is a need for innovation) of the organisation and the prevailing mindset (which is stuck in a previous stage of development because of emotional attachment). Support for this view may be seen in the proposal that it is the presence of a 'negative mindset' with regard to change amongst managers and employees that causes failure of the implementation of well-established methodologies. It is further suggested that this negativity means that when there are changes in market circumstances there are increased levels of control and a general increase in panic management rather than improvement. This reinforces the existing mindset as a self-fulfilling prophecy (Barker 1998). It is also suggested that these forces become most powerful, that latent features of the mindset become manifest, as the change process triggers them (Isabella 1992). At one level the resolution of these issues lies in the need to develop the emotional capability to be able to unfreeze the fixed or negative mindset. There is also a need to integrate the mindset with a dynamic understanding of the issues that confront the organisation not only in practical ways, but also at an emotional level.

This preoccupation with the integration of emotion and issues of managing change has led to an interest in the concept of emotional intelligence at the individual level and emotional capability as something embedded within the organisation. From the point of view of the individual, emotional intelligence refers to the development of such characteristics as self-awareness, self-regulation, motivation of self and others, empathy and social skill (Goleman 1998). Goleman suggests that 'intellect was a driver of outstanding performance. Cognitive skills such as big-picture thinking and long-term vision were particularly important. But when I calculated the ratio of technical skills, IQ, and emotional intelligence as ingredients of excellent performance, emotional intelligence proved to be twice as important as the others for jobs at all levels' (1998: 93).

It is suggested that the development of emotional intelligence is related to the concept of emotional capability. In this latter state there is an understanding, at an organisational level, of 'the relationships between emotion and change, institutionalises routines that attend to emotions in situated contexts, and selectively devotes appropriate resources to achieving organizationally relevant outcomes' (Huy 1999). At the heart of the argument is a notion that members' emotional relationships to the organisation and to the processes of change are highly differentiated. For example, some may be very tightly integrated with the organisation as it is, others relatively alienated from it. At an organisational level, the capable organisation is one that deals with differences. Huy suggests a number of interrelated propositions some of which are highly relevant to the concerns of this chapter.

The first is to suggest that, at an emotional level, change happens more readily if members do not see it as a confrontation with their present emotional attachments. Thus if there are ways in which members can see the change state, no matter how radical, as representing at least some degree of continuity with the old, they have the opportunity to make the emotional bridge. Where there are aspects that must be given up, then, he suggests, there needs to be sufficient grieving time. A related proposition is that an emotionally capable organisation will, however radical the change, ensure that 'there is a certain level of stability: emotional equanimity – a state of evenness of mind – has to be present. In order to maintain a sense of identity, individuals have to feel a basic level of security and comfort, which is achieved by being strongly attached to symbolic objects' (Huy 1999: 335). Huy also suggests that a crucial issue is that the development of authenticity comes in the expression of emotion. This requires, at an organisational level, 'the ability to facilitate the variety of authentic emotional that legitimately can be displayed [and felt] in the organization during a radical change process'. This proposition accords with Nevis's (1987) suggestion that resistance to change can be seen as energy which can be embedded into the change process if it is acknowledged and understood by the change agents. Huy also discusses the development of what he calls playfulness, and what we have called flow, as an essential component of enabling members to deal with the change process.

A sceptical reading of the literature on emotional intelligence and on emotional capability suggests that one could perhaps take them both with a pinch of salt. Tossman (1999) suggests that the concept of emotional intelligence, in particular, can be seen as a management fad, a prescriptive device that joins the long ranks of similar, basically mechanistic, techniques which are designed to enable change to happen. However, at their heart, these interests do indicate a trend towards at least attempting to develop some understanding of the deeper elements in the mindset.

CONCLUSION

What has been suggested in this chapter is that the mindset is an orientation, a way of making sense of the world for the individual and the communities of practice that are part of his or her way of life. It is an individual and group thing, although there may be ways in which an organisation (or even society) can be characterised as having a mindset. There are in it elements of the conscious and the unconscious. There is also the filtering experience of the preconscious, that part of the mind that rejects conflicting materials even if there is a dim awareness that the absorption of these materials might make our lives better. In discussions on the concept of the mindset in relation to issues of change there are quite polar positions. At one end there is a notion that at a *prima facie* level the mindset is constricted. Emanating from the unconscious is an understanding of life in organisations that 'we do not always want to know, or want to know, why we do what we do; it is just too painful' (Fineman 1993: 24). In this view, at its most extreme, all change is incredibly arduous. Indeed, organisational life is itself experienced as an awesome tension in which change occurs only through the intervention of external agencies bringing into the organisation a therapeutic milieu (Obholzer and Roberts 1994) to overcome basic resistances to the challenges of change. At the other end of the polar position there is an acknowledgement that members may start with a mindset that is not aligned to the change process, but that emancipation is possible.

The concepts of emotional intelligence, emotional capability and spiritual intelligence represent a resurgence of themes that have been around for many years in terms of the humanisation of the organisation. These suggest the possibility of the development of self-understanding leading to the understanding of others as potent features of developing the organisation. In some ways akin to psychoanalytic method, the hermeneutic cycle or spiral (Gummesson 2000: 71) invites the organisational member (especially those with responsibility for shaping the mindset) to achieve an understanding of the present through appreciation of the past. As Gummesson suggests, the 'relationship between preunderstanding and understanding is influenced by our conscious as well as unconscious intentions, our *intentionality*' (2000: 71). Our ability to grasp the implications of our understanding and pre-understanding enables us to explore realistically aspects of the mindset. The development of this capability, through the learning organisation and other means, is the topic of later chapters.

REFERENCES

Alvesson, M. and H. Willmott (1992) 'Critical Theory and Management Studies: An Introduction', in M. Alvesson and H. Willmott, *Critical Management Studies*, London: Sage.

Argyris, C. (1990) *Overcoming Organizational Defences*, London: Allyn and Bacon.

Barker, B. (1998) 'The Identification of Factors Affecting Change towards Best Practice in Management', *Management Decisions*, 36(8): 549–57.

Belmiro, T.R., P.D. Gardiner and J.E.L. Simmons (1997) 'Business Process Re-engineering – a Discredited Vocabulary?', *International Journal of Information Management*, 17(1): 21–33.

Broekstra, G. (1996) 'The Triune – Brain Evolution of the Living Organization', in D. Grant and C. Oswick (eds), *Metaphor and Organizations*, London: Sage.

Brown, J.S. and P. Duguid (1998) 'Organizing Knowledge', *California Management Review*, 40(3): 90–111.

Buchanan, D. and R. Badham (1999) *Power, Politics, and Organizational Change: Winning the Turf Game*, London: Sage.

Cohen, L., J. Duberley and J. McAuley (1999) 'The Purpose and Process of Science: Contrasting Understandings in UK Research Establishments', *R&D Management*, 29(3): 233–45.

Collingwood, P.C. (ed.) (1997) *IT Strategies for Information Overload* (Digest no. 97/340), London: Institute of Electrical Engineers.

Collins, J.C. and J.I. Porras (1996) *Build to Last: Successful Habits of Visionary Companies*, London: Century Business.

Csikszentmihalyi, M. (1975) *Beyond Boredom and Anxiety*, San Francisco: Jossey Bass.

Csikszentmihalyi, M. (1988) 'The Flow Experience and Human Psychology', in M. Csikszentmihalyi and I.S. Csikszentmihalyi, *Optimal Experience: Psychological Studies of Flow in Consciousness*, Cambridge: Cambridge University Press.

Csikszentmihalyi, M. (1997) *Finding Flow: The Psychology of Engagement with Everyday Life*, New York: Basic Books.

Dale, B.G., C.L. Cooper and A. Wilkinson (1997) *Managing Quality and Human Resources: A Guide to Continuous Improvement*, Oxford: Blackwell Business.

Fineman, S. (1993) 'Organizations as Emotional Arenas', in S. Fineman, *Emotion in Organizations*, London: Sage.

Frankfurt Institute for Social Research (1973) *Aspects of Social Research*, London: Heinemann.

Frisby, D. and M. Featherstone (1997) *Simmel on Culture*, London: Sage.

Gear, M.C., E.C. Liendo and L.L. Scott (1989) *Changing Mind-Sets: The Potential Unconscious*, New York: New York University Press.

Gibbons, M., C. Limoges, H. Nowotny, S. Schwartzman, P. Scott and M. Trow (1994) *The New Production of Knowledge: The Dynamics of Science and Research in Contemporary Societies*, London: Sage.

Goffman, E. (1956) *Presentation of Self in Everyday Life*, Harmondsworth: Penguin.

Goleman, D. (1998) 'What Makes a Leader?', *Harvard Business Review*, 76(6): 92–102.

Goss, T., R. Pascale and A. Athos (1996) 'The Reinvention Roller Coaster: Risking the Present for a Powerful Future', in J. Champy and N. Nohria, *Fast Forward: The Best Ideas on Managing Business Change*, Harvard, MA: Harvard Business School.

Gummesson, E. (2000, 2nd edition) *Qualitative Methods in Management Research*, Thousand Oaks, CA: Sage.

Hammer, M. (1996) *Beyond Reengineering: How the Process-centred Organization is Changing Our Work and Our Lives*, London: HarperCollins Business.

Horkheimer, M. (1937) 'Traditional and Critical Theory', in P. Connerton (ed.), *Critical Sociology*, Harmondsworth: Penguin.

Huy, Q.N. (1999) 'Emotional Capability, Emotional Intelligence, and Radical Change', *Academy of Management Review*, 24(2): 325–45.

Isabella, L.A. (1992) 'Managing the Challenges of Trigger Events', *Business Horizons*, 35(5): 59–67.

Johnson, P. and K. Smith (1999) 'Contextualising Business Ethics: Anomie and Social Life', *Human Relations*, 52(11): 1351–76.

Johnston, D.J. (1997) 'A New "Mind Set" for Social Policy', *The OECD Observer*, 205 (April/May): 4–5.

Jospin, L. (1999) 'Only on Our Terms', *The Guardian*, 16 November.

Kaiser, L.R. (1986) 'Organizational Mindset – Ten Ways to Alter Your World View', *The Healthcare Forum*, 29(1): 50–4.

Knights, D. and D. McCabe (1998) 'When Life is but a Dream: Obliterating Politics through Business Process Reengineering', *Human Relations*, 51(6): 761–99.

Lave, J. and E. Wenger (1991) *Situated Learning: Legitimate Peripheral Participation*, Cambridge: Cambridge University Press.

Lewin, K. (1947) 'Feedback Problems of Social Diagnosis and Action. Part II: Of frontiers in Group Dynamics', *Human Relations*, 1: 147–53.

Lewin, K. (1951) *Field Theory in Social Science*, New York: Harper Brothers.

Liedtka, J. (1991) 'Organizational Value Contention and Managerial Mindsets', *Journal of Business Ethics*, 10: 543–57.

Locke, R.L. (1996) *The Collapse of the American Management Mystique*, New York: Oxford University Press.

Mak, W.M. (1999) 'Cultivating a Quality Mind-set', *Total Quality Management*, 10(4/5): 622–6.

Marcuse, H. (1941) 'Some Social Implications of Modern Technology', in A. Arato and E. Gebhardt (1978) *The Essential Frankfurt School Reader*, Oxford: Basil Blackwell.

McAuley, J. (1994) 'Exploring Issues in Culture and Competence', *Human Relations*, 47(4): 417–30.

McAuley, J., J. Duberley and L. Cohen (2000) 'The Meaning Professionals give to Management . . . and Strategy', *Human Relations*, 53(1): 87–116.

McCabe, D., D. Knights, D. Kerfoot, G. Morgan and H. Willmott (1998) 'Making Sense of "Quality?" Toward a Review and Critique of Quality Initiatives in Financial Services', *Human Relations*, 51(3): 389–413.

Merton, R.K. (1968) *Social Theory and Social Structure*, New York: The Free Press.

Mirvis, P.H. (1997) '"Soul Work" in Organizations', *Organization Science*, 8(2): 193–206.

Mitroff, I.I. and E.A. Denton (1999) 'A Study of Spirituality in the Workplace', *Sloan Management Review*, 40(4): 83–93.

Nevis, E.C. (1987) *Organizational Consulting: A Gestalt Approach*, New York: Gardner Press.

Nonaka, I. and H. Takeuchi (1995) *The Knowledge Creating Company: How Japanese Companies Create the Dynamics of Innovation*, Oxford: Oxford University Press.

Obholzer, A. and V.Z. Roberts (1994) 'The Troublesome Individual and the Troubled Institution', in A. Obholzer and V.Z. Roberts (eds), *The Unconscious at Work: Individual and Organizational Stress in the Human Services*, London: Routledge.

Oram, M. and R.S. Wellins (1995) *Re-engineering's Missing Ingredient: The Human Factor*, London: Institute of Personnel and Development.

Rassam, C.C. (1993) *The Second Culture: British Scientists Speak out*, London: Aurum Press.

Reed, B.D. and B.W.M. Palmer (1975) *An Introduction to Organisational Behaviour*, London: Grubb Institute of Behavioural Studies.

Reed, B. and T. Watson (1999) 'New Managerialism and the Management of Higher Education', *Presentation to the Association of Business Schools*, Manchester.

Reed, M. (1985) *Redirections in Organizational Analysis*, London: Tavistock Publications.

Rhinesmith, S. (1992) 'Global mindsets for global managers', *Training & Development*, (October): 63.

Robins, J. (2000) 'Daisy replaces the flowcharts at new caring corporation', *The Independent*, 4 April.

Ryan, W.P. (1999) 'The New Landscape for Nonprofits', *Harvard Business Review*, 77(1): 127–36.

Sartre, J.-P. (1948) *Existentialism and Humanism*, London: Methuen.

Schwartz, H.S. (1990) *Narcissistic Process and Corporate Decay: The Theory of the Organizational Ideal*, New York: NYU Press.

Senge, P.M. (1993) *The Fifth Discipline: The Art and Practice of the Learning Organization*, London: Century Business.

Sievers, B. (1994) *Work, Death and Life Itself: Essays on Management and Organization*, Berlin: Walter de Gruyter.

Smith, P.A.C. and H.S. Saint-Onge (1996) 'The Evolutionary Organization: Avoiding a *Titanic* fate', *The Learning Organization*, 3(4): 4–21.

Smith, S., D. Tranfield, M. Foster and S. Whittle (1994) 'Strategies for Managing the TQ Agenda', *International Journal of Operations & Production Management*, 14(1): 75–89.

Spinelli, E. (1989) *The Interpreted World: An Introduction to Phenomenological Psychology*, London: Sage.

Stacey, R.D. (1996, 2nd edition) *Strategic Management and Organisational Dynamics*, London: Pitman Publishing.

Stacey, R.D. (2000, 3rd edition) *Strategic Management and Organisational Dynamics*, London: Financial Times/Prentice Hall.

Stapley, L.F. (1996) *The Personality of the Organisation: A Psycho-dynamic Explanation of Culture and Change*, London: Free Association Books.

Stokes, K. (1994) 'Institutional Chaos and Personal Stress', in A. Obholzer and V.Z. Roberts, *The Unconscious at Work: Individual and Organizational Stress in the Human Services*, London: Routledge.

Strauss, A., L. Schatzman, R. Bucher, D. Ehrlich and M. Sabshin (1964) *Psychiatric Ideologies and Institutions*, Glencoe, IL: The Free Press.

Strauss, A., L. Schatzman, R. Bucher, D. Ehrlich and M. Sabshin (1981) *Psychiatric Ideologies and Institutions*, New Brunswick: Transaction Books.

Takahashi, N. (1997) 'A Simple Garbage Can Model and the Degree of Anarchy in Japanese Firms', *Human Relations*, 50(1): 91–109.

Tossman, D. (1999) 'EQ – Vogue or Value?', *New Zealand Management*, 46(5): 34–6.

Warner, M. and M. Witzel (1998) 'General Management Revisited', *Journal of General Management*, 23(4): 1–19.

Weick, K.E. (1993) 'Sensemaking in Organizations: Small Structures with Large Consequences', in J.K. Murnighan (ed.), *Social Psychology in Organizations*, Englewood Cliffs, NJ: Prentice Hall.

Weiss, J.W. (1996) *Organizational Behavior and Change: Managing Diversity, Cross-Cultural Dynamics and Ethics*, St Paul, MN: West.

Zohar, D. and I. Marshall (2000) *SQ: Connecting with Our Spiritual Intelligence*, London: Bloomsbury.

Part 2

NEW APPROACHES TO CHANGE AND POWER

Chapter 4

CONCEPTUALISATIONS OF MANAGEMENT POWER IN STRATEGIES FOR CHANGE

The aims of this chapter are to:

1 Outline how the issue of management power is conceptualised and applied in various approaches to strategy and change.

2 Review and critique how management power is variably understood according to three competing sets of assumptions: the unitary, the pluralist and the radical.

3 Indicate how the epistemological problems encountered by the radical perspective, around the concepts of 'false consciousness' and 'real interests', have provided some impetus to the development of a postmodern stance which problematises the radical concern with emancipation of the oppressed.

INTRODUCTION

Conceptualising management power is notoriously difficult, not least because many managers seem reluctant to admit publicly that they exercise power (see Kanter 1979). This denial may occur because managers closely associate the exercise of power with engaging in the 'illegitimate discipline' (Thompkins 1990) of organisational politics to secure personal advantage by doing harm to others. Not only do such activities have an unsavoury and dysfunctional aura, they negate a presentation of self that alludes to rational decision-making. Topically, engaging in organisational politics substitutes the recent management discourse of openness and trust with what seem to be cynical, self-serving machinations.

Nevertheless, it may be argued that managers need to understand how power operates in order to be able to intervene and change organisations (Buchanan and Badham 1999). However, the issue of management power can be about far more than exposing the unbridled pursuit of self-interest by some managers or enabling innovation. Much depends on how power is conceptualised in the first place. But here we immediately confront a problem, for as Clegg (1989: xv) has indicated, power is the most 'contested of concepts', where competing definitions and operationalisations of power employed in empirical research continue to provoke much heated debate and little agreement. Hence any attempt to relate management power to the processes of strategy and change immediately confronts how different implicit and explicit conceptualisations of this phenomenon are drawn on by scholars. In this chapter we shall trace these conceptual variations and their practical implications for how strategies for organisational change are understood. In so doing we attempt to reveal the constitutive importance of competing underlying assumptions about organisations and society. We begin with the unitary non-zero-sum perspective.

THE UNITARY NON-ZERO-SUM PERSPECTIVE

An important point of departure in any discussion of power has to be a consideration of whether or not the exercise of power benefits one organisational group at the expense of another. For instance, a common notion underlying much strategy writing (e.g. Porter 1990) is that the exercise of power is something that benefits the whole membership of an organisation: that power is a non-zero-sum phenomenon. Such a view is exemplified in the work of Parsons (e.g. 1951, 1956). In this he treats power as a 'generalised resource', created by society, for regulating and stabilising social relations. Power is thereby assumed to be of functional importance since it appertains to a collective ability to maintain a social system by achieving 'its' goals.

From this Parsonian perspective organisations are presented as unitary, as harmonious, consensual entities that exist for the pursuit of common purposes where there is no inherent conflict of interest between members since all are seen to depend upon the revenues which flow from the organisation's activities. But like all successful teams, any organisation requires leadership. This is the responsibility of management, who exercise command in the interests of all since they are the best qualified to decide what these common interests are and how they might be best pursued. Metaphorically, management is thereby often likened to the nervous system of the body corporate. They are portrayed as meritocratic arbiters of collective interests whose accumulated expertise accords legitimate custodial prerogative. They are claimed to seek optimal solutions to secure unambiguous organisational goals in the discharge of their fiduciary responsibilities to shareholders (see e.g. Donaldson 1987, 1995).

Here a key assumption is that managers understand the relationships between their actions and 'organisational' goals so that they can rationally select and implement strategies that are likely to realise such unproblematic goals. But of course, as is argued in Chapter 3 with regard to Business Process Re-engineering, such an assumption is contestable. Cappelli et al. (1997) have noted how there is little evidence for the existence of such an understanding with regard to the recent vogue for restructuring and downsizing: indeed there is 'no systematic information about what works or does not work in terms of performance' (Cappelli et al. 1997: 222). Yet, as Mintzberg (1987: 58) observes, the keynote for the unitary perspective is the appearance of 'reason – the systematic analysis of competitors and markets, of company strengths and weaknesses, the combination of these analyses producing clear, explicit, full blown strategies'. Moreover, as Buchanan and Boddy (1992) note, through force of logical argument the production of clear and objective plans is often thought to counteract the perceived aberration created by political behaviour. Indeed the appearance of being able rationally to justify decisions may be necessary, but probably not sufficient, to protect any initiator of organisational change from criticism.

An important aspect of such appeals to reason and logic is that they can enable managers to argue that they are powerless, as their hands are tied by objective reality. The demands of legislation and the 'hidden hand' of market forces, which prioritise shareholder needs, cannot be gainsaid if the organisation is to compete and survive. Two outcomes arise here. The first is to enable the presentation of change strategies such as 'downsizing' as natural and inevitable, thereby masking the possibility that they do not realise presumed shareholder benefits by improving performance (see McKinley et al. 1998). The second is to distance the initiators of change strategies from culpability for any detrimental effects on employees. Indeed, Galbraith makes the more general point that 'nothing is so important in the defence of the modern corporation as the argument that power does not exist – that all power is surrendered to the impersonal play of the market, all decision is in the response to the instruction of the market' (1983: 120).

Such an abnegation of power beyond a technocratic expertise is evident in Porter's work (e.g. 1990) where he argues that 'great strategists' immerse themselves in analysing competitors, suppliers, customers, etc. and then design strategies that provide competitive advantage. Presumably, because of their privileged (i.e. superior) understanding of the situation, they can 'perceive something about reality that has escaped others' (Porter 1990: 130). As such practices and their outcomes are defined as 'technical'; they are taken-for-granted and remain unchallenged (Scott and Meyer 1994; Grey and Mitev 1995). But through invoking such technicism managers may lose sight of much of their own agency in strategic choice and organisational change. Instead, the decision to downsize in the face of globalised competition and the like become experienced as 'natural', as inevitable objective necessities from which there is no viable escape.

So from the unitary perspective, power as a concept is rarely mentioned. When it is it appears only as an impersonal mechanism through which organisations secure their survival. In this way power becomes inextricably linked to 'authority' – the legitimate exercise of command in the rational planning and implementation of change so as to achieve what are presented as unproblematic collective goals. So while Parsons may have claimed that 'the central phenomenon of organizational life is the mobilization of power' (1956: 225), his conceptualisation of power is limited to being 'directly derivative of authority: authority is the institutionalised legitimation which underlies power' (Giddens 1968: 260).

A necessary outcome of equating management power with authority is the idea that all employees owe a loyalty to their managers as the latter are of functional importance in enabling the survival of the organisation. As management-inspired organisational change is construed as a technical necessity in the interests of all, any conflict, disobedience or resistance to change is readily explained in terms of it being caused by various irrational pathologies (e.g. ignorance or stupidity) which illegitimately challenge managerial authority. So because organisations failed in practice to fit the prescribed harmonious vision, Reed observes how this Parsonian perspective was modified to incorporate 'elements of ideological indoctrination and structural control to deal with an irredeemable human recalcitrance on the part of "lower participants"' (1985: 6). Simultaneously, any explanation of resistance to change, etc. in terms of rational outcomes created by incompatible differences of perceived or vested interest is not countenanced.

Clearly the application of such unitary non-zero-sum assumptions about organisations has ideological utility for managers. Their invocation may be largely self-directed and self-serving in that they privilege managerial versions of reality upon which their decisions are based and, crucially, establishes their prerogative to manage (see Box 4.1).

Box 4.1

Management prerogative

Management prerogative might be likened to the 'divine right of kings'. The historian Christopher Hill (1969) describes how English monarchs and many of their subjects, prior to the Civil War, believed in the divine origin of the king's authority. For instance, according to Hill, the clergy were ordered in 1640 to tell their congregations that 'the most high and sacred order of kings is of divine right ... a supreme power ... given to this most excellent order by God himself' (Hill 1969: 86). Hence it was almost inconceivable that people could challenge the King or Queen, for that was to challenge divine authority. Thus as Fox in a wide ranging critique of management has suggested 'rulers of all kinds in all societies and at all times have been and are much exercised as to how to secure legitimation from their subjects and thereby promote willing compliance with their rules, policies and decisions' (1985: 53).

Hence as Willmott (1984) has noted, it would seem that the rhetoric which managers use in practice to describe and formally account for their activities as merely technical, apolitical and rational is reflected in, and reinforced by, this unitary non-zero-sum perspective. The result is that the role of vested interests, power and politics in strategy and change is effectively concealed. It is a clever masquerade that hides the everyday realities that managers face (see Buchanan and Badham 1999) where part of a power play may be a rhetorical appeal to such technicism. However, according to Peattie (1993), this rhetoric simultaneously stifles strategic dialogue, debate and ultimately creativity.

So while the non-zero-sum perspective may have some ideological utility it may simultaneously be both dysfunctional and pragmatically naïve. Indeed, there are alternative understandings of managerial power, which do not relegate resistance and conflict to the realm of wilful irrationality, but see them as natural, everyday part of organisational life. Here what is rational is relative to the particular values, beliefs and interests deployed by different groups of organisational members. This point is succinctly summarised by Pfeffer's observation:

> It is difficult to think of situations in which goals are so congruent, or the facts clear-cut that judgement and compromise are not involved. What is rational from one point of view is irrational from another. Organizations are political systems, coalitions of interest, and rationality is defined only with respect to unitary and consistent ordering of preferences. (1978: 11–12; quoted in Burnes 1996: 121)

Here Pfeffer seems to be questioning the epistemological possibility of an overarching rationality grounded in objective apprehension of the world while hinting at the importance of cultural relativity in the social construction of what is thought to be 'rational'. Moreover, in some respects, Pfeffer's stance accords with Giddens' (1968) critique of Parsons, where he emphasises how Parsons ignored the hierarchical nature of power and the clash of the divisions of interest that characterise modern society. In other words, the exercise of power in organisations is better construed as a zero-sum game played out by conflicting coalitions of interest for high stakes in which there are winners and losers. Zero-sum perspectives are to some degree based on Weber's view of power in which power is seen as the 'probability that one actor within a social relationship will be in a position to carry out his own will despite resistance' (1968: 53). Within this general zero-sum orientation it is possible to differentiate between the pluralist and radical frames of reference. We shall now review the contribution of each of these in turn.

THE PLURALIST PERSPECTIVE

From the vantage point of a pluralist perspective organisations, and society in general, are perceived as being constituted by diverse socio-economic groups whose pursuit of disparate sectional interests inevitably produces manifestations of conflict. Therefore, conflict between management and various organisational stakeholders (e.g. shareholders, employees, etc.) is not abnormal; rather it is to be expected. This constitutes a considerable departure from the non-zero-sum unitary perspective since the latter privileges one stakeholder group, the shareholder, whose presumed interest used to legitimate certain forms of managerial action – for example, the profitable use of the capital entrusted to management by shareholders (see Friedman 1962).

In contrast, pluralists recognise the need for managers to 'satisfice' (March and Simon 1958) the demands of a variety of stakeholders: 'those groups without whose support the organization would cease to exist' (Freeman 1984: 31). Due to the constraints created by such mutual dependency, pluralists emphasise that the differences of interest between various stakeholders are not so great that they cannot be accommodated and harmonised through negotiation and compromise – processes in which management plays a pivotal role.

Central to the pluralist argument that the non-zero-sum unitary perspective is pragmatically naïve, and hence unhelpful to managers, is their view of power. Power, for the pluralist, is the medium through which conflicts of interest are resolved as different groups and individuals secure and mobilise different power resources in their pursuit of their sectional interests. However, because organisations are seen to be composed of a multiplicity of unstable interest groups, who draw their power from a plurality of different sources, these groups cancel each other out. Thus pluralists assume that countervailing power exists so that one particular group can never continuously dominate all other groups. The stalemate in effect reinforces the need for managers to facilitate negotiation and compromise. Obviously part of the pluralist agenda has been to test and demonstrate the validity of their position by empirically registering the observable outcomes of the exercise of power in both organisations and wider society (see Box 4.2).

Box 4.2

Observing power outcomes

One possible way of simultaneously demonstrating and defending the pluralist thesis could be to observe the exercise of power in conflict situations and identify who 'wins'. If over a period of time no one group constantly wins, this would provide empirical support for the pluralist thesis of countervailing power. On the other hand, if one group appears to win every time, this would suggest that the notion of countervailing power does not hold. It is in the work of Dahl (1957, 1961) that we can discern a concerted attempt to study such outcomes by empirically registering wins and losses, in order to see who prevails in conflict situations. His approach thus scrutinised the exercise of power when two parties were in overt, observable conflict. In doing so he developed from Weber the view that 'A has power over B to the extent that he can get B to do something that B would not otherwise do' (1957: 202). In order to explain this operational definition of power, Dahl used the example of the power that a police officer (i.e. A) has to make car drivers (i.e. B) do what they would not otherwise do when s/he directs traffic. Therefore, Dahl focused on observable behaviour in overt conflict situations, with the assumption that a decision will be made that favours a particular party. The winner is, by that fact, the more dominant or powerful because they have been able to realise their objectives in the face of opposition. His most famous empirical research (1961) concerned the decision-making processes regarding urban development, public education and political nominations in New Haven. His findings seemed to show how a diversity of individuals and groups exercise power in different areas and, importantly, how no elite persistently dominated. It seemed to follow that the countervailing power thesis held.

However, rather than investigating the observable outcomes of the exercise of power, much organisational research has attended to an alternative pluralist agenda to investigate how power derives from a multiplicity of sources which vary from situation to situation and over time. Thus some writers tend to focus on distinguishing different power resources at the disposal of different coalitions of interest that form and re-form according to the issues at stake. Meanwhile, others concentrate on how the distribution of power resources within an organisation can vary over time. Regardless of their primary focus, an underlying assumption is that because power resources are so dispersed, so many and so unstable, they cannot be concentrated in the hands of particular organisational elites – hence organisations become construed as 'political' expressions of the countervailing power thesis. But it is also evident that many of these writers tend to adopt a managerial perspective by distinguishing the power resources available to managers and/or considering the implications for management practice of intra-organisational political processes. It is almost as if, in the endemic political struggles waged by organisational groups who are construed as equals, managers are the group most worthy of advice about the forms of power available to them and their effects upon others. It would seem that from the pluralist perspective some are more equal than others – yet it is unclear why this should be so.

MANAGEMENT'S POWER RESOURCES

Given the pluralist agenda outlined above, a key concern has been to identify the power resources available to managers in the discharge of their responsibilities. An early example of this focus is provided by French and Raven (1959), who attempted to categorise the 'social bases of power' used by supervisors to influence the behaviour of their subordinates. Their five-fold taxonomy depends on the responses of those on the receiving end of the exercise of power (see Box 4.3).

Box 4.3

French and Raven's taxonomy (1959)

1   Rewards are defined as cash, promotions, recognition and job satisfaction where the recipient values the chosen method and believes that s/he will benefit and that it will be available.
2   Coercive resources are the capacity to enforce discipline and rest on the fear of the likelihood of psychological or material punishment.
3   Referent power comes about when subordinates who like the supervisor identify with him/her. This is similar to the power exercised by a charismatic leader.
4   Expert power is exercised by those believed to have specialised knowledge or technical skill which others feel obliged to accept as they defer to what is taken to be superior knowledge.
5   Legitimate power is where subordinates defer to the right of leaders to exert influence over them by virtue of their formal authority.

For French and Raven all five social bases of power can occur in a work organisation – indeed all could be 'possessed' by a manager even though the use of one power base (e.g. coercion) may simultaneously undermine alternatives (e.g. referent). Except for the treatment of legitimate power, their taxonomy closely correlates with Etzioni's (1961) description of coercive, remunerative and normative (i.e. referent and expert) power resources in organisations. But for Etzioni, legitimate power is not the discrete category that French and Raven claim; rather, it is a variable quality that each of his three power resources might have. So, for instance, coercive power or expert power might be used legitimately or illegitimately. Furthermore, legitimacy is not an absolute quality as the unitary perspective claims; rather, it is related to the culturally derived meanings other participants project on managerial actions. Such an observation opens up the opportunity to investigate how legitimacy is socially established and maintained in organisations – a point to which we shall return.

Derived from French and Raven's original formulation there are other taxonomies of the power resources available to management which vary in their complexity (e.g. Kotter 1977; Kanter 1983; Mintzberg 1983; Handy 1985; Kakabadse et al. 1987). A common dimension to these different taxonomies is that they indicate possible approaches to the management of change through the manager wielding particular power resources according to the situation in order to overcome resistance to change. Perhaps one of the most famous change management models is Kotter and Schlesinger's (1979) contingency approach. Here they identify six change strategies – communication, participation, facilitation, negotiation, manipulation and coercion – on a continuum, beginning with the less intrusive and less potent (communication) through to the more overt and potent (coercion). Accordingly, it is for the manager to choose which change strategy is most appropriate given the level and nature of the resistance as well as the power resources available.

However, the power dynamics with which managers must cope are not limited to dealing with subordinates' resistance to their innovations. For instance, a logical outcome of the pluralist approach is not to construe management themselves as a homogeneous organisational constituency united by shared interests or by a selfless service to shareholders. Instead, managers are seen to be more likely to engage in organisational politics than other employees as they cope with the conflicts that arise with other managers. Pfeffer defines organisational politics as involving:

> those activities taken within organizations to acquire, develop, and use power and other resources to obtain one's preferred outcomes in a situation in which there is uncertainty or dissensus about choices. (1981: 7)

While Pfeffer emphasises that political activity is that 'which is undertaken to overcome some resistance or opposition' (1981: 7), others have emphasised how it also entails resistance to the power of others. So, for instance, Mintzberg (1983, 1989) outlines the political strategies deployed by managers to protect or enhance their own organisational careers by manipulating peers, subordinates and superiors. These Machiavellian 'games' include: resisting authority; countering resistance; building power bases; changing the organisation; and defeating rivals. For Mintzberg all involve organisational behaviour that is 'informal, ostensibly parochial, typically divisive, and above all, in the technical sense, illegitimate – sanctioned neither by formal authority, accepted ideology, nor certified expertise (though it might exploit any of these)' (1983: 172).

It follows from this perspective that management strategies for changing organisations are characterised by hidden political processes which entail conflicting goals, bargaining and compromise through a process of 'logical incrementalism' (Quinn 1980). The message is that power and politics may be undesirable but are endemic and inevitable parts of everyday life in organisations; a 'distasteful' reality with which managers must cope (Kumar and Thibodeaux 1990: 364). Indeed, to eschew politics may entail a misplaced sentimentality and is pragmatically naïve. Therefore, the key to 'good' management becomes construed in terms of the aims which managers pursue in their politicking. It is the extent to which they aim to secure personal gain through 'empire-building' as opposed to the more responsible aim of 'institution-building' – motivational differences which some commentators take to be an outcome of personality variables (e.g. McClelland and Burnham 1995).

The picture of organisations replete with the political machinations of managers underplays the likelihood that not all managers are willing or equipped to engage consciously in such behaviour. Indeed, it is also evident that some managers, especially women (Arroba and James 1987; Mann 1995; McKenna 1997), who often are excluded from male networks, are both disadvantaged in and by political behaviour, and importantly are reluctant to engage in such behaviour. Nevertheless, some writers have been concerned to help managers cope with the complexities created by political behaviour and, as Dalton (1959) observed over forty years ago, attempt to reconcile the 'rational, emotional, social and ethical claims' which arise. While some writers provide self-interested checklists for building power resources (e.g. Senior 1997: 183), others (e.g. Buchanan and Badham 1999) advise managers and change agents to become 'political entrepreneurs'. This means they 'need to' combine political astuteness with critical and ethical self-reflection, if they are to drive any organisational change effectively.

Hence many pluralists have overtly undermined the notion that technical aspects to managerial work exist that are politically neutral and that phenomena such as organisational politics are mere pathological aberrations and are of limited importance. In practice, however, managers must not be seen to be 'political' – maintaining an aura of legitimacy is essential. In this vein Pfeffer (1981, 1992) and Pettigrew (1977, 1987) have observed that political behaviour has to be concealed under a veneer of rational/analytical testimony; otherwise, if the players' actual motives were revealed, they would be condemned as illegitimate and thus resisted. To preserve the appearance of rationality, information may be sought not to make a decision but 'after the fact to ratify a decision that has been made for other reasons' (Pfeffer 1992: 248) so that it 'seems to have been made in the "correct" fashion' (1992: 250).

So, it is not the case that anything goes in managing the meanings attached to decisions to secure consent. Indeed, the processes noted by Pfeffer say much about the value placed on the appearance of rational decision-making in a search for socially acceptable goals, such as economic efficiency and profit. Here it would seem that change processes which institutional theorists (e.g. Di Maggio and Powell 1983) call 'coercive isomorphism' may be at play in two interrelated respects. The first is at the public level of testimony where managers rhetorically portray themselves as conforming to the dominant rationalist conventions, present in wider society about 'good' management, with regard to how they have arrived at a decision. This is necessary to preserve and enhance the legitimacy of that decision (see also Porac et al. 1995) as well as where necessary to 'delegitimate' (Pettigrew 1977: 85) any opposition. The second is where the need to maintain legitimacy may move managers beyond processual rhetorical ploys and rituals to prompt an actual convergence in organisational practices as managers feel compelled to incorporate the latest recommendations for work and organisational design (see Scott and Meyer 1994), regardless of their efficacy.

However, as we have already indicated, analysing the cut-throat machinations of some managers is merely one part of the pluralist agenda. Many pluralists have focused on the significant influences on change processes, which derive from the power resources deployed by coalitions of 'lower participants' in organisations to produce temporary order in organisational affairs, which can be a source of resistance to management-inspired change initiatives. Such power, and its deployment, is critical in demonstrating and constituting the pluralist notion of countervailing power as well as a phenomenon that managers must take into account when formulating their strategies for change.

LOWER PARTICIPANTS' POWER RESOURCES

Pivotal to the pluralist agenda is the contribution of researchers (e.g. Mechanic 1962; Crozier 1964; Pettigrew 1973; Batstone et al. 1978; Wilson 1982) who focused on the countervailing power of 'lower participants', either generally or in dyadic relationships. Countervailing power derives from their ability to create dependencies through their control over information and/or uncertainty.

Crozier's (1964) study of the behaviour of maintenance engineers in a French tobacco factory demonstrated how they had more power than their colleagues who operated the factory's machinery. The maintenance engineers controlled, and tried to ensure that they continued to control, the only source of uncertainty for management in an otherwise highly routinised production process. The uncertainty was located in the engineers' ability to repair breakdowns in a mechanised plant. Indeed, management was aware of these dependencies and tried to reduce them through preventative maintenance to avoid breakdowns, but manuals were lost and machinery was sabotaged! Of course, lower participants may also attempt to develop their power resources by proactively increasing others' dependency. Mechanic (1962) found that, by taking over aspects of the administration, hospital orderlies had succeeded in acquiring the skills, knowledge and information needed by their hierarchical superiors. They had then used the power to improve their organisational status and conditions of service. Similarly, both Pettigrew (1973) and Wilson (1982) studied organisational decision-making and found that their control over information was important to subordinates in that it allowed them to influence organisational events to their personal advantage. Generally, the picture that emerges is one where 'lower participants' can themselves draw on, maintain and develop a variety of sources of power in defending and furthering their own perceived interests. A necessary precursor to such activity may well be the development of a 'collective consciousness' so that the power deriving from dependencies can be realised (Marchington and Armstrong 1983) – a point to which we shall return.

For the pluralist, the problematic scenario created by 'lower participants' is further complicated by the way the distribution of power resources in an organisation can vary temporally, under the impact of several contingencies. Hickson et al. (1971) argue that the division of labour within organisations can cause differences in power to arise amongst the resultant functional sub-units according to how critical they are in enabling the organisation's success and survival. This pattern of dependencies is in turn related to the situations faced by an organisation. So as the environment, or the technology, etc., of an organisation changes, so will the distribution of power amongst its constituent parts. In this fashion Hickson et al. built on, and consolidated, a number of previous studies (e.g. Landsberger 1961) by developing their 'Strategic Contingencies Theory of Power'. This thesis suggests that the power of an organisational sub-unit, or department, depends upon three variables: its ability to cope with uncertainty; its centrality; and its substitutability.

The division of labour in an organisation results in some departments, or groups of members, coping with ambiguous and unpredictable situations. By being able to cope with uncertainty, they make other parts of the organisation dependent on them, and thus accrue more influence and power. Centrality refers to the extent to which the workflows of an organisational sub-unit are interlinked to the activities of other units. Hickson et al. split this variable into two elements: workflow pervasiveness and workflow immediacy. Workflow pervasiveness refers to the degree to which a sub-unit's activities connect with those of other sub-units; workflow immediacy relates to the extent to which, and the speed with which, the cessation of a unit's activities disrupts the rest of the organisation. Substitutability refers to whether or not the activities of a sub-unit are readily replaceable by other parts of the organisation. So, for instance, the argument would be that the dependence of other parts of an organisation on the activities of a particular sub-unit would be reduced if there were alternative providers of those activities.

Therefore, for Hickson et al., the strategic relationships that develop out of an organisation's division of labour create imbalances in the interdependencies between organisational sub-units, which confer greater or lesser amounts of power. So Hickson et al. argue that a sub-unit will have more power according to the extent that it is more central, and/or the more uncertainty it copes with, and/or the less substitutable it is. However, as the activities, technologies and environment of an organisation change, so will the division of labour and hence the amount of power a sub-unit may have at its disposal. It follows that organisational initiatives that affect the division of labour may intensify political dynamics as they confront an arena composed of supportive potential winners and resistant potential losers as power becomes redistributed – something managers could exploit in the development of their change strategies.

Thus while the amount of power available to departments and groups may well be influenced by shifts in an organisation's division of labour, Hickson et al. are much too deterministic in their approach. Members might be unaware of the power available to them in the pursuit of their perceived interests and thus there may be a gap between the 'possession' of power and their exercise of that power. Hickson et al. ignore the implications of this issue and thereby appear deterministically to assume that members have perfect knowledge and will act on that knowledge in the light of their vested interests. These problems are compounded by their implicitly unitary view of relationships within organisational sub-units. That is, they appear to assume that within an organisational sub-unit consensus exists over members' interests and goals. This fails to recognise the impact of internal hierarchical relationships on members' behaviour. It is in the context of these problems that Marchington's (1979, 1982) contribution might be best understood.

Marchington begins by suggesting that the four variables considered by Hickson et al. may be regrouped into two main factors. Thus he collapses work-flow pervasiveness and immediacy into what he calls disruption – the ability to halt production. Substitutability and coping with uncertainty are reduced to replaceability – the long-term ability to increase indispensability. Although he proceeds to apply this model specifically to analysis of workgroup power, what is most important in Marchington's work is his attempt to resolve some of the problems already noted with Hickson et al. He avoids their determinism by noting the potential gap between structural power resource possession (i.e. capacity) and the subsequent exercise of that power (i.e. realisation). His argument is that capacity and realisation are mediated by the consciousness of individual actors and their cohesiveness as a group. He thereby draws attention to the impact of ideology and culture on power relations; and the likelihood that even if a group is aware of its power, it may be unwilling to use it for ideological reasons.

Nevertheless, Marchington does share with Hickson et al. one major limitation that has been the concern of writers who might be broadly classified as 'radical'. This is the tendency to relate power capacity to structural position within an organisation through the development of, and changes in, the division of labour. Clegg (1975) has pointed out that such an understanding of power is rather like attempting to understand a game of chess by thinking that 'the pieces gain their power through their current position, rather than gaining their current position through their power to make moves according to the rules of the game. In short, the power that a piece has is defined totally in terms of its relationship. This definition entirely neglects the progress of the game in terms of its history and rules' (1975: 49).

Thus Clegg implies that strategic position may well be an expression of power in itself. Therefore, it is imperative to consider the power needed by groups to achieve their structural positions and consider members' differential ability to structure and control situations by setting the 'rules of the game'. For consideration of Clegg's argument, as well as more explicit analysis of the role of culture and ideology, we have to turn to those writers who may broadly be classified as 'radical'. But in doing so it is important to begin by considering their initial point of departure.

THE RADICAL PERSPECTIVE

As we have shown, the flavour of the pluralist approach is based on the understanding that organisations are constituted by diverse interest groups who vie with one another for position in the pursuit of perceived self-interest. As Pfeffer and Salancik (1978: 26) have described it, organisations may thus be seen as 'settings in which groups and individuals with varying interests and preferences come together and engage in exchanges'. In doing so participants knowingly draw on different power resources which are often in a state of flux under the impact of various contingencies. Thus for the pluralist, during both the formulation and implementation of organisational change, power is the medium through which overt conflicts of interest are ultimately resolved. But central to this conceptualisation is the notion of countervailing power. Thus there cannot be one continual winner and, moreover, conflicting parties have to negotiate and compromise because of their mutual dependency.

In contrast to the pluralist view of organisations being composed of a multiplicity of negotiable interests, a radical view of power is grounded in the assumption that society and its institutions are characterised by a confrontation between fundamentally opposed and irreconcilable class-based vested interests. Although they would agree that power is of fundamental importance in understanding human behaviour in organisations, they would also argue that it is a phenomenon that is unequally distributed – that the material and symbolic power of owners and their surrogates (i.e. management) far outweighs that of labour. Thus it is hardly surprising that the focus of the radical critique of pluralism has been the latter's notion of countervailing power. The radical perspective has many theoretical strands, but the most important largely derive from attacks on Dahl's (1961) original concern to analyse the exercise of power in observable decision-making situations, which involve overt conflict, where A purposefully gets B to do something she or he would otherwise not do.

In their critique of this pluralist view, Bachrach and Baratz (1963, 1970) draw our attention to a subtler and less visible activity where power is also exercised by preventing decisions being taken over potential issues in which there would be a conflict of interests. So they argue that power has two faces. The first more or less corresponds to that investigated by Dahl, but they argue that power is also exercised when:

> A devotes his energies to creating or reinforcing social and political values and institutional practices that limit the scope of the political process to public consideration of only those issues which are comparatively innocuous to A. To the extent that A succeeds in doing this B is prevented for all practical purposes from bringing to the fore any issues that might in their resolution be seriously detrimental to A's set of preferences. (Bachrach and Baratz 1970: 7)

For Bachrach and Baratz, management would usually be in a much stronger position to exercise this kind of power, based on agenda-setting, for they are better placed strategically than employees and their representatives. So Bachrach and Baratz seem to expose a serious limitation of certain pluralist themes. By noting how grievances expressed outside the decision-making arena fail to be translated into demands within it, they draw our attention to situations where 'the dominant values, the accepted rules of the game, the existing power relations among groups, and the instruments of force singly, or in combination, effectively prevent certain grievances from developing into full-fledged issues which call for decisions . . .' (1963: 641). Such a 'non-decision making situation' (1963: 641), therefore, involves aspects of what Schattschneider (1960) called 'the mobilisation of bias'. This refers to the exercise of power through the conscious creation of areas of non-decisions, which result in the 'suppression or thwarting of a latent or manifest challenge to the values or interests of the decision maker' (Bachrach and Baratz 1970: 44). Knowledge and its processes of production are a pivotal influence on what is organised into and out of organisational politics. As Gaventa and Cornwall observe:

> scientific rules are used to declare the knowledge of some groups more valid than others, for example 'experts' over 'lay people'. . ... Certain issues and certain groups receive more attention than others; clearly established 'methods' or rules of the game can be used to allow some voices to enter the process and to discredit the legitimacy of others. (2000: 71)

No doubt we all are aware of many examples in our organisations of cases of this sort where the action of an individual, or group, exploits non-decision-making processes. That is to say, the making of decisions in particular areas, where there is cause for grievance or the potential for resistance, is circumvented precisely because it would have an adverse effect on the interests of the more powerful, for example: where 'unacceptable' or 'controversial' items are excluded from the decision-making agenda, which in turn becomes restricted to 'safe' issues; where some members' opinions or grievances are dismissed as 'trivial' or 'unjustified'; where critical organisational decisions are made informally by elites, who then arrange for them to be rubber-stamped in formal committees; where information is suppressed and hidden from the public domain. Of course such 'non-decisions' may fail to limit the scope of organisational politics. They can cause conflict over the agenda, or promote resistance through calculative compliance, especially where those promised involvement and participation through various employee empowerment strategies realise that they have been excluded from certain decision-making agendas and their expectations created by the discourse are left unfulfilled (Rosenthal et al. 1997; Wilkinson et al. 1997).

Although Bachrach and Baratz have made an important contribution to our understanding of power in organisations by effectively undermining Dahl's approach, they too have been subject to criticism. This is because their methodology confines investigation to an examination of overt, and thus observable, conflict (i.e. the ways in which grievances, about which there is conflict, are excluded from the decision-making agenda and are thereby suppressed). What it therefore tends to ignore is the ways in which bias might be mobilised to forestall the generation of conflict in the first place. It is precisely in this context that Lukes (1974) provides a most important contribution, which both extends and complements Bachrach and Baratz's earlier analysis.

Basically Lukes (1974) regards Bachrach and Baratz as not going far enough and adds a further aspect which he denotes as the 'third dimension of power' (the first being Dahl's and the second Bachrach and Baratz's). His critique of the first two dimensions of power focuses on their concern with the exercise of power in situations of conflict. Although he notes that this is important, what it ignores is the insidious exercise of power that serves to forestall the generation of conflict in the first place. As Lukes put it:

> A may exercise power over B by getting him to do what he does not want to do but he also exercises power over him by influencing, shaping or determining his [*sic*] very wants. Indeed is it not the supreme exercise of power to get another or others to have the desires you want them to have – that is to secure their compliance by controlling their thoughts and desires? (1974: 23)

So Lukes' third dimension of power entails consideration of the ways in which potential issues are suppressed by both agenda-setting and 'the socially constructed and culturally patterned behaviour of groups and practices of institutions' (Lukes 1974: 24). The implication is that drawing on the leverage provided by the various power resources noted by the pluralists to push through organisational change is only one aspect of managing change. Besides non-decision-making through agenda-setting, Lukes draws our attention to how managing change may rely primarily on the avoidance of conflict in the first place by (re)configuring employees' vocabularies and attitudes so that new practices seem inevitable and irresistible. This focuses attention on how managers are forever searching for new ways of instilling self-discipline in employees by 'manufacturing consent' (Burawoy 1979) to prevent opposition from arising. (This issue is explored in more detail in Chapters 5 and 6.) The result may be that certain ideas become unthinkable – not being flexible, customer-centred, business-like, cost-conscious, and so on. By including some ideas as normal, logical or rational, alternatives are excluded or displaced as abnormal, illogical, naïve or irrational – sometimes as things of the past no longer possible or relevant.

While such inclusion/exclusion operates in the agenda-setting of the second dimension, Lukes' key point is that they can prevent conflict developing in the first place through what amounts to a process which we shall call 'cultural doping' (Chapter 5). Here he argues that the shaping of preferences, perceptions and cognitions operates so that subordinates 'accept their role in the existing order of things either because they can see or imagine no alternative to it, or because they see it as natural and unchangeable, or because they value it as divinely ordained and beneficial' (Lukes 1974: 24). What we may have here, he suggests, is a latent conflict where there may be a contradiction between the interests of those exercising power and the 'real interests' of those employees who are complicit in their own subordination. Indeed, this form of power may be so masked that its beneficiaries may themselves be unaware of their role in its application and perpetuation. Moreover, as one moves away from the pluralist, one-dimensional approaches, to the second and third dimensions, the main beneficiaries of the power distributions are organisational elites such as shareholders and management. This undermining of pluralism is well illustrated by the way in which Lukes draws our attention to the fundamental role of management prerogative.

MANAGEMENT PREROGATIVE

According to Storey (1983: 58–9) the second and, particularly, the third dimensions of power are interwoven with, and supportive of, the fabric of authority embodied in management's right to manage – managerial prerogative. As he contends, the boundaries of managerial prerogatives, or rights, serve to demarcate those functional tasks which give management its distinctiveness. It is not, therefore, surprising that such rights are carefully defended. These boundaries are constantly shifting and have been the subject of much discussion by academics (e.g. Dunn 1990; Guest 1991; Keenoy 1991; Antony 1994). It has been pointed out that since the earliest days of the industrial revolution, owners and managers have sought to legitimate what they regarded as their essential managerial function of control. Some form of subordination and domination is portrayed as essential to ensure the control of employment relationships in modern complex organisations and this is secured by ideas and statements known collectively as managerial ideology. McGivering et al. (1969), for example, defined managerial ideology as 'a set of beliefs which management seeks to propagate in order to inspire acceptance and approval of managerial autonomy by the general public and by specific groups of workers' (1969: 91).

Managerial ideology serves to conceal the exercise of power from those who suffer its consequences. For instance, Golding's ethnography (1980) shows how management's right to manage is a taken-for-granted and tacit assumption of those conversing within an organisational setting. But the maintenance of such a prerogative depends on its not being overtly recognised or challenged – the sheer symbolic status of being a manager was enough to ensure subordinates' compliance to orders. The result is that management prerogative is depoliticised and naturalised: employees rarely challenge the right of managers to manage and control their activities in the first place. An aspect of this is that

> non-negotiable demands are not generated in the first place. Workers, in the main, accept the configurations of industrial hierarchy, the extreme division of labour, production for profit and not for need, market rationality and material and symbolic inequality. These are by and large perceived as 'givens' in the taken-for-granted world order. (Storey 1983: 59)

Thus it would appear that the reason why management prerogative tends to go unchallenged lies primarily in employees' prior socialisation, which inculcates a tendency to accept most aspects of the status quo and narrow down any challenges to, at most, an 'aggressive economism'. This points to the dyadic nature of Lukes' third dimension of power: which is precisely the point that Storey (1983) seems to make when he provides a brief analysis of Paul Willis's (1977) work (see Box 4.4).

Box 4.4

Learning to labour

Willis presents an ethnographic study, based primarily on the conversations of twelve working-class youths who display 'anti-school' attitudes. These self-styled 'lads' reject the school's values of academic success and career achievement as expressions of fulfilment and individuality; and disparage the other boys who conform and subscribe to those values as 'the ear'oles'. In its place they defer to a rebellious, anti-intellectual and macho 'counterculture' characterised by an 'entrenched, general and personalized opposition to authority'. This entailed derogation of those who conform to the school's conventional values, by a celebration of having a 'laff', drinking, fighting and womanising. These activities they perceive as endowing adult status, something, *ipso facto*, that is denied to the 'ear'oles'. To finance their activities the 'lads' had part-time jobs which further symbolised their adulthood. So upon graduating from this counter-school culture the 'lads' enthusiastically (and realistically, given their lack of qualifications) sought manual work, which matched their assessment of personal worth in terms of masculine physical toughness, rather than contemptible mental work and white-collar employment. Willis argues that this counterculture 'fits' with the culture of the workplace and made the 'lads'' transition to work relatively painless. Willis thus claims that their counterculture is rooted in the beliefs predominant in their class background – an anti-authority masculine chauvinism that emphasises a distinction between 'us and them'. For Storey (1983), such prior social conditioning, with its acceptance of the 'cash nexus', instrumental attitudes towards work and the celebration of manual work over contemptible white-collar work, serves both to ease their passage into the world of work with its divorce of conception from execution and culturally precondition them to accept their lot and accept management's right to manage. In effect the 'lads' become entrapped and disempowered by their own rebellion!

Although Willis's work has been subject to some methodological (e.g. Hammersley and Atkinson 1985) and theoretical (e.g. Clegg 1989; Knights and

Willmott 1985) criticism it does lend support to the view that the establishment of management control and prerogative relies on dyadic aspects of power. Aspects of employees' culture, may, in effect, forestall the generation of non-negotiable demands in the first place in a way that is independent of managerial actions and strategies. This can lead us only to conjecture that perhaps any management may be impossible without the prior establishment of such prerogative that legitimates the right to manage in the first place.

In sum, Lukes' approach appears to present a thoroughgoing challenge to the pluralist notion of countervailing power. He draws attention to how the proactive ability to shape cognitions and the existence of particular cultures promotes the interests of some groups (e.g. management) over others (e.g. employees). The result is that the disempowered become complicit in their own subordination by being unaware of their own best interests and thereby incapable of challenging the organisational status quo.

But some of Lukes' critics (e.g. Benton 1981; Clegg 1989) have pointed to the way he sustains his development of Bachrach and Baratz by making a distinction between the culture(s) to which employees defer in making sense of their world(s) and their objectively identifiable 'real', or 'true' interests. That is, his articulation of the third dimension is based on the development of employee cultures that obscure and subvert their 'real' interests by inculcating what amounts to a 'false' consciousness. Thus he argues that to associate the absence of conflict with genuine consensus is to rule out 'the possibility of false or manipulated consensus by definitional fiat' (Lukes 1974: 24). Because conflict has been successfully averted, Lukes argues that one may have a situation of 'latent conflict', which consists of 'a contradiction between the interests of those exercising power and the real interests of those they exclude' (1974: 24–5). So Lukes bases his argument on an appeal to the existence of interests outside situations in which power is insidiously exercised (see Knights and Willmott 1985). But how can Lukes know what these real interests might be? Surely, according to his own analysis, real interests would be articulated only in circumstances free from constraint and hegemonic domination? Indeed, it would seem that justification for his argument can be acquired only through an appeal to privileged knowledge on his own part, something that seems incommensurable with his earlier analysis.

This notion of 'real interests' is, in Clegg's (1989) view, a serious weakness of Lukes' analysis. Clegg states his objections in the form of a conundrum. Judgements of what are 'real interests' must be made by actors or by observers of that action. If made by the observer, it will be according to some standard of 'real interests', or capriciously, or inconsistently. If by the actor, it is impossible to differentiate an authentic, real articulation of interest that is made from 'without' power, from an inauthentic, false articulation of interest, which is made as a result of the constraints of power. If actors cannot know their own minds, how can observers (Clegg 1989: 100)? So for Clegg (1989: 114) Lukes fails to discuss adequately the role of ideology in determining interests.

This creates two key problems. First, it puts Lukes in the position of assuming that powerful organisational elites somehow know their own interests and can intentionally realise them through shaping preferences and cognitions while the oppressed do not. This amounts to a privileging of those elites' cognitions – albeit through a very different argument from that put forward by the techno-cratic rationalism of the unitary perspective discussed earlier in this chapter. Second, by imputing 'false consciousness' as a key dynamic to inequality in power relations in organisations, Lukes presumes to know what the interests of the oppressed really are. This leads Lukes to assume that the oppressed can be emancipated from their false consciousness through what amounts to their assimilation of his own analysis of real interests. But how would we know whether such real interests are not just another ideology? Indeed Lukes' analy-sis seems to imply that there cannot be any intellectual space free from ideo-logical distortion and so must presumably include his own analysis in this realm.

According to Clegg (1989), in order to resolve the ambiguities inherent in Lukes' formulation of the third dimension we must develop a perspective that can question and discuss the mechanisms that influence members' social con-struction of organisational reality without imposing yet another ideology. Such an ideology would, for example, presume what the 'real' interests of the 'oppressed' really are. As we shall see in Chapter 6, it is precisely this concern that leads to the development of the postmodernist perspective on power.

CONCLUSION

In this chapter we have traced how managerial power has been construed in sev-eral contradictory ways by a variety of commentators. Depending upon the per-spective adopted, management power has been presented as: a legitimate expression of authority as opposed to a means of producing and reproducing the appearance of legitimacy; a means of pursuing collective goals, as opposed to a means of securing sectional self-interest; dependent upon conflict occurring, as opposed to a means of forestalling the generation of conflict; being realised through intentional acts, as opposed to being grounded in unconscious pro-cesses; being countervailed by dispersed power resources throughout organis-ations, as opposed to being hierarchically ordered and concentrated in the hands of the upper echelons.

Each presentation of managerial power depends on and articulates different constitutive assumptions about organisations and society as well as epistemo-logical assumptions about the knowledge of both the manager and the researcher. For instance, the unitary approach privileges and naturalises the rationality of the manager. The pluralist privileges and naturalises stakeholder coalitions' ability to identify their own interests. The radical privileges both the ability of the researcher to discern the true interests of the disempowered and the ability of the powerful to discern and act in their own best interests.

The epistemological problems encountered by Lukes, and outlined by Clegg, also bedevil the focus of our next chapter. In this we shall show how critical theorists present a distinctive social constructivist analysis of strategies for organisational change whose normative dimension focuses on the development of a critical consciousness amongst the oppressed in organisations as pivotal to a programme of emancipation, resistance and organisational change. In Chapter 6 we move on to consider postmodernism and how it undermines Critical Theory and its largely radical perspective on power and change at an epistemological level.

As we shall show, the development of postmodernism depends on complex epistemological and ontological commitments that are at variance with those of the perspectives considered in this chapter. The result is a distinctive postmodern conceptualisation of power where power is not a property possessed by actors, but is an all-pervasive quality that is present in, constitutive of and constituted by social relationships where some participants are advantaged while others resist, without knowing that they are doing so. So, rather than liberating the oppressed from the psychic prison of their false consciousness, postmodernists are concerned to identify and unsettle the discursive processes by which such relationships are produced and reproduced as 'normal' or 'natural'. However, in order to understand the postmodern approach we must first turn to the social constructivist commitments out of which both critical theory and postmodernism emerge to develop their distinctive positions upon power, strategy and change.

REFERENCES

Ansoff, H.I. (1991) 'Critique of Henry Mintzberg's Design School', *Strategic Management Journal*, 12: 449–61.

Antony, P.D. (1994) *Managing Culture*, Buckingham: Open University Press.

Arroba, T. and K. James (1987) 'Are Politics Palatable to Women Managers?', *Women in Management Review*, 3(3): 123–30.

Bachrach, P. and M.S. Baratz (1963) 'Decisions and Nondecisions', *American Political Science Review*, l57: 641–51.

Bachrach, P. and M.S. Baratz (1970) *Power and Poverty: Theory and Practice*, Oxford: Oxford University Press.

Batstone, E. et al. (1978) *The Social Organisation of Strikes*, Oxford: Basil Blackwell.

Benton, T. (1981) '"Objective" Interests and the Sociology of Power', *Sociology*, 15(2): 161–84.

Brown, R.K. (1978) 'Work', in P. Abrams (ed.) *Work, Urbanism and Inequality*, London: Weidenfeld and Nicolson.

Buchanan, D. and R. Badham (1999) *Power, Politics and Organizational Change: Winning the Turf Game*, London: Sage.

Buchanan, D. and D. Boddy (1992) *The Expertise of the Change Agent: Public Performance and Backstage Activity*, Englewood Cliffs, NJ: Prentice Hall.

Burawoy, M. (1979) *Manufacturing Consent: Changes in the Labour Process under Monopoly Capitalism*, Chicago: Chicago University Press.

Burnes, B. (1996) *Managing Change: A Strategic Approach to Organisational Dynamics*, London: Pitman.

Cappelli, P., L. Bassi, H. Kahtz, D. Knoke, P. Osterman and M. Useem (1997) *Change at Work*, Oxford: Oxford University Press.

Clegg, S.R. (1975) *Power, Rule and Domination; A Critical and Empirical Understanding of Power in Sociological Theory and Organisational Life*, London: Routledge and Kegan Paul.

Clegg, S.R. (1979) *The Theory of Power and Organisation*, London: Routledge and Kegan Paul.

Clegg, S.R. (1989) *Frameworks of Power*, London: Sage.

Crozier, M. (1964) *The Bureaucratic Phenomenon*, Chicago: University of Chicago Press.

Dahl, R.A. (1957) 'The Concept of Power', *Behavioural Science*, 2: 209–15.

Dahl, R.A. (1961) *Who Governs? Democracy and Power in an American City*, New Haven and London: Yale University Press.

Dalton, M. (1959) *Men who Manage*, New York: Wiley.

Di Maggio, P.J. and W.W. Powell (1983) 'The Iron Cage Revisited: Institutional Isomorphism and Collective Rationality in Organizational Fields', *American Sociological Review*, 48: 147–60.

Donaldson, L. (1987) *In Defence of Organization Theory*, Cambridge: Cambridge University Press.

Donaldson, L. (1995) *American Anti-management Theories of Organization: A Critique of Paradigm Proliferation*, Cambridge: Cambridge University Press.

Dunn, S. (1990) 'Root Metaphor in the Old and New Industrial Relations', *British Journal of Industrial Relations*, 28(1): 1–31.

Etzioni, A.A. (1961) *Comparative Analysis of Complex Organisations*, New York: Free Press.

Fox, A. (1985) *Man Mismanagement*, London: Hutchinson.

Freeman, R.E. (1984) *Strategic Management: A Stakeholder Approach*, London: Pitman.

French, J.R.P. and B.H. Raven (1959) 'The Social Bases of Power', in D. Cartwright (ed.) *Studies in Social Power*, East Lansing, MI: University of Michigan Press.

Friedman, M. (1962) *Capitalism and Freedom*, Chicago: University of Chicago Press.

Galbraith, J.K. (1983) *The Anatomy of Power*, Boston, MA: Houghton Mifflin.

Gaventa, J. and A. Cornwall (2000) 'Power and Knowledge', in P. Reason and H. Bradbury (eds), *Handbook of Action Research: Participative Inquiry and Practice*, London: Sage.

Giddens, A. (1968) '"Power" in the Recent Writings of Talcott Parsons', *Sociology*, 3(2): 257–72.

Golding, D. (1980) 'Establishing Blissful Clarity in Organisational Life: Managers', *Sociological Review*, 28(4): 763–83.

Grey, C. and N. Mitev (1995) 'Management Education: A Polemic', *Management Learning*, 26(1): 73–90.

Guest, D.E. (1991) 'Personnel Management: The End of Orthodoxy', *British Journal of Industrial Relations*, 29(2): 149–75.

Hammersley, M. and P. Atkinson (1985) *Ethnography: Principles in Practice*, London: Tavistock.

Handy, C.B. (1985, 3rd edition) *Understanding Organizations*, Harmondsworth: Penguin.

Hickson, D.J., C.R. Hinings, C.A. Lee, R.E. Sneck and J.M. Pennings (1971) 'A Strategic Contingencies Theory of Intraorganizational Power', *Administrative Science Quarterly*, 16(2): 216–29.

Hill, C. (1969) *The Century of Revolution*, London: Sphere.

Kakabadse, A., R. Ludlow and S. Vinnicombe (1987) *Working in Organizations*, Harmondsworth: Penguin.

Kanter, R.M. (1979) 'Power Failure in Management Circuits', *Harvard Business Review*, 57(4): 65–75.

Kanter, R.M. (1983) *The Change Masters: Innovation and Entrepreneurship in the American Corporation*, New York: Simon and Schuster.

Keenoy, T. (1991) 'The Roots of Metaphor in the Old and New Industrial Relations', *British Journal of Industrial Relations*, 29(2): 313–28.

Knights, D. and H. Willmott (1985) 'Power and Identity in Theory and Practice', *Sociological Review*, 33(1): 22–46.

Kotter, J.P. (1977) 'Power Dependence and Effective Management', *Harvard Business Review*, 55(4): 125–36.

Kotter, J.P. and L.A. Schlesinger (1979) 'Choosing Strategies for Change', *Harvard Business Review*, 57(3): 106–14.

Kumar, K. and M. Thibodeaux (1990) 'Organizational Politics and Planned Organizational Change', *Group and Organizational Studies*, 15(4): 357–65.

Landsberger, H.A. (1961) 'Parsons' Theory of Organisations', in M. Black (ed.), *The Social Theories of Talcott Parsons*, Englewood Cliffs, NJ: Prentice Hall.

Lukes, S. (1974) *Power: a Radical View*, London: Macmillan.

Mann, S. (1995) 'Politics and Power in Organizations: Why Women Lose Out', *Leadership and Organization Development Journal*, 16(2): 9–15.

Marchington, M. (1979) 'The Issue of Union Power', *Employee Relations*, 1(4): 3–7.

Marchington, M. (1982) *Managing Industrial Relations*, London: McGraw-Hill.

Marchington, M. and P. Armstrong (1983) 'Shop Steward Organisation and Joint Consultation', *Personnel Review*, 12(1): 24–31.

McClelland, D.C. and D.H. Burnham (1995) 'Power is the Great Motivator', *Harvard Business Review*, 73(1): 126–39.

McGivering, I.C., C.G.J. Mathews and W.H. Scott (1969) *Management in Britain*, Liverpool: Liverpool University Press.

McKenna, E.P. (1997) *When Work Doesn't Work Anymore: Women, Work and Identity*, New York: Hodder and Stoughton.

McKinley, W., M.A. Mone and V.L. Barker (1998) 'Some Ideological Foundations of Downsizing', *Journal of Management Inquiry*, 7: 198–212.

Mechanic, D. (1962) 'Sources of Power of Lower Participants in Complex Organisations', *Administrative Science Quarterly*, 7(4): 349–64.

Mintzberg, H. (1983) *Power in and around Organizations*, London: Prentice Hall.

Mintzberg, H. (1987) 'Crafting Strategy', *Harvard Business Review*, (July–August): 65–75.

Mintzberg, H. (1989) *Mintzberg on Management: Inside Our Strange World of Organizations*, London: Free Press.

Parsons, T. (1951) *The Social System*, New York: Free Press.

Parsons, T. (1956) 'Suggestions for a Sociological Approach to a Theory of Organizations: Parts I and II', *Administrative Science Quarterly*, 1(1): 63–85 and 1(2): 225–39.

Peattie, K. (1993) 'Strategic Planning: Its role in Organizational Politics', *Long Range Planning*, 26(3): 10–17.

Pettigrew, A. (1973) *The Politics of Organisational Decision-making*, London: Tavistock.

Pettigrew, A. (1977) 'Strategy Formulation as a Political Process', *International Studies of Management and Organization*, 7(2): 78–87.

Pettigrew, A. (1987) 'Context and Action in the Transformation of the Firm', *Journal of Management Sciences*, 24(6): 649–70.

Pfeffer, J. (1978) *Organizational Design*, Arlington Heights, IL: AHM Publishing.

Pfeffer, J. (1981) *Power in Organizations*, Cambridge, MA: Pitman.

Pfeffer, J. (1992) *Managing with Power: Politics and Influence in Organizations*, Boston, MA: Harvard Business School.

Pfeffer, J. and G.R. Salancik (1978) *The External Control of Organisations: A Resource Dependent Perspective*, New York: Harper and Row.

Porac, J.F., H. Thomas, F. Wilson, D. Paton and A. Kanfer (1995) 'Rivalry and the Industry Model of Scottish Knitwear Producers', *Administrative Science Quarterly*, 40: 203–27.

Porter, M. (1990) *The Competitive Advantage of Nations*, New York: Free Press.

Quinn, J.B. (1980) *Strategies for Change: Logical Incrementalism*, Homewood, IL: Irwin.

Reed, M. (1985) *Redirections in Organizational Analysis*, London: Tavistock.

Rosenthal, P., S. Hill and R. Peccei (1997) 'Checking out Service: Evaluating Excellence, HRM and TQM in Retailing', *Work Employment and Society*, 11(3): 481–503.

Schattschneider, E.E. (1960) *The Semi-Sovereign People: A Realist's View of Democracy in America*, New York: Holt, Rheinhart and Wilson.

Scott, W.R. and J.W. Meyer (1994) *Institutional Environments and Organizations*, London: Sage.

Senior, B. (1997) *Organizational Change*, London: Pitman.

Storey, J. (1983) *Managerial Prerogative and the Question of Control*, London: Routledge and Kegan Paul.

Thompkins, J.M. (1990) 'Politics – the Illegitimate Discipline', *Management Decision*, 28(4): 23–8.

Weber, M. (1968) *The Theory of Social and Economic Organization*, New York: Oxford University Press.

Wilkinson, A., G. Godfrey and M. Marchington (1997) 'Bouquets, Brickbats and Blinkers: TQM and Employee Involvement in Context', *Organization Studies*, 18(5): 799–22.

Willis, P. (1977) *Learning to Labour: How Working Class Kids Get Working Class Jobs*, London: Saxon House.

Willmott, H.C. (1984) 'Images and Ideals of Managerial Work', *Journal of Management Studies*, 21(3): 347–68.

Wilson, D.C. (1982) 'Electricity and Resistance; A Case Study of Innovation and Politics', *Organisation Studies*, 3(2): 119–40.

Chapter 5

CRITICAL THEORY AND SOCIAL CONSTRUCTIVISM

The aims of this chapter are to:

1 Contextualise the development of Critical Theory in a distinctive form of social constructivism.

2 Show how Critical Theory, as developed by Habermas, offers a philosophically grounded critique of the dominant ideologies which pervade Western organisations so as to emancipate people from domination.

3 Elucidate the implications of critical theory for our understandings of organisational change.

INTRODUCTION

As we enter the twenty-first century significant changes are occurring in the frames of reference we have available for understanding strategy and change. Though varied, these increasingly popular epistemological orientations are simultaneously united by their acceptance that an objective and disinterested foundation for science cannot exist. Commitment to truth and knowledge as the authoritative outputs of a singular scientific rationality has been problematised through acknowledgement of epistemological relativity and plurality. Since there can be no indubitable fixed foundation for our knowledge about the world, scepticism abounds regarding the Cartesian analytical system described in Chapter 1. The 'fable' of the Cartesian dualism between knower and known is replaced by the view that knowledge develops within evolving social traditions, or, as we have called them in Chapter 3, mindsets. As Burr elaborates, 'knowledge is ... seen not as something a person *has* (or does not have), but as something that people *do* together' (1995: 8; emphasis in the original). So all there can be are socially constructed narratives based on particular paradigms, or discourses, or language-games, and so on – a claim that has devastating implications for any management practices and how we understand them.

However, even a cursory review of the management strategy and change literature would suggest that its mainstream remains reluctant to jettison foundationalism in some form. Clearly, there must be much to lose. For instance, a key implication of social constructivism is the undermining of any claim that management theory and practice are morally founded on a technical imperative, to improve efficiency, justified and enabled by objective analyses of how things really are (see Grey and Mitev 1995; Fournier and Grey 2000). At an epistemological stroke, social constructivism in any form makes the moral authority of managers to impose their will on others, during processes such as strategy and change, highly precarious. If all knowledge is a variable and socially contingent output, why should the culturally relative products of one socio-economic group (e.g. managers) accumulate epistemic privilege, social prestige and financial reward at the expense of alternative ways of knowing and acting, whether the latter are in existence or merely constitute an as yet unrealised potential?

Nevertheless, the challenges posed by social constructivism have begun to filter through via a process of epistemological critique which replicates a well-trodden path in other disciplines. Here the main target for these social constructivist attacks has been what is usually construed as the prevailing, if rarely explicitly discussed, philosophical orthodoxy in management that expresses the Cartesian dualism – the various emanations of positivism. Indeed, it is in relation to positivism and its core assumptions that social constructivists most clearly define themselves.

Briefly, positivism assumes that there is a foundational point at which an observer can stand and observe the external world objectively. Here truth is to be found in the observer's passive registration of what Auguste Comte (1853) called the 'positively given' – the facts that constitute external social and natural reality. So, provided that managers deploy knowledge developed through the application of the appropriate methodological protocols, their subsequent practices are construed as technically neutral activities, grounded in objective representations of reality. In essence, managerial prerogative becomes enshrined in a claim to superior knowledge, which in turn depends on the assumption that such privileged access to reality is possible. Pivotal to this positivist epistemological assumption is the role of language in enabling the neutral representation of reality.

In his early work, Wittgenstein (1922) argued that language gains its meaning from its direct correspondence with the objects of an independent external reality. In this 'picture theory' of language, a sentence can be meaningful in only two ways: either by picturing a fact, or by analysis, breaking it down into more basic sentences which picture facts. The relationship between language and reality is called picturing because words stand for objects just as points on the surface of a picture represent physical space. In order to justify this 'representational' view of language, Wittgenstein claimed that the character of external reality and the language used to describe it must match, otherwise our propositions about the world would be meaningless. At the time positivists construed Wittgenstein's picture theory of language as legitimising empiricism by justifying the assumption that experience constructs language, and not vice versa. This in turn sustains the possibility of a neutral observational language, something that Hindess sees as making . . .

> possible a very precise conception of the testing of theory against observation. The testing of theory against irreducible statements of observation is equivalent to a direct comparison between theory and the real. If they fail to *correspond* then the theory is false and therefore may be rejected. (1977: 18; our emphasis)

As we have noted, these positivistic epistemological commitments have been increasingly undermined in both the natural and social sciences by a disparate group of critics broadly known as 'social constructivists'. Just as these critics are united by their repudiation of a theory-neutral observational language, so they are also divided over the implications of their epistemological stance. Although Burr (1995: 10) identifies the publication of Berger and Luckmann's (1967) work as announcing a social constructivist manifesto to social scientists, it would seem that the philosophical roots of social constructivism might be also traced back to Immanuel Kant.

For instance, key themes in social constructivist epistemology were expressed by Kant's undermining of empiricism in his *Critique of Pure Reason*, which was first published in 1781. Here Kant distanced himself from the empiricist forebears of positivism by arguing that our minds are not passive receivers of sense data. Rather we automatically select, limit, organise and interpret our experience of external reality. We endow the world with meaning, and not vice versa as the empiricists then claimed. Kant tried to show how our knowledge always contained components deriving from ourselves prior to any experience. Although the categories, concepts and meanings we use seem to originate in what we take to be the external world, Kant claimed that they naturally derive from our innate *a priori* (i.e. prior to experience) cognitive structures. Hence Kant rejects the Cartesian dualism – that it is possible for the mind neutrally to access and contemplate the objects of external reality. Instead, for Kant, the so-called external world is a construction of the mind working on our sensory inputs. Any separation between the knower from what is known, as proposed by the Cartesian dualism and accepted by all forms of positivism, is undermined in Kant.

Meanwhile social constructivist ideas in the natural sciences also pre-date Berger and Luckmann's work. For instance, social constructivism was articulated by Heisenberg's (1958) 'uncertainty principle' – that it is impossible to observe and investigate something without that influencing what is seen. For Heisenberg what a scientist observes is not independent of the process of observing but is an outcome of the scientists' methodological interaction with, and conceptual constitution of, his/her objects of knowledge. A classic statement of this position had already been provided by Ludwik Flek's idea (1935/1979), that during inquiry natural scientists construct not only their accounts of the empirical facts but also the facts themselves. So for Flek every scientific fact is a social fact, the negotiated product of the collective thinking of a community united by a 'thought style'.

In a similar manner the older Wittgenstein (1958) repudiated his 'picture theory' of science by arguing that language does not allow access to reality; instead our renditions of reality are located in language itself rather than anything independent of it. He claimed that scientists' 'representations' of reality are thus the product of 'language-games' through which they socially construct their realities by deploying a particular game's concepts and theories. For Hanson (1958: 8) this means that 'there is more to seeing than meets the eyeball'. There cannot be any neutral foundation for natural science located in the passive registration of sensory inputs since the scientist's language-in-use, their theories and hypotheses, influence what will be observed before any observations are made. This is a thesis which in effect socialises science and which was subsequently highly influential on a key figure in social constructivist thought, the physicist Thomas Kuhn, whose theory of scientific development (1957, 1962, 1970) simultaneously gained avid appreciation and cultivated considerable indignation amongst audiences in the social sciences.

Controversy developed because Kuhn's thesis used historical examples to demonstrate how, in practice, natural science neither proceeds inductively through verification and proof of theory nor deductively through falsification of theory – a thesis that became a key source of social constructivist ideas in the social sciences. Especially during the 1970s and 1980s, social constructivists popularised the view that the positivist ideal of a neutral, detached observer was a quixotic one – what counts as warranted knowledge, truth and reason is always conditioned by the socio-historical context of the scientist. Far from articulating universal scientific truths any scientists' account will be a local social construction created through the operation of community language-games (e.g. Rorty 1979), paradigms (e.g. Burrell and Morgan 1979), metaphors (e.g. Ortony 1979), interests (Habermas 1972, 1974a), traditions (Gadamer 1975), discourses (Foucault 1977), inescapable frameworks (Taylor 1985), or worldviews (Geertz 1989), and so on. Besides using different terminology, where such writers disagree is regarding the ontological implications of their constructivism – a matter illustrated by Kuhn's own earlier equivocation.

Kuhn's rejection of a theory-neutral observational language leads to two very different implications, which are both tacitly invoked by his statement that after a change in paradigm 'scientists are responding to a different world' (1970: 135), by which he means that any scientific statement is the social construction of the scientist. However, are these statements just different versions of an independently existing social/natural reality that we can never fully know because our theories are always underdetermined, or does it mean that reality is created and determined by the socially constructed theory? In other words, what does Kuhn mean by 'scientist ... responding' in the passage quoted above? The question is whether those 'responses' are grounded in an intersubjective consensus that is based *either* on the paradigm's reactive mediation of an independently existing reality (i.e. ontological realism) *or* on the paradigm's proactive creation of a reality that has no independent ontological status (i.e. ontological subjectivism). While some social constructivists seem inadvertently to oscillate between ontological realism and subjectivism (e.g. Morgan 1986; 1993), many are firmly in the realist camp (e.g. Beck 1996), while others (e.g. Baudrillard 1983) embrace ontological subjectivism. In this chapter we shall focus on one ontologically realist version of social constructivism – broadly termed critical theory – and its implications for how we construe strategy and change. In Chapter 6 we shall turn to the implications of the recent development of an ontologically subjectivist stance which is broadly called postmodernism.

THE THEMES OF CRITICAL THEORY

Critical Theory (CT) should not be confused with the notion that to be critical is merely to evaluate others' work by pointing to its methodological flaws or theoretical mistakes and contradictions – a process possible only because the critic presumes to occupy an epistemic position superior to that of the criticised. So while noting Reed's (1992) observation that there is a variety of approaches which may be called 'critical', here we locate CT in the social constructivist attacks on positivism described above, because this allows us to identify it clearly as a distinctive approach to analysing organisational relations.

By pursuing an ontologically realist version of social constructivism, CT undermines the epistemological authority of management and demands consideration of the social processes which underpin and legitimise any knowledge claim. Hence the received image of management as a technical, politically-neutral activity (see Willmott 1984) is rejected by CT as this image serves to conceal the knowledge-constituting role of partisan interests. Following Alvesson and Deetz (1996), we use the term CT to refer to studies that draw concepts, principally though not exclusively, from the Frankfurt School. Here we will focus primarily on the work of Jürgen Habermas who not only built on the ideas of earlier critical theorists, such as Marcuse (1964) and Horkheimer and Adorno (1947), but also set out to 'reconstitute the whole paradigm of critical theory' (Pursey 1987: 33), thereby providing social science with a new theoretical stance and sense of purpose (Delantey 1997: 94).

Like Kuhn, Habermas (1972, 1974a and b) presents a powerful critique of positivist epistemology and its underlying commitment to a Cartesian dualism. Thus he argues that a correspondence theory of truth obfuscates the relationship between 'knowledge' and 'interest' by presupposing the possibility of a theory-neutral observational language that unproblematically reconstitutes reality for examination. While Habermas admits that positivism's limitation of the sciences to entities that were assumed to be immediately available to sensory experience has helped to remove metaphysical and religious dogmas from the realm of science, he sees such epistemic commitments as problematic.

Positivism's presupposition of a theory-neutral observational language allows positivists to ignore the effects of the epistemic subject (i.e. the knower) on what is known and thereby protects it from any form of epistemological reflexivity. For Habermas such positivist pretensions are a masquerade. All knowledge is contaminated at source by the influence of socio-cultural factors upon sensory experience:

> even the simplest perception is not only performed pre-categorically by the physiological apparatus – it is just as determined by previous experience through what has been handed down and through what has been learned as by what has been anticipated through the horizon of expectations. (1974b: 199)

Habermas eschews positivism's 'objectivist illusions', which conceal the processes by which knowledge is constituted, by drawing attention to the socio-cultural factors that influence sensory experience. In this manner he substitutes the naïve empiricism of the correspondence approach to truth with a social constructivism based on the object-constituting activity of epistemic human beings. In this Habermas accepts the existence of a reality independent of human subjectivity which imposes limitations upon human endeavours through 'the contingency of its ultimate constants' (1972: 33). Like Kant, Habermas puts forward a phenomenalist position that human cognition shapes reality through its imposition of *a priori* cognitive principles. This 'externality' can become an object of human knowledge only through our imposition of object-constituting epistemological 'categories' which derive from our fundamental 'anthropologically deep seated interests', which 'determine the aspects under which reality is objectified and can thus be made accessible to experience to begin with' (1974a: 8–9).

For Habermas, it is only through reference to fundamental interests that it becomes possible to understand: first, the criteria that are applied in identifying what is taken to be 'real'; and, second, the criteria by which the validity of such propositions may be evaluated. Hence he identifies two 'object-constituting' epistemological categories, each of which involves specific interests and constitutes the object-domains of two forms of knowledge:

> in the functional sphere of instrumental action we encounter objects of the type of moving bodies; here we experience things, events, and conditions which are, in principle, capable of being manipulated. In ... [social] ... interaction we encounter objects of the type of speaking and acting subjects; here we experience persons, utterances and conditions which in principle are structured and understood symbolically. (1974a: 8)

Following from this, Habermas identifies two forms of knowledge with their attendant ontological domains, each deriving from specific human interests which, he suggests, have naturally developed during human evolution.

The first knowledge-domain, empirical-analytical science, emphasises the human interest in our creative interplay with and attempts at exerting control over, the natural environment. This can be linked to evolution in that the need for physical survival leads to the development of knowledge about and control over the environment. This is 'not only a fundamental category of human existence but also an epistemological category ... [which] ... signifies a scheme both of action and apprehending the world' (1972: 28). For Habermas this instrumental interest in 'technical' control over nature sets limits on how we apprehend nature by placing parameters on the theoretical concepts of the empirical-analytical sciences. For instance, because empirical-analytical science is oriented towards the establishment of technical control over nature, warranted knowledge becomes restricted to procedures that 'permit the deduction of law-like hypotheses with empirical content ... [which] ... make predictions possible' (1972: 308).

The second knowledge-domain, historical-hermeneutic science, emphasises the human 'practical' interest that arises out of the need for interpersonal communication where humans encounter other speaking, thinking and acting subjects who have to be understood symbolically. This interest is 'designed to guarantee, within cultural traditions . . . self understanding of individuals and groups as well as reciprocal understanding between different individuals and groups' (1972: 176). Where communication fails, a condition for human survival is disturbed. Thus the historical-hermeneutic sciences are structured so as to facilitate the apprehension of the meanings of actions and communications.

To his taxonomy of interests and sciences Habermas adds what he calls 'critical science', which derives from 'emancipatory interest'. This third form of science is best illustrated by Habermas's critique of Gadamer (1975), who had also rejected the possibility of an ahistorical neutral position on the part of the observer/knower and claimed that our knowledge is therefore socio-historically relative and context-bound. What Habermas (1977) specifically objects to in Gadamer's perspective is the relativist contention that there cannot be any independent ground from which it is possible to criticise ongoing tradition. Habermas clearly thinks that this relativism leads to the uncritical acceptance of the status quo and its repressive authority relations.

Habermas, therefore, identifies a third knowledge constitutive interest – an emancipatory interest that seeks to free people from domination – the systematic distortion of interaction and communication – and liberates their rational capabilities. The form of knowledge for this project is self-knowledge and understanding generated through self-reflection. When accomplished this self-reflection 'leads to insight due to the fact that what was previously unconscious is made conscious in a manner rich in consequences: analytic insights intervene in life' (1974a: 23). Self-reflection demystifies previously unacknowledged distortions and enables awareness of the link between knowledge and interest. As such the emancipatory interest is 'derivative' in that it can exist only under conditions of 'systematically distorted communication and thinly legitimated repression' (1973: 176). The resultant critical science seeks to free people from overt and covert forms of domination. It unites aspects of the empirical-analytical and the historical-hermeneutic sciences within a project aimed at self-reflective understanding (Geuss 1981: 2).

In sum, Habermas challenges positivism by arguing that the object domains of forms of knowledge and their criteria of validity are constituted by interest. Therefore, reality is knowable only through the operation of interest-laden modes of engagement. Subsequent accounts of reality are not objective or neutral but rather express interest – an expression obfuscated by appeals to neutrality and objectivity. But as McCarthy (1978: 295) points out, by tying knowledge to the imperatives of human life, Habermas effectively undercuts notions of objectivity and encounters relativism: 'how can Habermas claim anything more than an interest-relative truth for his own theories?' (1980: 293). It is evident that Habermas was aware of this problem and he tries to rescue the status of his own critique by finding an epistemological refuge from which that very critique might be pursued and defended.

Habermas (1970a and 1971) asserts that universal unconstrained consensus is implicit in human communication. He argues that when two speakers engage with one another, even if only to disagree, they take for granted certain assumptions about the organisation of speech. They necessarily assume that they could reach an agreement, if they were to debate specific issues with one another under conditions free of distorting factors – in other words, free from domination. The ability to communicate linguistically in a fashion that satisfies what he calls 'validity claims' produces 'communicative competence'. These validity claims are: that the sentences speakers utter are comprehensible and their propositions are true; their overtly expressed intentions are honest; and the norms referred to in speech are correct. In everyday communication the validity claims which are inevitably made by speakers are usually accepted unquestioningly by hearers. This consensus is disturbed either by a misunderstanding or by a challenge to these claims. Such a situation may be remedied by clearing away misunderstanding or by testing the 'validity claims' by speakers and hearers undertaking analysis. Discourse occurs when analysis is made explicit and entails the application of canons of argument and evidence with the intention of coming to agreement over the validity claims that have been disputed or misunderstood.

According to Habermas any communication rests on the assumption that speakers can justify their tacit validity claims through recourse to argument and discourse. However, in what he calls 'systematically distorted communication', validity claims are maintained through the exercise of power which prevents justification through engagement in discourse and produces a pretence of consensus. The problem for Habermas is to elucidate how we might differentiate between systematically distorted communication and discursively produced 'rational' consensus.

Box 5.1

Habermas's ideal-speech situation

McCarthy interprets the ideal-speech situation as freedom from internal and external constraint: 'that there must be for all participants a symmetrical distribution of chances to select and employ speech acts, that is an effective equality of chances to assume dialogue roles. If this is not the case, the resultant agreement is open to the charge of being less than rational, of being the result not of the force of better argument but, for example, of open or latent relations of domination, of conscious or unconscious strategic motivations. The ideal of truth points ultimately to a form of interaction that is free from all distorting influences.' (1978: 308)

Habermas's solution is directly relevant to the issue of strategy formulation and organisational change practices. It is the 'ideal-speech situation' (see Box 5.1) in which discursively produced 'rational consensus' is induced when that consensus derives from argument and analysis without resort to coercion, distortion or duplicity. For Habermas, although such a consensus is not attained in everyday social interaction due to the operation of power and domination, it is both pre-supposed, and a potential in any communication. Thus the extent to which actual communication deviates from the ideal, and hence from the truth, depends on the degree of repression in society. In this sense, Critical Theory seeks to show the practical, moral and political significance of particular communicative actions. It also investigates how a particular social structure may produce and reinforce distorted communicative actions that practically and subtly shape its members' lives. Forrester incisively summarises Critical Theory as a structural phenomenology:

> It is a phenomenology because it attends to the skilled and contingent social construction and negotiation of intersubjective meanings. It is structural because it attends to the historical stage on which social actors meet, speak, conflict, listen, or engage with one another. . . . Human actors make sense of daily life subjectively, through communicative interaction but 'sense' depends on context or setting – the objective social structure in which those actors work and live. (1983: 235)

As we shall illustrate, this controversial task permeates both the attempts of critical theorists to analyse current strategy-change practices and their concerns with emancipation.

STRATEGY FORMULATION AND ORGANISATIONAL CHANGE

Propelled by its epistemological commitments, the aim of CT is to understand how management practices, such as strategy and change, are developed and legitimised within the shifting terrain of asymmetrical power relations. For Jermier (1998) the resultant agenda for Critical Theory is committed to attempting to access actors' culturally derived worldviews while revealing the socio-economic conditions which create and maintain asymmetrical power relations. The reader here will note the similarity between this agenda and Lukes' (1974), whose work was reviewed in Chapter 4. For instance, according to Jermier, the most controversial task for CT is

> to go beyond informants' reports to articulate the socio-economic context that envelops their informants' accounts without relying exclusively on either pre-existing theory or mere speculation. A hallmark of critical research is the blending of informants' words, impressions and activities with an analysis of the historical and structural forces that shape the social world under investigation. (1998: 242)

So far from construing strategy and change merely as a set of neutral technical activities that benefit all by serving an assumed unitary organisational interest, a primary concern of CT is to unmask their lack of objectivity. It does so by exposing the creative role of underlying social values, partial interests and power relations in producing those practices. In doing so CT reveals previously hidden structures of oppression and counteracts the discursive closure brought about by acceptance of any knowledge, managerial or otherwise, as privileged and therefore unchangeable. By such an analysis CT opens up the possibility of alternative interest and value-laden modes of practice located in democratic discourse which subverts and displaces the orthodox, top-down, technocratic image of management by asking ethical questions concerning collective priorities (Forrester 1989).

Hence CT seems to offer a solution to the problem of identifying 'real' interests which bedevils Lukes' work (1974). Indeed, a goal of Habermas's Critical Theory is 'a form of life free from unnecessary domination in all its forms is inherent in the notion of truth' (McCarthy 1978: 273). This is a social constructivist position which deploys a consensus theory of truth, as a regulative democratic standard, to assess the extent of systematically distorted communication. Central to CT is the possibility that any established practice can itself be challenged and changed – that people are able to emancipate themselves from asymmetrical power relations through the power of reason which is located in processes of critical reflection. So while the scrutiny of management practice is important, of equal significance is to give voice to those interests currently excluded by mainstream management discourses. A vital step in this process is the realisation that the status quo is neither natural nor inevitable.

The two themes evident in CT will now be considered: the first analyses the mainstream orthodoxy evident in management discourses about strategy and change so as to reveal structures of oppression primarily by undercutting its positivist epistemological stance; the second expresses CT's normative concern with emancipation and the possibility of a life free from exploitation and oppression through what amounts to a demand for the democratisation of organisations and consideration of how this might be achieved. Within each theme it follows that if critical theorists must reject the hubris of scientific detachment, they must also accept their role as partisan participants in interest-laden discourse. Hence critical theorists must also be self-reflexive about their own analyses and, as Kinchloe and McLaren observe, put their 'assumptions on the table so that no one is confused concerning the epistemological and political baggage they bring with them' (1994: 140). It is in dealing with the demands of such self-reflexivity that the epistemic conundrums that critical theorists create for themselves are exposed.

CRITICAL THEORY AS ANALYSIS OF MAINSTREAM ORTHODOXY

Although the discipline of strategy may suffer from a confused amalgam of taxonomies, deductive logic and empirical observation (Kay 1993), as we have already implied, positivist epistemological commitments generally underpin the mainstream conceptualisations which have been articulated in best-selling text-books (e.g. Johnson and Scholes 1993) and which have notionally colonised the practices of many business communities – at least at the public level of testimony (Cappelli et al. 1997). Now some terminological confusion arises here because commentators on this mainstream insist on using the term 'rationalism' to describe its epistemology (see Chapter 4). For instance, Mintzberg (1990) advises us that this orthodoxy is composed of three distinct prescriptive schools: the 'design', the 'planning' and the 'positioning'; and it is 'rationalism' that is taken to unite this 'eclectic forum' (see also Knights and Morgan 1991; Whittington 2001; Calori, 1998). In this context Browne and his colleagues define rationalism as entailing the epistemic stance

> that science and reason can enable humans to understand nature and things 'out there' and that our capacity to generate knowledge about the world we live in, especially laws and principles, is related to achieving progress. Dominant theories of strategy are embedded in this context and 'accurate' representations of the business environment overwhelmingly use 'rational' criteria like sales, market share, return on assets and profitability. (Browne et al. 1999: 401)

If we take a theory-neutral observational language to be the key epistemic commitment of positivism, it is evident from the above quote that rationalism and positivism are mutually interdependent. For instance, positivism accepts the rationalist belief that the human mind can discover the innate laws that govern the workings of the universe. Both agree that application of those laws, through the development of technically explicit rules and procedures, can eliminate uncertainty and disorganisation as well as ensure material progress. What positivism provides is the methodological operationalisation of the theory neutral observational language to enable the development of the requisite knowledge. (For fuller explanations see Slife and Williams 1995; Delanty, 1997.)

So, despite the risks of oversimplifying, it is worth briefly reprising the key features of this orthodoxy since CT is best understood as a distinctive heterodox counterpoint to positivism/rationalism. According to this orthodox wisdom, organisations interact with environments which independently exist outside their boundaries and on which they rely for a variety of resources (e.g. Learned et al. 1965). By proffering opportunities and threats, different environmental sectors exert varying demands for adaptation on different organisational segments. For the mainstream it is, therefore, incumbent on the strategist (usually senior management) to be able to understand the relationships that their organisation has with different environmental sectors, predict how those relationships might change and develop modes of adaptation which cope with, or exploit, those demands (e.g. Porter 1990). Sometimes this view of environment relations expresses social Darwinist assumptions. For instance, population ecologists (e.g. Hannan and Freeman 1977) argue that populations of organisations compete with one another and the 'hidden hand' of their shared environments acts to select and allow those organisations to survive that best serve its demands. Those that are unfit do not survive such natural selection.

Although natural selection may be capricious and haphazard, there is an emphasis on achieving strategic fit whereby an organisation meets environmental demands, achieves competitive advantage, and thereby improves its likelihood of survival. Such a fit is thought to be achievable through the strategist's objective transcription and subsequent analysis of external and internal, cognitively accessible, empirical realities. For instance, according to Calori (1998), by employing the binary rationalist logic (described in Chapter 1) the strategist begins with an external appraisal of the environment to identify current and future opportunities and threats. This can then be compared with an internal appraisal of the organisation's strengths and weaknesses to reveal its core competencies and how they might be improved. Indeed, for some commentators, such processes of strategic choice and fit are played down in favour of an emphasis on the strategic development of these competencies since ecological niches are too difficult to identify, particularly in times of rapid change and unpredictability (e.g. Hamel and Prahalad 1989). Based on these analyses strategy should be formulated by identifying appropriate courses of action that ensure strategic fit and/or enhance strategic core competencies. Either formulation may in turn be implemented through management's mobilisation of resources and the development of structures and control systems to facilitate and monitor the realisation of the cascaded strategic objectives.

For Porter (1985, 1990) there are different generic strategies from which managers should select to sustain competitive advantage whose implementation will put particular demands on the internal configuration of organisational practices and relationships. By being alert to the need to adapt to external pressures and/or the necessity to develop critical competencies, management also has to act as change agents by purposively inducing planned change in their organisations. This prescriptive thrust of much mainstream academic discourse has been questioned by those (e.g. Quinn 1980; Pettigrew 1985; Johnson 1987) who have observed that in practice strategy is much more about the incremental enactment of culturally derived preferences in contexts of negotiation and political compromise with the demands which emanate from various internal and external stakeholders. Nevertheless, although the prerogative of management may be constrained by those demands, the necessity for change management in the light of strategic objectives has still become a rhetorical *leitmotif* of much recent management discourse and practice. Indeed Mintzberg (1990) has surmised that the appeal of orthodoxy's standardised techniques may lie in how they countervail the apparently chaotic and irrational practices that arise during political struggle. According to Stacey (1993), such techniques privilege the cognition of the strategic designer as ultimate arbiter of the collective good and guardians of progress.

Thus although it may often be painful and disruptive, and may even fail, managers are increasingly exhorted to implement changes to gain or maintain competitive advantage, increase productivity and improve organisational performance. These are processes which require analysis of the factors within an organisation which may facilitate or forestall the necessary changes (e.g. Porras and Hoffer 1986; Robertson et al. 1993; Champy 1995) and the development of appropriate control systems (Goold and Quinn 1990; Simons, 1991, 1994; Coad 1995). For instance, the reported failure fully to exploit the potential benefits of new manufacturing strategies has been related to implementation problems in which the inability to adapt control systems is significant (Tayles and Drury 1994). The result can be a lack of alignment of the everyday concerns of managers and the behavioural standards of employees with the company's new strategy.

From this synopsis of the orthodox orientation it is hardly surprising that strategy is construed by the mainstream as a rational force for positive organisational change by enabling improved performance, and hence is a pivotal tenet of 'good' management (see Ansoff 1965; Porter 1985). Not planning for change is a mistake that damages organisations (Drucker 1995). Indeed, failure to give organisations a sense of direction and/or to implement the necessary changes can only be the product of incompetence, negligence, irrationality or moral turpitude (e.g. Karger and Malik 1975). On the other hand, resistance to change expresses a wilful failure to appreciate the collective interest – something that must be eradicated.

In sum, rationalists implicitly and explicitly award epistemological privilege to the strategic analyses and prognostications of managers provided, as Pollitt (1993) observes, they attend to the advice and outcomes of the appropriate academic discourse. Such a perspective is, of course, anathema to critical theorists as it aligns an image of 'science' with what CT construes as the sectional interests of management (Grey and Mitev 1995) and simultaneously reduces employees to 'strategic tools of the competitive battle their supreme command is fighting' (Sievers 1994: 80). So, rather than seeking to sustain the management practices which they perceive as routinely occurring in organisations, critical theorists are distrustful of the status quo and judge the technically neutral imagery the mainstream propagates as both untenable and ideological (e.g. Shrivastrava 1986).

Alvesson and Willmott (1996: 133–7) observe from a CT perspective how 'strategy talk' has colonised and framed managers' understandings of themselves and management. Similarly, Oakes and her colleagues claim that strategy is a profound mechanism of control which can be coercively executed through organisational hierarchies, but also 'provides and sanctions legitimate forms of discourse and language and thus serves as a mechanism of knowledge that produces new understandings of the organization' (1998: 258). In order to appear competent, managers have to demonstrate a command of the 'strategy talk'. In this manner 'strategy talk' has become a benchmark for legitimising managers' activities by demonstrating their comprehension of the need to pursue competitive struggle and thereby subordinate themselves and other employees to its incontestable demands for organisational change. A key element in strategy talk is the elitist exclusion of most of those who are affected by strategic decisions because they lack the requisite (i.e. privileged) knowledge and expertise – whether they be employees, local communities or customers, etc. For the orthodox it is managers who make the difference by identifying strategic direction and becoming the architects of 'positive' change which ensures organisational 'alignment' (e.g. Greenwood and Hinings 1993; Trahant et al. 1997). Although many managers are expected to 'talk the talk', in theory and practice it is senior managers who exercise a monopoly over strategic decision making (see Mintzberg 1990). For Alvesson and Willmott, the issue becomes 'one of calculating how employee or customer support can be cost-effectively engineered, rather than how their concerns can best be appreciated or addressed' (1996: 136). For critical theorists, such a calculation expresses an instrumental rationality (see Box 5.2). This raises two problems: first, it is self-defeating; and second it relies on a foundationalism that has no epistemological justification and, through discursive closure, serves to prevent any epistemological self-reflection and the articulation of alternative discourses.

Box 5.2

Instrumental rationality

Instrumental rationality is pivotal to the technicism of the mainstream. It is a rationality that is concerned only with identifying and implementing the most appropriate means for achieving given ends. The appearance that is created is one of technical neutrality. For critical theorists it is a façade since by failing to reflect on the nature and desirability of those ends, an instrumental rationality, through default, inevitably accepts value- and interest-laden ends as *a priori* givens. The values and interests those ends express are thus masked and subliminally encoded into the ostensibly morally- and politically-neutral technical fixes which managers claim to deploy. Debate about the organisation's purposes is thereby stifled. It is precisely the nature of such ends, and their underlying ethical justification, which is of direct concern to critical theorists (see Alvesson 1987; Grey and Mitev 1995).

For Habermas, top-down orthodox approaches to strategy and change would be self-defeating since they entail what he has called 'systems integration' (1987), which demands compliance with a normative order imposed by 'experts' through the impersonal media of rules and sanctions rather than through members' active consent. In contrast to 'social integration', which relies on a consensually determined normative order through members' unconstrained engagements, systems integration engenders a purposive-rational attitude which makes it possible 'to exert generalised, strategic influence on the decisions of other participants while *bypassing* processes of consensus orientated communication' (1987: 183, emphasis in original). Indeed, in the mainstream literature, control systems seem often to be conceptualised as analogous to independent variables that can be manipulated to engender change in the dependent variable – members' everyday task behaviour. For instance, the mainstream popularity of notions such as strategic and subsystems fit as diagnostic devices (e.g. Tichy 1983; Donaldson 1987; Cummings 1993; Harrison 1994) implies the ability on the part of management contingently to adjust the alignment between organisational variables to change and promote particular behavioural requirements in order to implement strategy. Critical theorists have traced the various ways in which attempts at systems integration have historically varied from bureaucratised labour processes (e.g. Ritzer 1993) to the more recent development of culturally based forms of control (e.g. Willmott 1993) which contrive to re-engineer the value premises of employee behaviour often so as to engender responsible autonomy (Friedman 1977). A renewed surge of management theorising aimed at such cultural homogenisation rose to prominence in the 1980s (Barley and Kunda 1992). This can be seen to have derived from a number of sources. First, there is a concern to analyse and replicate what are assumed to be the adoptable aspects of the organisational underpinnings of Japan's apparent competitive edge (e.g. Pascale and Athos 1981). Second are attempts to seek out indigenous (mainly North American) 'excellent' management practices (e.g. Peters and Waterman 1982). Third, there was a perceived need to move away from increasingly ineffective bureaucratic modes of control, towards 'clan' (e.g. Ouchi 1980) forms of control that instil personal commitment. Such rules and procedures 'stifle initiative and creativity' in an atmosphere that is 'emotionally repressive' (Kanter 1989: 280) and hence were seen to be inappropriate in the uncertain environmental conditions which were and are thought to prevail.

Regardless of the source of inspiration, the effect was to cultivate a fixation, for example articulated in Human Resource Management and Total Quality Management programmes, with cultural renewal and charismatic leadership as the determinants of entrepreneurial success (see Blunt 1990; Legge 1995). In response, critical theorists have questioned the ends this fixation serves. Specifically, they have examined how such ostensibly benign organisational innovations are aimed at manufacturing consent through regulation of the cognitive and affective spheres, thereby extending the scope of managerial domination of the oppressed in organisations (e.g. Knights and Willmott 1989; Alvesson 1991). Critical theorists liken the manner in which such 'cultural doping' may occur to the operation of 'newspeak' in George Orwell's (1963) vision of a future dystopia (e.g. Willmott 1993; Jermier 1998). Thus Du Gay suggests that:

> Culture Excellence is a struggle for identities, an attempt to enable all sorts of people from the highest executive to the lowest shop-floor employee, to see themselves reflected in the emerging conception of the enterprising organization and thus to come increasingly to identify with it. (1991: 54; quoted in Willmott 1993: 519)

Indeed, culture management boils down to the idea that if the appropriate values and attitudes are internalised, a common sense of purpose, or 'moral involvement', activated through emotion and sentiment, develops. This makes the constant surveillance of employees, as a form of control, redundant since employees will discipline themselves (Mitchell 1985). Since such cultural re-engineering is often couched in a rhetoric of 'responsible' self-determination and empowerment, some employees may be persuaded that they will benefit from the discipline of prescribed norms and values (see Knights and Willmott 1989). Clearly, such an analysis resonates with Marcuse's (1964) view that industrial societies exhibit oppressive totalitarian characteristics under the guise of democratic freedom. Therefore, some critical theorists fear that exposure to culture management may well result in the further subjugation of many employees as they transform themselves into corporate clones happy in their ideological domination (e.g. Willmott 1993). However, others have noted that the effectiveness of culture management will always be limited (e.g. Antony 1994) and how employees may resist the snares of false consciousness (see Box 5.3) through a variety of strategies which include a cynical calculative compliance with the prescribed norms without internalisation (e.g. Ogbonna and Wilkinson 1988; Kunda 1992).

Box 5.3

False consciousness and Critical Theory

Although CT begins by accessing members' self-understandings, critical theorists assume that the meanings, which many members use in making sense of their organisational experiences, derive from the systems of asymmetrical power which pervade organisational life. Thus false consciousness refers to the interpretations and meanings, held by many employees, for instance, that are disseminated through the distorted communication of powerful organisational groups to justify and reproduce their domination. Critical theorists believe that through false consciousness such employees not only remain unaware of their subjugation, but are complicit in imposing its distortions on themselves. For instance, the ideological camouflage provided by the apparently factual basis and technical neutrality of management's strategic analyses may make those social constructions appear so reasonable and incontestable that it is difficult for employees to imagine alternative possibilities. Members thus become entrapped by the logic of those demands. So, for instance, by showing how strategic analyses are distorted and explaining how they have arisen, the analytical dimension of CT aims to expose the sources and effects of false consciousness. Meanwhile CT's normative element builds on such accounts by facilitating the development of a critical consciousness which expresses employees' true interests and frees them from the ideological hegemony of others' interests. The result is that CT embraces the possibility of itself becoming a force for ideological and, by implication, organisational change.

At a more general level, Habermas (1987: 363) argues that instrumental rationality, expressed through the various forms of systems integration, continuously confronts problems of intra-organisational legitimisation. This is because it can engender routinised compliance only with technocratic norms which subsume all forms of social interaction within a means–ends calculus. For instance, this calculus engenders the cynical adoption of a sanctioned moral vocabulary often divorced from enacted moralities, which suffer from 'the logical result of alertness to expediency ... the elimination of any ethical guidelines at all' (Jackall 1988: 195), save for 'what the guy above wants from you' (Jackall 1988: 6). In a similar vein Willmott observes that

> instead of producing committed, enthusiastic, self-disciplining subjects, a possible effect of corporate culturist programmes is a reinforcement of instrumentality amongst employees who comply with their demands without internalizing their values.... Mere compliance is insufficient since it signals a failure to mobilize the emotional energies of staff in ways that inspires them to embody and live out corporate values. (1993: 536–7)

One reason why such calculative compliance emerges is provided by Knights and Roberts' observation that authority

> cannot be imposed or individually possessed, but always remains only a quality of the relationship between people, in which both are personally committed to, and see as legitimate, the reciprocal rights and obligations realized through their interaction. As soon as one individual seeks to elevate his/her own instrumental ends above concern for the other then mutual trust is quickly destroyed, and transformed into attempts at mutual manipulation. (1982: 50)

Hence, from the point of view of Critical Theory, the authority of 'strategists', 'change agents', and the like is often problematised by modes of systems integration which fail to induce the mutuality necessary for 'desired change' to be translated into effective forms of cooperation.

In sum, CT's analyses of strategy and change turn on how reputedly rational models appear to be scientific and thereby provide management practices with an aura of technical neutrality. Such assured respectability and the rationalists' provision of off-the-shelf techniques eases their adoption by practitioner audiences. In line with their epistemological commitments, and as a first step towards emancipation, critical theorists are keen to reveal this putative mandate as a masquerade that has detrimental effects upon employees. This project can entail both the consideration of the social conditions that enable the articulation of certain recipes of knowledge (Miller 1991) and the analysis of the proactive and serendipitous efforts of various 'carrier groups' (Law and Lodge 1984) of strategy-change knowledge to secure and aggrandise their authority in the cognition of potential clients and patrons. Such appeals to legitimacy may be greatly influenced by the relative strengths of carrier groups who calculatively use a variety of cognitive and social resources both to advance their ideas and (according to Shapin 1984) eventually ensure the closure of debate. Latour (1987) demonstrates how knowledge claims are constituted as factual by carrier groups through their establishment of networks of association and alliances with supportive significant others, as well as their success in overcoming opposition and resistance. As Rouse (1987) has pointed out, epistemic power derives in part from the ability to silence opposing accounts of the same phenomena. To borrow Tinker's terminology, in the 'horse race of ideas' some horses 'never reach the starting gate, others are excessively handicapped, and still others may be nobbled ... before the race' (1986: 377).

However, in their analyses of the mainstream, critical theorists face an epistemological conundrum. On the one hand, CT research attempts to provide an account of the socially constructed knowledge and meanings that actors deploy in making sense of organisational reality – whether they are management theorists, practitioners or employees. On the other hand, critical theorists are equally concerned to locate any actor's (false) consciousness in an analysis of how particular values and interests are expressed in, and shape, that lived experience, thus revealing its particular social origins as well as how it blinds people to their own potentialities.

Thus power is central to this analysis. According to CT, social constructions produced outside the ideal-speech act must be ideologically distorted by asymmetrical power relations and hence serve to stabilise and legitimate the control of dominant organisational groups (e.g. Steffy and Grimes 1992; Oakes et al. 1998) through the production of false consciousness. However, this movement beyond describing actors' lived experiences, to explaining their development and analysing their effects, creates the conundrum noted above: if any description or analysis has to be socially constructed and hence is value- and interest-laden, surely the critical theorist's own endeavours must be equally problematic. As we noted with Lukes (1974) in Chapter 4, surely there is a danger that critical theorists privilege their own analyses by default and thus contradict their own epistemic commitments. This danger also lurks in CT's normative view of strategy and change where CT tries to make a difference to members' lives.

CRITICAL THEORY AS A NORMATIVE VIEW OF STRATEGY AND CHANGE

Driven by philosophical commitments which suspect any claim to epistemic authority, CT expresses unease and scepticism regarding the technical solutions to ostensible organisational 'problems' developed through the knowledge-constituting lens of the rationalist orthodoxy. CT's normative dimension expresses Habermas's emancipatory interest which, located in the principle of self-reflection on their organisational predicaments, aims to liberate people from asymmetrical power relations, dependencies and constraints. As a consequence, the mainstream loses its practical relevance for it is not tied to this emancipatory interest but instead works within and propagates the hegemonic status quo. It follows that CT has a direct concern with organisational change. This is not just in the form of a distinctive analysis and critique of current management theory and practice but also in the form of a moral imperative to engender organisational change in a direction justified by CT's particular social constructivist orientation.

From Habermas we can infer that if directions and implementation of strategy and organisational change are to avoid the problems of epistemic authority delineated previously, they must be grounded in the intersubjective consensus achievable in an ideal-speech situation. As we shall see in Chapter 11, some forms of action research enthusiastically embrace this agenda. For critical theorists, since one absolute truth cannot be accessed, legitimate knowledge and the practices it enables are 'accessible to rational discussion only within the . . . horizon of a concrete historical form of life' (Habermas 1990: 108). This communal consensus implies agreement not only on the outcomes of discourse, but also on the rules and logics of reasoning that lead to them. Legitimate knowledge and practice cannot be the outcome of privileged access and dissemination by the authoritative few. Rather, legitimacy can be accorded only if knowledge and practice are the outcomes of unconstrained public debate and agreement where validity claims are assessed by self-reflective participants and conflict is resolved through participants' exploration of each other's claims and which allows the force of the better argument to decide (see Alvesson and Willmott 1992: 13–14). Here what is rational is what results from what Gergen calls 'negotiated intelligibility' (1985: 272) and what Habermas calls consensus. Rationality is not conceived as the 'entitative and egocentric reasoning' of an epistemically privileged individual (see Dachler and Hoskin, 1995). Rather, socio-rational knowledge and practice occur when democratic social relations have already been established.

Here, although her idiom is different, there are evident parallels with Sinclair's (1993) normative stance on organisational change. By commencing with a recognition of the inevitability of cultural plurality within organisations, Sinclair proceeds to argue that organisations should tolerate diversity and can benefit from the discourses that will develop. Although fearful that this could lead to the anarchic proliferation of diversity that leaves no basis for consensus, she argues that it does avoid both the intolerance of diversity and the cultural imperialism encouraged by forms of systems integration. Hence she (re)constructs management's moral authority. Instead of trying to institutionalise standards that derive from their own cultural particularism and drive out alternative social values, the task of management becomes one of understanding the configurations of existing cultures and their areas of potential consensus, which could form the basis of a core of organisation-wide cultural norms and practices. Thus Sinclair eschews systems integration articulated through the imposition of putatively privileged management derived strategies. Instead, by fostering and sponsoring cultural coexistence, the task of management is reconfigured to one of encouraging members' reflexive and critical thought through processes that entail self-scrutiny, debate and the establishment of consensus prior to action. According to Sinclair (1993: 69–70), it is through such processes that members weigh up personal and organisational obligations and responsibilities before finally applying the resultant standards and making a decision.

In a similar vein, Senge argues for reflexivity and dialogue. Here,

> a group explores complex difficult issues from many points of view. Individuals suspend their assumptions but they communicate their assumptions freely. The result is a free exploration that brings to the surface the full depth of people's experience and thought, and yet can move beyond their individual views. (1990: 241)

Although the processes prescribed by Sinclair and Senge are akin to Habermas's (1987) social integration, CT's normative dimension has far more radical implications for organisations. As we have noted, Habermas's ideal speech situation portends unforced consensus about ends and means in democratic conditions of public argument. However, it is also evident to Habermas that such a consensus is not attained in everyday social interaction in organisations due to the operation of power and domination which systematically distort communication, etc. This raises two important questions. First, who are the potential communicants in any discourse about strategy and change in an organisation? And second, how could communicants ever be certain that systematic distortions were not taking place given the insidious nature of power and domination?

Instead of the mainstream's devaluation of the versions of reality held by many groups within an organisation, CT requires that those individuals and groups whose perspectives are ordinarily silenced in organisations must be given voice. The demand is for members' conscious self-determination of social values. Therefore, identification and involvement of all potential communicants presumably must start with the mobilisation of every organisational stakeholder. While this in itself is highly problematic, the subsequent power relations between communicants could pose insurmountable problems. Following Marcuse (1964), the danger is that notionally democratic communication becomes a façade in which the more powerful deploy a rhetoric of democracy to impose their own (ethical) preferences upon, and silence or marginalise the less powerful. By persuading the less powerful that they have more rather than less power (see Coopey 1995), the result may be what Pastin (1988: 11) has called an 'agreement racket' where those who disagree are excluded, opposed or their influence nullified by the more powerful. In mobilising organisational stakeholders currently silenced by modes of systems integration, it is possible to identify a new pedagogical role for change agents, which starkly contrasts with the mainstream norm.

Critical theorists question the dominant assumption that perceived organisational problems exist independently of a change-agent's processes of perception. Rather, critical theorists would argue that problem definition, its causal analysis, the subsequent identification and implementation of remedial interventions, all express particular tacit assumptions, values and interests specific to the local understandings of the community to which the change agent belongs (see Gergen 1995). Other communities may well perceive issues in different ways depending on their own local, taken-for-granted understandings. Hence the common view of the change agent as a detached expert who exercises a legitimate role as an architect of change is taken to be a process that disenfranchises the less powerful, who have as much claim to epistemic authority as any putative change agent. So, from the perspective of CT, most organisation members are only too often reduced to the objects of organisational change. They are reduced to objects who are seen by many commentators (e.g. Scase and Goffee 1989; Greenwood and Hinnings 1996; Agocs 1997) as irrationally resistant to the changes demanded by experts because of their fear of the unknown, their lack of trust, their pursuit of self interest, and so on. In this manner, the prevailing orthodoxy (e.g. Kotter 1996; Kotter and Schlesinger 1979) separates the subjects of change (change agents in their parlance) from the objects of change (other members) who have to be manipulated by the contingent deployment of the power resources available to management: coercion or persuasion or cultural doping, and so on.

From the stance of CT, due to the problematic status of any epistemic authority, the role of the putative change agent is fundamentally reconstructed to one of facilitating democratic agreement. It thus becomes an educational role that must focus on the processes of agreement rather than the substantive content. This point is worth clarifying here through reference to the educational work of Paulo Friere.

Friere (1972a and b) articulates a view of knowledge that is in line with CT: knowledge is relational – an outcome of inter-subjective processes. The focus of Friere's critique is a conception of learning which parallels mainstream views of strategy and change as this orthodoxy construes knowledge as an asocial commodity which is held, and where appropriate is imparted to students, by epistemically privileged pedagogues. According to this tradition, pedagogues are the subjects of learning processes and the 'student' the object. Such educational practices are underpinned by what Friere considers to be a 'digestive' concept of knowledge in which the 'undernourished' are 'fed' with the epistemologically privileged knowledge of the expert pedagogue as if their consciousness were 'empty space' (Friere 1972b: 23–6). For Friere the passivity engendered by such 'education for domestication' entails the 'introjection by the dominated of the cultural myths of the dominator' (1972a: 59) and fails to enable the development of a 'critical consciousness' (1972a: 46) so central to the operationalisation of the ideal speech-act. In contrast, Friere argues that the prerequisites for the development of a critical consciousness, which dismantles the current hegemony, are not only the recognition by actors of their present oppression through that hegemony, but also the understanding that a liberating education programme must eschew a preprocessed and prescriptive character. In sum a critical consciousness is constitutable only through an authentic dialogue with the educator/change agent, in which both educators and learners are 'equally knowing subjects' (Friere 1972b: 31).

In following the implications of these prerequisites, Friere develops his 'problem-posing' model of pedagogy for the 'oppressed' in which the educator's role 'is to propose problems about the codified existential situations in order to help the learners arrive at an increasingly critical view of their reality' (1972b: 36). The aim is to initiate understanding of how certain taken-for-granted renditions of reality have been socially constructed through a locally hegemonic culture. Critical appraisal of these renditions tries to reveal the interests that are served, the practices they legitimate and those that are dismissed as irrational, unrealistic or illogical. Here Friere's 'educative' programme conceives relations between 'teacher' and 'student' as dialogic in the sense that the content of the programme is based on the student's personal experience. By examining how particular interest-laden discursive practices sustain, for instance, particular strategic preferences and change manoeuvres, Friere would see such a programme as an educative and therapeutic catalyst because the intent is to engender, through reflection, new (theory-laden) self-understandings.

Geuss (1981) calls such an educational experience an 'inquiry for change' because it should enable people to attach new meanings to the strategy change practices that they encounter and simultaneously expose the interests which produce and disseminate taken-for-granted management knowledge. People should thereby begin to: understand those practices as social constructions; become aware of their own role in production and reproduction of those practices; construe those practices as mutable; and identify how they might intervene in the evolution of their organisations and society. The result would be a challenge to traditional management prerogatives and the negotiation of alternative renditions of reality which create novel questions, inaugurate new problems and make new forms of organisational practice sensible and therefore possible.

So, as we have noted with Habermas's critical science, Friere's aim is to free people from the domination of distorted communication through the development of self-reflective understandings which allow them to participate in the social construction of new meanings (see Box 5.4).

Box 5.4

Self-reflection

For Habermas a prototype for critical science is psychoanalysis. This is because psychoanalysis involves 'depth-hermeneutics' (1972: 218) in which the distorted texts of the patient's behaviour become intelligible to him or her through self-reflection. This self-reflection is facilitated by the analyst's attempts at interpreting the patient's speech, behaviour and experiences in terms of unconscious causal variables that are identifiable through reference to the Freudian theory of neurosis. Through reflection on the analyst's interpretations during therapy, the patient may begin to see 'himself through the eyes of another and learns to reflect on these symptoms as off shoots of his own behaviour' (1972: 32). In this fashion emancipation occurs as the patient becomes liberated from the terror of his or her own unconscious as previously suppressed and latent determinants of behaviour are revealed and thereby lose their power.

Therefore, through what amounts to a dereification of social practices (see also Unger 1987; Beck 1992), Friere argues that a liberated phenomenological world might arise, which could be utilised to identify and pursue alternative practices, dispositions and ends that result in 'socially transformative' actions which are commensurable with subjects' interests. Thus it is inappropriate for a pedagogue to attempt to deposit putatively privileged strategic or change recipes into a learner. The role of the educator change agent is to facilitate democratically grounded reality reconstructions, not to prescribe them. Legitimate knowledge arises only where it is the outcome of such democratic collective agreement. The educational process must develop those subjects' ability to assess their circumstances through developing a self-conception in which they are epistemic subjects who are able to determine and change their situation, as opposed to powerless objects determined by an immutable situation presented to them by the supposedly authoritative analyses of (senior) managers, change agents and the like.

CONCLUSION

CT aims to be emancipatory by enabling the analysis and problematisation of organisational communities' varying taken-for-granted social constructions of reality which express their varying practices, interests and motives. In doing so critical theorists attempt to establish the conditions necessary for the development of differential constructions of reality and to show the possibility of alternative accounts. This enables people to 'alter their lives by fostering in them the sort of self-knowledge and understanding of their social conditions which serve as a basis for such an alteration' (Fay 1987: 23).

Because different knowledge products have different interest-laden implications, it follows that our knowing selection of one knowledge product as opposed to an alternative becomes a matter of ethical priority. Such choices and priorities can be decided only through what Arrington and Puxty (1991: 45) call 'the best available model of democracy ... in which an intelligible public will takes shape as a consensus-of-belief about how to co-ordinate actions through the unconstrained arguments of the citizenry' – Habermas's ideal-speech act. As Singer (1994) observes, rationalist models of strategy appear to dismiss ethical considerations since they assume that strategy is exclusively about profit-maximisation. Indeed, business is often seen as the rightful preserve of an economic rationality that was somehow ethically neutral even though it was evident that Friedman's (1962) exclusive view of management's fiduciary responsibilities to shareholders was in itself an ethical argument. In contrast, CT radicalises stakeholder approaches through a commitment to democracy and the articulation of interests silenced and unrealised by the orthodoxy. Justified by commitment to a social constructivist epistemology critical theorists argue that if we are concerned to develop new modes of engagement that allow subjects who are currently excluded to contribute to the democratic development of strategic consensus, it follows that those subjects must determine and develop the substantive basis of that strategic direction so that their interests and ethical concerns become metaphorically permitted and encoded into its 'gaze'.

Although CT may be seen as the best model available for democratisation it also may be seen as idealistic: as far removed from the everyday problems that confront organisational members and impractical because of the vertical command and control demands which arise during organisations' routine engagement in the competitive struggle. Jejune assumptions about organisational democracy may underlie the dismissal of CT as fanciful – a stance implicitly justified by the lens provided by militaristic metaphors (see Whipp 1996) which underpin many mainstream contributions (i.e. ordinary people must obey the directions of those with strategic insight). Here it is worth pointing out that although military modes of organisation are usually taken to be antithetical to any notion of democracy, this has not always been the case. Grint (1991) uses Rodger's (1986) work on the 85,000-strong eighteenth-century British navy to illustrate how, contrary to the popular myth, some participative practices were far from anathema, even during engagements with the enemy:

> The *Penguin*, a twenty-gun sloop, found herself chased by two French thirty-six gun frigates, which head-reached on her and ranged up on either side. Captain Harris summoned his officers and men and asked their advice whether to fight or not; they replied they would have taken on one thirty-six but two was too much. So the *Penguin* struck her colours without firing a shot, and at the court martial Harris was honourably acquitted, as having done everything that a good officer could do. (Rodger 1986: 237, quoted in Grint 1991: 56)

Perhaps Rodger's snapshot of what amounts to a hidden, or even suppressed, military history suggests that democracy and its possibilities are not at all fanciful, even in the most perilous circumstances.

However, CT's programme for strategy and change is not without its problems and contradictions. Geuss questions whether there are any clear public criteria for success and failure of emancipation, making the point that

> emancipation can miscarry: the agents may steadfastly refuse to accept the views about freedom embodied in critical theory or they may recognise that they acquired certain beliefs or traits under conditions of coercion but maintain they would have acquired them anyway, even if they had been in circumstances of complete freedom; finally when they have experi-

enced the state of freedom the critical theory proposes they may discover that it imposes unexpected and intolerable burdens on them and must be abandoned. (1981: 89)

With regard to Friere's pedagogical operationalisation of Habermas's ideal-speech act, Taylor (1993) notes that dealing with problems similar to those noted above by Geuss can undermine Friere's philosophical stance to the extent that it becomes manipulative, monological and anti-dialogical in the sense that they militate against self-determination. Perhaps the causes of these problems derive from the epistemological contradictions that lurk within the ideal-speech. The most significant of these relates to the claim that any consensus must arise out of discourse, for this implies the possibility of the neutral adjudication of knowledge claims by rational investigators. Fay argues that participants

cannot know for certain whether they have provided the best interpretation of their experience – indeed they cannot even be certain what their experience is. There is nothing given to them, neither the meaning of their experience, nor what is to count as evidence, nor the relations of this evidence to their theories. In a situation of this sort, it is folly to think that all competent rational participants will ultimately agree on a particular theory as uniquely the best. (1987: 178)

As Fay observes, without the prior assumption of the possibility of a theory-neutral observational language, socio-rational analysis will not dictate to them 'the single answer to which any rational agent must adhere' (1987: 179). Therefore, Habermas's attempt to develop a regulative ideal based on unconstrained consensus cannot be sustained without recourse to the contradictory presupposition of the availability and use of a theory-neutral observational language to resolve disputes. Indeed Habermas's epistemological position seems inadvertently to restore the epistemic privilege embraced by positivists through a critique aimed at repudiating all forms of epistemic privilege based on positivism.

Hence the possibility that any strategic intent or change initiative can ever attain consensual grounding of its normative standards, may well be forlorn – a point to which we shall return in Chapter 11. Moreover, it is unclear how communicants could ever be certain that systematic distortions of Pastin's agreement racket were not taking place, given CT's own analyses of the insidious and ubiquitous nature of asymmetrical power relations. So if the ideal-speech act cannot practically live up to its promises, perhaps it is best treated as an ideal-type with which actual strategies of change may be compared and thereby sensitise potential communicants to the distortions arising from the exercise of power.

However, even the proposition of an ideal-type fails to deal with a second epistemological contradiction within CT: the extent to which CT itself can be separated from relations of power and thereby stand outside what critical theorists construe as false consciousness. As Hammersley (1992) observes, this problem raises the point that the notion of an ideal-speech act is based on a circular argument: it is defined in terms of freedom from the effects of ideology yet presumably we need to be free from ideology to recognise the situation. The danger is that critical theorists begin to 'assume the validity of their own truth claims' (Rosenau 1992: xii) and present an arbitrary privileging inconsistent with the emancipatory pursuit of critical theory (Grice and Humphries 1997). As Geuss (1981: 58) argues, CT 'doesn't merely give information about how it would be rational for agents to act if they had certain interests; it claims to inform them about what interests it is rational for them to have'.

Thus the views and values of the critical theorist may come to be privileged over the 'false consciousness' of those agents who have failed to realise their own true interests. Hence critical theorists have been criticised for their tendency to impose their voices and values on others (Quantz 1992: 471; Denzin, 1994: 509). While this problem is 'writ large' in the normative dimension of CT it is also evident in its analytic concerns. As we have noted, CT is committed to a structural phenomenology that accesses members' meanings yet locates them in a formative context of asymmetrical power relations largely unrecognised by those actors. Given CT's own social constructivist epistemology, the analysis of that formative context must be problematic unless grounded in consensus. But this begs the question – whose consensus?

This brings us to the heart of a paradox within CT. As presumably we do not yet live in societies free from domination, and therefore ideal-speech acts are not yet possible, what then is the epistemological status of Habermas's and other critical theorists' own work? Are they just more examples of systematically distorted communication or are they somehow exempt from such processes? Any claim to such an exemption is itself based on the exercise of epistemic authority and hence power. For some commentators this is precisely the case as Habermas's own notion of rational consensus in conditions of communicative competence invokes values that are derived from the Enlightenment tradition which he calls 'Old European Dignity' (1971: 143). Given his own critique of Gadamer's uncritical acceptance of 'tradition' and hence repressive power and authority relations referred to earlier, Habermas appears to be contradicting himself. As Arbib and Hesse point out with regard to the Enlightenment:

> the liberal values of freedom and equal rights are derived from this tradition, as are the norms of participatory democracy and the search for truth by means of rational argument. Ideal speech resting on Enlightenment values is not too far from Gadamer's grounding in tradition with some Western Ethnocentrism thrown in. (1986: 198)

In sum critical theory develops a distinctive brand of social constructivism which focuses on a perceived interconnection between politics, ethics and knowledge, thereby provoking a deeper consideration of the values and partiality which underpin and legitimise the authority of mainstream strategy and change discourses. Inherent in the approach is the hope that knowledge grounded in consensus can lead to emancipation and progress. How such concerns have been variably operationalised in action research and whole systems interventions will be considered in Chapter 11. However, as we have argued, some caution is needed here: CT is not immune to problems that arise from its own epistemology, which problematise its accounts of current management practice and its own normative practices. The result is that CT wages a war on two fronts: while positivists would attack CT for being irrational and anti-scientific as we shall see in Chapter 6 postmodernists accuse CT of being grounded in an Enlightenment tradition which expresses the very rationalism that critical theorists seem to attack. Ironically, as we shall show in Chapter 6, similar problems assail postmodernist analyses of strategy and change although postmodernism articulates a very different form of social constructivism.

REFERENCES

Agocs, C. (1997) 'Institutionalized Resistance to Organizational Change: Denial Inaction and Repression', *Journal of Business Ethics*, 23(9): 917–31.

Alvesson, M. (1987) *Organization Theory and Technocratic Consciousness*, Berlin/New York: Walter de Gruyter.

Alvesson, M. (1991) 'Organization: From Substance to Image', *Organization Studies*, 11(3): 374–94.

Alvesson, M. and S. Deetz (1996) 'Critical Theory and Postmodernism Approaches to Organization Studies', in S.R. Clegg, C. Hardy and W.R. Nord (eds), *Handbook of Organization Studies*, London: Sage.

Alvesson, M. and H.C. Willmott (eds) (1992) *Critical Management Studies*, London: Sage.

Alvesson, M. and H.C. Willmott (1996) *Making Sense of Management: A Critical Introduction*, London: Sage.

Ansoff, H.I. (1965) *Corporate Strategy*, Harmondsworth: Penguin.

Antony, P. (1994) *Managing Culture*, Milton Keynes: Open University Press.

Barley, S.R. and G. Kunda (1992) 'Design and Devotion: Surges of Rational and Normative Ideologies of Control in Managerial Discourse', *Administrative Science Quarterly*, 37: 363–99.

Baudrillard, J. (1983) *Simulations*, New York: Semiotext(e).

Beck, U. (1992) *The Risk Society: Towards a New Modernity*, Cambridge: Polity Press.

Beck, U. (1996) 'World Risk Society as Cosmopolitan Society? Ecological Questions in a Framework of Manufactured Uncertainties', *Theory, Culture and Society*, 13(4): 1–32.

Berger, P. and T. Luckmann (1967) *The Social Construction of Reality*, London: Allen Lane.

Blunt, P. (1990) 'Recent Developments in Human Resource Management: The Good, the Bad and the Ugly', *International Journal of Human Resource Management*, 1(1): 45–59.

Browne, M., B. Banerjee, L. Fulop, and S. Linstead (1999) 'Managing Strategically', in L. Fulop and S. Linstead, *Management: A Critical Text*, London: Macmillan Business.

Burr, V. (1995) *Introduction to Social Constructionism*, London: Routledge.

Burrell, G. and G. Morgan (1979) *Sociological Paradigms and Organizational Analysis*, London: Heinemann.

Calori, R. (1998) 'Philosophizing on Strategic Management Models', *Organization Studies*, 19(2): 281–306.

Capelli, P., L. Bassi, H. Kahtz, D. Knoke, P. Osterman and M. Useem (1997) *Change at Work*, Oxford: Oxford University Press.

Champy, J. (1995) *Re-engineering Management*, New York: HarperBusiness.

Chia, R. (1996) *Organisational Analysis as Deconstructive Practice*, Berlin: De Gruyer.

Clegg, S.R. (1989) *Frameworks of Power*, London: Sage.

Coad, A. (1995) 'Strategic Control', in A.J. Berry, J. Broadbent and D. Otley (eds), *Management Control: Theories, Issues and Practices*, London: Macmillan.

Comte, A. (1853) *The Positive Philosophy of Auguste Comte*, London: Chapman.

Coopey, J. (1995) 'The Learning Organization: Power, Politics and Ideology', *Management Learning*, 26(2): 193–214.

Cummings, T.G. (1993) 'Sociotechnical Systems Consultation', in R.T. Golembiewski (ed.), *Handbook of Organizational Consultation*, New York: Dekker.

Dachler, H.P. and D.M. Hoskin (1995) 'The Primacy of Relations in Socially Constructing Organizations', in D.M. Hoskin, H.P. Dachler and K.J. Gergen, *Management and Organization: Relational Alternatives to Individualism*, Aldershot: Avebury.

Delanty, G. (1997) *Social Science: Beyond Constructivism and Realism*, Buckingham: Open University Press.

Denzin, N.K. (1994) 'The Art and Politics of Interpretation', in N.K. Denzin and Y.S. Lincoln (eds) *Handbook of Qualitative Research*, London: Sage.

Donaldson, L. (1987) 'Strategy, Structural Adjustment to Regain Fit and Performance: In Defense of Contingency Theory', *Journal of Management Studies*, 24(2): 1–24.

Drucker, P.F. (1995) *Managing in a Time of Change*, New York: Truman Talley Books, Dutton.

Du Gay, P. (1991) 'Enterprise Culture and the Ideology of Excellence', *New Formations*, 13: 45–61.

Fay, B. (1987) *Critical Social Science*, Cambridge: Polity Press.

Flek, L. (1935/1979) *Genesis and Development of a Social Fact*, Chicago: University of Chicago Press.

Forrester, J. (1983) 'Critical Theory and Organizational Analysis', in G. Morgan (ed.) *Beyond Method*, London: Sage.

Forrester, J. (1989) *Planning in the Face of Power*, Berkeley, CA: University of California Press.

Foucault, M. (1977) *Discipline and Punish: The Birth of the Prison*, Harmondsworth: Penguin.

Fournier, V. and C. Grey (2000) 'At the Critical Moment: Conditions and Prospects for Critical Management Studies', *Human Relations*, 53(1): 7–32.

Friedman, A.L. (1977) *Industry and Labour*, London: Macmillan.

Friedman, M. (1962) *Capitalism and Freedom*, Chicago: University of Chicago Press.

Friere, P. (1972a) *Pedagogy of the Oppressed*, Harmondsworth: Penguin.

Friere, P. (1972b) *Cultural Action for Freedom*, Harmondsworth: Penguin.

Gadamer, G. (1975) *Truth and Method*, London: Sheed and Ward.

Garrick, J. (1998) *Informal Learning in the Workplace: Unmasking Human Resource Development*, London: Routledge.

Geertz, C. (1989) 'Anti Anti-Relativism', in M. Krausz (ed.) *Relativism: Interpretation and Confrontation*, Notre Dame, IN: Notre Dame University Press.

Gergen, K.J. (1985) 'The Social Constructivist Movement in Social Psychology', *American Psychologist*, 40: 266–75.

Gergen, K.J. (1995) 'Relational Theory and the Discourses of Power', in D.M. Hoskin, H.P. Dachler and K.J. Gergen, *Management and Organization: Relational Alternatives to Individualism*, Aldershot: Avebury.

Geuss, R. (1981) *The Idea of Critical Theory: Habermas and the Frankfurt School*, Cambridge: Cambridge University Press.

Goold, M. and J.J. Quinn (1990) 'The Paradox of Strategic Controls', *Strategic Management Journal*, 11: 43–57.

Greenwood, R. and C. Hinings (1996) 'Understanding Strategic Choice: The Contribution of Archetypes', *Academy of Management Journal*, 36(5): 1052–81.

Grey, C. and N. Mitev (1995) 'Management Education: A Polemic', *Management Learning*, 26(1): 73–90.

Grice, S. and M. Humphries (1997) 'Critical Management Studies in Postmodernity: Oxymorons in Outer Space?', *Journal of Organisational Change Management* 10(5): 412–15.

Grint, K. (1991) *The Sociology of Work: An Introduction*, Cambridge: Polity Press.

Habermas, J. (1970a) 'On Systematically Distorted Communication', *Inquiry*, 13: 205–18.

Habermas, J. (1970b) 'Towards a Theory of Communicative Competence', *Inquiry*, 14: 360–75.

Habermas, J. (1971) *Towards a Rational Society*, London: Heinemann.

Habermas, J. (1972) *Knowledge and Human Interests*, London: Heinemann.

Habermas, J. (1973) 'A Postscript to Knowledge and Human Interests', *Philosophy and the Social Sciences*, 3(2): 157–9.

Habermas, J. (1974a) *Theory and Practice*, London: Heinemann.

Habermas, J. (1974b) 'Rationalism Divided in Two: A Reply to Albert', in A. Giddens (ed.) *Positivism and Sociology*, London: Heinemann Educational Books.

Habermas, J. (1977) 'A Review of Gadamer's Truth and Method', in F.R. Dallmayr and T.A. McCarthy (eds) *Understanding Social Inquiry*, Notre Dame, IN: Notre Dame University Press.

Habermas, J. (1987) *The Theory of Communicative Action. Volume 2: Lifeworks and System: A Critique of Functionalist Reason*, London: Heinemann.

Habermas, J. (1990) *Moral Consciousness and Communicative Action*, Cambridge: Polity Press.

Hamel, G. and C.K. Prahalad (1989) 'Strategic Intent', *Harvard Business Review*, 67: 63–76.

Hammersley, M. (1992) *What is Wrong with Ethnography?*, London: Routledge.

Hannan, M. and J. Freeman (1977) 'The Population Ecology of Organizations', *American Journal of Sociology*, 83: 929–64.

Hanson, N.R. (1958) *Patterns of Discovery*, Cambridge: Cambridge University Press.

Harrison, M.I. (1994, 2nd edition) *Diagnosing Organizations: Methods, Models and Processes*, London: Sage.

Heisenberg, W. (1958) *Physics and Philosophy*, New York: Harper Brothers.

Hindess, B. (1977) *Philosophy and Methodology in Social Science*, Hassocks: Harvester Press.

Horkheimer, M. and T. Adorno (1947) *The Dialectics of the Enlightenment*, London: Verso.

Jackall, R. (1988) *Moral Mazes: The World of Corporate Managers*, Oxford: Oxford University Press.

Jermier, J.M. (1998) 'Introduction: Critical Perspectives on Organizational Control', *Administrative Science Quarterly*, 43(2): 235–56.

Johnson, G. (1987) *Strategic Change and the Management Process*, Oxford: Basil Blackwell.

Johnson, G. and K. Scholes (1993) *Exploring Corporate Strategy*, London: Prentice Hall.

Kanter, R.M. (1989) *When Giants Learn to Dance: Mastering the Challenges of Strategy, Management and Careers in the 1990s*, London: Unwin Hyman.

Karger, D.W. and A.A. Malik (1975) 'Long-range Planning and Organizational Performance', *Long Range Planning*, 8(2): 60–4.

Kay, J. (1993) *Foundations of Corporate Success*, Oxford: Oxford University Press.

Kinchloe, J.L. and P.L. McLaren (1994) 'Rethinking Critical Theory and Qualitative Research', in N.K. Denzin and Y.S. Lincoln (eds) *Handbook of Qualitative Research*, London: Sage.

Knights, D. and G. Morgan (1991) 'Corporate Strategy, Organizations and Subjectivity: A Critique', *Organization Studies*, 12(2): 251–73.

Knights, D. and J. Roberts (1982) 'The Power of Organization or the Organization of Power', *Organization Studies*, 3(1): 47–63.

Knights, D. and H.C. Willmott (1989) 'Power and Subjectivity at Work: From Degradation to Subjugation in Social Relations', *Sociology*, 23(4): 535–58.

Kotter, J.P. (1996) *Leading Change*, Boston, MA: Harvard Business School.

Kotter, J.P. and L.A. Schlesinger (1979) 'Choosing Strategies for Change', *Harvard Business Review*, (March/April).

Kuhn, T. (1957) *The Copernican Revolution*, Cambridge, MA: Harvard University Press.

Kuhn, T. (1962; 2nd edition 1970) *The Structure of Scientific Revolutions*, Chicago: Chicago University Press.

Kunda, G. (1992) *Engineering Culture: Control and Commitment in a High Tech Corporation*, Philadelphia: Temple University Press.

Latour, B. (1987) *Science in Action*, Milton Keynes: Open University Press.

Law, J. and P. Lodge (1984) *Science for Social Scientists*, London: Macmillan.

Learned, E.P., R. Christensen, K.R. Andrews and W.D. Guth (1965) *Business Policy: Text and Cases*, Homewood, IL: Irwin.

Legge, K. (1995) *Human Resource Management: Rhetorics and Realities*, London: Macmillan.

Lukes, S. (1974) *Power: A Radical View*, London: Macmillan.

Marcuse, H. (1964) *One-dimensional Man*, Boston, MA: Beacon Press.

McCarthy, T. (1978) *The Critical Theory of Jürgen Habermas*, Cambridge: Polity Press.

Miller, P. (1991) 'Accounting Innovation beyond the Enterprise: Problematising Investment Decisions and Programming Economic Growth in the UK in the 1960s', *Accounting, Organizations and Society*, 16(8): 733–62.

Mintzberg, H. (1990) 'Strategy Formulation: Schools of Thought', in J. Fredrickson (ed.) *Perspectives on Strategic Management*, Boston, MA: Ballinger.

Mitchell, T. (1985) 'In Search of Excellence versus the Hundred Best Companies to Work for in America: A Question of Values and Perspective', *Academy of Management Review*, 10(2): 350–5.

Morgan, G. (1986) *Images of Organization*, London: Sage.

Morgan, G. (1993) *Imaginization*, London: Sage.

Oakes, L.S., B. Townley and D.J. Cooper (1998) 'Business Planning as Pedagogy: Language and control in a changing institution', *Administrative Science Quarterly*, 43(2): 257–92.

Ogbonna, E. and B. Wilkinson (1988) 'Corporate Strategy and Corporate Culture: the View from the Checkout', *Personnel Review*, 19(4): 9–15.

Ortony, A. (ed.) (1979) *Metaphor and Thought*, Cambridge: Cambridge University Press.

Orwell, G. (1963) *1984*, Harmondsworth: Penguin.

Ouchi, W.G. (1980) 'Markets, Bureaucracies and Clans', *Administrative Science Quarterly*, March: 129–41.

Pascale, R.T. and A.G. Athos (1982) *The Art of Japanese Management*, Harmondsworth: Penguin.

Pastin, M. (1988) *The Hard Problems of Management: Gaining the Ethics Edge*, San Francisco: Jossey Bass.

Peters, T. and Waterman, R.H. (1982) *In Search of Excellence*, London: Harper and Row.

Pettigrew, A. (1985) *The Awakening Giant: Continuity and Change at ICI*, Oxford: Basil Blackwell.

Pollitt, C. (1993) *Managerialism and the Public Services: Cuts or Cultural Change in the 1990s*, Oxford: Blackwell Business.

Porras, J.I. and S.J. Hoffer (1986) 'Common Behaviour Changes in Successful Organizational Development Efforts', *Journal of Applied Behavioural Science*, 22(4): 477–94.

Porter, M. (1985) 'The Management of Innovation: Controlled Chaos', *Harvard Business Review*, (May–June): 73–84.

Porter, M. (1990) *The Competitive Advantage of Nations*, New York: Free Press.

Pursey, M. (1987) *Jürgen Habermas*, Chichester: Ellis Horwood and Tavistock.

Quantz, R.A. (1992) 'On Critical Ethnography (with Some Postmodern Considerations)', in M.D. LeCompte, W.L. Millroy and J. Preissle (eds) *The Handbook of Qualitative Research in Education*, New York: Academic Press.

Quinn, J.B. (1980) *Strategies for Change: Logical Incrementalism*, Homewood, IL: Irwin.

Reed, M. (1992) *The Sociology of Organizations*, Hemel Hempstead: Harvester Wheatsheaf.

Ritzer, G. (1993) *The McDonaldization of Society*, Newbury Park, CA: Pine Forge.

Robertson, P.J., D.R. Roberts and J.I. Porras (1993) 'Dynamics of Planned Organizational Change: Assessing Empirical Support for a Theoretical Model', *Academy of Management Journal*, 36(3): 619–34.

Rodger, N.A.M. (1986) *The Wooden World: An Anatomy of the Georgian Navy*, London: Fontana.

Rorty, R. (1979) *Philosophy and the Mirror of Nature*, Princeton, NJ: Princeton University Press.

Rosenau, P. M. (1992) *Postmodernism and the Social Sciences: Insights, Inroads and Intrusions*, Princeton, NJ: Princeton University Press.

Rouse, J. (1987) *Knowledge and Power*, Ithaca, NY: Cornell University Press.

Scase, R. and R. Goffee (1989) *Reluctant Managers: Their Work and Life Styles*, London: Routledge.

Senge, P.M. (1990) *The Fifth Discipline: The Art and Practice of the Learning Organization*, London: Century.

Shapin, S. (1984) 'Talking History: Reflections on DA', *Isis*, 18: 533–50.

Shrivastava, P. (1986) 'Is Strategic Management Ideological', *Journal of Management*, 12: 363–77.

Sievers, B. (1994) *Work, Death, and Life Itself: Essays on Management and Organization*, Berlin: Walter de Gruyter.

Simons, R. (1991) 'Strategic Orientation and Top Management Attention to Control Systems', *Strategic Management Journal*, 12: 49–62.

Simons, R. (1994) 'How New Top Managers Use Control Systems as Levers of Strategic Renewal', *Strategic Management Journal*, 15: 69–189.

Sinclair, A. (1993) 'Approaches to Organizational Culture and Ethics', *Journal of Business Ethics*, 12: 63–73.

Singer, A.E. (1994) 'Strategy as Moral Philosophy', *Strategic Management Journal*, 15(2): 191–213.

Slife, B.D. and R.N. Williams (1995) *What's behind the Research? Discovering Hidden Assumptions in the Behavioural Sciences*, London: Sage.

Stacey, R.D. (1993) *Strategic Management and Organization Dynamics*, London: Pitman.

Steffy, B.D. and A.J. Grimes (1992) 'Personnel/Organizational Psychology: A Critique of the Discipline', in M. Alvesson and H.C. Willmott (eds) *Critical Management Studies*, London: Sage.

Tayles, M. and C. Drury (1994) 'New Manufacturing Technologies and Management Accounting: Some Evidence on the Perceptions of Accounting Practitioners', *International Journal of Production Economics*, 36(1): 1–17.

Taylor, C. (1985) *Philosophy and the Human Sciences: Philosophical Papers 2*, Cambridge: Cambridge University Press.

Taylor, P.V. (1993) *The Texts of Paulo Friere*, Milton Keynes: Open University Press.

Tichy, N.M. (1983) *Managing Strategic Change: Technical, Political and Cultural Dynamics*, New York: Wiley.

Tinker, A.M. (1986) 'Metaphor or Reification: Are Radical Humanists Really Libertarian Anarchists?', *Journal of Management Studies*, 23(4): 165–90.

Trahant, B., W.W. Burke and R. Koonce (1997) 'Twelve Principles of Organizational Transformation', *Management Review,* 86(8): 17–21.

Unger, R. (1987) *Politics: A Work in Constructive Social Theory: Its Situation and its Task*, Cambridge: Cambridge University Press.

Whipp, R. (1996) 'Creative Deconstruction: Strategy and Organization', in S. Clegg, C. Hardy and W.R. Nord (eds) *Handbook of Organizational Studies*, London: Sage.

Whittington, R. (2001, 2nd edition) *What is Strategy and Does it Matter?*, London: Thompson Learning.

Willmott, H.C. (1984) 'Images and Ideals of Managerial Work', *Journal of Management Studies*, 21(3): 347–68.

Willmott, H.C. (1993) 'Strength is Ignorance; Slavery is Freedom: Managing Culture in Modern Organizations', *Journal of Management Studies*, 30(4): 515–52.

Wittgenstein, L. (1922) *Tractatus Logico-Philosophicus*, London: Routledge and Kegan Paul.

Wittgenstein, L. (1958) *Philosophical Investigations*, Oxford: Basil Blackwell.

POSTMODERNIST VIEWS OF STRATEGY AND CHANGE

The aims of this chapter are to:

1 Establish the differences between Critical Theory and postmodernism.

2 Outline postmodernism as a philosophy that undermines notions of objectivity and neutrality in management practice.

3 Illustrate the implications of postmodernism for our understanding of strategies for change in terms of the deconstruction of texts, genealogy and the powerful truth-effects of narratives/discourses.

4 Review the tensions that are created by the relativism inherent in postmodernist analysis.

INTRODUCTION

As we indicated in Chapter 5, a distinctive form of social constructivism called 'postmodernism' has recently emerged and has attracted considerable interest. Writers such as Michel Foucault, François Lyotard and Pierre Baudrillard have all found avid audiences in many of the disciplines concerned with management practice. Perhaps this attention arose because of a growing disillusion with the positivistic assumptions that still dominate these disciplines and the apparent demise of traditional critical alternatives, such as Marxism. Alternatively, Alvesson wryly observes that the interest in postmodernism may be a result of academic entrepreneurship. He suggests it is 'a new brand image ... on the edge of the intellectual frontier'. It is a fad which has advantages for those concerned to market their 'knowledge products' by 'defining out earlier work and creating space for new careers' (1995: 1068). Regardless of academic motives, an evident outcome has been much rethinking of the meaning of management. Yet despite this interest (and perhaps because of it) any definitive characteristics of a postmodernist approach remain notoriously nebulous and postmodernism remains 'a mine-field of conflicting notions' (Harvey 1989: viii) with 'no agreed meaning' (Featherstone, 1988: 207).

This appearance of disorientation and chaos may be due in part to the complexity of the language that is used to convey unfamiliar ideas in often elliptical ways. Indeed, some positivist critics have focused on just such tendencies to justify their accusation that postmodernists use meaningless jargon to intimidate readers and disguise an intellectual paucity (e.g. Sokal and Bricmont 1997). But what makes postmodernism particularly opaque is that some avowed postmodernists paradoxically reject a single correct position in favour of a multiplicity of perspectives which are so steeped in relativism and scepticism that a continual unsettling of received conventional ideas seems to be the only postmodern 'norm'.

Therefore, establishing any clear border with critical theory becomes problematic, indeed some commentators purposely blur any distinction (e.g. Marsden and Townley 1995; Fournier and Grey 2000). We feel that such obfuscation is a mistake since, as we illustrated in Chapter 5, critical theorists fear and attempt to avoid the spectre of relativism. In contrast, postmodernists disavow such escape attempts and instead willingly embrace, celebrate and reinvigorate relativism to end all 'totalities'. In this spirit postmodernists often accuse CT of 'essentialism'.

For instance, CT's essentialism is seen to lie in its guiding theoretical presuppositions that structurally based oppression and exploitation lie hidden beneath appearances – an essentialism that is further articulated in its concern with enabling emancipation through, for instance, democratisation. CT's guiding theoretical presuppositions are dismissed by postmodernists as unsustainable 'grand' or 'meta' narratives which arbitrarily 'assume the validity of their own truth claims' (Rosenau 1992: xi). Furthermore, in their depiction of the world critical theorists merely replace the old voices of authority (e.g. managers) with a new hierarchy of truth – presumably with the critical theorist at the apex. So while critical theorists strive to make a practical difference by supporting the democratisation of organisations, postmodernists eschew any prescription for organisational change beyond 'the search for instabilities' (Lyotard 1984: 54) which unsettle established discourses and express 'tolerance of a range of meanings without advocating any of them' (Rosenau 1992: 139). In effect truth, whether in terms of rationally grounded consensus or of correspondence to an independent reality, is no longer considered a worthwhile epistemological goal.

Of course, postmodernism's scepticism about any form of authority is itself an expression of a distinctive epistemological argument. So despite postmodernism's approbation of dissensus and indeterminacy, this chapter will present the main themes of postmodernism by identifying its unifying epistemological and ontological assumptions which justify that postmodernist ambivalence. The implications of these philosophical underpinnings for how we understand strategies for change will then be considered. Finally, postmodernism will be subject to a critique that focuses upon the ambiguities created by its relativistic tendencies.

POSTMODERN PHILOSOPHY

The postmodern is usually seen as a culturally innovative challenge to the ordered structures associated with modernism, a move away from modernism to something explicitly eclectic and indeterminate. In this sense the 'post' in post-modern means 'after' the modern, but it can also mean 'against', or a 'denial', or a 'transcendence', of the modern tradition. Of course, this begs the question – what is signified here by the terms 'modern' or 'modernism'?

The modern is associated with the dramatic changes to society which followed the Enlightenment. Industrialisation, urbanism, scientific and technological development promised human emancipation from the terrors inflicted by the capricious vagaries of the world. As expressed by the Cartesian–Newtonian synthesis described in Chapter 1, progress was assured by our increasing ability to exercise control over our natural and social environments allowed by our development of a newly enhanced reason that swept away knowledge derived from metaphysical speculation and theocratic revelation. As Harvey observes, this Enlightenment project 'took it as axiomatic that there was only one possible answer to any question. From this it followed that the world could be controlled and rationally ordered if we could only picture and represent it rightly' (1989: 27).

Thus under the benevolent guidance of the technocratic elites who act as guardians of 'reason' order and progress is assured (Harvey 1989: 35). Hence this Enlightenment project – the *leitmotif* modernism – would locate the authority of management in their potential to access a body of privileged and uncontaminated knowledge which reveals the essentials of the world thereby allowing causal explanation, prediction and ultimately management control. However, as we have already indicated, the postmodern may be defined 'as an incredulity' (e.g. Lyotard 1984: xxiv) towards such notions as they are metanarratives which assume the validity of their own truth claims and surreptitiously organise and legitimate more specific substantive domains of knowledge and associated practice.

For instance, both Lyotard (1984) and Bauman (1989) attack the Enlightenment metanarrative that science enabled human progress and emancipation through rational control located in the production of reliable knowledge. As Gergen (1992) suggests, these modernist promises advanced management's absorption of a machine metaphor which assumed that it was possible for hierarchical elites to design organisations rationally so as to minimise uncertainty and maximise efficiency through the elaboration of (bureaucratic) rules to govern members' tasks. However postmodernists claim that the promise of the Enlightenment to emancipate humanity from poverty and ignorance died in the Nazi concentration camps (e.g. Lyotard 1984). Indeed, Bauman (1989) argues that it was the modern rational bureaucracy which allowed and enabled the Holocaust. Therefore, how can rationality guarantee its promises?

Accordingly, postmodernists see scientific objectivity, social progress and human emancipation as self-legitimising myths, as 'essentialist' delusions based on taken-for-granted metanarratives which are unattainable. Hence a recurrent theme in postmodernism is the rejection of the positivist metanarrative (see Berg 1989; Parker 1992): for postmodernists it is impossible to develop a rational and generalisable basis to management that enables the regulation of organisations from an objective standpoint. As Cooper and Burrell (1988: 100) argue, any claim to be 'rational' is merely an attempt 'to canonise the discourse of the normal over the abnormal' (see Box 6.1).

Ironically, the seeds of this postmodern scepticism towards any authority, scientific, managerial or otherwise, were sown by positivism itself. By extolling the power of human reason and holding out the promise of progress, the Enlightenment project of positivism had paradoxically institutionalised scepticism about what the criteria of progress should be, the methods by which it might be obtained, and whether it is even desirable. Indeed, the increasing secularisation of Western society, as a product of the Enlightenment dictum 'dare to know', may have only replaced the premodern belief in the providence of an immutable God-given order to life with a growing realisation of the frailty of the human reason it propagated. As everything became open to the critique spawned by positivism's articulation of a sceptical calculating reason, ultimately that reason itself became open to critique. In this manner positivism eroded the versions of reality that it promulgated and which had made the fragility of the human condition easier to bear (Berger et al. 1973; Giddens 1991). In other words, positivism, the epistemological basis of modernism, began to exhaust itself under the impetus of its own critique. It is in this realisation where lies the development of postmodernist epistemology.

So while postmodernists point to the disrepute into which modernism has fallen, they also use this revelation to repudiate the positivist's epistemological and ontological claim to be able to stand outside their own cultural tradition, and thereby neutrally apprehend the facts of an independent reality. Through what is called the 'linguistic turn', postmodernists replace positivism with an anti-empiricist position that argues that all knowledge is indeterminate – where there can only be narratives or discourses based on particular perspectives (see Box 6.1). It follows that there is a need for a 'war on totality' and its pretentious search for the 'true' dynamics of change (Lyotard 1984: 81).

Box 6.1

Language games, narratives and discourses

The terms 'language-game', 'narrative' and 'discourse' tend to be used interchangeably in postmodern writings. The most commonly used seems to be discourse. A discourse is a system of thought and practice which conditions our ways of experiencing and acting on particular phenomena: a discourse will be expressed in all that can be thought, written or said about a particular topic, which by constituting phenomena in a particular way (objectification) influences behaviour. In these respects a discourse constrains and stabilises our subjectivity – our sense of ourselves and social reality – into a particular gaze. Thus discourses structure knowledge and practice by producing rules that systematically delimit what can be articulated. Prevailing discourses are experienced as fact, and make alternatives difficult to articulate and comprehend. For Foucault (1977) all aspects of life are subject to observation, investigation and regulation through the media of discourse. Therefore, the history of management is one of how particular discourses have come to dominate particular socio-historical contexts and thereby dictate what counts as legitimate knowledge and practice, and what does not. Regardless of their organisational status, the person, and his or her experience, are taken to be social products, while the notion that an autonomous individual is the origin of experience must be mistaken. Indeed, the idea of the 'individual' is taken to be the output of a particular discourse.

The linguistic turn is where language is never innocent; where no meaning exists beyond language; where knowledge and truth are linguistic entities constantly open to revision; where the 'social bond' is linguistic but it is not woven with a single 'thread' (Lyotard 1984: 40). So while positivists assume that language can neutrally picture reality, the linguistic turn construes the relationship between a concept (the signifier) and its object (the signified) as arbitrary – for the postmodernist nothing exists outside the articulation of arbitrary signs which manufacture a profusion of images. The result is a 'fundamental uncontrollability of meaning' which means that the '"out there" is constructed by our discursive conceptions of it and these concepts are collectively sustained and continually renegotiated in the process of making sense' (Parker 1992: 3). Therefore, any communication is polysemous – there is no single discoverable true meaning only numerous different interpretations. In sum this free play of signifiers means that they get their meaning only from other signifiers in and through language and thus do not refer to anything outside themselves, such as an independent reality.

Hence via the linguistic turn postmodernists dissolve positivism's separation of subject and object to advocate a de-differentiation of their relationship (e.g. Jeffcutt 1994; Chia 1995; Kilduff and Mehra 1997). While critical theorists would agree with such de-differentiation they would not accept the postmodernist's subsequent deployment of subjectivist ontology. As Latour (1990) observes, for postmodernists de-differentiation dissolves the distinction between reality and its representation in the sense that our linguistic schemes are thought to create reality. For instance, Baudrillard (1983) claims that all that we are left with are 'simulacra' – images that refer to nothing but themselves; a 'hyper-reality', divorced from extra-linguistic reference points, in which there is nothing to see save simulations which appear to be real. Thus through what has been called 'the twilight of the real' (Wakefield 1990) or 'reality's erasure' (Gergen 1992) the epistemological fulcrum provided by a commitment to reality as an independently existing reference point is destroyed, since 'the world is not already there, waiting for us to reflect it' (Cooper and Burrell 1988: 100). Of course, critical theorists would retort by arguing that just because we cannot reflect reality in our knowledge it does not inevitably mean that reality isn't already there: being an antimodernist does not necessarily lead to postmodernism.

In the postmodern spirit, Rorty (1979: 357–61) claims that whatever counts as truth, or reality, is a changeable socio-linguistic artefact where justification lies in the consensus arising out of the culturally specific 'language-games' of a 'form of life'. For Rorty different language-games constructed in diverse forms of life are incommensurable – the knowledge of one community cannot be judged by the standards of another (Rorty 1982: 188–9). It follows that there is a need to focus attention on arguments that are reasonable and persuasive to members of a particular community. Likewise, Lyotard (1984, 1988) sees knowledge as being produced by particular language games which, via their own rules and structures, produce a plurality of localised understandings which offer no epistemological basis for preferring one such manifestation over alternatives. He uses the term 'agon' (e.g. 1984: 16) to refer to the unresolvable contest between different communities' language games and he argues that postmodernists must accept this diversity and be concerned to gain knowledge of these variable and socially contingent understandings.

Thus Lyotard differentiates modernism's 'expert's homology' from what he calls postmodern science. The latter 'refines our sensitivity to differences and reinforces our ability to tolerate the incommensurable' (1984: xxv). Here postmodernists further part company with critical theorists since their view that incommensurability is inevitable and irresolvable means that consensus as an epistemic standard or aim 'has become an outmoded and suspect value' (Lyotard 1984: 66). Indeed it is a preference-less toleration of the polyphonic (many voices) which is pivotal for the postmodernist since any discursive closure, whether grounded in CT's democratic consensus or otherwise, implies the arbitrary dominance of a particular narrative, discourse or language-game. This would serve to silence alternative voices and prevent the heteroglossia of discursive practices that would otherwise ensue (see Gergen 1992: 222–4).

Chia (1995) reviews the implications for organisational analysis of the postmodernist position outlined above. Here he develops the notion that knowledge has no secure vantage point outside socio-linguistic processes by drawing on Woolgar (1988) to argue that there is a tendency to reify, invert and then forget built into the positivist's differentiated view of subject–object relations. This is similar to Berger and Luckmann's view that man forgets 'his own authorship of the world ... and ... the dialectical relationship between man the producer and his products is lost to consciousness' (1971: 106). For Chia (1995) the movement from the socially constructed and overtly precarious to the fixed and independ-

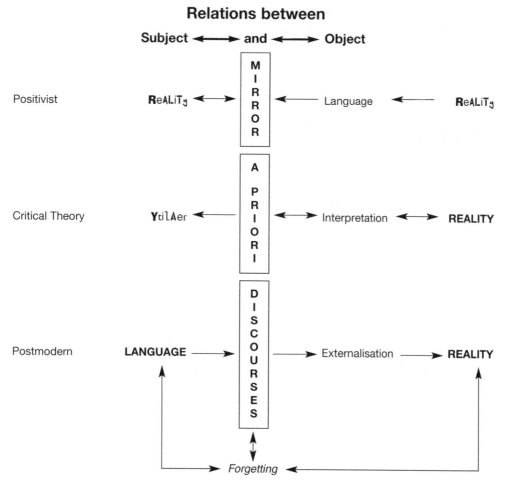

Relations between

Subject ←——→ and ←——→ Object

Figure 6.1 Positivist, Critical Theory and postmodern approaches compared

ent means that the postmodern always precedes the modern's 'false concrete-ness' – its antecedence is merely forgotten, ignored or denied (see Figure 6.1).

So for postmodernists, whatever knowledge is it cannot be justified through metaphors which commit us to thinking that it is an accurate representation of the external world. Hence the positivist 'myth of transparency' (Vattimo 1992: 18), of unmediated access to reality, is an illusion which must be set aside along with the aim to find a single totalising truth. For postmodernists multiple truths are always possible – the question is which truths are being allowed to be voiced; and how, why and what are their effects upon people? Conversely, an equally important question is how and why the status of truth is withheld from the other accounts which are always possible and therefore immanent in any context.

Hence for Gergen (1990) and Rosenau (1992) the postmodernist's mission is to deploy their rhetorical skills in order to: unsettle and reconstitute the language of representation; erode epistemic hegemony and undermine traditions and orthodoxies; and carve out the new domains of intelligibility, thereby giving voice to 'truths' previously suppressed. At first sight this programme of erosion seems to promise a form of emancipation located in how a plurality of usually silenced voices may be given audibility.

POSTMODERN ANALYSIS OF STRATEGY AND CHANGE

As all knowledge is understood as the product of socio-linguistic construction, postmodernists undermine the manager's right to manage by pointing to how notions of expertise, truth, objectivity, facticity and science are merely prestigious discursive constructs which are rhetorically deployed to establish that prerogative. As Jeffcutt observes, '"reality" or "truth" becomes an "effect" and not an absolute position, an outcome of a particular reading ... of a text' (1993: 27). Because there can be 'no standards worthy of universal respect dictating what to think or how to act' (Shweder 1984: 47) those who argue that epistemic privilege is still possible are dismissed as 'cultural overseers' (Rorty 1979: 317). It follows that the growing importance of strategic change to practitioners and academics cannot be the result of recently enhanced epistemological faculty. Indeed, rather than viewing strategy as a resource for analysing and changing organisations, postmodern analysis treats strategy as a phenomenon for critical examination by focusing attention on how it constitutes, and is constituted by, social relations.

For instance, by drawing heavily on Foucault (1970, 1972, 1977, 1980, 1986), Knights and Morgan (1991) locate the seductive impact of the mainstream view of strategy in its claim to provide certain knowledge practically relevant for managing complex organisations. In order to present strategy as a topic for critical investigation they construe it as a set of discourses. These discourses result in particular outcomes by transforming subjects' self-understandings (i.e. identity) and sense of reality through their participation as 'strategic actors' (Knights and Morgan 1991: 260) in the formulation and implementation of strategy. Discursive activity produces the behaviour it seeks to describe (Turner 1987: 61) since notionally empirical findings 'reflect pre-existing intellectual categories' (Hassard 1993: 12). Any strategic knowledge as such is seen as the outcome of a distinct discourse with its own mode of engagement constituted by its own rules, structures and epistemic criteria: a social product that produces social relations.

If the legitimacy of strategic change is primarily located in a modernist claim to a rational picturing of organisations in their environments so as to ensure improved performance, and so on, postmodernists erode these apparently self-evident metanarratives through undertaking several interrelated tasks. One task is to identify the particular ways of seeing and acting that a discourse takes and excludes. Another is to analyse the social processes that make it possible for a particular discourse to be historically constituted and by which a discourse is reconstituted into new discursive formations. A third task is to identify the effects of a particular discourse on people. Below we review how postmodernists have dealt with these tasks with regard to the discourses of corporate strategy – first, through deconstruction, second, through genealogy, and third, by examining truth effects.

The deconstruction of discourses

As we have shown, the outcome of the linguistic turn is the notion that since language cannot depict the real it must rhetorically produce what we take to be real. Phenomena such as organisational structure, competencies or environment, etc. cannot refer to real objects which the strategist may act on, but are merely linguistic constructs which people take to be real. Simultaneously, any appeal to unavoidable empirical realities by strategists become interesting but incredulous rhetorical ploys. For postmodernists 'reality' can have an infinite number of attributes since there are as many realities as there are linguistic modes of describing and explaining. Here postmodernists draw upon Derrida's (1973) argument that any meaning includes identity (what something is) and difference (what something is not). He combines two senses of the term difference – to differ in space and to defer in time – to produce what he calls '*différance*'. By this he means that the meaning of a word 'is derived from a process of deferral to other words . . . that differ from itself' (Gergen 1992: 219). If meaning can be attained only by looking at the relationship of one word to others (e.g. in a dictionary), then the accomplishment of meaning is continually deferred as each consultation of the dictionary merely leads to further words, which in turn have to be looked up. According to Derrida (1973) such unending deferral means that communication is polysemous – any signifier can relate to many signifieds and hence its meaning can never be pinned down. For Derrida there are always deferred and marginalised meanings within any communication which can be revealed in a text by a reader.

The deconstruction of discourses focuses on language and the social negotiation of meaning themselves so as to display and unsettle their underlying constructive properties and processes (Cooper 1989; Linstead and Grafton-Small 1992; Chia 1995), thereby demonstrating the relativity of any discourse and creating space for alternatives (Bradshaw 1996). By stressing the indeterminacy of language, Derrida dismisses the view that 'the truth' can be discovered by rationalist or empiricist methods as an example of modernist logocentricism. Derrida critiques logocentricism by arguing that for every 'fixed' idea, there is also an 'absent' idea. In other words, how we make sense of the world inevitably entails partiality – by interpreting experience in a particular way we inadvertently exclude alternative renditions.

As the term implies, deconstruction is the dismantling of constructions – or more precisely, linguistic constructions. It derives from literary criticism where texts are analysed in order to reveal their inherent contradictions, assumptions and different layers of meaning: to address issues which are hidden from the naïve reader and unrecognised by the author as they strive to maintain unity and consistency. In an epistemological sense any body of knowledge, any human subjectivity, behaviours, conversations or organisational practices can be treated as a text which can be deconstructed (see Czarniawaska-Joerges 1996). So, in conducting a deconstructive reading of a text, several questions are asked:

> Why are certain authors, topics or schools excluded from the text? Why are certain themes never questioned, whereas other themes are condemned? Why, given a set of premises, are certain conclusions not reached? The aim of such questions is not to point out textual errors but to help the reader understand the extent the text's objectivity and persuasiveness depend upon a series of strategic exclusions. (Kilduff 1993: 15–16)

Therefore, the aim of deconstruction is to reveal the assumptions, omissions and contradictions inherent in any text since all texts are understood to contain elements that counter their author's assertions. Kilduff (1993) deconstructs March and Simon's *Organisations* (1958) to identify its gaps and silences and show how the Tayloristic assumptions it overtly condemns are simultaneously utilised elsewhere in the text to produce their narrative. Deconstruction also entails showing how texts contain taken-for-granted ideas which depend on the exclusion of something. Often this will involve identifying the assumptions that underpin and thereby produce the 'fixed' truth-claim. These assumptions are then disrupted through their denial and the identification of the 'absent' alternatives whose articulation produces an alternative text, or re-reading, of reality. Here a helpful example is Boje's (1995) deconstruction of the various stories told about Walt Disney through his comparison of the 'happy' official stories produced by the Disney organisation with the 'dark' unofficial stories 'to show how each version covered up a great deal of ambiguity' (1995: 1007).

Gergen provides the following example of deconstructing the hidden meanings within an organisational text of corporate rationality whose meaning at first sight seems self-evident but whose polysemous aspects mean that it could mean virtually anything:

> 'Let's be logical about this; the bottom line would be the closing of the Portsmouth division' does not carry with it a transparent meaning. Rather, its meaning depends on what we make of words like 'logical', 'bottom line' 'closing' and the like. These meanings require that we defer to still other words. What does the speaker mean by the term 'logical' for example? To answer we must defer to other words like 'rational' 'systematic' or 'coherent' . . . at the outset it is clear that there are many meanings for such terms . . . they have been used in many contexts and thus bear 'the trace' (in Derrida's terms) of many terms. For example 'logical' can also mean 'right thinking', 'conventional' or 'superior'. Which does the speaker really intend? . . . each term employed for clarifying the initial statement is itself opaque until the process of differance is again set in motion. 'Right thinking' can also mean 'morally' correct, 'conventional' can also mean 'banal', and so on. And in turn these terms bear the traces of numerous others in an ever-expanding network of significations. (1992: 219)

So, on the one hand, 'a manager's words . . . are like authorless texts; once the words are set in motion, the manager ceases to control their meaning' (Gergen 1992: 220). On the other hand there 'are constraints over the free play of signi-fiers' generated by participants which 'confine their activities to those which fit the language so constrained' (Gergen 1992: 221).

Linstead (1993: 69) radicalises Gergen's demand that signifiers be set free to ensure organisational vitality. He calls for a deconstructive ethnography in order to 'resuscitate the subordinate terms, to elevate them, to amplify the silent voices in order to problematise the dominant understanding and rather than create a new hierarchy, re-construct a duality of awareness within conventional consciousness'. In a similar vein Cooper (1989) observes that deconstruction involves two movements: overturning, where terms are shown to suppress their binary opposites; and metaphorisation, which involves recognition that posi-tively and negatively valued terms are defined in relation to each other and inhabit each other. Hence, in order for the positively valued concept 'logical' in Gergen's example to make any sense it can be defined only in terms of its nega-tively valued binary opposite i.e. 'illogical'. Nevertheless, this binary opposite is devalued, excluded and suppressed in the text – a hierarchy that deconstruction overturns by 'centring the marginal and marginalising the central' (Linstead 1993: 58).

Knights (1992) provides an interesting example of such repressive textual pro-cesses when he argues that strategic discourse and practice reflect and reproduce a masculine regime of rationality which excludes and suppresses the binary opposite of women as irrational:

> the discourse on rationality itself, of which strategy is one of its latest manifestations, sustains a 'particular kind of masculinity based on the exclusion of the personal, the sexual and the fem-inine from any definition of rationality' (Pringle 1990: 88). It is a form of rationality in which the masculine preoccupations with conquest and domination are exalted (Kerfoot and Knights, 1991). Strategy establishes that cause through which 'a masculine ethic of independence and commitment assumes a power over the environment and a sense of control' (Bologh 1990: 229) . . . . Although these 'externalities' can never be controlled and are for this reason a threat to managerial masculinity, the existence of a strategy provides an occasion whereby such externalities can be continually (re)constituted as objects of conquest. (1992: 528)

Hence deconstruction denies that any text can ever be settled or stable: it can always be questioned as layers of meaning are removed to reveal those meanings which have been suppressed. So in organisational life, meaning is always pre-carious and local (Linstead and Grafton-Small 1992) and any construct may be deconstructed even, as Cooper (1990) shows, the notion of organisation itself. Simultaneously deconstruction leads to questions about *how* something becomes seen as factual and about the consequences of such privileging. Usually we remain blithely unaware of these constructive socio-linguistic processes as we construct our objects of perception rapidly, automatically and unconsciously. Although the ontological result may appear as objective and separate from our-selves, as 'out there', through the action of discourse we are participants in cre-ating what we apprehend. So in Chia's (1995) terms postmodern deconstruction is about remembering these formative socio-linguistic processes that attribute a false concreteness to our objects of analysis and which modernists have sublimated or forgotten.

The result is a relativistic position for deconstruction which does not get the deconstructor closer to a 'fixed', or privileged, truth. At most it can offer only alternative social constructions of reality within a text, which then become amenable to further deconstruction to expose their underlying ideology. Thus no text should be allowed to rest in any finalised truth. With reference to Lukes' (1974) third dimension of power, Fletcher observes that by challenging the processes used to fix truth, deconstruction 'moves the concept of unobtrusive power away from discovering truth, and exposing one ideology by imposing another, towards unpacking the ways that all social reality is constructed' (1992: 33). In these respects postmodernist rhetorical analysis is parasitic in that it can feed off existing texts only – including its own deconstructions.

Genealogy of discourse

As we have shown, deconstruction is concerned with examining the logics and contradictions embedded in discourses – a process that for Linstead (1993) is consistent with Foucault's genealogical method. According to postmodernists, during their constitution discourses become naturalised – that is, they begin to operate as inevitable, immutable and self-evident truths which make the organisational practices they justify appear to be natural and necessary. For Foucault discourses can be deconstructed by revealing how they are constructed, highlighting the tacit metanarratives that underpin them, and opening up the potential for articulating alternative ways of knowing.

In undertaking a genealogy of strategy the first task is to isolate and describe the discourses of strategy, their ways of seeing organisations and members, and excavate the systems of rules that enable and limit what is knowable. This analysis disrupts the claims of mainstream strategic discourse to report observed reality and to be essential tools for rendering the management of organisational processes and environments more rational by pointing to how those discourses create the objects which they presume to analyse, such as the 'environment', 'competitive advantage', 'organisation', 'employees', and so forth.

Knights (1992) shows how Porter (1980, 1985) presents a distinctive view of business by first representing organisations as sets of value chains which are separate from the members and consumers who constitute them; second, ignoring how the truth of his thesis is dependent on its being only selectively adopted by those with privileged access to its nostrums otherwise its universal adoption would cancel out any competitive advantage; and third, transforming managers and employees into subjects who gain a sense of meaning, purpose and identity from the practices informed by Porter's discourse. As Knights summarises it:

> Porter constitutes the problems (e.g. cost leadership, cost differentiation, the value chain) that his theory is designed to resolve. But his work is attractive to management also because

it contributes to the transformation of management practice into an expertise that is supported by knowledge. As a rational basis for managerial prerogative, this expertise provides some illusion of control, legitimacy, and security in the face of uncertainty.... Insofar as a successful implementation of strategy is expected to generate competitive advantage, it promises 'security' for both the organisation and its members. This is so only because competitive advantage is a condition of the possibility of growth in a market economy that ordinarily results in an expansion of resources (e.g. incomes, career promotions). Accordingly, employees readily accept delegated responsibilities for the business strategy when they are cascaded down the hierarchy and, in doing so, collaborate in the constitution, or self-formation, of their own identity as subjects of strategy. (1992: 527–8)

The next step in Foucault's genealogical deconstruction of discourses is to examine the socio-historical conditions which make it possible for a particular discourse to emerge and develop thereby further unsettling its epistemological authority. Hence a genealogy of strategy would not be a history of strategy *per se*; rather, it would be a history about how such phenomena became socially constructed and came to be taken-for-granted. Here the task is not to identify some 'essential origin, but has to be seen as emerging out of a set of accidental and unpredictable conditions that happen to coincide at a particular point in history' (Knights 1992: 528).

Accordingly, Knights and Morgan (1991) argue that a discourse of strategy arose in a set of local conditions peculiar to post-1945 North America. These conditions included: the separation of ownership and control, which created the need for managers to be able systematically to articulate their corporations' objectives to external shareholder audiences; the development of multinational corporations and the consequent need to manage geographically dispersed operations in culturally diverse markets; and the development of multidivisional corporations where each plant was treated as a profit centre subject to market forces. These conditions required managers to be able to explain how their companies were going to succeed in more complex conditions and appear to be able to exert control over what lay outside the organisation. As Knights and Morgan observe, a strategic discourse met these needs and provided managers 'with a rationalisation of their successes and failures, while generating a sense of personal and organisational security for managers' (1991: 262).

Genealogy is, however, not only concerned with the emergence of discourses, but also with how existing discourses are adapted and transformed into new discourses. These changes are the focus of Barry and Elmes (1997) who explore the narrative forms that different strategic discourses take. They present a view of strategy as types of story embedded in a positivistic metanarrative. This metanarrative serves to enable and justify more specific narratives, as they are dependent on its own validity being taken-for-granted and remaining unchallenged. Barry and Elmes use narrative theory (Martin 1986) to highlight how different rhetorical devices can increase or decrease strategic credibility in the eyes of any audience/readership and can provide a veneer of epistemic authority which can mask its subjectivities. In other words, strategic credibility has nothing to do with the truth of a narrative, but is located in audience approval and participation by their appropriation of the characterisations and plot provided by the story.

Barry and Elmes argue that all effective narrativists have to achieve two outcomes: the first is to appear credible by convincing the audience that the narrative is plausible; the second is to defamiliarise by the narrative seeming novel and thereby engendering a new way of perceiving things. For Barry and Elmes there is an ambiguous relationship between these outcomes: narratives which are credible but familiar are unlikely to get much attention, whereas narratives which are unfamiliar may get plenty of attention but have difficulty in establishing their credibility when first introduced. Thus authors and narrators must continuously cope with the tensions between credibility and defamiliarisation which arise by reframing each dimension in the light of the other if an effective strategic narrative is to be recounted.

To ensure strategic credibility strategists have to employ a series of narrative devices (see Table 6.1) – the more unusual the strategy the more these devices will be used. For instance, the use of classical archetypal characterisations (e.g. the hero, the martyr, the wanderer) 'might provide a deeper sense of meaning and purpose than can be achieved through, for example, spreadsheet modelling' (Barry and Elmes 1997: 430). Meanwhile, the novelty of a narrative causes us to see things differently, thereby making a story more effective.

However, the novelty of a story will wane with telling as the audience becomes bored with it. So, no matter how initially exciting, familiarity can breed contempt. While new venues for and formats of strategy presentation may sustain some defamiliarisation, Barry and Elmes claim that different strategic discourses arise and succeed one another precisely because of the need for novelty. Hence each successive framework may be seen as a genre – a unique way of constructing and representing texts. They argue that Mintzberg's (1994) discussion

Table 6.1 Narrative credibility devices

Materiality	A story's material existence (e.g. being written down) and/or in terms of its reference to familiar concepts and phenomena accessible to the audience.
Voice and perspective	Who is telling the story and from what perspective – for instance, strategic narrators will often tell their stories using the detached third person so that the audience will see the content as objective and uninfluenced by the narrator.
Ordering and plots	Strategic narratives are ordered according to familiar plot lines (e.g. the heroic company fighting a number of threats and enemies) so as to enhance their credibility.
Readership	Ensuring that the audience interprets the strategic context as the narrator intends by the narrator inculcating in them logics underpinning the strategic stories (e.g. SWOT, PEST, 7Ss).

Source: Adapted from Barry and Elmes 1997

of 'strategy schools' suggests ten genres, each with its own distinctive style, content and structure. So as to highlight processes of change they examine three genres: the epic (i.e. Mintzberg's design); the technofuturist (i.e. Mintzberg's planning); and the purist (i.e. Mintzberg's positioning). With regard to the first two genres Barry and Elmes argue that while epic accounts rely on hierarchically-based authority to achieve adoption, the technofuturist narratives deployed a positivist orientation which uses scientific referencing to achieve credibility. However, by the mid-1970s, 'both genres had lost their lustre and became stale ... this explains why the next genre, the purist style, achieved such popularity. It was everything the epic and technofuturist genres were not ... [it] ... offered a defamiliarised, relatively atemporal character-based narrative' (1997: 440).

As exemplified by Miles and Snow (1978) and Porter (1980), the purist genre was effective because it reframed organisations as personalities (e.g. leaders, defenders, prospectors, etc.) with distinct characteristics (e.g. defenders are conservative while prospectors continually change) and claimed to guarantee how companies could succeed in competitive markets by choosing an ideal strategic personality. However, as with previous genres, Barry and Elmes note how the novelty of the purist narrative declined as practitioners found it difficult to operationalise and was replaced by new emergent genres.

Box 6.2

Lyotard's view

Barry and Elmes' approach concurs with Lyotard's (1984) more general observations about science. In a review of Lyotard's work, Kallinikos (1997: 117) observes that 'science needs to demonstrate its usefulness and practicability and to bespeak the meaningfulness of its own game in terms that can be apprehended by society's other linguistic games. This is, Lyotard claims, the major problem of legitimation. The contemporary "language game of science desires its statements to be true but does not have the resources to legitimate their truth on its own" (1984: 28).... It is at this crossroads that science resorts, wittingly or unwittingly, to traditional knowledge (mainly narrative knowledge) which it otherwise despises and condemns as an anachronistic fable, a relic of the past.'

In sum, genealogy focuses on the description of strategic discourses/narratives and the analysis of their development use and change. From this perspective:

> If some members can manage change, it is only possible because of their ability to hegemonise through a particular discursive formation a socially constructed version of reality.

> From a strictly normative standpoint, managers should have no ontological priority over any other possible social agents when it comes to decision making. Unfortunately, traditional organisation theory has perpetrated the falsehood that they do. (Hetrick and Boje 1992: 55)

Hence genealogy poses several important questions. Who writes and reads strategy? Who is marginalised and subjugated by that writing and reading? How is the writing and reading of strategic discourses linked to power in organisations? Pivotal to answering these questions is what postmodernists call the 'truth effects' of strategy.

Discursive truth-effects

As we have illustrated, postmodernists cannot claim to produce truths about strategy, rather they would see truth as a subjective outcome or effect of the social relationships that underlie strategic discourses and narratives. All the writers reviewed (e.g. Knights and Morgan 1992; Barry and Elmes 1997) suggest that strategic discourses and narratives represent a set of power-knowledge relations that constitute the subjectivity of managers and employees. Like any discourse it 'produces reality ... domains of objects and rituals of truth' (Foucault 1977: 194) which in effect suppress and even destroy the articulation of alternative possible 'truth-effects'. Power is not seen as being possessed by conscious agents, whether they are individuals or collectivities; rather, like knowledge, power is seen to be the outcome of and reside in discourses themselves. In Cooper's (1989) terminology knowledge and power 'inhabit each other'. For Foucault, 'the exercise of power perpetually creates knowledge and, conversely, knowledge constantly induces effects of power' (1980: 52).

So by what is called the decentring of the subject Foucault rejects the individual knower as the autonomous origin of meanings and as the focus of any analysis. Instead, through the language we use in, and gain through, social interaction we obtain and propagate shared discourses through which we give meaning to the world. The individual is thereby constituted through exposure to historically and socially contingent discourses: through learning to speak a discourse, the discourse speaks to the individual by structuring their experiences and definitions of who they are. The result is that people are not free to make their own interpretations; rather they are constrained by existing discourses. Human beings are thereby construed not as self-directing but deterministically, as mere conduits for discourses which produce the 'subject' by restricting what is thinkable, knowable and do-able within a discursive domain. By implication postmodern writers themselves cannot stand outside such social processes. Thus Foucault, for instance, decentres the notion of the 'author' as an outcome of 'the privileged moment of individualisation in the history of ideas, knowledge, literature, philosophy and the sciences' (1984: 101).

We shall return to the relativistic tensions decentring creates. For the time being it is important to note how a key postmodernist activity has been to apply the Foucauldian notion of decentring to investigate how all forms of work-based identity and subjectivity are discursively constituted and hence vary. For instance, by examining contemporary retailing Du Gay (1996) traces how contemporary discourses of organisational change take hold in particular contexts and 'make up' the identities of employees in their everyday working lives. He shows how an all-pervasive enterprise-excellence discourse has, through the image of the sovereign consumer, reimagined and blurred the distinction between the identities of consumers and employees. Both are now constituted as autonomous, responsible, calculating individuals seeking to maximise his/her worth through self-regulated acts of choice in a market-based world. So within this discourse:

> an active, 'enterprising' consumer is placed at the moral centre of the market based universe. What counts as 'good', or 'virtuous', in this universe is judged by reference to the apparent needs, desires and projected preferences of the 'sovereign consumer'. Thus, an enterprise culture is a culture of the customer, where markets subordinate producers to the preferences of individual consumers. Success and failure in this market based universe are supposedly determined by the relative ability of competing producers to satisfy the preferences of the enterprising consumer. (Du Gay 1996: 77)

Du Gay associates the enterprise-excellence discourse with a series of organisational changes, which displaces bureaucracy as an organisational form and set of values by construing it as dysfunctional and by reconstituting the employee as entrepreneurial. Thus for Du Gay an employee's sense of identity is negotiated, constituted and confirmed by his or her positioning within relations of power. Employees become inscribed with the ethos of enterprise in all aspects of their lives: an ethos which encourages them to transform themselves by building 'resources in themselves rather than rely[ing] on others' (Du Gay 1996: 183), through presenting characteristics such as initiative, risk-taking, self-reliance and the ability to accept responsibility for oneself and one's actions and so on, as virtuous.

Another helpful example of research informed by Foucauldian concepts is provided by Covaleski et al. (1998). They examine how, through the use of management by objectives (MbO) and mentoring, accounting firms have shaped professionals' identities and transformed them into self-disciplining members whose work goals, language and lifestyles reflect the strategic and entrepreneurial imperatives of their organisations. Drawing heavily on Foucault's account of Jeremy Bentham's panopticon (see Box 6.3), Covaleski and his colleagues characterise MbO as a 'disciplinary technique' which replicates the organisation in

---

Box 6.3

The Panopticon

'We know the principle on which [the Panopticon] was based: at the periphery, an annular building; at the centre, a tower; this tower is pierced with wide windows that open onto the inner side of the ring; the peripheric building is divided into cells, each of which extends the whole width of the building; they have two windows, one on the inside, corresponding to the windows of the tower; the other, on the outside, allows light to cross the cell from one end to the other. All that is needed, then, is to place a supervisor in a central tower and shut up in each cell a madman, a patient, a condemned man, a worker or schoolboy. By the effect of backlighting, one can observe from the tower, standing out precisely against the light, the small captive shadows in the cell of the periphery.... Hence the major effect of the Panopticon: to induce in the inmate a state of conscious and permanent visibility ... in the peripheral ring, one is totally seen; in the central tower, one sees everything without ever being seen' (Foucault 1977: 200–2).

the professional's identity. As with the inmates of the panopticon, MbO objectified the accountants they interviewed through a regime of calculability and surveillance in which the individual recognised him/herself relative to peers by assimilating the organisational goals transmitted through MbO:

> Here the exercise of power lies in making a multitude of subjects visible to an unseen source through documentation. More generally, writing, documentation, marking, and notation are the media by which subjects are objectified, individualised, rendered visible, and subjected to the norm.... With the dynamic action of norms carried by disciplines and exemplified in the 'examination' human activity can be 'judged' as to normality.... The expert or professional who exercises professional judgement, who embodies impartiality and acts objectively, can thus be seen as an agent of the norm. (Covaleski et al. 1998: 297)

In contrast, mentoring is presented as a 'technique of the self', which relies mainly on what Foucault calls 'avowal' (1986: 58). Analogous to the Catholic confessional, avowal is where, through a process of self-disclosure and self-examination, 'individuals are incited to change themselves, aided by the categories, criteria and languages of experts' (Covaleski et al. 1998: 322) so that organisational imperatives become their own. Here the expert mentor acts as an arbiter of the truthful by providing the protégé with the language of self-examination and by acting as a therapeutic agent who, through normative evaluation and correction, guides any remedial action. As such 'mentoring was complicit in subjectivising the protégé and transforming the protégé from partner as "professional" to partner as "business person"' (Covaleski et al. 1998: 322).

Importantly, Covaleski et al. found that a countervailing discourse of professional autonomy fuelled resistance to pressures towards such 'corporate cloning'. Just as MbO was used to constrain autonomy, mentors and their protégés simultaneously subverted MbO practices to their own ends, thereby making it a form of power/knowledge which limited the original disciplinary practice. So 'in transforming MbO into a means for advocating for the protégé, mentors at once avowed commitment to MbO, in that they acknowledged the legitimacy of talking about it, as they were in the very act of resisting it' (Covaleski et al. 1998: 327). As Linstead and Grafton-Small (1992: 344) put it, corporate cultures are texts that members read, and in doing so bring their awareness of alternative cultural texts that enter the corporate text 'changing its nature and reproducing it as they consume it'. For Knights and Vurdabakis the result is resistance to discursive truth-effects since any new discourse will always encounter a 'terrain already occupied by a variety of social relations and forms of subjectivity' (1994: 185).

Another effect arises here. People within organisations may be differentiated according to their participation in a discourse that shapes their subjectivity. For instance, those groups that accept and deploy strategic discourses enjoy an aura of expertise and material privilege within organisational hierarchies, while those that are unable, or unwilling, to deploy that discourse lose status. Moreover, the ability to deploy a strategic discourse reflects a command of knowledge of a particular domain which is employed in relation to employees who lack such a command and who have no socially legitimated claim to such knowledge. Indeed, the deployment of any discourse is seen as empowering those people with the right to speak and analyse while subordinating others who are the object of the knowledge and disciplinary practices produced by the discourse. Such experts – as Hollway (1991) has noted with regard to work psychologists and Townley (1994) has noted with regard to HRM practitioners – together with the knowledge that they articulate, serve to mask the arbitrary nature of their normative judgements which subordinate employees. Thus not all people are equal within the web of power relations which defines and orchestrates them. Here claims to detached reason and objective analysis merely serve to mask the self-aggrandisement of the 'speaker' who, through the discourse, dominates and oppresses those whom he or she analyses and categorises. Indeed in the case of strategic discourses, Knights and Morgan (1991: 271) note how the speaker secures and embellishes the material and symbolic privileges of particular individuals and groups, thus helping him/her to legitimise 'strategic inequalities'.

The disempowered may collude in the establishment of this power relationship in two ways. First, they accept the authority of discourse speakers to analyse and categorise thereby empowering those speakers. Second, as Du Gay (1996) notes, a discourse defines and constrains the subjectivities and identities of the disempowered to the extent that they engage in self-surveillance and correction of their behaviour towards the norms it articulates. Likewise, those managers with privileged access to the strategic discourse gain a sense of meaning and identity from the practices it sanctions – as Knights and Morgan observe, they feel like subjects who can 'make a differance in managing uncertainty as part of what it means to pursue success' (1991: 264). So, as with other types of discourse, strategic discourses are drawn on by managers to: construct a sense of identity; make sense of what is going on; and exercise control over other employees. Such processes are in a continuous state of flux as ever-emerging discourses develop and serve to shape and reshape members' organisational realities and practices (see Watson 1994).

In sum, postmodernists portray human subjectivity as an outcome of the exercise of power – 'a game in which the rules are never revealed or understood by the players' (Delanty 1997: 106). In this sense postmodernists see power as being everywhere yet nowhere in a world that is 'irreducibly and irrevocably pluralistic, split into a multitude of sovereign units and sites of authority, with no horizontal or vertical order, either in actuality or potency' (Bauman 1992: 35). This raises three important points.

First, power is construed as a relationship between subjects yet also independent of subjects where 'it is not possible for power to be exercised without knowledge it is impossible for knowledge not engender power [*sic*]' (Foucault 1980: 52). Thus power and knowledge are intimately intertwined: they produce one another and cannot escape one another. In this manner individuals and collectivities become socially inscribed, classified, known and transformed into self-disciplining subjects through a power that they may exercise but do not possess. Hence Foucault rejects conceptions of power in 'zero sum and negative terms – as power over, the traditional representation of "A" getting "B" to do something they would or should not otherwise do' (Townley 1994: 7).

Second, unlike for critical theorists, power is not systematically patterned into a structurally-based hegemony which obfuscates exploitative employment relationships by shaping employees' cognitions and preferences. So, as we have shown, a postmodern analysis of relations between subjects' identity and power is not a matter of analysing the ways in which our autonomy is suppressed by capitalist institutions. Instead, it is one of investigating the ways in which our subjectivity has become the object of regulation through the development of particular discourses, such as that of enterprise-excellence, which 'normalise' culturally specific notions of identity and punish deviations from that norm. There may be a vertical power order within a discourse, but the point is that there are always multiple discourses at play. Intriguingly, by making people more aware of the discursive aspects of everyday life, postmodernist discourse may well empower people to challenge and resist the discourses at play by asserting previously silent alternatives.

Third, despite its deterministic tendencies decentring does not necessarily mean that resistance is always absent and the subversion of discourses is impossible. As Du Gay observes, 'the official discourse of enterprise ... cannot completely close off the processes of the production of meaning.... What cannot be guaranteed in advance are the articulations that may result from the meeting and mixing of entrepreneurial discourse with already existing cultural practices ... and the meanings and identities they constitute' (1996: 160–1). Because people are exposed to a variety of discourses in different aspects of their lives, their identities can be unstable due to the conflicting requirements which enmesh them (Rose 1996). This can create the conditions for resistance against particular discourses, through, for instance, the reassertion of traditional employee discourses noted by Du Gay. In the case of strategy, Knights and Morgan (1991) argue that not everyone has taken up a strategic discourse: some managers reject its rationalism, preferring intuition; many employees remain incorrigibly cynical; there is a time lag between different parts of the world in the uptake of strategic discourses.

CONCLUSION: REBELS WITHOUT A CAUSE?

At first sight postmodernist approaches pose a significant sceptical challenge to positivistic views of strategy and change, or indeed any other totalising meta-narrative. Postmodernism demands that people think about and be suspicious of how they engage with the world; the categories they deploy; the assumptions that they impose and the interpretations that they make. By 'not finding answers to problems, but ... [by] ... problematising answers' (Cooper and Burrell 1988: 107) postmodernism makes people think about their own and others' thinking to question the familiar and taken-for-granted. It encourages irony and humility as well as rebellion against the imposition of any unitary scientific discourse which expunges plurality by forcing discursive closure.

So while postmodernism's reflexive value should not be underestimated, since it can at least sensitise us to alternative ways of apprehending strategy and change, it also sanctions relativism. Through what Thompson calls 'a retreat into the text' (1993: 202) epistemology is collapsed into ontology, resulting in the world becoming whatever we wish to make it. The intellectual mirroring of reality that underpins positivism is thereby replaced by the relativist's intellectual production of reality (see Figure 6.1, p. 155). Here truth is relative to the socially derived discourses everyone must deploy for which no independently existing evaluative criteria exist. As Parker (1995) reports, the result of relativism can be absurd claims such as Baudrillard's denial that the Gulf War took place. Apparently it was a media simulation. While such excesses appear to be easy targets, what is important is to consider how relativism creates several problems within postmodernism's own project.

If we accept the postmodernist claim that all knowledge is the outcome of social construction, what is the epistemological status of the postmodernist's own account? Can the conduct of deconstruction and genealogy, etc. be accomplished without invoking a metanarrative of epistemic privilege constituted by the very act of authoring? Through their own project is there a danger that postmodernists construct discourses about discourses that contradictorily, and tacitly, assert a claim to privilege through some epistemological backdoor? We have illustrated how postmodernists see strategies for change as mere rhetorical constructions ripe for deconstruction. However, such a postmodernist enterprise can be carried out only through language which, unless some tacit claim to epistemic privilege is deployed, should in turn also be deconstructed in terms of rhetoric, as some, like Linstead (1993), advise but most fail to live up to in practice. The danger is that if postmodernists eschew Linstead's advice a paradox lurks. Surely from a postmodern stance, their own analyses must constitute discourses which could sustain and contribute to the cultural impact of the discursive forms they (re)present. For instance, with regard to Du Gay's work, Fournier and Grey (1999: 115) make the point that Du Gay's analysis has contributed to constituting and reproducing enterprise-excellence as an accomplished fact! The inference must be that the truth-effects of postmodernists' own discourses may have unforeseen consequences.

According to critical theorists, postmodernists cannot avoid these charges. Habermas (1987) accuses postmodernists of surreptitiously deploying positivistic metanarratives. For Kellner (1988) the contradiction is evident in the work of both Baudrillard and Lyotard, who make general statements about external cultural conditions and then deny the possibility of reality and its representation. Indeed, the tacit notion that we should accept the 'truth-effects' of postmodernists' accounts is expressed by default in both Du Gay's (1996) and Knights' (1992) work – otherwise how can they justify their own ending of deconstruction and reflexivity through the closure of their own accounts? This poses the question of whether some postmodernists tacitly assume that their deconstructing intellectual stands outside the discursive knowledge–power relations which embed everyone else and that we should complacently accept their truth-effects? The danger is a double standard in that some postmodernists seem to apply their relativism only to the texts of others.

Second, if postmodernists remain faithful to their relativism there remains the problem that the assertion of relativity, like positivism's notions of privilege, is still a metanarrative which assumes its own validity and about which postmodernists advise us to be incredulous! Moreover, if we agree with the postmodernist's epistemic commitment that all knowledge claims are untrustworthy, why should we trust the postmodernists' claims about the relativity of knowledge? In other words, the nihilistic anti-dogmatic dogmatism of postmodernism's relativistic metanarrative nullifies itself, since why should anyone accept a metanarrative that rejects its own foundations? Such an outcome seems a contradiction: the articulation of an anti-totalising relativistic metanarrative which imperialistically seeks to ban all other metanarratives but its own discursive totalisations.

Third, even if it were possible to avoid the contradictions and paradoxes noted above, the postmodernist must accept that there are no good reasons for preferring one representation over another – including, presumably, their own genealogies and deconstructions. However, if we accept that we cannot and should not judge others (and their discursively produced realities and truths), the basis of critique and the choice of interventions to change things must be simultaneously undermined. To put it bluntly, if there is no possibility of adjudicating between different realities because there are no independent criteria with which to judge, it follows that there are no criteria through which we can engage in any form of criticism of the status quo. For the postmodernist, criticism becomes a pointless exercise since all that happens is either the mere jux-taposition of incommensurable alternative narratives, or the critic's attempted imposition of a discourse on others through a metanarrative of privilege.

Indeed, under the mantle of relativism it is difficult to see how anyone can have anything to say that is significant, or even worth listening to, never mind critical. The practical effect is that 'the problems of [fictional] individuals in [mythical] organisations are safely placed behind philosophical double glazing and their cries are treated as interesting examples of discourse' (Parker, 1992: 11). Any intervention, organisational or otherwise, implies the exercise of choice based on some kind of evaluative criteria. But as Newton observes, the problem for a postmodernist would be 'in determining that basis, since this implies the end of endless reflexivity and a move towards the postmodernity abhorrent notion of closure' (1996: 15). But, of course, the decision not to inter-vene, or not to criticise, is in itself a political act, which by default serves to sup-port the status quo and could promote a conservative disinterestedness in the guise of a radical posturing.

However, the fear of discursive closure has not prevented some scholars from considering how a postmodern stance might be used to inform organisational interventions and change. Barry (1997) outlines how 'narrative therapy': eschews expert-imposed solutions; entails careful reading, acknowledgement and reflection of client stories; and opens space for the authoring of alternative stories which counter hegemonic discourses so that there is no longer a sole dominating account of the problem. Hence Barry implies that discursive closure may not be the outcome of intervention – indeed, intervention may reopen dis-cursive opportunities so that 'if organisation members can better understand how they construct themselves and their organisation, they will be better able to address their problems' (Barry 1997: 31). This is an important point, which we shall address in the next chapter when we consider complexity theory.

So where does postmodernism leave us? Generally, postmodernists do seem like rebels without a cause as 'resistance and alternative readings rather than reform or revolution become the primary political posture' (Alvesson and Deetz 1996: 195). This lends force to Harvey's (1989) observation that the postmodern image of individuals being empowered to manufacture their own identities and realities is not a critique of capitalism, but its apotheosis! Rather than develop a critique, it would seem that the postmodern imperative is a mandatory non-judgemental rhetorical skill. Multivocal authors playfully manipulate signifiers to create new textual domains of intelligibility redolent with 'poetic awe' and 'linguistic tension' (Tsoukas 1992: 645). It is a game in which scientists become 'balloon craftsmen – setting aloft vehicles for public amusement' (Gergen 1992: 216). Narratives of organisational change may exude imagery, but they lack any substance. In many respects anything goes save that the text must provoke some pleasure, interest and excitement in terms of aesthetic appeal and rhetorical play (Kilduff and Mehra 1997: 465). But just as this aesthetic imperative serves overtly to relativise everyone's narratives, what it ignores is the likelihood that claims to epistemic authority by particular organisational groups will not suddenly disappear (Berg 1989: 205–6). The result may be that any (re)presentation of reality becomes a matter of taste where knowledge is commodified and reason is replaced by subtle forms of seduction. This is where the more reflexively aware postmodern manager uses his or her narrative skills to manipulate their organisational audiences into supporting particular change agendas, ensure discursive closure and snuff out resistance. *Plus ça change, plus c'est la même chose!*

REFERENCES

Alvesson, M. (1995) 'The Meaning and Meaninglessness of Postmodernism: Some Ironic Remarks', *Organisation Studies*, 16(6): 1047–75.

Alvesson, M. and S. Deetz (1996) 'Critical Theory and Postmodernism Approaches to Organisation Studies', in S.R. Clegg, C. Hardy and W.R. Nord (eds) *Handbook of Organisation Studies*, London: Sage.

Barry, D. (1997) 'Telling Changes: From Narrative Family Therapy to Organisational Change and Development', *Journal of Organisational Change Management,* 10(1): 30–46.

Barry, D. and M. Elmes (1997) 'Strategy Retold: Toward a Narrative View of Strategic Discourse', *Academy of Management Review,* 22(2): 429–52.

Baudrillard, J. (1983) *Simulations*, New York: Semiotext(e).

Bauman, Z. (1989) *Modernity and the Holocaust*, Oxford: Polity.

Bauman, Z. (1992) *Imitations of Postmodernity*, London: Routledge.

Bauman, Z. (1995) *Life in Fragments: Essays in Postmodern Morality*, Oxford: Basil Blackwell.

Berg, P.O. (1989) 'Postmodern Management? From Facts to Fiction in Theory and Practice', *Scandinavian Journal of Management*, 5(3): 201–17.

Berger, P.L. and Luckmann, T. (1971) *The Social Construction of Reality*, Harmondsworth: Penguin University Books.

Berger, P.L., B. Berger and H. Kellner (1973) *The Homeless Mind: Modernization and Consciousness*, Harmondsworth: Penguin.

Boje, D.M. (1995) 'Stories of the Story Telling Organisation: A Postmodern Analysis of Disney as "Tamara-land"', *Academy of Management Journal*, 38(4): 997–1035.

Bradshaw, P. (1996) 'Women as Constituent Directors: Re-reading Current Texts Using a Feminist-Postmodern Approach', in D.M. Boje, R.P. Gephart Jr and T.J. Thatchenkery (eds) *Postmodern Management and Organisation Theory*, London: Sage.

Burrell, G. (1988) 'Modernism, Postmodernism and Organisational Analysis 2: The Contribution of Michel Foucault', *Organisation Studies*, 9(2): 221–35.

Chia, R. (1995) 'From Modern to Postmodern Organisational Analysis', *Organisation Studies*, 16(4): 579–604.

Clegg, S.R. (1990) *Modern Organisations: Organisation Studies in the Postmodern World*, London: Sage.

Cooper, R. (1989) 'Modernism Postmodernism and Organisational Analysis 3: The Contribution of Jaques Derrida', *Organisation Studies*, 10(4): 479–502.

Cooper, R. (1990) 'Organisation/Disorganisation', in J. Hassard and D. Pym (eds) *The Theory and Philosophy of Organisations: Critical Issues and New Perspectives*, London: Routledge.

Cooper, R. and G. Burrell (1988) 'Modernism Postmodernism and Organisational Analysis: An Introduction', *Organisation Studies*, 9(1): 91–112.

Covaleski, M.A., M.W. Dirsmith, J.B. Heian and S. Samuel (1998) 'The Calculated and the Avowed: Techniques of Discipline and Struggles over Identity in Big Six Public Accounting Firms', *Administrative Science Quarterly*, 43(2): 293–327.

Czarniawaska-Joerges, B. (1996) *Narrating the Organisation: Dramas of Institutional Identity*, Chicago: Chicago University Press.

Delanty, G. (1997) *Social Science: Beyond Constructivism and Realism*, Buckingham: Open University Press.

Derrida, J. (1973) *Speech and Phenomena*, Evanston, IL: Northwestern University Press.

Drucker, P.F. (1993) *Post-Capitalist Society*, New York: Harper and Row.

Du Gay, P. (1996) *Consumption and Identity at Work*, London: Sage.

Featherstone, M. (1988) 'In Pursuit of the Postmodern: An Introduction', *Theory, Culture and Society*, 5(2–3): 195–216.

Fletcher, J.K. (1992) 'A Poststructuralist Perspective on the Third Dimension of Power', *Journal of Organisational Change Management*, 5(1): 31–8.

Foucault, M. (1970) *The Order of Things: an Archaeology of the Human Sciences*, London: Tavistock.

Foucault, M. (1972) *The Archaeology of Knowledge*, London: Routledge.

Foucault, M. (1977) *Discipline and Punish: The Birth of the Prison*, Harmondsworth: Penguin.

Foucault, M. (1980*) Power/Knowledge*, Brighton: Harvester.

Foucault, M. (1984) 'What is an Author?', in P. Rabinow (ed.) *The Foucault Reader*, Harmondsworth: Penguin.

Foucault, M. (1986) *History of Sexuality*, Harmondsworth: Penguin.

Fournier, V. and C. Grey (1999) 'Too Much, Too Little and Too Often: A Critique of Du Gay's Analysis of Enterprise', *Organisation*, 6(1): 107–28.

Fournier, V. and C. Grey (2000) 'At the Critical Moment: Conditions and Prospects for Critical Management Studies', *Human Relations*, 53(1): 7–32.

Gergen, K. (1990) 'Social Understanding and the Inscription of Self in Cultural Psychology', in J. Stigler et al. (eds) *Essays on Comparative Human Development*, Cambridge: Cambridge University Press.

Gergen, K. (1992) 'Organisation Theory in the Postmodern Era', in M. Reed and M. Hughes (eds) *Rethinking Organisation*, London: Sage.

Giddens, A. (1991) *Modernity and Self-identity: Self and Society in the Late Modern Age*, Cambridge: Polity Press.

Habermas, J. (1987) *The Theory of Communicative Action Volume 2; Lifeworlds and System: A Critique of Functionalist Reason,* London: Heinemann.

Harvey, D. (1989) *The Condition of Postmodernity: An Enquiry into the Origin of Social Change*, Oxford: Basil Blackwell.

Hassard, J. (1993) 'Postmodernism and Organisational Analysis', in J. Hassard. and J. Parker (eds) *Postmodernism and Organisations,* London: Sage.

Hassard, J. and M. Parker (eds) (1993) *Postmodernism and Organisations*, London: Sage.

Hetrick, W.P. and D.M. Boje (1992) 'Organisation and the Body: Post-Fordist Dimensions', *Journal of Organisational Change Management*, 5(1): 48–57.

Hollway, W. (1991) *Work Psychology and Organisation Behaviour*, London: Sage.

Jeffcutt, P. (1993) 'From Interpretation to Representation', in J. Hassard and M. Parker (eds) *Postmodernism and Organisations*, London: Sage.

Jeffcutt, P. (1994) 'The Interpretation of Organisation: A Contemporary Analysis and Critique', *Journal of Management Studies*, 31: 225–50.

Kallinikos, J. (1997) 'Classic Review, Science, Knowledge and Society: The Postmodern Condition Revisited', *Organisation*, 4(1): 114–29.

Kellner, D. (1988) 'Postmodernism as Social Theory: Some Challenges and Problems', *Theory, Culture and Society*, 5: 239–69.

Kilduff, M. (1993) 'Deconstructing Organisations', *Academy of Management Review*, 18(1): 13–31.

Kilduff, M. and A. Mehra (1997) 'Postmodernism and Organisational Research', *Academy of Management Review*, 22(2): 453–81.

Knights, D. (1992) 'Changing Spaces: The Disruptive Impact of a New Epistemological Location for the Study of Management', *Academy of Management Review*, 17(3): 514–36.

Knights, D. and G. Morgan (1991) 'Corporate Strategy, Organisations and Subjectivity: A Critique', *Organisation Studies*, 12(2): 251–73.

Knights, D. and T. Vurdabakis (1994) 'Foucault, Power, Resistance and all that', in J. Jermier, D. Knights and W. Nord, *Resistance and Power in Organisations*, London: Routledge.

Lash, S. and J. Urry (1987) *The End of Organised Capitalism*, Cambridge: Polity Press.

Latour, B. (1990) 'Postmodern? No Simply Modern! Steps toward an Anthropology of Science', *Studies in History and Philosophy of Science*, 21: 45–71.

Linstead, S. (1993) 'Deconstruction in the Study of Organisations', in J. Hassard and M. Parker (eds) *Postmodernism and Organisations*, London: Sage.

Linstead, S. and R. Grafton-Small (1992) 'On Reading Organisation Culture', *Organisation Studies*, 13(3): 331–55.

Lukes, S. (1974) *Power: A Radical View*, London: Macmillan.

Lyotard, J.-F. (1984) *The Postmodern Condition: A Report on Knowledge*, Manchester: Manchester University Press.

Lyotard, J.-F. (1988) *The Differend: Phases in Dispute*, Minneapolis: University of Minnesota Press.

March, J.G. and H.A. Simon (1958) *Organisations*, New York: Wiley.

Marsden, R. and B. Townley (1995) 'Power and Postmodernity: Reflections on the Pleasure Dome', *Electronic Journal of Radical Organisation Theory*, 1(2); <http://tui.waikato.mngt.ac.nz/leader/journal/ejrot.htm>.

Martin, W. (1986) *Recent Theories of Narrative*, Ithaca, NY: Cornell University Press.

Miles, R. and C. Snow (1978) *Organisation Strategy, Structure and Process*, New York: McGraw-Hill.

Mintzberg, H. (1994) *The Rise and Fall of Strategic Planning*, New York: Free Press.

Newton, T. (1996) 'Postmodernism and Action', *Organisation*, 3(1): 7–29.

Parker, M. (1992) 'Post-modern Organisations or Postmodern Organisation Theory', *Organisation Studies*, 13(1): 1–17.

Parker, M. (1995) 'Critique in the Name of What? Postmodernism and Critical Approaches to Organisation', *Organisation Studies*, 16(4): 553–64.

Porter, M.E. (1980) *Competitive Strategy*, New York: Free Press.

Porter, M.E. (1985) *Competitive Advantage*, New York: Free Press.

Rorty, R. (1979) *Philosophy and the Mirror of Nature*, Princeton, NJ: Princeton University Press.

Rorty, R. (1982) *Consequences of Pragmatism (Essays: 1972–80)*, Minneapolis: University of Minnesota Press.

Rosenau, P.M. (1992) *Post-modernism and the Social Sciences: Insights, Inroads and Intrusions*, Princeton, NJ: Princeton University Press.

Shweder, R. (1984) 'Anthropology's Romantic Rebellion against the Enlightenment, or There's More to Thinking than Reason and Evidence', in R. Shweder and R. Levine (eds) *Culture Theory: Essays on Mind, Self and Emotion*, Cambridge: Cambridge University Press.

Simons, J. (1995) *Foucault and the Political*, London: Routledge.

Sokal, A.D. and J. Bricmont (1997) *Intellectual Impostors: Postmodern Philosophers' Abuse of Science*, London: Profile.

Stacey, R.D. (1993) *Strategic Thinking and Management of Change*, London: Kogan Page.

Thompson, P. (1993) 'Postmodernism: Fatal Distraction', in J. Hassard and J. Parker (eds) *Postmodernism and Organisations*, London: Sage.

Townley, B. (1994) *Reframing Human Resource Management: Power Ethics and the Subject at Work*, London: Sage.

Tsoukas, H. (1992) 'Postmodernism: Reflexive Rationalism and Organization Studies', *Organisation Studies*, 14(3): 323–46.

Turner, B.S. (1987) *Medical Power and Social Knowledge*, London: Sage.

Vattimo, G. (1992) *The Transparent Society*, Cambridge: Polity Press.

Wakefield, N. (1990) *Postmodernism: Twilight of the Real*, London: Pluto.

Watson, T. (1994) *In Search of Management: Culture, Chaos and Control in Managerial Work*, London: Routledge.

Woolgar, S. (1988) *Science: The Very Idea*, Sussex: Ellis Horwood.

Chapter 7

COMPLEXITY, POWER AND CHANGE

The aims of this chapter are to:

1 Review the contribution that complexity theory can make to the management of change.

2 Identify key principles emerging from complexity theory, and relate these to logic and language, leading in turn to consideration of the use of metaphor, paradox and dialogue in management.

3 Link this debate to the role of power in and between organisations.

4 Show how complexity theory can implicitly draw on both Critical Theory and post-modernism to offer an approach to change management and organisational development which is richer than that premised on conventional thinking of the type discussed in Chapter 1, and that this approach is more than a set of inter-esting or provocative ideas – it can be put into practice, and is therefore worthy of consideration by those involved in the management of change.

INTRODUCTION

There has been a rapid growth of interest in complexity theory and its relevance to organisations, and this has led a number of writers to set out the implications for managers (see, for example, Kiel 1994; Bettis and Prahalad 1995; Darwin 1996a and b; Stacey 1996b; Laszlo and Laszlo 1997; Kelly and Allison 1999; Lissack and Roos 1999). There is a tendency, however, for them to focus on one, albeit an important, aspect: the need to understand the management mindset and to become exposed to other mindsets beyond the still dominant approach to much contemporary 'modernist' management thinking, which is rooted in the Cartesian–Newtonian synthesis.

There is a danger here of two valued thinking. Rittel and Webber (1973) once distinguished the problems of natural sciences – tame problems – from the prob-lems faced in public policy, which 'are inherently wicked'. They identify ten characteristics of the latter (reformulated as questions in Table 7.1), concluding that 'the problems that planners must deal with are wicked and incorrigible ones, for they defy efforts to delineate their boundaries and to identify their causes, and thus to expose their problematic nature. The planner who works with open systems is caught up in the ambiguity of their causal webs' (Rittel and Webber 1973: 167).

Table 7.1 Tame or wicked?

- Can you provide an exhaustive formulation of the problem, containing all the information the problem solver needs for understanding and solving the problem?
- Can you be sure when you have found a/the solution?
- Can you provide decision rules which determine whether or not a proposed solution is the correct one?
- Can you undertake a controlled test of a proposed solution, without waves of consequences which also need to be considered?
- Can you experiment without penalty?
- Can you identify all the possible solutions?
- Is it possible to use the same set of techniques in solving this problem as in another?
- Is the problem independent, or a symptom of another problem?
- Is the nature of the problem's resolution independent of the choice of explanation?
- Is it acceptable to be wrong?

Source: Based on Rittel and Webber (1973: 161–6).

It is useful to develop Rittel and Webber's thesis in two ways. First, we should move away from dichotomy. Managers are not presented with 'either/or' choices; they face a variety of contexts. We could, for example, conceive of a spectrum ranging from Tame → Tricky → Wild → Wicked. Conventional 'rational' approaches work well at the Tame end; decreasingly so as we move to the Wild and Wicked.

Second, as the above implies, we can extend their argument from 'problems' to 'contexts' – by which is meant the dynamic interaction between an organisation, its enacted environment and the issues being addressed. This also points to a distinction between the approach being suggested here and the one that identifies different organisational environments, such as Emery and Trist's (1965) four 'ideal types' of causal texture or Ansoff and Sullivan's (1993) five levels of increasing environmental turbulence. Here the environment is not seen as something external to and distinct from the organisation and its situation; managers need to recognise in their analysis the extent to which they create (enact) that environment by their approach and actions.

There is also the danger that discussion will be confined to the realm of ideas. When teaching strategic management and change, a frequent response from managers is that they are comfortable with the rational planning approach, which they find straightforward in approach. But when we get on to all this other stuff . . . what does it mean and how is it used? Those who break through this recipe-led mindset may find the ideas arising from complexity theory stimulating, but confronted with the immediate requirements of their work, and the political nature of organisations, they still prefer the recipes and toolkit offered by the conventional textbooks on strategic management. After all, the perspective in these texts has been enriched over the years, as authors have recognised the limitations of the narrow strategic planning approach, and the need to address power and organisational dynamics – the latter through the wide-ranging concept of organisational culture. What does complexity theory offer to take us beyond this? Here we put forward some ideas, through an integration of the theory with several other strands of thinking, and suggest that this inter-linking has relevance to managers in the inseparable realms of thought and action.

Vignette 7.1

A wicked issue

As an example of a wicked situation, consider the issue of rising crime rates on housing estates. The stakeholders in this include residents, young people, local employers and shopkeepers, the police, the probation service, churches, tenants and residents groups, black and Asian groups. Within the local authority itself relevant departments include Housing, Social Services, Education, Youth Service, Leisure, Economic Development and Planning (and therefore outside unitary authority areas there will be at least two Councils involved). The value systems of stakeholder groups will vary considerably, with causal factors cited including 'human nature', unemployment, poverty, racism, family breakdown, lack of role models. Solutions offered will advocate resource allocation to the youth service, to education and schools, to police on the streets, to police detection, to more deterrent devices, tougher sentencing in courts and harsher prison regimes, to job creation, to family planning, to improving race relations. The list of frequently conflicting, often contradictory, causal factors and proffered solutions could be greatly extended.

The argument takes as its starting point the challenges to conventional thinking reviewed in Chapter 1. We begin, therefore, with a recognition that no solid foundations exist. Indeed, the alternative metaphor to the building with solid foundations would be that of weaving a pattern that connects strands of thinking from a number of disciplines, each reinforcing the others, but none providing the 'base'. The ideas discussed below thus provide a framework for a coherent and fruitful approach to strategic management, and can be used in discussion with people when advocating the value of this approach. But there is no solidity.

The argument also challenges the tendency to slip into two-valued frames: to set up, for example, tables which contrast 'old' thinking with 'new' thinking, as well as the contrast raised in the literature between descriptive and prescriptive approaches to strategy – a contrast which again shows the dominance of crisp logic. Outlined here are a number of frameworks and strategic techniques. While some of these are intended to help in description, as well as in analysis, none is intended to be prescriptive: rather, they are heuristic. That is to say, they are put forward as helpful ways by which those interested in change management can think and act (most commonly simultaneously).

COMPLEXITY THEORY

In 1948 Weaver wrote an article on 'Science and Complexity', in which he identified three kinds of problem. First, there are those of Organised Simplicity, usually involving two variables; before 1900 science was primarily concerned with these – indeed, this was the terrain explored within the Cartesian–Newtonian synthesis.

From 1900 onwards problems of a second kind – Disorganised Complexity – were tackled, using the techniques of probability theory and statistical mechanics then being developed. These are problems in which the number of variables is very large, and each of these variables has a behaviour which is individually erratic, or perhaps totally unknown. Despite this, the system as a whole possesses certain orderly and analysable average properties.

Weaver argued that scientific methodology in effect went from one extreme to the other, and left a vast middle ground untouched. In this ground there may be many variables, but what is really important is that these problems 'show the essential feature of organisation' (1948: 539). These are the problems of Organised Complexity, and they are to be found 'in the biological, medical, psychological, economic and political sciences.... Science must, over the next 50 years, learn to deal with these problems of organized complexity' (1948: 540). He saw two promising developments which might help science begin to deal successfully with these problems. The first was 'the wartime development of new types of electronic computing devices' (1948: 541), the second the 'mixed team' approach of operations analysis.

Weaver would no doubt be intrigued by what has happened since then. His call for interdisciplinary teamworking has become a familiar one in management texts. As to the other promising avenue, there is no doubt that computers have made a massive contribution. But as Klir and Bo Yuan have argued:

> Initially, it was the common belief of many scientists that the level of complexity we can handle is basically a matter of the level of computational power at our disposal. Later, in the early 1960s, this naive belief was replaced with a more realistic outlook. We began to understand that there are definite limits in dealing with complexity, which neither our human capabilities nor any computer technology can overcome. (1995: 2)

Today a group of interconnected ideas (some emerging through the use of computer power) are seen by many as offering the route to addressing the problems of organised complexity. This new approach – complexity theory – provides a distinct challenge to the Cartesian–Newtonian Synthesis; it involves a different landscape, mindset, language and toolkit. At the same time, it is consistent with a number of arguments put forward in the management literature, and may be seen as giving theoretical support to them. (See Table 7.2).

Complexity theory is the third wave of ideas introduced into a wider setting from mathematics in recent years – its predecessors were catastrophe theory and chaos theory. Each time this happens, initial excitement about the new approach is followed by reservation as people seek – and fail to find – 'hard evidence' that this is more than hype, more than metaphorical rhetoric. It is, after all, easy to see chaos and complexity in much that organisations do, and it is a commonplace to argue that the past was predictable and relatively static, while the future is uncertain and unpredictable; new ways of thinking which offer signposts in this dangerous environment are therefore attractive. The parallel with the taste for management fads is obvious.

By way of cautious reminder, consider Marx and Engels' words:

> Constant revolutionising of production, uninterrupted disturbance of all social conditions, everlasting uncertainty and agitation distinguish the bourgeois epoch from all earlier ones. All fixed, fast-frozen relations with their train of ancient and venerable prejudices and opinions are swept away; all new-formed ones become antiquated before they can ossify. All that is solid melts in air. (1848)

It is not the perception of a move towards increasing turbulence that stimulates our discussion; rather, the recognition that change is always there – 'becoming' is the constant – and it merits consideration.

A number of attempts have been made to relate these new ideas to management, strategy and organisations. Here we review several such contributions and consider their implications. Critically, the argument will be that complexity theory does have promise and offers exciting new ways of thinking. But while it is *necessary* to an adequate approach to strategic management, it is not *sufficient* – it needs to be integrated into the wider dimensions of strategy and change explored in this book. The language of complexity is illustrated in Table 7.2.

As we saw in Chapter 1, one of the oldest features of the Cartesian–Newtonian Synthesis is the use of bipolar, crisp logic – the 'either/or' approach which has dominated Western thinking for more than two millennia. The desire to polarise is strong. Since the argument here must be presented in part by contrast, it would be easy for this also to fall into such a dichotomous trap. It is important to note immediately, therefore, that while in some cases the two columns represent contrasts, in others the concept on the right may be seen to embrace that

Table 7.2 Central concepts compared

Cartesian–Newtonian synthesis	The Complexity Approach
Certainty	Chaos, complexity and self-organised criticality
Structure preserving systems	Dissipative systems and complex adaptive systems
Independent existence	Codependent existence and Autopoiesis
Equilibrium	Far from equilibrium; at the edge of chaos
Reduction	Emergence
Crisp (two-valued) logic	Four-valued logic and fuzzy logic
Body/mind split	Body/mind link
Command and control	Self-organisation
Linear thinking	Systems thinking; triple lens vision
Competition	Mutualism and coevolution

on the left. Thus two valued logic (which will be explored below) is a special case of both four valued logic and fuzzy logic. Similarly, linear thinking may be considered a special case of systems thinking. This parallels the situation in both science and mathematics. Newtonian physics may be seen as a special case of the physics of Einstein, applicable in certain circumstances, or Euclidean geometry as a subset of the full family of geometries.

Referring to Weaver's approach, we can see that organised simplicity is itself a subset of organised complexity, where the number of variables has been kept very low. Similarly, the Modern Paradigm is a special case of a wider, complexity-based framework, applicable in contexts where the number of variables is low, perhaps allowing predictability, or where uncertainty is at a minimum. But just as the Cartesian–Newtonian methods become less relevant as we move away from organised simplicity, so the methods of the Modern Paradigm – including strategic planning, control techniques and the management of culture – become less relevant as levels of uncertainty and complexity increase in organisations.

COMPLEX ADAPTIVE SYSTEMS

Perhaps the central concept that allows us to explore the implications of complexity theory is the Complex Adaptive System (CAS). Once again, the application of this has its precursors in earlier writings. Thus in 1968 Buckley argued that 'the mechanical equilibrium model and the organismic homeostasis models of society that have underlain most modern sociological theory have outlived

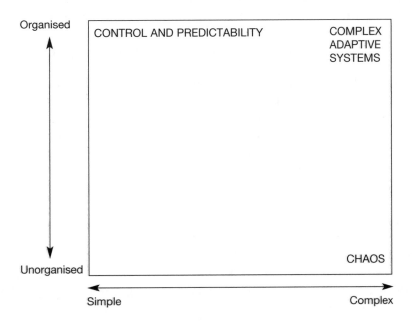

Figure 7.1 Control, chaos and complexity

their usefulness' (in Jun and Storm 1973: 198). Equilibrial systems are relatively closed and entropic, losing structure in going to equilibrium. Homeostatic systems are open and negentropic, maintaining a moderate energy level within controlled limits. Their main characteristic is that they function to maintain the given structure of the system within pre-established limits, using negative feedback loops with the environment to achieve this. The complex adaptive system is also open and negentropic, but is open 'internally' as well as externally in that the interchanges among its components may result in significant changes in the nature of the components themselves with important consequences for the system as a whole. In Figure 7.1 (see p. 181) it is shown in relationship to the two areas identified by Weaver.

The following expansion of this concept is based closely on the discussion by Holland (in Waldrop 1992), together with the explanation of CAS given by Gell-Mann (1995). Each part of the description is given (see Table 7.10), and followed by comment. A CAS is a network of many 'agents' acting in parallel. The CAS is not a single entity – like an organisation, it has many 'agents'; but these are not in a hierarchical system of command and control – they form an interconnecting network. This idea parallels one that has become very popular in discussions on new forms of organisation, the network or cluster, which is seen to offer an alternative to the hierarchy/market dichotomy (Darwin 1992).

- They are 'adaptively intelligent' – constantly seeing and imagining patterns, testing ideas, acting upon them, discarding them again–always evolving and learning.
- Constant change occurs through learning, adaptation and evolution. The connection with the vogue concept of the 'learning organisation', and with emergent theories of strategy, is apparent.
- The control of a complex adaptive system tends to be highly dispersed.

Here again we have the contrast with a hierarchical structure. But this does not imply an absence of layers and levels, as the discussion below illustrates.

Coherent behaviour in the system arises from competition and cooperation among the agents themselves. Competition can produce a very strong incentive for cooperation, as agents spontaneously forge alliances and symbiotic relationships with each other for mutual support. It happens at every level and in every kind of complex, adaptive system, from biology to economics to politics. Competition and cooperation are closely interrelated.

Evolutionary theory in the nineteenth century stressed the 'survival of the fittest', and in economic theory this was reflected in the emphasis given to competition. Cooperation was regarded with some suspicion for a long time. In the life sciences the role of symbiosis and mutualism today is given much greater emphasis. The same applies to thinking about strategic management, where the virtues of cooperation are more widely accepted, and the search is for new linkages. We explore this further in Chapter 9. Organisms in an ecosystem coevolve.

In the natural world this has produced flowers that evolved to be fertilised by bees, and bees that evolved to live off the nectar of flowers. It has produced cheetahs that evolved to hunt gazelles, and gazelles that evolved to escape from cheetahs. In the human world, the dance of coevolution has produced equally exquisite webs of economic and political dependencies – alliances, rivalries, customer–supplier relationships, and so on. Coevolution is a powerful force for emergence and self-organisation in any complex adaptive system.

Emergence and self-organisation are important concepts in complexity theory. Reductionism is an important tenet of the traditional paradigm; the scientific method involved is to disaggregate everything to the lowest level, and then investigate the properties of those 'corpuscles', in the belief that a full understanding of these parts allows a full understanding of the whole. This is a belief as simple as it is mysterious, since emergence is to be found everywhere, and emergent properties in turn often produce emergent behaviours. If you cool liquid water molecules, for example, at $0°C$ they will suddenly stop tumbling over one another at random. Instead they will undergo a 'phase transition', locking themselves into the orderly crystalline array known as ice. By going in the other direction and heating the liquid, those same tumbling water molecules will suddenly fly apart and undergo a phase transition into water vapour. Neither phase transition will have any meaning for one molecule alone.

Harré (1984) has described emergent properties as those properties of a group or aggregate that are not properties of the individuals of which they are a collection. This has implications for understanding and for action. It means, for example, that attempts to develop management strategy by systematic (reductionist) analysis of individual elements – resources, capability, position, the environment – are likely to miss important emergent themes.

> The ability to reduce everything to simple fundamental laws does not imply the ability to start from those laws and reconstruct the universe. In fact, the more the elementary particle physicists tell us about the nature of the fundamental laws, the less relevance they seem to have to the very real problems of the rest of science, much less society. (Anderson 1972, quoted in Waldrop 1992: 81)

It means also that in taking action we have to recognise that issues will arise – emerge – as action takes place: 'At each level of complexity, entirely new properties appear. [And] at each stage, entirely new laws, concepts, and generalisations are necessary, requiring inspiration and creativity to just as great a degree as in the previous one. Psychology is not applied biology, nor is biology applied chemistry' (Anderson, 1972: 82). This suggests that emergent strategy has an important role to play in complexity-based management.

Capra (1996) has traced the concept of self-organisation to the early years of cybernetics. In the 1950s, when binary networks were built using an array of lamps which could flicker on or off, experimenters discovered that after a short period of random flickering, ordered patterns would emerge in most networks. This spontaneous emergence of order became known as self-organisation. Later work explored this phenomenon, and identified three common characteristics of models of self-organisation. First, there is the spontaneous emergence not only of order, but also of new structures and new modes of behaviour, including processes of learning and evolution. Second, they deal with open systems which are operating far from equilibrium, and third, there are internal feedback loops described mathematically by nonlinear equations.

A complex adaptive system has many levels of organisation, with agents at any one level serving as the building blocks for agents at a higher level. For example : proteins, lipids, nucleic acids → cell → group of cells → tissue → collection of tissues → organ → association of organs → whole organism → group of organisms → ecosystem.

The same applies in organisations, especially large ones. Thus local authorities may have within them a number of directorates, each including a number of departments, each having divisions, each having sections (or more likely these days, business units). And each of these exists within a wider environment with which it is constantly interacting.

Complex adaptive systems are constantly revising and rearranging their components as they gain experience. Examples are to be found in the evolution of organisms, the brain-changing neuron connections, firms reshuffling organisational charts, countries realigning in alliances. At some fundamental level, all these processes of learning, evolution and adaptation are the same. And one of the fundamental mechanisms of adaptation in any given system is this revision and recombination of the building blocks.

Within this constant change there are layers. In particular, the distinction between structure and organisation is important – a distinction which plays a key role in a theory closely related to complexity: autopoiesis. We shall return to this below.

All complex adaptive systems anticipate the future. They build models that allow them to anticipate the world. These may not be conscious models, but implicit predictions. In the cognitive realm implicit models include skills and expertise – huge, interlocking sets of standard operating procedures that have been inscribed on the nervous system and refined by years of experience. Consider, for example, the skill of the medieval architects who designed the great Gothic cathedrals. They had no way to calculate forces or load tolerance; they built high vaulted ceilings and flying buttresses using standard operating procedures passed down from master to apprentice.

In part the interest in complexity theory in management has arisen from disillusion with planning systems that seek to predict the future. This does not, however, imply a disinterest in the future, nor a process of 'just muddling through'. This different approach to the future has been described by Bartlett and Ghoshal as 'Beyond Strategy to Purpose', a move from emphasis on a strategic plan to building 'a rich, engaging corporate purpose' (1994: 81).

This approach to the future is also illustrated by Ingvar (1985), whose research suggests that the human brain keeps trying to anticipate the future through what he calls 'memories of the future', which help us to prepare to meet possible futures and provide a filter through which we pass the data with which we are constantly barraged.

Complex adaptive systems typically have many niches, each one of which can be exploited by an agent adapted to fill that niche. New opportunities are always being created by the system. It is, therefore, essentially meaningless to talk about a complex adaptive system being in equilibrium. The system can never get there; it is always unfolding, always in transition. In fact, if the system ever does reach equilibrium, it isn't stable; it's dead. Agents in the system can never 'optimise' their fitness or their utility. The space of possibilities is too vast; they have no practical way of finding the optimum. The most they can ever do is to change and improve relative to what the other agents are doing. In short, complex adaptive systems are characterised by perpetual novelty (Holland, quoted in Waldrop 1992). A complex adaptive system functions best in a situation between order and disorder (Gell-Mann 1994: 249).

The argument within complexity theory that systems are never in equilibrium has been one that has particularly attracted interest. It challenges the equilibrium theory so important to neoclassical economics and taken into strategic management, for example, by Rumelt et al.:

> The challenge is to retain the power of thinking. . . . Equilibrium assumptions are the cornerstone of most economic thinking. Researchers who eschew equilibrium assumptions risk gross errors in the causal interpretation of data. . . . While equilibrium assumptions often drive out consideration of innovation, change, and heterogeneity, this is not invariably the case. . . . More sophisticated views now permit more sophisticated equilibria. (1994: 43, 537)

In complexity theory the language is of systems which are 'far from equilibrium', sometimes expressed as being on the 'edge of chaos'. The idea of a 'transition zone', an area of instability which is neither order nor chaos, is one which has been well developed by Miller (1990) in his analysis of the 'Icarus Paradox'. His four trajectories of decline include two where the change is towards excess stability – decoupling and focusing – and two where the change is towards excess instability – venturing and inventing – even though the momentum driving change is associated with orderliness, or the search for greater internal consistency. He identifies a number of factors which cause this – the 'lenses' through which people view, and indeed create, reality, retrospective rationality (such as attributing success to previous personal action), overconfidence, and defence mechanisms.

Another to explore this territory is Pascale (1991), who uses one of the metaphors arising from complexity theory when he advocates 'managing at the edge', which involves avoiding excessive consensus, stimulating 'creative conflict' and encouraging a state of dynamic tension in organisations.

A complex adaptive system acquires information about its environment and its own interaction with that environment, identifying regularities in that information, condensing those regularities into a kind of 'schema' or model, and acting in the real world on the basis of that schema. In each case, there are various competing schemata, and the results of the action in the real world feed back to influence the competition among those schemata (Gell-Mann 1994: 17).

There are other important concepts in complexity theory, but we hope we have enough to see that there is here a very different conception of an organisation from that of the machine or clockwork (order), and different also from the 'snakepit' (chaos). The landscape here is that of the rainforest – a complex ecosystem made up of multiple interacting agents. This suggests that we move beyond a binary approach and recognise that in addition to order (organised simplicity) and chaos (disorganised complexity) there is the possibility of organised complexity. We now take that challenge to binary thinking a stage further by considering crisp and fuzzy logic.

LOGIC

Logic is important because it plays a significant part in the way people think. As Ford and Ford (1994) have argued, logic refers to the underlying assumptions, deeply held, often unexamined, which form a framework within which reasoning takes place. It provides the lens through which we view everything: it tells us what is real, what is true, what is beautiful and what is the nature of things. When someone is 'operating' in a particular logic, he or she takes its rules and boundaries for granted. Logic poses the problems, provides the language for explaining and understanding them, and determines their solutions. In this section we begin by looking at two-valued, or crisp, logic. We then consider fuzzy logic and four-valued logic. Both take us into the realm of language and concepts, and this is developed by examining prototypes and schemata, and then the role of metaphor and paradox in management. Recognising the crucial place which language has in management – arguably, it is the most important single tool used by all managers – we move on to a review of dialogue. Crisp logic has the binary code True/False, Yes/No, Right/Wrong, and is a persistent theme in Western thinking. The three key axioms of this logic are:

- Axiom of Contradiction: A thing cannot be itself and something else.
- Axiom of Identity: A thing is equal to itself.
- Axiom of the Excluded Middle: A thing is one of two mutually exclusive things.

In recent years this has become a popular theme to challenge in management writings, with the exhortation that we shift from 'either/or' to 'both/and', and take paradox more seriously (see for example Pascale 1990; Bate 1994; Collins and Porras 1994; Stacey 1996a). In effect, what we have here is a revival of dialectics, whose equivalent three axioms are:

Table 7.3 Dialectics

A	Not A
True	False
False	True
True	True

- Axiom of Transformation: A qualitative shift occurs from a gradual increase or decrease in quantity.
- Axiom of Oppositional Struggle: Each entity is a unity of contradictory opposites.
- Axiom of Negation: Change occurs in the negation of the previous form.

These axioms allow for 'both/and' as well as 'either/or'; we thus have an extension of the truth table as shown in Table 7.3.

This debate, however, does not take us much beyond two-valued logic, which tends to reappear in other aspects of the same writers' work. Thus Stacey, who has many useful things to say about paradox, retains a binary structure when he considers organisations and management. Similarly, Collins and Porras in effect create a new bifurcation of either/or vs. both/and ('Tyranny of the Or' vs. 'Genius of the And').

This can even stretch to the work of those concerned with fuzzy logic, which we explore next. Kosko (1994: 24, 69–78) sets up a polarity between the Aristotle 'prophet of A or Not-A' and the Buddha 'prophet of A and Not-A'. This illustrates a more general point: it is difficult to talk about new ideas without setting up a contrast with those being challenged.

FUZZY LOGIC

Beginning with Brouwer's intuitionist school of logic in the early twentieth century, there have been a number of alternatives to two-valued logic, involving many-valued logics. But the most extensive new area of thinking originated from Zadeh in 1965, with his first paper on the theory of fuzzy sets, which challenged Aristotelian two-valued logic. When A is a fuzzy set and x is a relevant object, the proposition 'x is a member of A' is not necessarily either true or false, as required by two-valued logic, but it may be true only to the degree to which x is actually a member of A. The degree of membership in fuzzy sets (as well as degrees of truth of the associated propositions) can be represented by numbers in the closed unit interval (0, 1). The extreme values in this interval, 0 and 1, then represent, respectively, the total denial and affirmation of the membership in a given fuzzy set as well as the falsity and truth of the associated proposition.

Fuzzy sets not only give us a powerful representation of measurement uncertainties; they also provide a meaningful representation of vague concepts expressed in natural language. As an example, we can take the set comprising all the delegates at the British Academy of Management, and ask how many of them are in the subset middle-aged delegates. A crisp definition is possible (all between the ages of X and Y), but will represent only the view of the person giving that definition. We could instead take particular ages: 20 would not be seen as middle-aged; 40 would be accepted as middle-aged. As we move from one to the other, at what point does middle age appear? If someone is young at 23, then she will still be young at 23 and one week, and therefore at 23 and two weeks ... an example of Wang's Paradox: If a number x is small, then $x + 1$ is also small. If $x + 1$ is small, then $x + 1 + 1$ is small as well. Therefore, a thousand billion is a small number; so too is infinity.

To resolve this paradox, the term middle-aged may introduce fuzziness by allowing some sort of gradual transition from youth to middle age, and beyond. This is, in fact, precisely the basic concept of the fuzzy set, a concept that forms a generalisation of the classical or crisp set.

The crisp set divides the individuals in a given universe of discourse into two groups: those that are in the set and those that are not. But many of our concepts do not allow this neat 'logic chopping'. Consider, for example, the set of dangerous dogs, expensive houses, highly contagious diseases, endangered species, modest profits, numbers much greater than 1, or cloudy days. These sets have imprecise boundaries that facilitate gradual transitions from membership to non-membership, and vice versa.

A fuzzy set can be defined mathematically by assigning to each possible individual in the universe of discourse a value (between 0 and 1) representing its grade of membership in the fuzzy set. This grade corresponds to the degree to which that individual is similar to or compatible with the concept represented by the fuzzy set.

Returning to our earlier example, a fuzzy set representing the middle-aged people at the BAM conference might assign a degree of membership of 1 to those aged 40–45, reducing this figure by 0.1 for each year above or below these boundaries. These grades signify the degree to which each age approximates our subjective concept of middle-aged, and the set itself models the semantic flexibility inherent in such a common linguistic term. Because full membership (40–45) and full non-membership (those below 30, or above 55) in the fuzzy set can still be indicated by the values of 1 and 0, respectively, the concept of a crisp set is a restricted case of the more general concept of a fuzzy set for which only these two grades of membership apply.

Research on the theory of fuzzy sets has been growing steadily since Zadeh's first papers were published in the mid-1960s. Interestingly, this is a field which has been more rapidly adopted in applied science than in the philosophy of science: video camcorders are often advertised as incorporating fuzzy logic in their software. This recognition led to a study by the US Department of Commerce in 1991. One of the issues that concerned the Department was why this approach, although developed in the West, was being most quickly applied in Japan: by 1992 the products from Japan and South Korea using fuzzy logic included air conditioners, car engines, chemical mixers, copying machines, cruise control, dishwashers, dryers, lift controls, factory controls, health management systems, microwave ovens, computers, refrigerators, televisions, video camcorders, translators and toasters.

The Department commented:

> From a philosophical viewpoint, the fuzzy logic concept is attuned to the fundamental teachings of Zen Buddhism, which perhaps contributed to the Japanese acceptance of this concept. There are others who believe that the fuzzy logic success in Japan is a result of that country's perceived need to become competitive in advanced technologies such as artificial intelligence, biotechnology, and optical computing. (*Fuzzy Logic: A Key Technology for Future Competitiveness*, quoted in Kosko 1994: 156–7)

Fuzzy boundaries can also be used to help give a better understanding of organisational structures and stakeholders, especially in strategic alliances and joint ventures. Thus instead of Mintzberg's sharp distinction between internal and external stakeholders, we can recognise partial membership of intersecting sets.[1] We can replace 'crisp' boundaries within and between organisations with fuzzy ones. It will rarely be necessary to employ the impressive mathematical structures that underpin this theory, but the concepts themselves can be of great value.

Fuzzy logic helps us to recognise the way in which apparently sharp and absolute dichotomies are socially constructed. Grint (1997) illustrates this in the field of medicine, applying fuzzy logic to the distinction between life and death. Transsexualism provides another example. Our conventions demarcate sharply between male and female, although this is complicated when we recognise the different categories involved: physical gender (male–female), behaviour patterns (masculine–feminine), sexual orientation (homosexual, bisexual, heterosexual). Lewins (1995) argues that the overall concepts of male and female are socially constructed, and that most transsexuals seek to locate themselves securely in one or other of the two: typically, they desire an 'alignment' between the mental and the physical (feeling themselves to be women trapped in the bodies of men, or vice versa).

But as Archer and Lloyd (1982) show by reference to Omani society, a third gender role is feasible (the same has also been found with the *berdache* in some Native American cultures). And Star (1991) identifies the way in which the dichotomy between male and female can be enforced on transsexuals. In a graduate class on feminist theory one participant had an ambiguous appearance and name (Jan). It turned out that Jan was considering transsexual surgery, but was currently enjoying the experience of being ambiguous: 'It's like being in a very high tension zone, as if something's about to explode' (1991: 45). (This comment illustrates an important link between fuzzy logic and complexity theory, in which the 'high tension' of the boundary between order and chaos is considered the most creative arena. Perhaps living on the boundary of a constructed dichotomy can be like living at this edge.)

Jan later underwent transsexual surgery, but discovered in the process that the 'gender identity clinic' required that 's/he dress more like a conventionally feminine woman to "prove" that s/he was serious in her desire for the surgery' (Star 1991: 46). Star refers to other gender clinics which require candidates for transsexual surgery to dress and act 'as stereotyped females', denying them surgery if they do not.

To date there have been few other attempts to employ this approach in management theory. One exception is Grint (1997), who employs fuzzy logic to allow a reconsideration of a number of management themes, such as measurement systems. Another is provided by Lerner and Wanat (1983), who have explored the implications for bureaucracy, and in particular the practice of categorisation. They argue that fuzzy sets allow a more realistic and humane public service. They see the crisp set as 'the appropriate perception for the Weberian bureaucracy-as-technical-tool whose discretionary decisions have been legitimately pre-empted by the legislature' (1983: 503). This is a familiar problem in local government, where the need for overt parity leads to the imposition of crisp rules that are also very inflexible. Overtly crisp rules are on occasion subverted by fuzzy interpretations, which, however, remain hidden to those most affected. Overt fuzzy rules might address this problem.

FOUR-VALUED LOGIC

Returning once more to two valued logic and its extension into dialectics, we can now take this a step further by reconsidering the Law of the Excluded Middle. Dialectics accepts a third possibility – that both A and Not-A may be true. What is interesting is to consider the fourth possibility – that neither is true (see Table 7.4). This has rarely been examined in Western thinking, but there are examples in Eastern thinking, especially in the work of Nagarjuna, the second-century Indian philosopher prominent in the Madhyamika School, who argued for an ontology based on this approach which has the potential to enrich the debate on postmodernism.

Nagarjuna had a specific purpose in developing this approach.

The method of the Madhyamika demonstrates the absurdity and uselessness of concepts and aims at showing the reality of emptiness as dealt with by the Prajnaparamita.[2] It is not a

Table 7.4 Four-valued logic

A	NOT-A
True	False
False	True
True	True
False	False

linguistic philosophy, a simple play of words, or an intellectual exercise. The aim of the Madhyamika is to reduce all concepts to absurdity in order to open the door to non-conceptual knowledge. It is not the intention of the Madhyamika to propose a view of reality in order to set it up in opposition to other views of reality. All views, according to the Madhyamika, are erroneous, because the views are not reality. (Thich Nhat Hanh 1994: 121)

This contrasts directly with one of the key principles of the Cartesian–Newtonian synthesis – the desire for firm foundations and certainty. For Nagarjuna argues against such foundations: this is a philosophy of groundlessness. Varela, Thompson and Rosch (1993) suggest that the philosophical analysis of Madhyamika is directly relevant to current preoccupations in part because it explicitly recognises that the search for an ultimate foundation is not limited to the notion of the subject ('I think therefore I am'); it also includes our belief in a pregiven or ready-made world.

Epistemologically, the Madhyamika approach is a critique of concept chopping, or, as Thich Nhat Hanh has eloquently put it, the use of the sword of conceptualisation:

Our concept of self arises when we have concepts about things that are not-self. Using the sword of conceptualization to cut reality into pieces, we call one part 'I' and the rest 'not I'.... We usually think of 'life span' as the length of our life, beginning the moment we are born and ending when we die. We believe that we are alive during that period, not before or after. And while we are alive, we think that everything in us is life, not death. Once again, the sword of conceptualisation is cutting reality into pieces, separating one side, life, from the other side, death. (Thich Nhat Hanh 1992: 38,40)

Again, what we see here is the possibility – and value – of stretching or breaking categories.

METAPHOR

Arguably, language is the most important tool that a manager has. She uses it in everything she does – in meetings, in presentations, in written material, in individual discussion. It is the medium through which strategy is discussed and developed, through which tacit knowledge becomes explicit, through which ideas are shared and thereby implemented within organisations.

Not surprisingly, there has, therefore, been much interest in the use of language in management, and metaphors have aroused particular excitement. This discussion is introduced here, not because anything new is to be suggested, but because metaphor has a role within the wider argument being developed. For it can be a powerful way of entrapping thought, as well as having the potential to assist in concept bending and breaking.

Most powerful of all in management, as we have seen in Chapter 1, is the mechanistic metaphor: 'The pervasive influence of machines remains beyond dispute ... this is nowhere more evident than in the modern organisation' (Morgan 1997: 12). Another important metaphor, also considered in Chapter 1, relates to building; this is so rooted in our thinking about thinking that in one book on metaphor (Grant and Oswick 1996) there is no direct reference to it, despite its use by several of the contributors.

Morgan identified eight metaphors, and argued for their use to generate multiple ways of thinking and acting. Alvesson and Willmott (1996) see danger in this 'supermarket approach' and argue that the underlying value orientations and associated commitments of a metaphor need to be considered in order to appreciate the significance and limitations of any metaphor. Without this, uncritical selection of familiar metaphors can confirm rather than challenge preconceptions and prejudices. They illustrate this through the presentation of four metaphors: management as distorted communication, management as mystification, management as cultural doping and management as colonisation.

The earlier argument on fuzzy categories provides a further dimension on this. We should recognise that metaphors themselves are fuzzy concepts. Thus presentations by managers on MBA courses, when they were asked to discuss their organisation using one of Morgan's metaphors, have revealed very different interpretations of each metaphor. We have only to consider the different conceptions of the machine, such as the clockwork, the computer and the engine. Supporting this, Lackoff and Johnson (1980) argue that full consistency across metaphors is rare, but coherence is typical. When metaphors are used in management debate, it may help if grounds for coherence are examined. This relates in part to the very nature of metaphor. The theory of enactment reinforces the view of Lackoff and Johnson that metaphor plays a very significant role in determining what we consider to be real, since much of our social reality is understood in metaphorical terms, and our conception of the physical world is partly metaphorical.

Lackoff (1987: 371) subsequently argued that human conceptual categories have properties that are, at least in part, determined by the bodily nature of the people doing the categorising, rather than solely by the properties of the category members, and that properties are a result of imaginative processes that do not mirror nature. Integrating these ideas suggests a view of enactment, which is a continual dynamic interplay between the embodied nature of the subject, perceptual processes and categories, which have arisen previously from this interplay, including imaginative processes such as metaphor. Absent from this is any firm foundation of knowledge, any source of certainty.

The interlinked theme of reframing has also been pursued by Bolman and Deal (1991) to encourage managers to think more holistically. They argue that, faced with problems in an organisation, people tend to adopt one of three limited perspectives: a people-blaming approach; a bureaucracy-blaming approach; and a thirst for power.

They then outline five perspectives, each of which provides a different way to reframe the organisation. Four of these are the structural (which relates closely to the machine form), the human resource frame (here they draw on the work of Argyris and Schon), the political frame and the symbolic frame, while the fifth frame integrates ideas from systems theory and cybernetics.

There has been much critical debate on the value of reframing and metaphor-based approaches to organisations. Palmer and Dunford (1996) raise a number of concerns, for example: Do managers actually use reframing? Can the benefits always be clearly articulated? Do the benefits continue over time? In light of these, it is worth reiterating that they are introduced here primarily for their heuristic value.

Vignette 7.2

The team with two kings

An example will illustrate both the strength and the limitations of a metaphorical approach. This example relates to a management team of which one author was a member. The OD consultant working with us at the time produced a chess set and asked team members to relate themselves and others to the pieces (and their respective power and influence). What emerged was a consensus that the team had two 'kings', the formal, hierarchically located, leader, and another member who was seen by several as even more central. The discussion that followed helped to illuminate a number of ambiguities in relationships and behaviour which could be seen as stemming from this. But it did not lead to any action: the situation changed only when one of the two concerned left the organisation a year later.

PARADOX

This statement is false.

We have already seen that the value of paradox is now widely espoused in management literature, and we have explored its roots in dialectics. The purpose of this section is to consider the use of paradox as a way of thinking about change, and link this to learning.

The argument begins with Watzlawick et al. (1974), whose frequently-cited book on change is well worth a revisit. They employ Russell's Theory of Types to distinguish first- and second-order change, illustrated by Ashby's application to a machine.[3] There is a change from state to state, which is the machine's behaviour, and there is the change from transformation to transformation, which is a change of its way of behaving and which occurs at the whim of the experimenter or some outside factor. They argue that there are two important conclusions to be drawn from the postulates of the Theory of Logical Types: 1) logical levels must be kept strictly apart to prevent paradox and confusion; and 2) going from one level to the next higher (i.e., from member to class) entails a shift, a jump, a discontinuity or transformation – in a word, a change of the greatest theoretical and practical importance, for it provides a way out of a system.

Earlier in their discussion, they employ Group Theory to illustrate aspects of change. A simpler model is to think of the game of chess. First-order change is movement within the laws of chess. These laws are about – they are meta to – the game itself. Any change in the rules would constitute second-order change, and 'remembering that second-order change is always in the nature of a discontinuity or a logical jump, we may expect the practical manifestations of second-order change to appear as illogical and paradoxical as the decision of the commandant of the castle of Hochosterwitz to throw away his last food in order to survive' (1974: 12). The story to which they refer is a good illustration of the theme, and is reproduced in Vignette 7.3. They identify a number of characteristics of second-order change:

- Second-order change is applied to what in the first-order change perspective appears to be a solution, because in the second-order change perspective this 'solution' reveals itself as the keystone of the problem whose solution is attempted.

- While first-order change always appears to be based on common sense (for instance, the 'more of the same' recipe), second-order change usually appears weird, unexpected and uncommonsensical, there is a puzzling, paradoxical element in the process of change.

- Applying second-order change techniques to the 'solution' means that the situation is dealt with in the here and now. These techniques deal with effects and not with their presumed causes; the crucial question is What? and not Why?

- The use of second-order change techniques lifts the situation out of the paradox-engendering trap created by the self-reflexiveness of the attempted solution and places it in a different frame.

Vignette 7.3

The siege of Hochosterwitz

When in 1334 the Duchess of Tyrol, Margareta Maultasch, encircled the castle of Hochosterwitz in the province of Carinthia, she knew only too well that the fortress, situated on an incredibly steep rock rising high above the valley floor, was impregnable to direct attack and would yield only to a long siege. In due course, the situation of the defenders became critical: they were down to their last ox and had only two bags of barley corn left. Margareta's situation was becoming equally pressing, albeit for different reasons: her troops were becoming unruly, there seemed to be no end to the siege in sight and she had similarly urgent military business elsewhere. At this point the commandant of the castle decided on a desperate course of action which to his men must have seemed sheer folly: he had the last ox slaughtered, had its abdominal cavity filled with the remaining barley, and ordered the carcass to be thrown down the steep cliff onto a meadow in front of the enemy camp. Upon receiving this scornful message from above, the discouraged duchess abandoned the siege and moved on.

This leads to a conceptualising of reframing in terms of class membership: 'In its most abstract terms, reframing means changing the emphasis from one class membership of an object to another, equally valid class membership, or, especially, introducing such a new class membership into the conceptualisation of all concerned.' (Watzlawick et al. 1974: 98) This has several implications. First, our experience of the world is based on the categorisation of the objects of our perception into classes, which are mental constructs and therefore of a totally different order of reality from the objects themselves. Second, once an object is conceptualised as the member of a given class, it is extremely difficult to see it as belonging simultaneously to another class. This class membership of an object is called its 'reality'; thus anybody who sees it as the member of another class must be mad or bad. Third, what makes reframing such an effective tool of change is that once we do perceive the alternative class membership(s) we cannot so easily go back to the trap and the anguish of a former view of 'reality'. Once again we see the power – but also the dangers – of conceptualisation.

Watzlawick et al. (1968: 252–3) point to the potential therapeutic effect of paradoxical communication. From our earlier discussion, we can see that the use of paradox in the way they outline can be enhanced in two ways: through the use of metaphor to encourage perception of alternative class membership, and through the use of fuzzy set theory to explore partial membership of sets.

The analysis developed by Watzlawick and his comments were inspired in part by Bateson's application of the Theory of Types to learning. We can take the approach further by moving beyond a two-level analysis of change, and using the multilevel approach which Bateson employed (and which has been borrowed in various forms by many writers on organisational learning since).

Table 7.5 shows this multilevel method, linking change and learning, and using another metaphor – motion – to illustrate the levels. We can further illustrate this by referring again to the chess example. Level 0 would be random moves by a player who is unable through these to learn the rules. Level I learning involves learning the rules, while Level I change is the application of these rules – the change move by move in the game itself as it is played out. Level II learning involves thinking about these rules – whether or not they constitute a good game perhaps – and Level II change involves changes to the rules – it is possible, for example, through a step-by-step alteration to the nature and powers

Table 7.5 Learning and change

		Learning	Change
0	Stasis	No learning	No or random change
1	Constant motion	Learning	Change within fixed rules
2	Constant acceleration	Learning to learn	Change of rules
3	Variable acceleration	Learning to learn to learn	Change of rule-set

Source: Based on Bateson (1973: 250–79).

of the individual pieces, the layout of the board, and the objectives of the game, to reach the game of Chinese chess.

Level III learning would reflect on the nature of games as such; Level III change could lead to a change of game, say to Pool. This is discontinuous, since the board, the equipment and the rules are quite different. Level IV would shift us out of the 'game' set completely, although Bateson comments: 'Learning IV would be change in Learning III, but probably does not occur in any adult living organism on this earth. Evolutionary process has, however, created organisms whose ontogeny brings them to Level III. The combination of Level phylogenesis with ontogenesis, in fact, achieves Level IV' (1973: 264).

Applying this elaboration to organisations and their markets, Level 0 would involve an organisation selling a product, but not learning as it does so. Level I would involve learning about how the product sells and seeking to improve performance within the 'rules' of the market. Level II would involve a change of market or product, while level III would be a change of the entire *raison d'être* of the organisation. Level IV would involve rethinking the very notion of being an organisation – an unlikely level for any organisation to reach (although aspects of this will be explored in Chapter 9, when we consider the link between organisations and ecology). Within this we can also envisage reference to the 'unwritten rules' of the game (Scott-Morgan 1994) and to other ways in which people might challenge or subvert the rules.

However, this extension requires us to refine a basic premise of the approach adopted by Watzlawick and colleagues – the discontinuity between levels (something that also appears extensively in discussions of paradigm shifts). Part of the confusion and paradox of change lies in the difficulty in seeing this discontinuity, which may only become fully apparent in retrospect.

We can see this by considering one of the best-known scientific revolutions – the shift from a geocentric to a heliocentric universe, one of the key steps in the shift toward the Cartesian–Newtonian Synthesis. Copernicus himself was extremely conservative, wishing to stick wherever possible to the old principles. Thus Kuhn argues that Copernicus tried to design an essentially Aristotelian Universe around a moving earth. Koestler cites one of Copernicus' successors, Johann Kepler, as saying that 'Copernicus tried to interpret Ptolemy rather than nature' (1959: 203).

But Copernicus was not the only participant in this revolution who clung to ancient principles. As Tarnus (1991) points out, Kepler was inspired by his search for the celestial 'music of the spheres', a search that began with Pythagoras. Galileo prepared astrological birth charts for his patrons. And Newton reported that his interest in astrology stimulated his mathematical research; he was also a student of alchemy.

This excursion into astronomy is intended to illustrate the complexities of changes in mindsets. Interpretations of Kuhn's theory of scientific revolution often see the paradigm shift as a discontinuous process, leading to notions of incommensurability between paradigms. Yet some of the key protagonists in a major shift sought to build, rather than break, the existing paradigm. The paradoxes that ensued were the stimulus to new creativity, leading ultimately to that shift.

As a final reflection on paradox, we may note that its value in stimulating people to think outside conventional frames and thereby induce change is well established in many cultures. The following vignette gives one further example of this.

Vignette 7.4

Paradoxical behaviour in Native American culture

Sometimes, in the midst of a sacred ceremony, a person will enter and make fun of what is going on. This is a clown, someone very different from our own familiar circus figure. In the West the clown has become a harmless figure of fun, but indigenous clowns are disturbing in the way they assault, frighten and even beat people. Clowns can also be openly sexual, waving giant phalluses and indulging in mock intercourse.

Clowns are disturbing because they turn the world upside down and openly challenge the order of nature and society. Wherever harmony and order are present, the clown intervenes. The clown makes boundaries explicit by crossing them; demonstrates the meaning of order through disorder. Most important of all, the clown reminds us that in the flux of the world nothing is certain. In Blackfoot ceremonies the circle is always open so that something new can appear.

A relative of the clown is the 'contrary' who does everything in reverse. The contrary will walk backward, face the rear of a horse when riding, and wash in dirt. The contrary's behaviour is also linguistic, with No used for assent, and Yes turned into a denial. Thus, through the medium of speech and action, a contrary teaches the limits and conventions of social behaviour and social inhibitions.

Source: Peat (1995: 83).

DIALOGUE

Concern about the negative effects of discussion has prompted a number of writers to develop the idea of dialogue, put forward by Bohm some years ago. Bohm suggested that there is an important difference between a dialogue and ordinary discussion. In the latter, people tend to hold relatively fixed positions and argue in favour of their views, trying to persuade others to change their own. This can lead to agreement, but is unlikely to produce anything positive. Indeed, if the positions involved are of fundamental importance to the people concerned, then discussion degenerates into confrontation, or at best a polite avoidance of the issues.

By contrast, as we have shown in Chapter 5 with regard to Critical

Theory, in dialogue individuals are prepared to listen to others with sufficient sympathy and interest to understand the meaning of their position, and are ready to change their own points of view if there is sufficient good reason to do so. Bohm and Peat (1987) argue that a spirit of goodwill or friendship is necessary for this to take place: it is not compatible with a spirit that is competitive, contentious or aggressive. Participants must be prepared to suspend their own point of view, while also holding other points of view in a suspended form and paying full attention to their meaning. This has the potential for 'concept breaking': 'when the rigid, tacit infrastructure is loosened, the mind begins to move in a new order' (Bohm and Peat 1987: 244). From a postmodernist stance, existing discourse becomes unsettled as alternatives emerge.

In a subsequent paper with Factor and Garrett (1991), Bohm extends this description, suggesting that people normally gather either to accomplish a task or to be entertained, both of which can be categorised as predetermined purposes. But by its very nature dialogue is not consistent with any such purposes beyond the interest of its participants in the unfoldment and revelation of the deeper collective meanings that may be revealed. These may on occasion be entertaining, enlightening, lead to new insights or address existing problems. Surprisingly, they argue, in its early stages the dialogue will often lead to the experience of frustration (a phenomenon which we shall find again in Chapter 11, when we explore Whole Systems Interventions).

Siding with critical theorists they point also to the democratic principle of dialogue: it is essentially a conversation between equals, and any controlling authority, no matter how carefully or sensitively applied, will tend to hinder and inhibit the free play of thought and the often delicate and subtle feelings that would otherwise be shared. Dialogue, they conclude, is vulnerable to being manipulated, but its spirit is not consistent with this. Hierarchy has no place in dialogue.

The development of the spirit of dialogue in a group can take time. Isaacs and Smith (in Factor and Garrett 1991: 374) say that it may take a year or more to develop the competencies required for dialogue and Isaacs identifies five paradoxes:

- Techniques that leave technique behind: while there are techniques of dialogue which can help build a container – an environment that promotes collective inquiry – technique in itself cannot get you to your goal.
- 'Don't just do something, stand there': 'in dialogue we don't think about what we're doing; we do something about what we're thinking.'
- Intention but no decision: it is best to approach dialogue with no result in mind, but with the intention of developing deeper inquiry.
- A safely dangerous setting: the issues being considered may be difficult and dangerous – the environment of dialogue is intended to be safe enough to allow this consideration.

- Being individual and collective: participants need to listen to themselves, as well as the group, and understand the roots of their perceptions, and of emergent collective meanings.

POWER

We now extend the debate to reintroduce and develop the role of power in and between organisations, first considered in Chapters 4 and 5. We shall argue that approaches to management based on complexity theory need to incorporate a view of power, just as any other approach does. Dialogue may be desirable, and in certain circumstances it may be attainable. But often circumstances require an understanding of the dynamics of power and the role managers can play in this.

The four arenas of power

The basic framework used here is simple. We start with the approach adopted by Flood and Jackson 'from the industrial relations literature' (1991: 35). This involves unitary, pluralist and coercive relationships between participants. Table 7.6 presents the characteristics of each as identified by them, with a number of changes. First, the word 'control' replaces 'coercive'; second, their framework is extended here by adding a fourth type of relationship, which will be called the open, and is also summarised in Table 7.6.

Coercion has been defined as 'To force to act or think in a certain way by use of pressure, threats, or intimidation; compel. To dominate, restrain, or control forcibly: coerced the strikers into compliance. To bring about by force or threat: efforts to coerce agreement' (American Heritage Dictionary). In the same source, control is defined as 'To exercise authoritative or dominating influence over; direct; Authority or ability to manage or direct.' Thus control includes coercion. In addition, there are a number of other ways by which one individual or group can require others to do things that they may not otherwise choose to do. This is reflected in Table 7.6 where the original 'Some coerce others to accept decisions' has been replaced by 'Some require others to accept decisions'.

We can now link these four types of relationship through the matrix presented in Table 7.7, where they are seen as four arenas of power. The vertical axis concerns the number of dominant belief and power system(s); the horizontal axis concerns the potential for agreement or consensus between the participants. While shown as a simple matrix, we should recognise from the outset that both these axes are in practice a spectrum, and there is scope for considerable movement both within and between the four arenas – indeed, this is often what management is about. In the language of fuzzy logic, the arenas are fuzzy sets, and any situation can have partial membership of more than one. These four arenas may also be represented pictorially as shown in Figure 7.2.

The approach taken here can be clarified by comparing it with Bate's (1994)

Table 7.6 Types of relationship

	Unitary	Control	Pluralist	Open
Summary	We all agree what to do	This is what we will do	We do our best to agree what to do, and then stick with it	We need to get some agreement so that we can take action, but it will be provisional
Communality of interest	Share common interests	Do not share common interests	Basic compatibility of interest	Compatibility of interest may well be partial
Values and beliefs	Highly compatible	Likely to conflict	Diverge to some extent	Divergence may be significant, including some conflict
Ends and means	Largely agreed	Not agreed, and 'genuine' compromise is not possible	Do not necessarily agree, but compromise is possible	Compromise may be provisional – subject to change when the opportunity arises for one or more participants
Decision-making	All participate	Some require others to accept decisions	All participate	All participate, although power differences mean some have more influence than others
Objectives	Act in accordance with agreed objectives	No agreement over objectives is possible given present systemic arrangements	Act in accordance with agreed objectives	Objectives may not be agreed, but action can be agreed by negotiation

Table 7.7 Arenas of power

		Potential for Agreement	
		High	Low
Dominant belief and	Single ↕	Unitary	Control
power system(s)	Multiple	Pluralist	Open

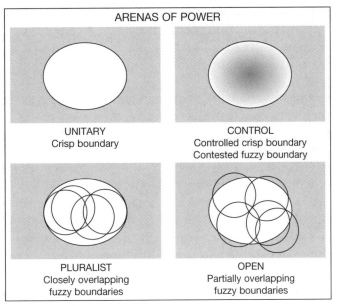

Figure 7.2 Arenas of power

identification of four approaches to culture change. We need to be clear about typology – Bate is concerned with approaches, not arenas, and with ways of changing culture, whereas the present debate is about power relationships; nevertheless, there are useful linkages. In broad terms, the aggressive approach is one likely to be adopted by dominant groupings in a Control arena, or by groups seeking to shift from Open to a Control arena. The conciliative approach will be found in the Pluralist arena, while the indoctrinative approach is most likely in the Unitary arena (it may also be used by groups seeking to shift from a Control to a Unitary arena).

On this basis we might expect the corrosive approach to correspond to the Open arena, but there is an important caveat here. Bate argues that the corrosives are fundamentally pluralists – something they have in common with the conciliatives. They see the organisation in terms of the informal network of power rather than formal authority. In this network power is diffuse and multi-directional; it is shared and there is no dominant party, no single individual or group who can impose a solution or course of action on the rest:

> However, corrosives and conciliatives differ in the way they manage that pluralism. Whereas conciliatives are prepared to be open and accommodating in outlook, corrosives tend to be covert and devious, skilfully manipulating relationships in order to achieve their ends. Theirs is a zero-sum game conception of life in which gains are made only at other people's expense. Sorokin puts it well when he says that people who hold to this frame of reference see the changing world as booty to be grabbed, and everyone within that world as a potential enemy rather than a brother. (1994: 186–7)

It is worth noting the values being imposed on this approach – it is covert, devious and manipulative. This is no doubt the normative position that would be taken by those facing such an approach – indeed, the corrosive approach is one to be used in a Control arena, by those in a subordinate position seeking to gain dominance.

The argument in this chapter is that strategies appropriate to the Open arena are much wider and deeper than the corrosive. Important to this is the question of legitimacy, which must always be seen as relative and multiple. In any context we can identify four types of legitimacy. At the first level, there is legal legitimacy – what is considered legitimate in the formal legal framework of the society within which the organisation is operating. At the second level, most commonly used in debates on power in organisations, there is the question of what is legitimate in the organisational context. In the Unitary and Control arenas strategies will be legitimate if they fit the dominant belief system. In the Pluralist and Open arenas different parties will have different views of legitimacy (although we can expect a greater convergence of view on this in the former, as compared to the latter). Part of the working agreement (tacit or explicit) will be an understanding of what activity is considered to be legitimate.

At the third level there will be a view on legitimacy by the various participant groups. In a Unitary arena this will coincide with the second level. In a Control arena the non-dominant groups will each have their own view of legitimacy, and this will influence the stand they take in relation to control (including acceptance, resistance or subversion). In the Pluralist and Open arenas group views on legitimacy will also vary, and relative influence will determine the extent to which they feed into legitimacy at the second level.

Finally, there will be individual views on legitimacy – what strategies an individual considers acceptable within their own ethical framework. At its simplest level, Christians or Jews who obey the Ten Commandments, or Buddhists who have taken the Ten Precepts, will have a somewhat different view of what is acceptable behaviour from those who have what Heirs (1986) has described as 'the Machiavellian mind', which is obsessed by internal politics and politicking.

It is useful to relate this to the different grounds for consenting or agreeing to something identified by Held (1987): coercion, or following orders; tradition; apathy; pragmatic acquiescence; instrumental acceptance; normative agreement; and ideal normative agreement. He reserves the term legitimacy for the last two: thus legitimacy is taken to imply that people follow rules and laws because they think them right and worthy of respect. The distinctions made above suggest that different partners will have different perspectives on this. For example, a dominant partner may consider that there is normative agreement. ('In the circumstances before us, and with the information available to us at that moment, we conclude it is "right" for us as an individual or member of a collectivity: it is what we genuinely should or ought to do' (Held 1987: 182). Another partner accepts through apathy ('We cannot be bothered one way or another'). A third accepts through pragmatic acquiescence ('Although we do not like a situation, we cannot imagine things being really different and so we accept what seems like fate'); while a fourth position is to accept through coercion ('There is no choice in the matter').

As we showed in Chapter 4, the question of the acceptability, or legitimacy, of 'political' activity in organisations is a central one in the debate on power, which is often identified as 'backstage activity' – something undoubtedly done, but not having the same public legitimacy as the rationally considered and logically phased public performance. This is the basis of the approach to strategic change put forward by Boddy and Buchanan (1992).

We would argue that this relegation of 'political' approaches to power is increasingly inappropriate. It rests on the assumption that there is a single rationality, either universally accepted or imposed (this, after all, is part of the belief system held by each party). But in many contexts there are multiple rationalities at play, based on divergent views of objectives, means and ends, and differing views of what is considered legitimate. At its simplest level one has only to listen to protagonists from different political parties debate in public – whatever the subject of debate, they will diverge dramatically in their treatment of it. A statistic will be shown to demonstrate diametrically opposite things; an event will be a tremendous success to one, a stupendous failure to the other. Leaving aside the question of how far this may be posturing, some divergence is inevitable in political debate, and the same applies at the organisational level.

Crucial to the present argument is the assertion that 'political' strategies are neither more nor less legitimate than others are, except in a relative context which depends on the relevant arena of power.

Power strategies

The arenas of power are the locations for the use of power strategies in and between organisations. Often the exercise of power takes place purely within a single arena, but there will be times, particularly in change management, when a shift between arenas is one of the objectives. We therefore need to consider strategies appropriate to work within and across boundaries, and in this chapter the focus is upon those that relate to interorganisational activity. For this reason we concentrate on the Pluralist and Open arenas. The Unitary arena will rarely be found in partnerships dealing with the wicked issues for the reasons discussed earlier. On occasion, a Control arena will be found where one partner effectively has the whip hand in determining what will happen. It is a moot point whether this can genuinely be called a partnership.

This is perhaps best illustrated by considering the difference between consultation and negotiation, as illustrated in Table 7.8, developed originally to illustrate the shift in stance which took place between the then South African government and the ANC at the time of the release of Nelson Mandela. When the relationship between the partners became one of negotiation, they entered the Open arena; before that, South Africa had been in the Control arena. If we

Table 7.8 Negotiation and consultation

Negotiation	Consultation
• It always costs you: be prepared for give-and-take • No one has complete control over the process, because everybody sitting around the table has equal status • The outcome is uncertain • When you sit down at the table, you want the people sitting opposite to be strong, and in a position to deliver on the agreement eventually negotiated when they report back to their people	• It need not cost you: you can always go back to square one because the final decision is in your hands • You can control the process • The outcome is uncertain but only on your own terms • The strength of the other parties is not central to the process; you are looking for their wisdom, not so much for their ability to deliver on the settlement

consider against this table the power strategies used in other 'peace initiatives' which have proved much less successful, such as Palestine/Israel, we perhaps get some clue as to one of the problems that exists.

When working in partnerships we need to think of three key questions we can ask in relation to the arenas of power. First, how do we work in an Open arena where power is zero sum? Second, when and how can we make an Open arena into a positive sum context? And third, when and how can we move it to become a Pluralist arena? It is naturally preferable to work in this arena where possible, but we always have to recognise that this may not be permanent. In considering these questions, we begin by looking at strategies appropriate in the Pluralist and Open arenas; out of this come some suggestions in response to both the first and the third questions. We then consider the notion of 'creative intelligence', which is the distinguishing characteristic between zero-sum and non-zero-sum Open arenas. This, therefore, helps us in answering the second question.

Just as the boundaries between the arenas are fuzzy, so are the distinctions between strategies. Many writers have produced lists of power strategies over the years, and these can be relevant to several of the groups discussed below. Thus an approach which seeks to shift from one arena to another is likely to embrace tactics used in both. In analysing what is happening, and what could happen, it is also necessary to consider intended shifts, unintended shifts, and shifts due to circumstances outside the volition or control of the participants.

The Pluralist arena

In this arena there are differences of view and no single dominant belief and power system, but the drive is towards agreement. Power strategies involving conciliation, compromise and consensus are therefore encouraged. Conflict is accepted – even encouraged – in formative stages of strategy and decision-making, but the assumption is that once a decision is taken, or a strategy set, there will be unity in executing it. The conciliative approach outlined by Bate will often be seen here.

Influence is an important root of power in this arena. Thus, effective participants need good negotiating skills. A valuable approach to this subject is the Harvard Negotiation Method (Fisher and Ury 1991; Fisher and Brown 1989) which takes as its starting point the contrast between soft and hard approaches to bargaining. Neither is satisfactory, and instead the principled approach is advocated. Central to this is the problem-solving approach: don't bargain over positions. The method has four key elements: separate the people from the problem; focus on interests, not positions; invent options for mutual gain; and insist on independent criteria. Grint (1997) also provides a number of guidelines for effective negotiating, inspired in part by the implications of fuzzy logic.

Lacking the ability to impose their views on others, participants in this arena need good influencing skills. Strategies to achieve and maintain agreement are also important in the Pluralist arena. Kanter (1989) suggests 'Eight I's that create successful We's', which can help in this.

One of the themes underpinning these approaches is that partnerships develop because something can be achieved which is not possible through individual action. But there is an important caveat to this discussion. The trust required in the Pluralist arena is often difficult to build, but easy to fracture. We will discuss below shifts from the Pluralist to the Open arena, which may be the intentional direction of one participant, or be a consequence of factors outside the control of the participants.

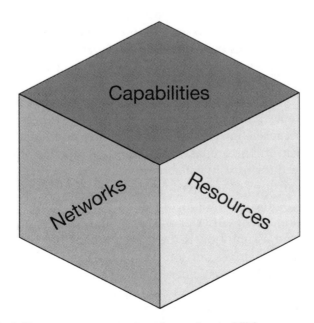

Figure 7.3 Black Box: resources, networks and capabilities

Participants need to bear these possibilities in mind, and an important aspect of this is what Lorange and Roos (1992) have called the 'Black Box' (Figure 7.3), whose contents keep the organisation in a stronger bargaining position, or ensure that it will not be totally stranded if the partnership does not work.

The Open arena

This is the most volatile arena. There is no dominant powerbase, and participants come from very different standpoints, so there is considerable room for conflict and the exercise of power plays. Unlike the Pluralist arena, this is likely to continue into the implementation phase – agreement will be achieved through negotiation, but will often be provisional. Strategy therefore will be 'emergent', and participants will continue to seek maximum advantage from their perspective.

The provisional nature of agreement is not necessarily a matter of participants always looking to what suits them best. This arena is often the one where wicked situations are played out. In these situations circumstances change, and each participant needs to recognise this and be able to respond. This can be seen on a day-to-day basis in two contemporary examples – Northern Ireland and Palestine/Israel.

Inter-organisational activity will often fall into this arena. If there are a number of different power bases involved, each with different values and rationalities, then only the most naïve is likely to argue that political strategies are illegitimate. Negotiating strategies will also be important, as in the Pluralist arena. This again highlights the contrast with Bate's corrosive approach, in which the players are operating in a zero-sum game. A fundamental principle of the Harvard Negotiating Method is to seek options for mutual gain, which can exist even where the participants have different values. Indeed it will on occasion be facilitated by this, since what is important to one because of their objectives and values may be far less important to another.

We now turn to shifts between arenas, and those relevant to this debate are summarised in Table 7.9. Here we can be briefer – not because they are less important, but because strategies will often involve combinations of those we have identified within the arenas. One important dimension that emerges is trust. Thus the need for trust in collaborative activity is a theme which emerges frequently in discussions of partnership. Barnes (1981: 108–10) identifies three assumptions which, in combination, prevent trust from forming. A person holds the first assumption when either/or thinking dominates choices and decision-making. The second assumption is the principle that hard is better than soft, which means that hard drives out soft. While the third holds that the world is a dangerous place requiring that a person adopt a position of pervasive mistrust to survive.

What is notable about these three assumptions, in terms of the present debate, is that they are rooted in the Cartesian–Newtonian paradigm, with its emphasis

Table 7.9 Crossing the boundaries

From	To	
Increased potential for agreement		
Open	Pluralist	One of the strongest features in the literature on strategic alliances is the emphasis on building and maintaining trust, and this is likely to be a key element of this strategy.
Move to multiple dominant power groups		
Unitary	Pluralist	This move may be desired if it is felt that the organisation is becoming too narrowly focused – as with those that are victims of the Icarus Paradox (Miller 1990). It will be necessary to create legitimacy for views other than the currently dominant one, whose primacy therefore needs to be challenged. In effect, there is an unfreezing job to be done here. The questioning of assumptions and the role of Devil's advocacy may both be appropriate.
Control	Open	Here the groups lacking dominance are seeking to change the balance of power, and weaken the power of the currently dominant power. The strategies suggested by Alinsky (1972) and Mintzberg (1983) will be relevant, and more generally tactics of sabotage, subversion, revolt, open challenge. This may well be the first part of a double act – first creating an Open arena, and then reverting back to Control, but with a new dominant power group.
Decreasing potential for agreement		
Pluralist	Open	This shift occurs as the views of participants come to diverge, and agreement becomes less sure, less binding. It may be a deliberate move by one or more participants due to changing strategic priorities, or the result of factors beyond the control of the participants.
Move to single dominant power group		
Pluralist	Unitary	The desire here is for unity, but through 'winning hearts and minds' rather than through coercion. Appeals to rationality may be appropriate, as will Bate's conciliative approach.
Open	Control	Here one of the currently rival camps is seeking dominance – a scenario familiar in revolutions, as for example in the Bolshevik rise to supremacy, and the subsequent rise of Stalin.

on crisp (two-valued) logic, quantitative approaches, and a competitive view of the world. A hypothesis that emerges is that trust may be easier to develop within the wider setting being developed here.

PROTOCOLS FOR DISCOURSE

We are moving from the Cartesian–Newtonian search for convincing arguments which require assent from all rationally thinking people to discourse in which persuasion and assent are central. In addition to dialogue and negotiating, already considered, we can draw on further interweaving strands, including rhetoric, principles of argumentation, and fair process.

Turning first to rhetoric, Shotter (1993) suggests that, in recent times, this has suffered at the hands of logic; in a debased form, it has been seen (from within a Cartesian perspective) as having to do with the emotional side of argumentation. Classically, however, rhetoric was seen as where a decision was needed and it was impossible to use methods of calculation aimed at absolute certainty. In such circumstances, because there are no agreed foundational truths or universal methods of inquiry, all conclusions must be arrived at by persuasion. An argument is settled, not by the production of calculations, but by giving good reasons to one's audience, particular reasons why they should, in that situation, assent to one's claims. (Good reasons are reasons which, at the time they are given, no one can challenge or criticise.) The role of the narrativist, outlined in Chapter 6, is very evident here.

The 'argumentative turn' in policy and planning (Fischer and Forester 1993) provides further ideas. We may take the argument of Healey (1993: 239) as illustrative. She suggests that

> We may shift our ideas, learn from each other, adapt to each other, and act in the world together. Systems of meaning or frames of reference shift and evolve in response to such encounters. But it can never be possible to construct a stable, fully inclusionary consensus, and the agreements we reach should be recognised as merely temporary accommodations of different, and differently adapting, perceptions.

In this, she sees herself as parting company with Habermas, by recognising the inherent localised specificity and untranslatability of systems of meaning. Shotter makes a similar comment:

> instead of the assumption that, given the appropriate background consensus, mutual understanding is normally obtained with ease and discourse about validity claims is only necessary during the breakdown of consensus, the assumption here is that understanding is always only partial and dispute about validity claims is an endemic part of everyday life activity. (1993: 176)

Our discussion is further enriched by considering the application of fair process to organisational theory, a subject which has been of growing interest in recent years and has been linked to business relationships (Kumar 1996; Chan Kim and Mauborgne 1997), entrepreneur–investor relation (Sapienza and Korsgaard 1996), organisational justice (Schminke, Amrose and Noel 1997), strategic decision-making in multinationals (Chan Kim and Mauborgne 1995, 1996) and long-term inter- and intra-organisational relationships (Darwin 1998).

The crucial distinction to be made in discussions of fair process is between distributive and procedural justice. People experience distributive justice when they believe that they have received the compensation or the resources they deserve. Procedural justice builds trust and commitment, which produce voluntary cooperation, which drives performance, leading people to go beyond the call of duty by sharing their knowledge and applying their creativity.

The approach outlined here allows us to escape the technocratic dichotomy, summarised by Fischer: 'Nothing is more irrational to technocratic theorists than the disjointed, incremental forms of decision-making (typically described as "muddling through") that result from a political commitment to democratic bargaining and compromise.... Technocratic writers see [these features] as a nightmare of irrationality' (1990: 22). The technocrat sees the alternative to the Modern/Cartesian–Newtonian approach of order and regulation to be irrationality and chaos, which at best leads to muddling through. What is proposed here is activity at the boundary – 'debate at the edge', embracing dialogue, rhetoric, argument and fair process.

Drawing on the various strands developed in this and earlier chapters, we can identify what may be called 'Protocols for Discourse':

- There will be no certainty or absolute truth.
- Self, environment and knowledge are mutually constructed, have fuzzy boundaries, and are in a state of becoming.
- Space needs to be created to allow self-organisation and emergence.
- Argument and methods of inquiry will usually be based on 'local', provisionally agreed premises.
- There will be multiple perspectives and multiple rationalities, and there is no expectation that these can be reduced to one.
- The search is for achievable levels of mutual understanding.
- Respectful, skilled discussion or dialogue is sought through:
  - Creating a process which is 'safely dangerous', especially when the context is Wicked. This process needs to interweave the individual and the collective, and to allow the space for reflection and inquiry.
  - Balancing advocacy with inquiry, which means that at times in the process there needs to be suspension of judgement.
  - Building shared meaning, by identifying assumptions, listening, exploring impasses, and using self-awareness and reflection as a resource.
  - Moving towards action through agreement.
- A reflexive and critical capacity should be maintained.
- The use of creative intelligence should be encouraged.
- Unanimity is not a requirement.
- Dissensus is as likely as consensus.
- Agreement will usually be provisional.

- Fairness is important, and both distributive and procedural justice are needed.

These contrast sharply with the style of thought and mode of inquiry that flow from the Cartesian–Newtonian paradigm. The latter has been summarised by Shotter (1993) as follows:

- True knowledge begins in doubt and distrust.
- Reality is studied as atomic matter in lawful mechanical motion.
- The world is treated as an 'external', physical world, devoid of any mental content.
- Proper knowledge, that is scientifically respectable knowledge, consists in beliefs that have been methodically shown to be true.
- Knowledge is a 'possession' and we are in an ownership relation to it.
- As true knowledge is a unified system of propositions, disagreement must be a sign of error.

Vignette 7.5

A public-private partnership

Some of the themes developed in this chapter can be illustrated by considering a partnership in practice. One of the authors was involved in a public-private partnership which had been set up to promote economic development in a major British city. For about three years this partnership worked extremely well, undertaking a number of activities, and at the same time, developing a growing sense of partnership between the public and private sectors, which had previously been at war with each other for a number of years. The different partners put different inputs into the partnership. The author was one of the representatives of the Local Authority, whose major input involved staff and their supporting costs. One of the other partners contributed a cash sum which was used for the various initiatives undertaken.

This latter partner changed its chief executive. The new person in post had a much less supportive view of the partnership than the woman who had previously been in post. He began to question what the partnership existed to do, and this led to every new activity becoming the subject of detailed discussion. What quickly became clear was that while this partner contributed less than 20 per cent of the total funding, it had the upper hand in negotiations. This was because the Local Authority's contribution was in kind, and was, in effect, unconditionally committed. By contrast their contribution, being in cash, was only available if projects were agreed. In effect, this partner had the power of veto over every activity.

There were two very clear lessons from this. The first was that it is not the size of resource that is important for a partner, but whether or not that resource is discretionary (see also Pfeffer 1992 on this). If it is discretionary, then it is part of their Black Box, since their continued involvement and continued agreement with the programme is necessary if the partnership is to receive this resource. By contrast, if the resource is already committed then it is, in effect, out of the Black Box.

The second lesson concerns the relationship between trust and contract. This was one of the first partnerships between the public and private sectors to be undertaken in this city. Before that there had been a period of almost open warfare. Perhaps because of this background, everyone proceeded very carefully, and sought to develop trust between the partners. At no time was a clear contractual arrangement established between the partners; instead the activity emerged and deepened as the trust deepened. This was fine as long as all the partners sought consensus and sought to work together. Once a single partner raised questions about the partnership's activities, it became very clear that trust in itself was not enough. If we had had a contract, or indeed any form of written agreement, however simple, to which we could refer, then the impasse which we experienced might not have occurred. Indeed to some extent a written agreement can be seen as a collective Black Box, tying together the various partners in a more or less formal way.

In effect, what had happened was that all participants had sought to act as though the partnership was in the Pluralist arena, when it needed just one change of stance to demonstrate that it was clearly in the Open arena. If participants had worked from the latter basis, then trust would not have been seen as a sine qua non: instead it would have been something to develop over time and thereby achieve the shift from Open to Pluralist arena. Meantime, it would still have been possible to undertake joint activity, because the partners were using creative intelligence.

Careful consideration from the outset of the organisational Black Box is not, on this reading, evidence of lack of trust in the other partners: it is a necessary precursor to the development of that trust. If this approach had been taken, then a more careful examination of the Local Authority's Black Box would have revealed how fragile it was, and led to action to strengthen it, so that when the testing time came, the Council representatives would have been in a much better position to meet it.

CONCLUSION AND DISCUSSION

We began this chapter by identifying the area of 'organised complexity' as one of growing interest to human inquiry. The central concept then introduced was that of the complex adaptive system, for which eleven properties were identified which bring together many of the key ideas in complexity theory. These are summarised in Table 7.10. Here the link is also made to Open arenas, drawing in part on the outline of the various arenas given in Table 7.6; this is done to reinforce the importance of power considerations. This is not to suggest that all Open arenas are complex adaptive systems – as the table suggests, this will be the case only if creative intelligence is present. Thus this is not a proposal of equivalence, but rather an argument that organisations operating as (or in) Open arenas will be (in) complex adaptive systems if there are real opportunities for the exercise of creative intelligence, thus allowing them to move from zero-sum situations.

We have here a conception of the organisation that differs radically from the two most common characterisations – the machine/clockwork and the

Table 7.10 Open arenas as complex adaptive systems

Complex adaptive systems	Open arenas
A network of many 'agents' acting in parallel	An Open arena is 'a network of many "agents" acting in parallel'
'Adaptively intelligent' – constantly seeing and imagining patterns, testing ideas, acting upon them, discarding them again–always evolving and learning	The summary position of the Open arena is that 'We need to get some agreement so that we can take action, but it will be provisional.' It is recognised that action requires some agreement, but through Creative Intelligence new ideas can emerge, to be tested, acted upon, perhaps discarded
Control tends to be highly dispersed	'All participate, although power differences mean some have more influence than others'
Coherent behaviour arises from competition and cooperation among the agents themselves. Competition can produce a very strong incentive for cooperation, and they are closely interrelated	'Competition can produce a very strong incentive for co-operation, and they are closely interrelated. 'Divergence may be significant, including some conflict' 'Objectives may not be agreed, but action can be agreed by negotiation'
Coevolution is a powerful force for emergence and self-organisation	If power and influence are dispersed, then development in the Open arena will take place only through self-organisation. As the agents involved develop a partial understanding of each other – coevolution – there is the possibility of emergence and self-organisation
Many levels of organisation, with agents at any one level serving as the building blocks for agents at a higher level	In an Open Arena there are not only different levels of organisation (especially in a multi-organisational or multi-divisional setting) but often there are also different Arenas at play (that is to say, one or more other Arenas may be nested within it).
Constantly revising and rearranging components as they gain experience. At some deep, fundamental level, processes of learning, evolution and adaptation are the same. And one of the fundamental mechanisms of adaptation in any given system is this revision and recombination of the building blocks	'Compromise may be provisional – subject to change when the opportunity arises for one or more participants'
Anticipate the future, building models and implicit predictions based on experience	Where creative intelligence is exercised, those involved in the Open arena have the possibility of anticipating the future, building models and developing implicit predictions

Table 7.10 *continued*

Complex adaptive systems	Open arenas
New opportunities are always being created by the system. It is therefore essentially meaningless to talk about a complex adaptive system being in equilibrium: the system can never get there. It is always unfolding, always in transition	The provisional nature of agreement in Open Arenas means that they are always unfolding (anticipating the next Chapter, a method based on action research and action learning is therefore appropriate)
Function best in a situation between order and disorder	An Open arena is unstable, as power, influence and interest shift
Acquire information about their environment and their own interaction with that environment, identifying regularities in that information, condensing those regularities into a kind of 'schema' or model, and acting in the real world on the basis of that schema.	The agents in an Open arena 'acquire information about their environment and their own interaction with that environment, identifying regularities in that information, condensing those regularities into a kind of "schema" or model, and acting in the real world on the basis of that schema'.

organism. It differs also from the snakepit (Schwartz 1990), although aspects of the snakepit will be present. Indeed, it is concern about the lack of a political dimension to complexity theory applications that has given rise to the discussion on power above. We can compare and contrast the complexity approach by considering again the four interrelated domains of the paradigm introduced in Chapter 1. This is done in Table 7.11.

Table 7.11 Domains of the paradigms

Modern	Snakepit	Complexity
Landscape		
Clockwork and machine Plan and map Foundations	The snakepit	Rainforest
Mindset		
Everybody knows what the organisation is about and is concerned solely with carrying out its mission; people are basically happy in their work; the level of anxiety is low; people interact with each other in frictionless, mutually supportive cooperation; and if there are any managerial problems at all, these are	Everything is always falling apart, and people's main activity is to see that it doesn't fall on them; nobody really knows what is going on, though everyone cares about what is going on because there is danger in not knowing; anxiety and stress are constant companions; and people take little pleasure in	Accept unpredictability and the likelihood of emergence. Search for and discover patterns beneath complexity. Accept fuzziness (and distinguish fuzzy thinking from sloppy thinking!). Identify and use both positive and negative feedback. Give due weight to the capacity for self-organisation, and the freedom that must

Table 7.11 *continued*

Modern	Snakepit	Complexity
basically technical problems, easily solved by someone who has the proper skills and knows the correct techniques of management.	dealing with each other, doing so primarily to use others for their own purposes or because they cannot avoid being so used themselves. Managerial problems here are experienced as intractable, and managers feel that they have done well if they are able to make it through the day.	be given to facilitate this. Address the need to develop the organisation's intelligence and ability to generate knowledge. Recognise codependent arising: the mutually interactive creation of the organisation and its environment. Accept the need for disruptive action. Exercise what the poet John Keats called Negative Capability: the ability to be 'in uncertainties, mysteries, doubts'. Recognise that strategy in complex situations (the Wild and Wicked) will almost always be action-driven. Recognise that we are talking here about the strategy of Becoming: of flux, change and transformation.

Language

Control	Chaos	Complex
Order	Disorder	Order within chaos
Modern	Postmodern	Constructivist
Objective	Subjective	Interconnected
Realist	Non-realist	Neither
Analytical	Instinctive	Evolving
Safe	Unsafe	Dynamic
Logical	Illogical	Fuzzy logic
Certain	Uncertain	Adaptive
Foundations	No foundations	Web or net
Predictable	Unpredictable	Pattern
One best way	Any way	Multiple approach
Structured	Unstructured	Pattern
Planned	Unplanned	Dynamic capability
Competitive	*Competitive*	*Coevolution*

Table 7.11 *continued*

Modern	Snakepit	Complexity
Toolkit		
SWOT	Many of those in the previous column, plus	All of those in the previous two columns, plus
PEST(EC)		
Five-force analysis		
Value chain	Stakeholder analysis	Whole systems intervention
Generic strategy	Levers of power	Colour thinking
Ashridge Mission models	Understanding the unwritten rules	Use of metaphor
Critical success factors	Understanding defensive routines	Principled negotiation
Balanced scorecard		Dialogue and skilful discussion
Plan		Critical action research and learning
Cultural web		Systems thinking
Stakeholder analysis		Using paradox
Levering and stretching resources		Ecological approaches
Force field analysis		Imaginisation
Organisation life cycle		
Structure: forms and forces		
Product portfolio mix		
Dynamics of globalisation		
Alliance development and maintenance		
Scenario planning		
Knowledge management		

We can integrate the ideas developed in this chapter into a number of principles and concepts that emerge from the varied theoretical debates that have been reviewed.

1 Encourage democracy – recognising that this may well be a contested arena

The first principle focuses on control. A commitment to emancipation and greater democracy in organisation implies a preference for the Pluralist and Open arenas of power, rather than the Unitary or Control arenas. This is equally implied by complexity theory. Complex adaptive systems need to be far from equilibrium – the characteristic of Unitary and Control arenas, by contrast, is stability (whether voluntary or enforced). New forms of organisation consistent with the thinking of complexity theory are, as we have seen, now widely espoused, but they are likely to fall foul of the entrenched power interests that they threaten. One of the advantages of the Cartesian–Newtonian synthesis for those in power is that it helps legitimate their position – it is an argument for control, which is seen as both possible and desirable. 'Mastery of nature' translates into management control and control of the environment.

Logic and language control in other ways. Crisp, two-valued logic facilitates a rigid perspective – the crisp boundary between organisation and environment, the neat categorisation of events and circumstances. It encourages groupthink – 'you are either with us or against us' – and hence acts as a driver towards a Unitary or Control arena. If there can be only right or wrong, then the notion of multiple perspectives becomes questionable – there are at most two perspectives, and one of these is invalid.

At the same time, the open arena is contested, for different perspectives relate not only to intent, but also to values and beliefs – not least, the value of discourse and the way in which it is conducted. This issue has been approached in earlier chapters from several directions, not in the belief that a definitive solution could be found, but on the basis that these different approaches offer mutual support. Out of them it is possible to develop protocols for discourse which will never be absolute, but can prove helpful in progressing it.

2 Facilitate multiple perspectives

The value of multiple perspectives is the second principle to emerge, and this relates to individuals as well as to groups.

3 Recognise fuzzy boundaries

Third, we have seen the importance of fuzzy boundaries. They make life more difficult, and the pressures towards 'concept chopping' are understandable. But this can deny us a richness of perspective. Thus the arenas of power are not distinct, although for the sake of exposition it was necessary to set them out in this way. The axes are not either/or – each is a continuum, and organisations shift along them. They are also holographic – within an organisation that is primarily a Control arena there will be pockets of pluralist or open behaviour, or people seeking the opportunity to shift in such directions. And equally within Pluralist or Open arenas there will be pressure towards the dominance of a single perspective, shifting upward on that axis.

4 Keep thinking and action in dynamic tension

Shifting far from equilibrium – in these ideas we have a fourth linking theme, that of dynamic tension, or dynamic poise, as outlined above. Dynamic tension is absent in the Unitary arena, and suppressed in the Control arena. It is ever-present where democracy is taken seriously. Multiple perspectives, democracy and participation are closely linked, and an important issue, therefore, is to consider methods that facilitate these, as well as barriers that hinder them. A number of these have been outlined, leading to the Protocols for Discourse.

Dynamic tension is about being at 'the edge'. This could be the edge between order and chaos: a number of writers, including Pascale (1991) and Miller (1990), have identified the value of the tension this can create (including 'constructive conflict'). Or it could be the boundary between two 'mutually exclusive' groups, described earlier as 'a very high tension zone'.

5 Value process and put trust in process

Fifth, we see the importance of process – strategy is about becoming, not being. But the insights of complexity theory allow us to take this further. Self-organisation is a direct challenge to control, and of course control mechanisms have frequently been used by management against it, as the history of trade unionism, as well as technocracy, Taylorism and Fordism, demonstrate. Self-organisation may be considered unnecessary, undesirable or something to be feared. Or it may be seen as desirable, but unpredictable, in danger of running 'out of control' – another form of fear (and another example of dichotomous thinking – control or chaos).

Complexity theory suggests that organisations should have 'trust in process'. We shall see later the implications of such an approach, which is undoubtedly one of the most difficult for managers to embrace. Consultation is safer than negotiation; involvement is safer than participation. 'Empowerment', whereby power is 'bestowed upon employees by progressive, enlightened managers' (Alvesson and Willmott 1996: 162), has within it the recognition that power can be taken back if the consequences prove undesirable. A closer look at empowerment, as we shall see, sometimes indicates that it is devolution only of responsibility, not power.

6 Allow for and encourage proactive emergence

Linked to 'trust in process' is a sixth theme, that of proactive emergence. In contrast to the reductive approach of traditional strategic planning, complexity theory takes emergence seriously. The approach to logic and language presented here, together with the approach to dialogue and discourse, are intended to facilitate emergence, and again the pluralist and open arenas will be those in which this is most likely to happen, since multiple perspectives can provide the catalyst for new thinking.

7 Facilitate learning

The seventh linking theme concerns learning. Complex adaptive systems are learning systems, and it may be argued that learning is more likely in Pluralist and Open arenas.

Bateson's treatment of learning was introduced earlier, in particular the idea that there are levels of learning that are different in type. It was argued that levels of change relate closely to this, but that there should be some caution about treating the levels as entirely distinct – the example of Copernicus was given. Where, for example, does 'first-order' incremental change end and 'second order' discontinuous changes begin? This is not to argue for blurring, but to stress again the value of thinking about the 'edge' – the fuzzy boundary between the two may itself offer potential for learning, as again the experience of the Copernican Revolution shows.

8 Accept (indeed embrace) the absence of certainty and foundations

The eighth, and final, theme is one that has underpinned the entire discussion: there is no certainty, there are no foundations, and there are no absolutes. For those imbued with the Cartesian–Newtonian synthesis (which in the Western world at least means pretty well everyone) this is not easy.

NOTES

1 A personal anecdote illustrates this. While working as a local government officer I was the Company Secretary of a public–private partnership. A dispute arose between the manager of the company and one of the local authority's departments, which was providing a contracted service to the company. I sought to protect the department's interests in discussions at the Company Board, and was criticised by another Board member who said that I should be representing the company's interests. But I was only on the Board by virtue of being a representative of the Council, and appointed by it. So was I internal or external?

2 The *Prajnaparamita Sutra* was developed in the second-century BCE and is the major text of the Madhyamika school. The words mean the 'Perfection of Wisdom Sutra'.

3 Once more the machine image returns to the analysis!

REFERENCES

Alinsky, S. (1972) *Rules for Radicals*, New York: Vintage Books.

Alvesson, M. and H. Willmott (1996) *Making Sense of Management*, London: Sage.

Ansoff, H.I. and P.A. Sullivan (1993) 'Optimizing Profitability in Turbulent Environments: A Formula for Strategic Success', *Long Range Planning*, 26(5): 11–23.

Archer, J. and B. Lloyd (1982) *Sex and Gender*, Cambridge: Cambridge University Press.

Barnes, L.B. (1981) 'Managing the Paradox of Organizational Trust', *Harvard Business Review*, (March–April): 107–116.

Bartlett, C.A. and S. Ghoshal (1994) 'Changing the Role of Top Management: Beyond Strategy to Purpose', *Harvard Business Review*, November.

Bate, P. (1994) *Strategies for Cultural Change*, London: Butterworth Heinemann.

Bateson, G. (1973) *Steps to an Ecology of Mind*, St Albans: Granada.

Bettis, R.A. and P.K. Prahalad (1995) 'The Dominant Logic: Retrospective and Extension', *Strategic Management Journal*, 16.

Boddy, D. and D. Buchanan (1992) *The Expertise of the Change Agent*, London: Prentice Hall.

Bohm, D. and F.D. Peat (1987) *Science, Order and Creativity*, London: Routledge.

Bohm, D., D. Factor and P. Garrett (1991) Dialogue: A Proposal [posted on the Internet] http://www.ratical.org/many worlds/K/dialogueProposal.html

Bolman, L.G. and T.E. Deal (1991) *Reframing Organisations*, San Francisco: Jossey Bass.

Capra, F. (1996) *The Web of Life*, London: Flamingo.

Chan Kim, W. and R. Mauborgne (1995) 'A Procedural Justice Model of Strategic Decision Making: Strategy Content Implications in the Multinational', *Organization Science*, 6(1).

Chan Kim, W. and R. Mauborgne (1996) 'Procedural Justice and Managers' In-role and Extra-role Behavior: The Case of the Multinational', *Management Science*, 42(4).

Chan Kim, W. and R. Mauborgne (1997) 'Fair Process: Managing in the Knowledge Economy', *Harvard Business Review* (July).

Collins, J.C. and J.I. Porras (1994) *Built to Last*, London: Century Business.

Darwin, J. (1992) *The Network Organization*, MBA Dissertation, Sheffield Business School.

Darwin, J. (1996a) 'Dynamic Poise: Toward a New Style of Management – Part One', *Career Development International*, 1(5).

Darwin, J. (1996b) 'Dynamic Poise: Toward a New Style of Management – Part Two', *Career Development International*, 1(7).

Darwin, J. (1998) 'Partnerships: What Type of Relationship?', in L.C. Montanheiro, R.H. Haigh, D.S. Morris and N. Hrovatin (eds) *Public and Private Sector Partnerships: Fostering Enterprise*, Sheffield: SHU Press.

Emery, F.E. and E.L. Trist (1965) 'The causal texture of organisational environments', *Human Relations*, 18(1): 21–32.

Fischer, F. (1990) *Technocracy and the Politics of Expertise*, Newbury Park, CA: Sage.

Fischer, F. and J. Forester (1993) *The Argumentative Turn in Policy Analysis and Planning*, London: UCL Press.

Fisher, R. and S. Brown (1989) *Getting Together*, London: Penguin.

Fisher, R. and W. Ury (1991, 2nd edition) *Getting to Yes*, London: Business Books.

Flood, R.L. and M.C. Jackson (1991) *Creative Problem Solving: Total Systems Intervention*, Chichester: John Wiley and Sons.

Ford, J.D. and L.W. Ford (1994) 'Logics of Identity, Contradiction, and Attraction in Change', *Academy of Management Review*, 19(4): 756–85.

Gell-Mann, M. (1995) *The Quark and the Jaguar*, London: Abacus.

Grant, D. and C. Oswick (1996) *Metaphor and Organizations*, London: Sage.

Grint, K. (1995) *Management: A Sociological Introduction*, Cambridge: Polity Press.

Grint, K. (1997) *Fuzzy Management*, Oxford: Oxford University Press.

Harré, R. (1984) *The Philosophies of Science*, Oxford: Oxford University Press.

Healey, P. (1993) 'Planning through Debate: The Communicative Turn in Planning Theory', in F. Fischer and J. Forester (1993) *The Argumentative Turn in Policy Analysis and Planning*, London: UCL Press.

Heirs, B. (1989) *The Professional Decision Thinker*, London: Grafton.

Held, D. (1987) *Models of Democracy*, Cambridge: Polity Press.

Ingvar, D. (1985) 'Memory of the Future: An Essay on the Temporal Organisation of Conscious Awareness', *Human Neurobiology*, 127–36.

Jacobs, R.W. (1994) *Real Time Strategic Change*, San Francisco: Berrett-Koehler.

Jun, J.S. and W.B. Storm (eds) (1973) *Tomorrow's Organizations: Challenges and Strategies*, Scott, Foresman and Company.

Kanter, R.M. (1989) *When Giants Learn to Dance*, London: Simon and Schuster.

Keizer, J.A. and G.J.J. Post (1996) 'The Metaphoric Gap as a Catalyst of Change', in C. Oswick and D. Grant (1996) *Organisation Development: Metaphorical Explorations*, London: Pitman Publishing.

Kelly, S. and M.A. Allison (1999) *The Complexity Advantage*, New York: McGraw-Hill.

Kiel, L.D. (1994) *Managing Chaos and Complexity in Government*, San Francisco: Jossey Bass.

Klir, G.J. and Bo Yuan (1995) *Fuzzy Sets and Fuzzy Logic: Theory and Applications*, London: Prentice Hall.

Koestler, A. (1959) *The Sleepwalkers*, Harmondsworth: Penguin.

Kosko, B. (1994) *Fuzzy Thinking*, London: HarperCollins.

Kumar, N. (1996) 'The Power of Trust in Manufacturer–Retailer Relationships', *Harvard Business Review* (November).

Lakoff, G. and M. Johnson (1980) *Metaphors We Live By*, Chicago: University of Chicago Press.

Laszlo, E. and C. Laszlo (1997) *The Insight Edge*, Westport, CT: Quorum.

Lerner, A.W. and J. Wanat (1983) 'Fuzziness and Bureaucracy', *Public Administration Review*, November: 500–9.

Lewins, F. (1995) *Transsexualism in Society*, South Melbourne: Macmillan.

Lissack, M. and J. Roos (1999) *The Next Common Sense*, London: Nicholas Brealey.

Lorange, P. and J. Roos (1992) *Strategic Alliances*, Oxford: Basil Blackwell.

Marx, K. (1973) *The Revolutions of 1848*, London: Penguin, in association with *New Left Review* (first published 1848).

Miller, D. (1990) *The Icarus Paradox*, New York: Harper Business.

Mintzberg, H. (1983) *Power in and around Organizations*, London: Prentice Hall.

Morgan, G. (1997) *Images of Organization*, London: Sage.

Nhat Hanh, T. (1994) *Zen Keys*, New York: Doubleday.

Pascale, R. (1991) *Managing on the Edge*, Harmondsworth: Penguin.

Peat, F.D. (1995) *Blackfoot Physics: A Journey into the Native American Universe*, New York: Fourth Estate.

Pfeffer, J. (1992) *Managing with Power*, Boston, MA: Harvard Business School Press.

Pratt, J., D. Plamping and P. Gordon (1999) *Partnership: Fit for Purpose?*, London: King's Fund Publishing.

Rittel, H.W. and M.M. Webber (1973) 'Dilemmas in a General Theory of Planning', *Policy Sciences*, 4: 155–69.

Rumelt, R.P., D.E. Schendel and D.J. Teece (1994) *Fundamental Issues in Strategy: A Research Agenda*, Boston, MA: Harvard Business School Press.

Sapienza, H.J. and N.A. Korsgaard (1996) 'Procedural Justice in Entrepreneur–Investor Relations', *Academy of Management Journal*, 39(3).

Schminke, M., M.L. Amrose and T.W. Noel (1997) 'The Effect of Ethical Frameworks on Perceptions of Organizational Justice', *Academy of Management Journal*, 40(5).

Schwartz, H.S. (1990) *Narcissistic Process and Corporate Decay*, New York: New York University.

Scott-Morgan, P. (1994) *The Unwritten Rules of the Game: Master Them, Shatter Them and Break Through the Barriers to Organizational Change*, New York: McGraw-Hill.

Senge, P.M. et al. (1994) *The Fifth Discipline Fieldbook*, London: Nicholas Brealey.

Sheppard, B.H. and M. Tuchinsky (1996) 'Micro-OB and the Network Organization', in R.M. Kramer and T.R. Tyler, *Trust in Organizations: Frontiers of Theory and Research*, London: Sage.

Shotter, J. (1993) *Conversational Realities: Constructing Life through Language*, London: Sage.

Spencer, L. (1989) *Winning through Participation*, Dubuque, IA: Kendall Hunt.

Stacey, R.D. (1996a) *Strategic Management and Organizational Dynamics*, London: Pitman.

Stacey, R.D. (1996b) *Complexity and Creativity in Organizations*, San Francisco: Berrett-Koehler.

Star, S.L. (1991) 'Power, Technologies and the Phenomenology of Conventions', in J. Law (ed.) *A Sociology of Monsters: Essays on Power, Technology and Domination*, London: Routledge.

Tarnas, R. (1991) *The Passion of the Western Mind*, London: Pimlico.

Ury, W. (1991) *Getting Past No*, London: Business Books.

Varela, F.J., E. Thompson and E. Rosch (1993) *The Embodied Mind*, Cambridge, MA: MIT Press.

Waldrop, M.M. (1992) *Complexity*, London: Viking.

Watzlawick, P., J.H. Beavin and D.D. Jackson (1968) *Pragmatics of Human Communication*, London: Faber and Faber.

Watzlawick, P., J. Weakland and R. Fisch (1974) *Change: Principles of Problem Formation and Problem Resolution*, New York: W.W. Norton.

Weaver, W. (1948) 'Science and Complexity', *American Scientist*, 36(4): 536–44.

Weisbord, M.R. and S. Janoff (1995) *Future Search: An Action Guide*, San Francisco: Berrett-Koehler.

Weisbord, M.R. et al. (1992) *Discovering Common Ground*, San Francisco: Berrett-Koehler.

Zadeh, L.A. (1965) 'Fuzzy Sets', *Information and Control*, 8: 338–53.

Part 3

LINKING CHANGE TO CURRENT THEMES

Chapter 8

CHANGE AND THE DESIGN OF ORGANISATIONS

The overall aims of this chapter are to:

1 Explore the contribution of ideas about organisational design as drives for organisational efficiency and effectiveness.

2 Enable the reader to develop analytical understanding of the design issues that lie behind management structures as a key aspect of the architecture of organisations. Particular attention, by way of example, will be given to delayering as part of a design strategy used by many organisations, as rhetoric, to restructure or re-engineer in order to become more effective.

3 Enable the reader to explore the ways in which the design strategy of downsizing has moved from fashion to strategic imperative and then to problematic status. This is the process by which the organisation sheds part of its labour force either through redundancy or through putting parts of its non-core business to be resourced by outside suppliers.

4 Enable the reader to develop an understanding of the significance of debates about organisational design that are located in the issues of modernism and postmodernism as underpinning philosophical and essentially practical aspects of organisational design.

5 Enable the reader to identify the ways in which these debates about organisational design can be located in issues of reflexive crafting, of understanding the design mindset from which one comes and its implications.

INTRODUCTION

It is a truism to observe that the design of organisations is the outcome of human will and intent, that 'the goals ... the rules ... and the status structures ... have not spontaneously emerged in the course of social interaction but have been consciously designed *a priori* to anticipate and guide interaction and activities' (Blau and Scott 1966: 5). In terms of conventional organisations this general statement aligns with the contestable (e.g. Bartlett and Ghoshal 1996) but traditional assertion that 'the primary responsibility of top management is to determine an organization's goals, strategy and design, therein adapting the organization to a changing environment. Middle managers do much the same thing for major departments within the guidelines provided by top management' (Daft 1995: 43). At the same time, however, the act of design – as with other aspects of the activities of members of the organisation – is pervaded by the mindset, the mental model brought to the activity. The approach to organisation design comes from emotional commitments, the tacit knowledge and aesthetic sentiments (Strati 2000: 91) of those responsible for the design and its enactment. These mediate the rational aspects, those 'clearly thought out, subtle, multi-factor model(s) of decision choices for the firm and its environment' (Clark 2000: 311) to which the designer may have recourse.

There are a number of discourses that explore, with varying degrees of intellectual rigour, reasons for new approaches to organisational design. Because the range of design ideas is so wide, we have chosen to identify only a few issues within this chapter in order to show that although some design issues achieve high status, they may prove to be somewhat transient. A key rhetoric, for example, has been the discourse of re-engineering. This focuses on the idea that organisations need to be more responsive to their customers. This suggests that the people who really matter in the organisation are those closest to the customers and they need to be able to 'feed back' to those with leadership responsibility without the cumbersome intervention of hierarchies. This represents a movement from organisations designed as task-oriented to organisations that are process-oriented. This involves what Hammer (1996) refers to as deep system design issues. These include such matters as development of the capability to learn, development of human processes that encourage depth of understanding of organisational change issues, the development of 'omnidirectional communication channels' (Hammer 1996: 223) and the development of appropriate values and beliefs to support the core customer facing ideology (Hammer 1996). This rhetoric is often aligned with that of the design opportunities brought about by Information Technology (e.g. Davenport 1993, among many others).

Another related rhetoric is to do with the idea that organisations are living in turbulent times. This is discussed in Chapter 6. Therefore, they need to reconstruct themselves so that they can be more responsive to an ever-changing environment, including issues such as globalisation. They need to adopt designs that mean that they can overcome the challenges of complexity. One of many approaches to this has been to take the principles of chaos theory (e.g. Stacey 1991) as a number of key concepts and to relate them in a more or less mechanistic manner to issues of organisational design. In this sense Stacey is following a long line of writers who have attempted to conceptualise organisation theory and design from the perspective of a scientific or biological metaphor with greater or lesser degrees of success (Morgan 1997).

It is argued that when people are liberated from the traditional controls that management imposes on them in the traditional organisation they will become liberated. If the purposes of the organisation are understood fully, they will begin to take on responsibility and fulfil the organisational mission – the organisation will become more effective and efficient. In order for the organisation to achieve complex purposes and to undertake change with maximum flexibility, there is a need to get away from the traditional division of labour, i.e. people undertaking specific and specialised tasks. Instead there is a need for people to be able to interact with each other and with the external environment in order to understand what is going on, both outside and inside the organisation. This means that people no longer have the familiar anchors of hierarchy. Instead they become self-organising. Organisation design is such that members 'in effect spontaneously communicate with each other and abruptly cooperate in coordinated and concerted common behaviour' so that the organisation can develop creativity so that it 'continually confronts instability and crisis' (Stacey 1996: 330). Stacey has subsequently clarified (or muddied, it depends on the reader's perspective) this position. He asserts that self-organisation relates to systems and not individual members. The design parameters of self-organisation are such that system members are engaged in co-creation with an understanding of the consequences of their actions. Despite the appearance of spontaneity there is a sense of order, a sense of purpose and priority in their actions. Members are constrained by, for example, the actions of others. The principle of self-organisation is independent of issues of power and empowerment (Stacey 2000: 234).

In order to facilitate personal responsibility in the workplace Stacey places his faith in 'extraordinary management'. This, he suggests, is about such things as 'questioning and shattering paradigms, and then creating new ones . . . a process of persuasion and conversion, requiring the contributions of champions ... the use of intuitive, political, group learning modes of decision-making and self organising forms of control in open-ended change situations' (1996: 72). In this design organisations are pervaded by a sense of networks with managers as the lynchpin around which the communities of practice get on with their work. Other writers see the leader who is charismatic or transformational as the key design agent in organisational change. They are able to give members an overriding sense of purpose and vision, and certainly in the delayered organisation a sense of shared purpose is what binds the place together. Hunt (1991) provides a comprehensive overview of the issues involved in this perspective. Other writers assert that the underpinning feature of organisational design is the way the architecture of the organisation is an expression, the embodiment, of the core ideology of the organisation. This in turn relates to the idea that organisation design should be geared to the development and facilitation of capability (e.g. Hamel and Prahalad 1994) and learning (e.g. Senge 1990).

These conceptions of organisational design slide into discourses that treat the idea of the postmodern organisation as a millennial dream and post-millennial achievement, and the modernist organisation as a morally undesirable construct (e.g. Gephart 1996). In Chapter 6 we saw how the postmodern perspective can be seen as a powerful philosophical rebuttal to and deconstruction of the underpinnings of modernism. As we saw in that chapter, the postmodern movement draws together many aspects of the *Weltanschauung* of the late twentieth and the early twenty-first centuries. Part of that debate comes from more concrete aspects of life than philosophy. Debates in modernism and postmodernism and their relationship to organisational theory and design can be located in, for example, architecture (McAuley 1996; Hatch 1997). Modernist architecture is highly structured and ordered. It tends to be linear and where there are curves they are designed to provide linkages with the linear. In this design, form always fits function. The absence of non-functional decoration is a statement of the rigour of modernism. There is no unnecessary distraction from the functionalist aesthetic. This aesthetic can accommodate both the elegance and purity of the line or the 'in your face' modernism of the new brutalism. Politically, also, modernism can show two faces. Commenting on a particular modernist building (the De La Warr pavilion) Deller comments that the architect 'achieved and put into practice what modernism was all about: the idea of democratising urban space and making the best of architecture available to the people is perfectly summed up in this beautiful building' (2001: 13). Its other face is the symbolisation of repression, as we noted in Chapter 1. Postmodernism, by contrast, in architecture, is a search to 'renew traditions of making built spaces symbolically rich and meaningful by invoking past styles and reinterpreting them using the marvellous new materials and construction techniques that inspired the functionalist movement' (Hatch 1997: 43). Of course, modernists would claim that *their* architecture is 'symbolically rich and powerful' as well. The two perspectives reflect different mindsets, different gazes at the world, different meanings in architecture.

These issues of modernism and postmodernism are also part and parcel of issues of organisational design. Whilst organisational theory itself has perhaps been more influenced by modernist and postmodernist philosophy from the French tradition (Hatch 1997), these realist themes of modernism and postmodernism that affect our appreciation and understanding of architecture, art, music and so on are part of the *Weltanschauung*. These issues inevitably affect those who design organisations. Thus, if we hold to the tenets of postmodernism we will tend towards a mindset that sees the ways in which people work together and the systems in which they operate as complex and interrelated. Because the postmodernist is not so concerned to see the linkage between form and function the postmodernist could envisage new systems and ways of working together constantly arising quite spontaneously and then disappearing as their purpose disappears. To the modernists this would not be appealing. It reflects a waste of energy and a refusal to craft carefully. An interesting part of the postmodern narrative is that there is – in management terms – no way in which there is an absolute right and wrong way of doing things. Management decision-making becomes subjective; organisation design needs to acknowledge that decisions made by members are the best that can be done in the circumstances. This is very different from the modernist perspective where what is legitimated, in the organisational design, is the degree of control exercised by the manager. The manager is responsible for the text, for authorial authority, so he or she is able to take an objective stance about the 'best' way to manage situations. It is an inbuilt aspect of the design that managers have the best interests of the organisation on their side. The ways in which these two mindsets produce profoundly different responses to the development of organisational designs will be discussed below.

A MORAL FABLE IN ORGANISATIONAL DESIGN – THE CASE OF DELAYERING

To think of organisations is to think of issues of design. In modern times, from Weber onwards, the achievement of requisite design has been a preoccupation of theorists about and actors within organisations. Their preoccupations reflect and shape the ways in which organisations relate to the society in which they are located. Weber (as we shall discuss later) takes the austere view of the macro sociologist in developing an understanding of the profound strengths and limitations of the bureaucratic form as design. Roethlisberger and Dixon (1939) are fascinated, at the level of design, with the relationship between the formal design, the informal organisation, and what they call the ideological organisation of the organisation. Their magnificent observation and theorising gently hints at the systems approach to design which was popularised in the 1960s (e.g. Katz and Kahn 1966) and which remains a pervasive image in many aspects of organisation design. There is, however, a more recent school that attempts to get away from systems-driven approaches to management and design to emphasise organisational processes. It is suggested that this approach to design, the so-called 'individualized corporation, does not mean stripping the organization of all its formal systems, policies and procedures. It does require redefining them so that they support rather than subvert top management's ability to focus on the organization's people' (Bartlett and Ghoshal 1996: 201).

In the midst of the great theorists and the actors are the gurus, the advocates of particular approaches to the design of organisation. Huczynski (1993) discusses the way business folk-heroes work on beleaguered managers. He suggests that their claims 'to create order out of disorder' and the provision to managers 'with new systems of coherence and continuity' (Huczynski 1993: 198) give managers a degree of temporary solace in a troubled world. Perhaps the first guru in management itself was Taylor – his tone of passionate advocacy rivals that of the great gurus of our own age. For example, in his advocacy of scientific management (the redesign of the management function) he promises that

> the initiative of the workman ... is obtained practically with the greatest regularity.... By far the greater gain under scientific management comes from the new, the very great and the extraordinary burdens and duties which are voluntarily assumed by those on the management's side. These new burdens and new duties are so unusual and so great that they are to the men used to managing under the old school almost inconceivable. (1912: 275)

The theme – that it is the managers who ultimately bear the burden of the maintenance of progress – is pervasive and renders them heroic. However, if managers take these recipes seriously they are liable, Huczynski (1993) suggests, to run into problems. A key problematic is the imposition on organisational members of 'recipes' that are frequently short-termist where the underlying issues are not. This will be illustrated by a discussion of two of the major themes of organisational design of the present period – delayering and downsizing.

In Chapter 3 we considered the relationship between the metaphors in use in organisations and the deeper ideological commitments held by members. It is, in the light of that discussion, useful to look at the language that lies behind the imagery of downsizing and delayering. Palmer and Dunford (1996) explored a range of what they termed popular management texts that explore these issues as core issues in organisational redesign. What they found was that by and large the imagery used to describe the pre-downsizing state suggested that 'the current state of organizations can be seen as akin to an overweight person' (1996: 100) existing in an environment that was threatening and which needs strong action. Lying alongside these metaphors of the body corporate as bloated, there are also, they suggest, counter-metaphors. These counter-metaphors do not deny the necessity for the core activity, but warn that the action needs to be taken judiciously. They provide the warnings against excess, almost like a government health warning, in that they do not stop the manager from undertaking the action but express nil liability if it ends in tears.

This process of shifting imagery and the way in which it affects organisation design may be seen in relation to the imagery surrounding the role of middle management. In many organisations the repository of truth – the model of organisational objectivity – lay with the middle managers. They were the people who really *cared* about the organisation (e.g. Campanis 1970; Floyd and Woolridge 1994; Grint and Case 2000), although there is evidence (Stroh and Reilly 1997) that as a consequence of the development of the philosophy of delayering, middle managers have also come to see their careers in rather a more instrumental, self-serving fashion. Traditionally, senior managers come and go, and the 'employees' have their own axes to grind. However *because* they care, these same middle managers may also be perceived to be deeply conservative in organisational matters. In the new organisation this conservatism is no longer required. Also, because the rhetoric is that the organisation has become so flexible and process-centred there emerge multiple hierarchies and teams which last for a short time, only to disappear to be replaced by new mini-hierarchical systems. One of the reasons cited for delayering and downsizing amongst the management cadre is that only a minority of middle managers have the skill or the capability to undertake the transition from the traditional tough management style to the more facilitative process management approach (Hammer 1996). So, within the dramaturgy of the new organisational design there is no place for that layer of management that separates the mission driven top of the organisation from the purposive bottom. Hence the impulse to delayer.

In the delayered organisation a key design concept is that individuals are made accountable for their own actions. Newton, who was Operations Director for the Harvester Restaurants, expresses this idea when she wrote: 'in order to delayer it is vital to identify the critical accountable job roles'. . . . This exercise should be carried out starting with the roles interfacing with the customer. This will identify the roles necessary in the organisation to get the job done. It is imperative that no accountabilities are shared, although everyone is responsible to a greater or lesser extent' (Newton 1994: 31). Because people understand the overall vision of the organisation through very clear communication of it, and because, within that vision, staff feel empowered to act, fewer managers are needed. Hammer suggests that the ratio of managers to staff can move from about 1:7 to 1:30 or even 1:50 – and as a result the responsibilities of managers change radically (Hammer and Stanton 1995: 210). We have already seen something of this theme expressed in Stacey's idea of 'extraordinary management'. In this vein advocates of re-engineering suggest that 'the manager's role switches from supervision to empowerment of team members, as work reorganises around core process and workers become self managed. Staff win greater autonomy and job satisfaction, as they move from being mere workers to becoming professionals' (Flood 1994: 36). However, to counter this view, there is the suggestion that there will, as a hidden consequence of this so-called facilitative approach, be a pressure, no less strong than that under a more coercive management style, towards high levels of consensual behaviour amongst employees. A sort of 'killing us softly with their song'. McCabe and Knights suggest that 'under the guise of discipline and surveillance, hierarchy will continue to thrive as it elevates those who conform whilst punishing those who rebel' (2000: 69).

Contra the delayering view, it could be argued that the traditionally structured organisation with appropriate layers of management is, in terms of the exercise of power and authority, legitimated in the distribution of roles and authority and that the very idea of the flat organisation is an aberration (Brown 1997). Jaques (1996) is a key representative of a continuing school that suggests that traditional hierarchies have considerable value. He suggests that traditional hierarchies provide members of the organisation with very clear boundaries and controls. In his view, the development of what he terms requisite organisation requires four key features. These consist of 'a hierarchical system of managerial layers, a system of accountability and authority in . . . working relationships. . . . A system of detailed managerial leadership processes. . . . An equitable differential structure using pay levels tied to the structure of managerial layers. . . . A newly-discovered system of evaluation of individual potential capability . . .' (1996: 2). Aligned with this view is the suggestion that management should, rather than being delayered, be regarded as a strategic asset (Morden 1997) through recognition of the linkage between middle management with organisational core capability and competitive advantage (Floyd and Woolridge 1994).

The story of the Spix's macaw

Apparently the last free-flying member of the Mexican Spix's macaw has died and this is a problem although there are some sixty of the species in captivity. The problem is that the dead parrot had the only mental map of 'how to survive, knowing how to find water, where to roost, which nuts to open when, and how to avoid predators. If this link could not be passed on it was a severe blow to hopes of restoring the species' (McCarthy 2000). As with the parrot, so the middle manager may be seen to be the repository of the organisational memory. That gives strategic advantage.

This view aligns with the emergence of management as profession in its own right (e.g. Dawson 1994) with its own distinctive mindset, which claims possession of a dominant, managerialist, discourse (Clarke and Newman 1997). Reed and Watson (1999) argue that managerialism, given the decline of socialism and the intellectual exhaustion of capitalism, has become the replacement global ideology. This is accomplished through the emergence of a pervasive and generalisable technical expertise in management. The management cadre are specialists in control through their knowledge of management and their skill in the implementation of their esoteric science and art. The ubiquity of this capability means that managers can claim that management work can be exercised as a culture-free phenomenon. They represent a core stabilising and pivotal role as between the essentially here today, gone tomorrow senior management and the essentially self-oriented employees. They can do this because they can make claims to be free from the impact of particular interest groups; they can make claims to be affectively neutral. Although Reed and Watson (1999) are, in this depiction, presenting it with gentle irony, the 'managerial monologue ... is an effort to integrate multiple meanings and alternative realities into one coherent voice.... There is one voice, one logic and one moral' (Salzer-Mörling 1998: 111) that flow from the managerial discourse. Whilst claims to managerial omniscience are vigorously contested (e.g. MacIntyre 1981; Locke 1996) and it is asserted that members can, indeed, overcome the claims of managerial dominance (e.g. Pritchard and Willmott 1997; McAuley, Duberley and Cohen 2000), the managerialist rhetoric has been powerful in issues of requisite design for organisations.

There are those, indeed, who would argue that the notion of delayering of management masks the growth, in quantitative terms, of management and supervisory activity. Gordon (1996) argues that the urge for control in organisations has led to the growth and development of what he terms corporate bureaucracies. These have, built within them, the very conditions for their expansion and development. What is more, he claims that far from exercising the claimed pivotal role, they erode, because of their interest in dominance and control, the bases of accountability to the most senior echelons of the organisation. Indeed, it is argued that the dominance of hierarchy is inevitable, that 'within a capitalist system that depends upon the extraction of surplus value, it is totally unrealistic to believe that hierarchy can be abandoned' (McCabe and Knights 2000: 64). Thus there is, it could be suggested, at the very heart of managerialism a paradox. This represents a disjunction between the claim that the managerial agenda is concerned with the logics of organisational efficiency and effectiveness and the actuality that the desire for control represents a regression to the very condition that the discourse was designed to avoid. This paradox is discussed further below.

A LINKED MORAL FABLE IN ORGANISATIONAL DESIGN – THE RISE AND FALL OF DOWNSIZING

As a moral fable, the story of downsizing as a design issue is fascinating. There is one view that downsizing will inevitably be with organisations over the long term. Its management will, for some writers, require leadership that is able to manage the tensions between organisational downsizing and the needs for organisational development (e.g. Bennis and Hodgetts 1996). Most writers in this tradition suggest that downsizing has not always been as effective as it might have been, but then suggest that if only the appropriate mechanisms were in place it would be an effective tool. To some purists downsizing is regarded as an investment (Mabert and Schemner 1997) which needs to be managed, contained and controlled like any other resource. In this sense downsizing becomes an end in itself with a keen regard for cost control of the activity itself and a regard for the avoidance of employment growth in the organisation once the optimum minimal organisation size has been achieved.

Another perspective is to regard downsizing as part of organisational long-term strategy, but with a view that the human resource is an asset rather than a cost. It is suggested that there are prescriptive approaches to the effective management of delayering (e.g. Band and Tustin 1996; Appelbaum, Everard and Hung 1997). This emphasis on a strategic and managed approach to downsizing is aligned to a view that 'for long-term sustained improvements in efficiency, reductions in headcount need to be viewed as part of a process of continuous improvement that includes organization redesign, along with broad systemic changes designed to eliminate redundancies, waste and inefficiency' (Cascio 1993: 95). In his study of organisational downsizing, Freeman (1999) saw two meanings given to downsizing – downsizing as a driver for organisational redesign (the investment approach) and organisational redesign as driver for downsizing (the human resource approach). These may be understood as generic strategies (in our terms mindsets) that underpin different approaches to the management of change.

A somewhat different school of thought reflects a view that downsizing has a certain air of inevitability, it is a feature of life, but that ameliorative process will mitigate its worst excesses. This strand of thought was present even in the very early days of the movement. Thus Lippitt and Lippitt (1984) saw it as an opportunity to re-examine priorities and engage in innovative approaches to the design of work and organisations. However, they felt that the key issue was to humanise downsizing through explanation, the participation of employees in change processes, values clarification and the encouragement of expressions of negative and positive emotion amongst employees. An analogous view stresses the need for management communication, to stress the positive aspects of the change and the opportunities (Kiechel 1985). In this view organisational renewal takes place in situations where the organisation is in touch with its environment and when the feelings of staff are taken into account. This ameliorative view is echoed in writers such as de Geus. He uses the image of the corporate organisation as ecology. He suggests that within this sensitive ecology, downsizing is a threat. He particularly looks at the semi-survivors – those whose contractual relationship to the organisation has changed, those who 'have been told, explicitly or implicitly, that they should no longer see their future as aligned with that of the company' (1997: 161). He suggests, somewhat ambivalently perhaps, that their shifting relationship to the organisation will be reflected in their increased allegiance to unionisation. This 'will inevitably have some impact on the corporate health; possibly benevolent, possibly malevolent, depending on whether these two personæ (the corporate and the union) will elect for symbiotic or inimical coexistence' (1997: 161). Well, there you go. This insight reflects an interest in the maintenance of the survivors in the organisation. Some writers (e.g. Kets de Vries and Balazs 1997) look at the issues of grieving and mourning as they affect all the parties in downsizing and emphasise the role of internal communications and a responsive human resource management strategy in the reduction of these effects. This may even be formalised as the concept of 'post-surgery' organisational therapy as an effort that is consciously directed towards the rebuilding of trust and commitment that will facilitate organisational competitiveness (e.g. Stoner and Hartman 1997).

An emergent theme, however, has been that the social and economic costs of delayering and downsizing are high in terms of their societal and psychological damage (Kets de Vries and Balazs 1997), and the physical costs of the process for those involved. Indeed it is claimed that the costs of unemployment and low-wage strategies that are a by-product of downsizing abut organisational effectiveness through the suppression of demand for goods and services (Roach 1996) and that the overall benefits to the organisation of downsizing are minimal when compared with the social cost (Morris, Cascio and Young 1999). There is a somewhat different view (cited, but not entirely endorsed, in Burke 1997) that downsizing, as rhetoric, was primarily experienced as a white-collar, executive phenomenon. It became drama only because it hit those echelons of society rather than blue collar workers who had always been prone to the vicissitudes of layoff. It is further suggested, in this view, that the general effect of downsizing has been a dispersal of these people into other sorts of organisation. Burke (1997) reflects a general consensus that emerged in the 1990s amongst academics if not practitioners that downsizing as design strategy is potentially damaging for both individuals and organisations. He suggests that the first responsibility of those who have a say in organisational design (in this case organisation development consultants) should be to 'challenge a potential downsizing decision ... and to test for the impact of social forces. ... Second, if other options have been thoroughly explored and downsizing is the only remaining choice, to push for dignity, humane treatment, and ultimate fairness' (Burke 1997: 12).

Significantly, perhaps, Burke suggests that such matters as downsizing and delayering are essentially symptoms of much deeper issues that confront the design of organisations. For him the issue of understanding the community and the development of the social fabric in which organisations are located is a touchstone issue. He suggests that within the current milieu the reframing of the employer–employee social contract, the development of personal capability in order to increase employability and the development of higher level of mutuality in trust are crucial. He also suggests that a key issue, when organisations merge and alter form, is to understand the issues of culture and culture clash, and crucially get to grips with the issues of corporate power and personal values that confront organisational members. This attempt to look at deeper issues of organisational life and design is echoed by other writers.

When Hamel and Prahalad looked at companies in the United Kingdom and the United States they suggested that although initially there might well have been good reason for a degree of delayering and downsizing, companies 'seemed to ask themselves: How will we know when we're done restructuring? Where is the dividing line between cutting fat and cutting muscle?' They add that these processes create situations in which morale – even for the survivors – can plummet, and that restructuring seldom results in fundamental improvement in the business. 'At best it buys time. ... Downsizing belatedly attempts to correct the mistakes of the past. ... The simple point is that getting smaller is not enough. Downsizing, the equivalent of corporate anorexia, can make a company thinner; it doesn't necessarily make it healthier' (1994: 11). They suggest, as the much more preferable alternative, that there is a need to look at resource leveraging. Whereas downsizing means 'cutting investment and head count in hopes of becoming lean and mean – in essence reducing the buck pays for the bang. ... [R]esource leverage seeks to get the most out of the resources one has – to get a much bigger bang for the buck. Resource leverage is essentially energizing while downsizing is essentially demoralizing' (Hamel and Prahalad 1993: 78). This implies looking at organisational design in relation to, for example, redeployment (Marshall and Yorks 1994) within the organisation in order to ensure continuity of knowledge and capability. In this light it is perhaps interesting that, on the basis of their empirical work, Morris, Cascio and Young suggest that where an organisation employs skilled people, 'it may be advantageous to maintain human resources even in slower periods in order to support flexibility' (1999: 86). This enables the maintenance of the stock of knowledge and capability within the organisation to meet the challenges of growth. They further suggest that the only examples where downsizing was effective were when it was part of 'aggressive asset restructuring' (1999: 84) which was geared to strategic goals of focus and vision. The emergent critique, then, suggests that downsizing has a detrimental effect on competitiveness (Hubiak and O'Donnell 1997). It destroys the interpersonal networks that are essential to knowledge exchange (Shah 2000); it has profoundly negative effects on product innovation (Dougherty and Bowman 1995), it needs to be replaced by the concept of the learning organisation (Shimko, Meli, Restropo and Oehlers 2000). So it is that downsizing comes to be regarded as a 'flawed paradigm' which needs to be replaced by, in this case, an 'alternative paradigm' of core competencies (Morden 1997). Here the process by which an aspect of design (whether downsizing or core competencies) becomes elevated to the status of paradigm (in the strict sense of a 'scientific achievement, a specific concrete *problem-solution* which has gained universal acceptance throughout a scientific field' (Barnes 1982: 17)) is in itself interesting and perhaps indicative of the way in which practices can become embedded as strong features of the mindset.

Although, as we have seen, even from the early days of downsizing and delayering doubts were expressed as to their efficacy, they persisted as a forceful aspect of design well into the 1990s. They are still, from time to time, seen as the only response to the modernisation agenda. In this sense, such design issues as downsizing and delayering are, it might be suggested, *aspects* of a pervasive mindset, model of organisations. Cascio suggests that the traditional approach to downsizing represents 'a failure to break out of the traditional approach to organization design and management – an approach founded on the principles of command, control and compartmentalization' (1993: 95). The pervasive features that lie behind this inability to move are identified by McKinley, Sanchez and Schick (1995) as three key forces that pervade, in our terms, the institutional mindset.

The first of these is 'constraining forces [which] pressure organisations to conform to institutional rules that define institutional rules that define legitimate structures and management activities' (McKinley, Sanchez and Schick 1995: 34). In the context of downsizing they suggest that whereas this started, as we discussed earlier, as a response to economic decline, it has become, for those who continue to believe in its efficacy, an institutional good in itself. As they comment, the ability to undertake downsizing can also be seen as enhancing shareholder value. This issue of the development of strategies that appeal to a real (or imagined) concept of shareholder value is one we discuss in Chapter 10. As an aspect of the processes of cultural communication of the culture of the dominating group in the organisation (Chapter 3), the ability to undertake downsizing has become, on the part of management role appropriate behaviour (the ability to downsize is a measure of managerial effectiveness). It becomes part of organisational common sense that downsizing is the automatic route to organisational efficiency. As a vehicle of culture stories may well be told of 'the old days' when there were members who 'idled away their days in mundane pleasures' and the heroic manager is the one who really pared his/her department to the bone. At the level of basic assumption downsizing is seen as 'the only way' to achieve organisational effectiveness. The constraining force becomes built into the culture, the psyche of the organisation.

The second of these forces is 'cloning ... which pressure organisations to conform to mimic the actions of the most prestigious, visible, members of their industry' (McKinley, Sanchez and Schick 1995: 34). They identify two key issues in the cloning mechanism. The first is that in industry or business partnerships the stronger will often influence the smaller to imitate their institutional patterns. A somewhat different reason for cloning is that if the environment is experienced as one of 'extreme uncertainty generated by global competition, rapid technological innovation, and a turbulent legal and political environment, organizations have a strong tendency to mimic the behavior of other organizations' (McKinley, Sanchez and Schick 1995: 35). In this sense the ways in which organisations undertake activities such as benchmarking, Business Process Re-engineering and other processes may have about them an air of trying to understand the 'successes' of others so that they can be embedded in the design of the organisation. It is part of a search for new patterns of order in what is experienced as a chaotic world that underpins this imitative behaviour.

The third of the forces is that of learning. This emerges as force 'through the management practices taught in universities or professional associations throughout the corporate world. . . . The spread of cost accounting techniques through business education and the professionalisation of accounting therefore plays a role in rationalizing downsizing as a legitimate activity' (McKinley, Sanchez and Schick 1995: 34–5). We would suggest, however, that another key learning force are management gurus and those heroic managers who then proselytise their understandings of the world and their success in it (Huczynski 1993). This points to a wonderful paradox in the development of the idea of the learning organisation. That is that although the *rhetoric* of the concept tends towards the humanistic, empowering aspects of learning, in *organisational* terms the quality and nature of the learning depends upon the holders of the dominant discourse.

The emergence of the managerialist agenda in the 1980s and 1990s pointed towards a 'bottom line', accountancy based (Hoskin 1998), utilitarian (McAuley 1996) understanding of business and industry as a core aspect of the basic assumptions for those organisations where the decision-makers are pervaded by this mindset. There are several aspects to the learning process that are significant in this context. Learning is essentially interactive. Those managers whose understanding of the world is essentially immobilised through fears of uncertainty will either take away from the learning experience what will fit their own mindset or undergo a process of dramatic conversion that will allay their fears (Huczynski

1993). In the case of the latter it is more than likely that the 'purity' of their learning will be subjected to political processes (Knights and Willmott 2000) which profoundly affect the initial intent. For example, in the specific case of Business Process Re-engineering, Hammer and Stanton protested that re-engineering is not about downsizing, 'no matter how many people persist in confusing the two' (1995: 179). However, the political processes involved in the implementation of BPR initiatives have meant that one effect has been the 'dramatic shedding of personnel through downsizing' (Knights and Willmott 2000: 9).

It should perhaps be added that, in a commentary on McKinley, Sanchez and Schick (1995), Higgs, a director of human resource for a large US insurance company, mounted a spirited defence of downsizing as an aspect of strategic decision-making. The main planks of her argument appear to be the development of intelligent robotics in industry and intelligent computing in business causes the displacement of workforces, and that delayered organisations have fewer places for those seeking management positions. She argues the rationalist case, that 'the same criteria should be used to determine the viability of a downsizing approach as are used in any other business case'. She sees downsizing as one aspect of the balanced scorecard approach to strategy formation, 'which simply states that when you lay out your strategy, you also specify the key indicators from multiple perspectives, including what business payoff you expect' (1995: 44). In their study of a large financial institution in the UK, however, Knights and Willmott (2000) found that downsizing was not undertaken in this manner. Rather it was one of a number of discontinuous shifts in strategic direction undertaken by the organisation in which management reacted to their understanding of external events with considerable uncertainty as to whether the change (downsizing or whatever) would work or not.

In these two sections on delayering and downsizing, we have taken two powerful design issues that have pervaded thinking about organisational design (particularly when related to design recipes such as Business Process Re-engineering) over recent times. We have shown how these issues were originally seen as a response to a perception of economic decline, but then became (quite rapidly) part of the (particularly Anglophone) mindset in large areas of business and industry. It has this appeal because it appeals to the logics of organisational efficiency as held by those who take an accountancy-based view of the nature of organisations and their responsibilities. We have tried to illustrate how this design became increasingly questioned but, perhaps, has not been replaced as a core issue in organisational design.

In the next section we shall explore issues of design of organisations from a different perspective. We will investigate the extent to which fundamental assumptions about the nature and form of organisations and their design have taken place.

ISSUES OF FUNCTION AND FORM – MODERNISM AND POSTMODERNISM AS ASPECTS OF THE DESIGN OF ORGANISATIONS

We have discussed in earlier chapters some of the underpinning issues in the contemporary debates of modernism and postmodernism. In this section we shall take a particular approach to the phenomenon. We shall suggest that we can regard modernism and postmodernism as narratives about particular forms of organisation. In other words, we shall deal with them as manifestations of concrete phenomena – ways of organising that are fundamentally different in form. The discussion of organisations as modernist or postmodernist is essentially a recent phenomenon. For example, a classic text from a previous generation discusses four key strands in organisational theory. Mouzelis discusses Weber and Marx in the same breath as theorists who provided analysis with a broad sociological sweep within which to explore organisations. He then suggests that the post-Weberians developed a theory of what are characterised as bureaucratic organisations in order to develop an understanding of the issues of 'democracy and individual freedom within a bureaucratised society' (1975: 167). Running alongside this tradition, Mouzelis suggests, is 'the movement of scientific management [which] reflects the confident ideology of American capitalism before the crisis of the thirties' (1975: 167). In this tradition there is an emphasis on the instrumental exploitation of the organisational member in order to increase productivity. Within this tradition it is useful to conceptualise the formal organisation as having a number of components amongst which are the aspects which are the domain of production, of management and those which are the domain of the administrative machinery – the bureaucracy (Blau and Scott 1963). This conceptualisation of organisations as domains of interest and communities of practice with their different rhetorics and discourses is echoed in, for example, the magnificent theorising of Mintzberg (e.g. 1983) and his understanding that all organisations have five key structures. The third strand Mouzelis discerns is that of the Human Relations School which has a concern for the individual and what are characterised as the informal aspects of organisation. He suggests that these three elements converge in interesting and insightful ways with greater or lesser rigour, but that the key organisational form is that of the bureaucratic milieu. He suggests that the key element in the synthesis of these different insights is the systems view of organisations. This indeed became a pervasive image in organisational design with perhaps the best-known example being the '7S' model with its claim that these systems are complex but with a central idea that 'organizational effectiveness stems from the interaction of several factors – some not especially obvious and some underanalyzed' (Waterman, Peters and Phillips 1980: 17).

Where there is an understanding of the contradictions contained within the modernist paradigm, alternatives tend to be expressed as 'a reflection of a deep-rooted aspiration for economic democracy in the major industrial countries'

(Doray 1988: 164). In this light, he suggests, if 'something new is "emerging", it is not really a thing, but a new and dynamic expression of the contradictions in the form of industrial society imposed by the dominant mode of production' (Doray 1988: 166). He suggests that this would call for a revaluation of the relationship between the subjective self and the very nature of society itself, a 'new form of "history", "politics" and "psychology" ' (Doray 1988: 166). It is perhaps interesting that Clegg (1990) certainly does not characterise postmodernism as necessarily this new way forward. He suggests that modernism and postmodernism are both organisational forms within which more general social dynamics of power and authority are played out. In this sense he takes a position analogous to that of Weber. It is interesting, however, that in Clegg's discussion of the active ingredients of modernism and postmodernism he takes a position that suggests a degree of positive normative bias towards the postmodern. For example, he suggests that the modernist perspective tends towards disempowerment and postmodernism tends towards empowerment (1990: 203). This is not necessarily so. At the heart of the modernist organisation lies the concept of legitimation, and as long as that rule is not breached the individual can be as empowered (or disempowered) as the social system within which the organisation is placed will allow. Here is another example. Clegg suggests that the basis of leadership is 'mistrust' within the modernist organisation and 'trust' within the postmodernist. We would suggest that there is nothing intrinsically embedded in postmodernism that would guarantee trust, whereas within modernism there is. That is, again taking its roots from Weber, at the very core of the bureaucratic organisation is the notion of legitimation.

It is in this context utterly fascinating to look at the claims and counterclaims of modernism and postmodernism. To take just one example, postmodernists claim, as we shall show, that the postmodern organisation has the flexibility to respond to an increasingly turbulent and chaotic external environment to enact the complex mission of the organisation as distinct from the built-in inflexibilities of modernism. However – and we write in a spirit of lively irony – history is pervaded by notions of the best way. Although Weber was always far too serious and critical to be a guru, his apparent advocacy of bureaucratic modernism has, to this writer, a wonderful air of recency. Weber, in a piece written in 1922, suggests that the bureaucratic, modernist organisation provides 'precision, speed, unambiguity, knowledge of the files [*OK – a responsive IT strategy*], continuity, discretion, unity, strict subordination, reduction of friction and of material and personal costs' (1922: 214). He states that

> above all the [need for] speed of operations ... is determined by the peculiar nature of modern means of communication.... The extraordinary increase in the speed by which public announcements, as well as economic and political facts, are transmitted exerts a steady and sharp pressure in the direction of speeding up the tempo of administrative reaction towards various situations. *The optimum of such reaction time is normally attained only by a strictly bureaucratic organization.* (1922: 215; emphasis added)

But then there is an irony in that for those living in that epoch the world was experienced as just as turbulent as it is for those of us in the current era (Christiansen 2000). After all, the period was witnessing the growth of electronic communications, rapid transport systems, globalisation (also known as colonisation), and premonitions of a world to be disturbed by war. Mintzberg (1994) writes of what he claims to be one of the myths of the present age – that of 'turbulence'. He suggests that every age makes claims to being turbulent and every age makes claims to be more turbulent than the age before. *Contra* this view of universal turbulence, Minzberg suggests that turbulence is relative and is unevenly distributed. Most organisations face periods of relative turbulence followed by periods of relative calm. His suggestion is that the best thing to do within the organisation is to recognise what is going on – and then create turbulence for the competitors.

DEVELOPING REQUISITE DESIGN FOR ORGANISATIONS AND APPROACHES TO MANAGEMENT: CHOICES AND PARADOXES

And so it is that there is this interest in the concept of the new paradigm for organisational design and approaches to management, this opposition between the older (mechanistic, modernist, Fordist, bureaucratic) and the newer (organic, postmodernist, post-Fordist, networking) forms of organisation and systems of management. Incidentally, we would suggest that a particular system or form of management in an organisation would have a profound effect on the organisational design, and that the design of the organisation would be in a close relationship with the form of management. In a systems sense, profound changes in management style would need to be accompanied by design changes in order for them to stick (Senge 1990). This comparative, dualist approach to design and form seems to be a manifestation of the early 1960s. Burns and Stalker (1961), for example, discuss what they call mechanistic and organic systems of management. They suggest that both 'types represent a "rational" form of organisation, in that they may both, in our experience, be explicitly and deliberately created and maintained to exploit human resources of a concern in the most efficient manner feasible in the circumstances of the concern' (1961: 119). Leavitt (1962), looking particularly at intra-organisational management style, compares and contrasts two perspectives – scientific management and participative management. He argues that there was a tendency to look at these two as ideological positions with adherents to one or the other regarding *their* position as axiomatically preferable. He argues, however, a more subtle position – one of differentiation in relation to task. The principles he explores could, we suggest, be translated easily into issues of design, a notion that any one organisation need not be designed according to one set of principles but that there can be requisite variety.

More recent writers (e.g. Clegg 1990; Hassard 1996) argue that the terms modernism and postmodernism can be used as convenient descriptors for the exploration of directly opposed forms of organisation. Clegg (1990) also seems to conflate the terms Fordism and post-Fordism with modernism and postmodernism. As we have suggested in the introduction to this chapter, however, these latter are arguments about organisational form, whereas the former represent debates about approaches to management (Reed and Watson 1999) and in this sense have some similarities but also differences. This dualist approach may also be represented as a paradigm shift. For example, Clark (1985) understands Weber's theory of bureaucracy as the point of emergence of a paradigm of organisation and organisation theory. When Weber discussed the concept of bureaucracy he did so as an ideal type. He was undertaking 'the construction of certain elements of reality into a logically precise conception. The term "ideal" has nothing to do with evaluations of any sort' (Gerth and Mills 1948: 59) and in that sense it can be claimed that this closely controlled non-normative model is paradigmatic. Clark (1985) then suggests that there is an emergent paradigm which 'ventures to the aphoristic core of the classical view' (Clark 1985: 76). He suggests that this new paradigm is as yet incomplete.

In the following vignettes we have taken elements of the two paradigms from Clark and from a number of other sources in order to demonstrate the key elements of the two models of organisational design.

Vignette 8.2

A thoroughly modernist organisational design

In this vignette we look at the issue of design where the mindset that underpins the parameters is modernist. The vignette, the design of which is influenced by Clark (1985), has been expressed as one that promotes the logics of efficiency and effectiveness.

A crucial aspect of the design is that it can be achieved through objective (Clark 1985: 53) criteria. There is an assumption that there is an organisational reality to be discovered 'out there' which can be specified in the form of organisational templates and designs that are maximally effective. The design can be expressed in 'calculable rules' to eliminate 'from official business love, hatred, and all purely personal, irrational, and emotional elements which escape calculation' (Weber 1922: 216). In this sense problem-solving, as a crucial aspect of design, is a process in which members undertake routines of finding the facts of the matter, applying objective criteria to those facts and then developing action plans and interventions. Design is based on the assumption that matters can be resolved in a linear manner with clear linkages between cause and effect. The search for certainty suggests that there is one 'best way' to effect organisational design.

This assumption of objectivity leads to a view that work routines can be arranged so that people can have detailed prescriptions of the nature of their work. The boundaries (Clark 1985: 53) between different sorts of work and different personnel are very clearly expressed. Members have a very clear understanding of the extent of their own role and the relationship of their role to others. Certainty is captured in such design elements as clear role and job design and through the establishment of clear lines of responsibility and authority. The relations between the different groupings are formally specified with distinctiveness and clarity. In this situation, members create consensus about the organisation through 'acquiescence to authority, rules, or traditions' (Heckscher 1994: 25).

Not only do these design features operate laterally; they are also established vertically through the critical design feature of hierarchy. Within the hierarchy a premium is placed on human will and agency – exercised in ways that are appropriate to the level in the hierarchy. Each layer of the hierarchy has its own rights and responsibilities. Breaches of hierarchical rectitude are liable to be sanctioned. The principles of legitimacy fix the leadership and followership roles.

In an overall sense organisational design is based on the premise that relationships between tasks and members can be organised in a mechanical manner (Clark 1985: 53). The relationships between tasks and people are gauged according to the logics of efficiency as defined by management. There is an emphasis on form fitting function; there is a division of labour, with each task assigned its own meaning. This means that there is a premium placed on the efficiencies of bureaucratic (Clegg 1990: 203) organisation. In a complex organisation there is *also* a high degree of interconnectedness, which relies on management, and unambiguous sets of instructions to coordinate the division of labour. There is a high degree of emphasis on created stability, control and discipline. Indeed, where it is possible, organisational design is also geared towards control of the external environment.

In relation to issues of change in organisational design, movement from one state of being to another tends to be transitional, incremental. Modernist design is essentially conservative. It is also aspirational in the sense that there is a belief that it is possible to achieve defined outcomes. Design respects that there are 'natural laws' of change (Clark 1985: 53). The rationalist mindset proposes that change can be controlled with the most appropriate changes being determined by the logic of the situation.

Then, by way of complete contrast, we have the postmodern design of organisation:

Vignette 8.3

The postmodern organisation made real

In this vignette we look at the issue of design where the collective, pluralist mindset that underpins the parameters is postmodernist. The vignette, the design of which is influenced by Clark (1985), has been expressed as one that promotes discourses of effectiveness in organisational design.

Design is permeated by an acknowledgement of the crucial importance of subjective understandings (Clark 1985: 53) of the nature of organisations and the environment. These understandings are expressed as discourses that may be articulated with great intellectual rigour but are expressions of choices rather than claims to be ultimate truths of design. Different bases of authority in the organisation are acknowledged by the members to be underpinned by subjective elements. This means that decisions about the design of the organisation or units of it are acknowledged as a judgement call. It is claimed that this lends to design flexibility and democracy (Clegg 1990: 203). The subjective element is apparent when members are willing to explore with each other emotional aspects of their work.

This assumption of subjectivity leads to an assumption that work routines can be based on the principles of networks and communities of practice. There is considerable merging and blurring of areas of expertise as between different members. Job design is essentially vague or relates to the activities of teams rather than individuals. Members develop consensus about organisational purposes and process through 'institutionalised dialogue' (Heckscher 1994: 25). The very idea of boundaries between different roles becomes meaningless particularly in organisations in which the dominant resource is knowledge. Thus one writer asserts that 'the postmodern university acts with increasing influence in the world, without existing anywhere in particular, for it may consist of all the knowledge into which its staff is linked. So the university may no longer be a site of knowledge as such, but rather a site of knowledge possibilities' (Smith 2000: 33).

Design is developed in order to optimise the performance of agreed tasks so that any conventional notions of hierarchy disappear. The idea of personalised legitimated agency through authority disappears. Authority becomes diffused (Clegg 1990: 203). Members of the organisation are 'voices' articulating 'texts' to be 'read' in complex ways. (Kirkbridge 1993). Each task has its own situational and flexible mini-hierarchy depending upon the need of the situation and the interplay of the discourses in relation to issues of authority.

Organisation design is based on the premise that relationships between the tasks and the members are collective (Clegg 1990: 203) and holographic (Clark 1985: 53). The organisation is made up of autonomous work groups interlinked by the strength of the organisation culture. Form and function are related through an understanding that the experience of work is a holistic experience. Because this interconnectedness is complex, it relies on people understanding the unwritten 'rules of the game' and their ability to deal with ambiguity. This is associated with a belief that the external environment is highly unpredictable and uncertain. There is also an assumption that if members of the organisation are to make a full contribution to the organisation, they should be empowered (Clegg 1990: 203) to undertake work in ways that they find fulfilling.

The holographic principle also suggests that design should be based on the basis of mutual causality (Clark 1985: 53), that all organisational matters are interconnected in different and more or less complex ways. Design is geared towards the appreciation of the value of complexity and interconnectedness. Serendipitous networks encourage strong emphasis on discussion and involvement of members, and there are potentially many different outcomes from the decision-making process. Change in design is based on a fluid strategy that allows operating assumptions to be questioned and altered. Change in the organisation is understood to be 'spontaneous, unpredictable and discontinuous' (Clark 1985: 53) with a belief in the ability to shift direction quickly and flexibly but at the same time maintaining central vision or integrity. Within the principle that change is a judgement call, 'one intervenes in a belief that something, generally better than worse might result' (Kirkbridge 1993: 50).

In the sense used in this chapter, the concepts of modernism and postmodernism are used in an essentially modernist, realist fashion: they are treated as serious concepts that can be applied, with greater or lesser rigour, to issues of substantive organisational design. In this sense the reflective designer will explore the issues that are contained in the two models and make decisions on issues of design that reflect the needs of the situations and tasks that confront them. In this sense it represents a leap of faith from the mindsets of either modernist or postmodern ideologies. There will also be a remembrance of the sheer mundane fact that both modernism and postmodernism have clockwork and snakepit aspects (Schwartz 1990). The representation of them in the vignettes above is intended to reflect their clockwork aspects – the different ways in which they can be functional in the operation of organisations within their different milieux. However, for each and every aspect there can also be the identification of ways in which that aspect can be dysfunctional. In the literature generally our attention is drawn, with an air of post-millennial optimism, to the deficiencies of modernism as we make the transition to postmodernism.

In this light it is perhaps interesting to see how, for example, modernist impulses can distort, for the unreflective, postmodernist intentions. In Table 8.1 we have suggested some of the ways in which an initial design impulse can lead to the opposite of what was initially intended. In the second column we have suggested that there can be impulses for efficiency or legitimate control that can lead to a distortion of the original intention. In universities, for example, there is, on the one hand, an encouragement that there should be diversity and risk-taking. On the other hand, there is a condition to this, that 'those risks need to be carefully considered and well managed.... "You can take risks and be accountable – by taking risks in a measured way"' (Goddard 2000: 44). From the perspective of the individual actor the reading of the postmodernist text with its modernist requirement for risk and assessment and risk mitigation can be a problematic task. It requires an understanding of how the agents in the discourse gauge the innovation/risk axis; it depends upon their assessment of the occupational fates of those who have taken 'risks' before.

Table 8.1 The desire for control can lead to unintended paradoxes in postmodernism and modernism (1)

Postmodernism proposes	Intervening need for	Reversion to modernism
Complex relationships	Simplicity	Clear boundaries
Dispersed control and diversity	Monitoring and audit	Hierarchies of control and uniformity
Holographic structures	Simplicity	Linear structures
Indeterminate environment	Focus	Managed environment
Mutual causality	Clarity	Linear causes and effect
Subjective understanding	Accountability	'Objective' judgement
Morphogenic change	Prescription	Engineered approach

Table 8.2 The desire for control can lead to unintended paradoxes in modernism and postmodernism (2)

Modernism proposes	Intervening processes	Unintended postmodernism
Clear boundaries	Role confusion	Complex relationships
Hierarchies of control	Political process	Dispersed control
Linear structures	'Robber barons'	Holographic structures
Managed environment	Loss of vision	Indeterminate environment
Linear causes and effect	Denial of responsibility	Mutual causality
'Objective' judgement	Denial of accountability	Subjective understanding
Engineered approach	Confused discourses	Morphogenic change

We would also suggest, however, that there can be situations in which effective modernism can be undermined by creeping postmodernism – in a sense a loss of the modernist plot as conflicting discourses are unconfined, lack boundaries and come to dominate the agenda (Table 8.2).

CONCLUSION

Throughout this chapter there has been an emphasis on the notion that in issues of organisational design, as in so many other aspects of organisational life, designers have choice. It has been suggested that although there may well be prescriptions and wisdoms about the 'best way' to achieve requisite design there are choices to be made and there are preferences to be exercised. An issue, to which we return in Chapter 10, is to consider why it is that very often these matters are decided as if there were no choice. In this light, downsizing was seen as (in some cases) a regrettable but inevitable response to downturn in Western (particularly Anglophone) economies and then seized upon as an accomplishment in its own right. Delayering was perhaps more enthusiastically seized upon from the start as a way of reducing the organisational fat. Similarly, the enthusiasm with which some advocates of change would move from, broadly speaking, modernist frameworks for their organisations to postmodern is a wonder to behold – and the ways in which structuralists (e.g. exponents of modernist forms of BPR) understand the need for control is also a wonder to behold.

An underpinning theme of this book has been an understanding of the mindset and the development of the habits of reflexivity as part and parcel of the stock of knowledge of organisational members. Hamel and Prahalad (1993) represent a burgeoning literature (reflected in many other chapters of this volume) which discusses the ways in which managers acquire what they call their frame of reference and we have called the mindset. Essentially, they suggest, the frame, which is gained through socialisation and is then reinforced by the self-fulfilling prophecy (Merton 1968) of experience, is, on the one hand, invisible but, on the other, pervades their every act. They argue, however, that increased diversity in the workplace and the impact of globalisation pushes for an imperative where there is a need to recognise difference in understanding issues of strategy. Given the relationship between strategy and design (that design is the internal agent and expression of strategy and core vision) a key theme of this chapter is that design issues require careful and reflective crafting rather than a reliance on straightforward recipes and prescriptions.

REFERENCES

Appelbaum, S.H., A. Everard and L.T.S. Hung (1997) 'Strategic Downsizing: Critical Success Factors', *Management Decision*, 37(7): 535–53.

Band, D.C. and C.M. Tustin (1995) 'Strategic Downsizing', *Management Decision*, 33(8): 36–46.

Barnes, B. (1982) *T.S. Kuhn and Social Science*, London: Methuen.

Bartlett, C.A. and S. Ghoshal (1996) 'Changing the Role of Top Management: Beyond Systems to People', in J. Champy and N. Nohria (eds) *Fast Forward: The Best Ideas on Managing Business Change*, Cambridge, MA: Harvard Business School Press.

Bennis, W. and R.M. Hodgetts (1996) 'A Conversation with Warren Bennis on Leadership in the Midst of Downsizing', *Organizational Dynamics*, 25(1): 72–9.

Blau, P.M. and W.R. Scott (1966) *Formal Organizations: A Comparative Approach*, London: Routledge.

Brown, M. (1997) 'The Survival of the Flattest (Organizational Structures)', *Human Resources*, (July/Aug) 31: 99–102.

Burke, W.W. (1997) 'The New Agenda for Organization Development', *Organizational Dynamics*, 26(1): 6–20.

Burns, T. and G.M. Stalker (1961) *The Management of Innovation*, London: Tavistock.

Campanis, P. (1970) 'Normlessness in Management', in J.D. Douglas (ed.) *Deviance and Respectability: The Social Construction of Moral Meanings*, New York: Basic Books.

Cascio, W.F. (1993) 'Downsizing: What Do We Know? What Have We Learned?', *The Academy of Management Executive*, 7(1): 95–107.

Christiansen, R. (2000) *The Visitors: Culture Shock in Nineteenth-century Britain*, London: Chatto & Windus.

Clark, D.L. (1985) 'Context of the Shift', in Y.S. Lincoln (ed.) *Organisation Theory and Inquiry*, Beverly Hills, CA: Sage.

Clark, P. (2000) *Organisations in Action: Competition between Contexts*, London: Routledge.

Clarke, J. and J. Newman (1997) *The Managerial State*, London: Sage.

Clegg, S.R. (1990) *Modern Organizations: Organization Studies in the Postmodern World*, London: Sage.

Collins, J.C. and J.I. Porras (1996) *Built to Last: Successful Habits of Visionary Companies*, London: Century Business.

Daft, R.L. (1995, 5th edition) *Organization Theory and Design*, St. Paul, MN: West Publishing Company.

Davenport, T.H. (1993) *Process Innovation: Reengineering Work through Information Technology*, Boston, MA: Harvard Business School.

Dawson, S. (1994) 'Changes in the Distance: Professionals Reappraise the Meaning of Management', *Journal of General Management*, 20(1): 1–22.

De Geus, A. (1997) *The Living Company: Habits for Survival in a Turbulent Business Environment*, Boston, MA: Harvard Business School.

Deller, J. (2001) 'Wonders and blunders', *The Guardian* (5 March).

Doray, B. (1988) *From Taylorism to Fordism: A Rational Madness*, London: Free Association Press.

Dougherty, D. and E.H. Bowman (1995) 'The Effects of Organizational Downsizing on Product Innovation', *California Management Review*, 37(4): 28–45.

Flood, G. (1994) 'Cut out the Middle Men', *Personnel Today*, (March): 36.

Floyd, S.W. and W. Woolridge (1994) 'Dinosaurs or Dynamos? Recognizing Middle Management's Strategic Role', *The Academy of Management Executive*, 8(4): 47–58.

Freeman, S.J. (1999) 'The Gestalt of Organizational Downsizing: Downsizing Strategies as Packages of Change', *Human Relations*, 52(12): 1505–42.

Gephart, R.P. (1996) 'Management, Social Issues, and the Postmodern Era', in D.M. Boje, R.P. Gephart Jr. and T.J. Thatchenkery (eds) *Postmodern Management and Organization Theory*, Thousands Oaks, CA: Sage.

Gerth, H.H. and C.W. Mills (1948) *From Max Weber: Essays in Sociology*, London: Routledge & Kegan Paul.

Goddard, A. (2000) 'Watchdog Culture Scares off Risk-takers', *Times Higher Education Supplement,* (11 August) 1,448: 2.

Gordon, D.M. (1996) *Fat and Mean: The Corporate Squeeze of Working Americans and the Myth of Managerial Downsizing*, New York: Simon & Schuster.

Grint, K. and P. Case (2000) '"Now where were we?" BPR Lotus-eaters and Corporate Amnesia', in D. Knights and H. Willmott, *The Reengineering Revolution: Critical Studies of Corporate Change*, London: Sage.

Hamel, G. and C.K. Prahalad (1993) 'Strategy as Stretch and Leverage', *Harvard Business Review*, 71(2): 75–85.

Hamel, G. and C.K. Prahalad (1994) *Competing for the Future: Breakthrough Strategies for Seizing Control of your Industry and Creating the Markets of Tomorrow*, Cambridge, MA: Harvard Business School.

Hammer, M. (1996) *Beyond Reengineering: How the Process-centred Organization is Changing Our Work and Our Lives*, London: HarperCollins Business.

Hammer, M. and S.A. Stanton (1993) *The Reengineering Revolution: The Handbook*, London: HarperCollins Business.

Hammer, M. and S.A. Stanton (1995) *The Reengineering Revolution Handbook*, London: HarperCollins.

Hassard, J. (1996) 'Exploring the Terrain of Modernism and Postmodernism in Organization Theory', in D.M. Boje, R.P. Gephart Jr. and T.T. Thatchenkery (eds) *Postmodern Management and Organization Theory*, Thousand Oaks, CA: Sage.

Hatch, M.J. (1997) *Organization Theory: Modern Symbolic and Postmodern Perspectives*, Oxford: Oxford University Press.

Heckscher, C. (1994) 'Defining the Post-bureaucratic Type', in C. Heckscher and A. Donnellon, *The Post-bureaucratic Organization: New Perspectives on Organizational Change*, Thousand Oaks, CA: Sage.

Higgs, A.C. (1995) 'Commentary on W. McKinley, C.M. Sanchez, A.G. Schick, Organizational Downsizing: Constraining, Cloning, Learning', *The Academy of Management Executive*, 9(3): 43–4.

Hoskin, K. (1998) 'Examining Accounts and Accounting for Management: Inventing

Understandings of the Economic', in A. McKinlay and K. Starkey (eds) *Foucault, Management and Organization Theory*, London: Sage.

Hubiak, W.A. and S.J. O'Donnell (1997) 'Downsizing: A Pervasive Form of Organizational Suicide', *National Productivity Review*, 16(2): 31–8.

Huczynski, A.A. (1993) *Management Gurus: What Makes Them and How to Become One*, London: Routledge.

Hunt, J.G. (1991) *Leadership: A New Synthesis*, Newbury Park, CA: Sage.

Jaques, E. (1996) *Requisite Organization: A Total System for Effective Managerial Organization and Managerial Leadership for the 21st Century*, Arlington, VA: Casson Hall & Co.

Katz, D. and R.L. Kahn (1966) *The Social Psychology of Organizations*, New York: John Wiley & Sons.

Kets de Vries, M.F.R. and K. Balazs (1997) 'The Downside of Downsizing', *Human Relations*, 50(1): 11–51.

Kiechel, W. (1985) 'Managing a Downsized Operation', *Fortune* (22 July).

Kirkbridge, P. (1993) 'Managing Change', in R. Stacey (ed.) *Strategic Thinking and the Management of Change: International Perspectives on Organisational Dynamics*, London: Kogan Page.

Knights, D. and H. Willmott (2000) 'The Reengineering Revolution? An Introduction', in D. Knights and H. Willmott, *The Reengineering Revolution? Critical Studies of Corporate Change*, London: Sage.

Leavitt, H.J. (1962) 'Management According to Task: Organizational Differentiation', *Management International*, 1: 13–22.

Lippitt, R. and G. Lippitt (1984) 'Humane Downsizing: Organizational Renewal versus Organizational Depression', *S.A.M. Advanced Management Journal*, 49(3): 15–22.

Locke, R.R. (1996) *The Collapse of the American Management Mystique*, New York: Oxford University Press.

Mabert, V.A. and E.W. Schmenner (1997) 'Assessing the Roller Coaster of Downsizing', *Business Horizons*, 40(4): 45–53.

MacIntyre, A. (1981) *After Virtue: A Study in Moral Theory*, London: Duckworth.

Marshall, R. and L. Yorks (1994) 'Planning for a Restructured, Revitalised Organization', *Sloan Management Review*, 35(4): 81.

McAuley, J. (1996) 'Ethical Issues in the Management of Change', in K. Smith and P. Johnson (eds) *Business Ethics and Business Behaviour*, London: Thomson Business Press.

McAuley, J., J. Duberley and L. Cohen (2000) 'The Meanings Professionals Give to Management . . . and Strategy', *Human Relations*, 53(1): 87–116.

McCabe, D. and D. Knights (2000) 'Such Stuff as Dreams are Made on: BPR up against the Wall of Functionalism, Hierarchy and Specialisation', in D. Knights and H. Willmott, *The Reengineering Revolution? Critical Studies of Corporate Change*, London: Sage.

McCarthy, M. (2000) 'World's Loneliest Bird is Missing, Feared Dead', *The Independent* (27 December).

McKinley, W., C.M. Sanchez and A.G. Schick (1995) 'Organizational Downsizing: Constraining, Cloning, Learning', *The Academy of Management Executive*, 9(3): 32–44.

Merton, R.K. (1968) *Social Theory and Social Structure*, New York: The Free Press.

Mintzberg, H. (1983) *Structure in Fives: Designing Effective Organizations*, London: Prentice Hall International.

Mintzberg, H. (1994) *The Rise and Fall of Strategic Planning*, London: Prentice Hall.

Morden, T. (1997) 'A Strategic Evaluation of Re-engineering, Restructuring, De-layering and Downsizing Policies as Flawed Paradigm', *Management Decision*, 35(3): 240–50.

Morgan, G. (1997) *Images of Organization*, London: Sage.

Morris, J.R., W.F. Cascio and C.E. Young (1999) 'Downsizing after all These Years: Questions and Answers about Who Did it, How Many Did it, and Who Benefited from it', *Organizational Dynamics*, 27(3): 78–88.

Mouzelis, N. (1975, revised edition) *Organisation and Bureaucracy: An Analysis of Modern Theories*, London: Routledge and Kegan Paul.

Newton, S. (1994) 'Organisational Delayering', *Training and Development*, (March): 30–2.

Palmer, I. and R. Dunford (1996) 'Understanding Organisations through Metaphor', in C. Oswick and D. Grant (eds) *Organisation Development: Metaphorical Explorations*, London: Pitman.

Pritchard, C. and H. Willmott (1997) 'Just how Managed is the McUniversity?', *Organization Studies*, 18(2): 287–316.

Reed, M. and S. Watson (1999) 'New Managerialism and the Management of Higher Education', Presentation to the Association of Business Schools Research Conference, University of Manchester Institute of Science and Technology.

Roach, S.S. (1996) 'The Hollow Ring of the Productivity Revival', *Harvard Business Review*, 74(6): 81–90.

Roethlisberger, F.J. and W.J. Dixon (1939) *Management and the Worker: An Account of a Research Program Conducted by the Western Electric Company, Hawthorne Works, Chicago*, Cambridge, MA: Harvard University Press.

Salzer-Mörling, M. (1998) 'As God Created the Earth . . . A Saga that Makes Sense?', in D. Grant, T. Kinnoy and C. Oswick (1998) *Discourse and Organization*, London: Sage.

Schwartz, H.S. (1990) *Narcissistic Process and Corporate Decay: The Theory of the Organization Ideal*, New York: New York University Press.

Senge, P.M. (1990) *The Fifth Discipline: The Art and Practice of the Learning Organization*, London: Century Business.

Shah, P.P. (2000) 'Network Destruction: The Structural Implications of Downsizing', *Academy of Management Journal*, 43(1): 101–13.

Shimko, B.W., J.T. Meli, J.C. Restrepo and P.F. Oehlers (2000) 'Debunking the "Lean and Mean" Myth and Celebrating the Rise of Learning Organizations', *The Learning Organization*, 7(2): 99–109.

Smith, A. (2000) 'New Life Amid Chaos', *Times Higher Education Supplement* (21 April).

Stacey, R. (1991) *The Chaos Frontier: Creative Strategic Control for Business*, London: Butterworth-Heinemann.

Stacey, R. (1993) *Strategic Management and Organisational Dynamics*, London: Pitman.

Stacey, R.D. (1996, 2nd edition) *Strategic Management and Organisational Dynamics*, London: Pitman.

Stacey, R. (2000, 3rd edition) *Strategic Management and Organisational Dynamics: The Challenge of Complexity*, London: Financial Times/Prentice Hall.

Stoner, C.R. and R.I. Hartman (1997) 'Organizational Therapy: Building Survivor Health and Competitiveness', *SAM Advanced Management Journal*, 62(3): 25–33.

Strati, A. (2000) *Theory and Method in Organization Studies: Paradigms and Choices*, London: Sage Publications.

Stroh, L.K. and A.H. Reilly (1997) 'Loyalty in the Age of Downsizing', *Sloan Management Review*, 38(4): 83–9.

Taylor, F.W. (1912) *Scientific Management*, cited in D.S. Pugh (ed.) (1997, 4th edition) *Organization Theory: Selected Readings*, Harmondsworth: Penguin.

Waterman, R.H., T.J. Peters and J.R. Phillips (1980) 'Structure is not Organization', *Business Horizons,* (June): 14–26.

Weber, M. (1922) *Bureaucracy*, in H.H. Gerth and C. Wright Mills (1948) *From Max Weber: Essays in Sociology*, London: Routledge & Kegan Paul.

Chapter 9

THE ECOLOGICAL METAPHOR

The aims of this chapter are to:

1 Explore the interrelationship between an organisation and its environment.

2 Explore the use of ecological themes as metaphor, and relate this to wider ecological themes.

3 Argue that ecological issues are of growing importance in strategic management and the management of change, and to consider the implications of taking ecological issues seriously.

4 Use this argument to illustrate the need to understand whole systems.

INTRODUCTION

Metaphors have long been a popular feature of change management and organisational development (OD); indeed, Oswick and Grant suggest that 'the use of metaphor in OD appears to be almost as old as the field itself' (1996: 1). The purpose of this chapter is to explore one particular type of metaphor – the ecological – and link this to the wider ecological debate. We take as starting points a number of themes developed in earlier chapters:

• The boundary between an organisation and its environment is fuzzy.

• An organisation and its environment can be seen to be in a process of continual mutual construction.

• A significant part of the organisational environment is the presence of other organisations, and the interrelationship between these organisations is of growing significance.

To these we now add the ecological theme. There is much controversy about the extent to which this requires serious concern. In the first vignette we summarise a number of the emerging concerns. It seems reasonable on the basis of these to share the conclusions of Held et al. that 'one thing seems beyond doubt: the capacity of environmental globalisation to create potential risks and threats to states in advanced capitalist societies greatly exceeds existing capacities to address them, and to construct alternative identities and effective international institutions at this time' (1999: 413).

Vignette 9.1

Ecological Concern

- Over-exploitation of fish stocks: all eighteen of the world's major fisheries have now reached or exceeded the maximum yields compatible with sustainability.
- Water tables are falling on every continent and major rivers are running dry.
- There is overgrazing and soil erosion.
- Concentrations of carbon dioxide are increasing in the atmosphere.
- Global average temperatures are rising.
- Extreme weather events are increasing in frequency and severity.
- Nitrogen overload is acidifying rivers and lakes.
- Ultraviolet radiation is rising due to stratospheric ozone depletion.
- Toxic heavy metals and persistent chemicals are building up in organisms and ecosystems.
- Forests are shrinking and wetlands are vanishing, especially in coastal areas.
- Coral reefs are dying.
- Invasions of non-native species are on the rise due to global traffic.
- Species are being exterminated about a thousand times faster than in earlier times.
- The problem of acid rain is growing, and the World Bank estimates that by 2010 there will be more than one billion motor vehicles in the world.
- Old diseases like TB are resurgent and new ones such as HIV AIDS, emergent.
- An estimated 37,000 infants will die today from poverty-related causes.
- More than 260 million children are out of school at the primary and secondary levels.
- 840 million people are malnourished.
- 850 million adults remain illiterate.
- 880 million people lack access to health services.
- One billion humans have inadequate shelter.
- 1.3 billion people (70 per cent female) attempt to live on less than US$1 a day – up by 200 million over the past decade.
- 2 billion have no access to electricity, and 2.6 billion lack basic sanitation.
- Some 1.2 billion adults are either unemployed or woefully underemployed earning below a living wage.
- More than 250 million children between 5 and 14 years of age are working as child labourers.
- *Forbes Magazine* estimates that the combined wealth of the 225 richest people in the world now equals the combined annual incomes of the poorest one-half of humanity.
- Problems emergent in the last half-century, in addition to the above, include nuclear risks, hazardous wastes, global warming and ozone depletion.

Sources: Various, including Clarke and Clegg (1998); Gladwin (1999); Held et al. (1999).

Table 9.1 Ecological images and relationships

Level		Image	Relationship
1	Reactive	Minimal – brought from other disciplines	Minimal – compliance
2	Proactive	Specific examples (Morgan 1997)	Opportunistic – linked to profit
3	Interactive	Fully articulated (de Geus 1997, Complex Adaptive System)	Seen as important in own right
4	Integrative	Ecological view of organisation integrated with ecological view of environment	

We can identify two distinct ways in which the ecological theme arises in discussion of organisations. The first is the metaphorical, where organisations, industries and the economic arena are variously characterised by reference to ecological or organic themes. The second is concerned with the relationship between the organisation and its environment. In strategic thinking this can still have a relatively narrow focused (evidenced in PEST analysis). But it is also possible to take a much richer view of this.

In Table 9.1 we suggest four levels at which each of these two ecological themes may be considered. As will be seen, in this framework it is only at the fourth level that they are integrated. This chapter outlines the nature of each of these levels, and finally speculates on the implications for organisations of a move to level 4.

LEVEL 1: REACTIVE

The reactive relationship between the organisation and its environment has been sharply characterised by Shrivastava (1994), who suggests that this 'organisational studies' (OS) view is CASTRATED – that is to say, it is characterised by the nine overlapping elements of Competition, Abstraction, Shallowness, Theoretical immaturity, Reductionism, Anthropocentrism, Time independent (ahistorical), Exploitable and Denaturalised. If we explore this in a little more detail (see Table 9.2), we can see in the acronym many of the characteristics of the Cartesian–Newtonian Synthesis discussed in Chapter 1.

Table 9.2 The CASTRATED environment

Competition	This refers to competition for environmental resources and antagonistic exploitative relations between organisations and their environments. Competition is regarded as an acceptable, legitimate and perhaps the only way of relating organisations to their environments.
Abstraction	These concepts regard the environment as an abstract social entity. It consists of abstract (and non-physical) economic, social, cultural, and technological components. Equally abstract ideas of 'uncertainty', 'stability', 'turbulence', 'domain consensus', etc. are used to characterise

it. The environment is operationalised and measured by even more abstract market and accounting measures or contrived social and perceptual attitude scales.

Shallow	Received concepts of organisational environment are shallow. They are simply semantic definitions that distinguish the firm from its external milieu. They attempt to describe the fuzzy boundaries of organisations, in simplistic terms.
Theoretical immaturity	The concepts of organisational environment do not go beyond mere empirical re-descriptions of immediate external influences on organisations. There is little analysis of the structural character of environmental influences, its historical origins, the interrelationships among structural and process elements, the complex dynamics of environmental changes, and relationships with larger social and historical processes.
Reductionism	While, in principle, the environment is seen to include all forces outside the firm that influence its actions and performance, in practice researchers reduce these forces to economic, social and technological forces that impact financial performance (PEST analysis). They ignore natural influences such as physical space, location, and time, which influence all aspects of organisations. In addition, positivist tendencies in OS place heavy emphasis on measuring organisational environments objectively. Measurement is necessarily a reductionist activity. It increases precision, but reduces descriptive richness.
Anthropocentrism	OS concepts of the environment presume that nature exists to fulfil human and organisational needs. Human needs unquestioningly receive priority over the natural environment. This view also fails to acknowledge any limits to the exploitation of nature.
Time-independent (ahistorical)	Organisational environment is regarded as a time independent, ahistorical idea. It is characterised by timeless dimensions, such as, uncertainty, heterogeneity and stability. These time neutral concepts obfuscate the historical roots and processes that shape organisational environments. Discussions of the environment sound as if they are equally valid at any period in time, and in any region of the world. The one exception to this is the organisational Population Ecology approach. This approach examines organisational survival patterns over time. However, it does so by excluding nature from its idea of organisational environment.
Exploitable	A fundamental assumption of these views is that the environment is a resource that may be exploited eternally for organisational benefit. Business organisations' sole objective is to exploit the environment to create economic value for its stockholders. No limits to this exploitation are ever acknowledged.
Denaturalised	The literature portrays organisational environment as being entirely a product of human institutions and actions. It has no natural component. People, organisations, and social and political institutions create it. It includes pressures from scientific and technological changes, changing international relations, and changes in demographic and social relations.

Source: Shrivastava (1994).

These days few companies remain at Level 1. Indeed, the consequences can be substantial if they do. Consider the following example from de Geus:

> Exxon let 15,000 people go in 1986, in the wake of the oil price collapse. They concentrated power in narrow chain of command and took away one side of their organisational matrix structure. In the process, they considerably reduced their managerial capacity. A year later, the Valdez oil spill incident took place. It took them 48 hours to react. That 48 hours has so far cost them $3 billion in cleanup costs, bad publicity, and legal fees. (1997: 127)

Attention to the environment has become part of an overall approach to risk management pursued by many organisations. Croker (1999) points to the need for this, and the consequences of not doing so. He gives as an example the natural gas explosion at Ford's River Rouge plant in Michigan, which cut off power to the 1,100 acre facility and ultimately resulted in the loss of six lives with fourteen more seriously injured, leading the Ford Motor Company Chairman to comment: 'This has got to be the worst day of my life.' To the deaths and injuries were added catastrophic loss of capacity and output in Ford plants and in Rouge Steel.

We can use Welford's (1995) five stage 'ROAST' scale to illustrate our levels. In his stage 1, 'Resistance', there is total resistance to environmental values and rules. Organisations are absolutely unresponsive and reactive to environmental initiatives. In stage 2, 'Observe and comply', the organisation observes environmental laws but actions reflect an unwilling attitude or lack of ability to comply. Actions are enforced through legislation or court decisions. Both these stages fit within our Level 1. We will return to the ROAST scale as we develop our argument.

Ecological metaphors at this level are equally impoverished. Perhaps the most familiar are those relating to the 'law of the jungle', envisaging an organisational environment in which there is 'survival of the fittest'. This 'social Darwinist' approach does little justice to evolutionary theory. Thus we should recognise that Darwin developed his theory within a dynamic tension between the Cartesian–Newtonian Synthesis and an alternative view which would fit well with the themes of complexity theory.[1] Howard Gruber has examined Darwin's development of his theory:

> The meaning of his whole creative life work is saturated with ... duality ... On the one hand, he wanted to face squarely the entire panorama of changeful organic nature in its amazing variety, its numberless and beautiful contrivances, and its disturbing irregularity and imperfections. On the other hand, he was imbued with the spirit of Newtonian science and hoped to find in this shimmering network a few simple laws that might explain the whole movement of nature. (quoted in Briggs 1992: 37–8)

Briggs comments: 'Darwin's admiration for complexity and his belief in the Newtonian model of simple natural laws brought him an important step toward the artist's aesthetic (sense of harmony and dissonance), but in the end the emphasis of evolutionary theory fell on the simplicity side of the equation – on scientific law' (1992: 39).

LEVEL 2: PROACTIVE

A proactive view of natural metaphor frequently occurs in management litera-ture, part of a wider use in many domains (See Vignette 9.2). Thus Mintzberg et al. (1998), in their characterisation of ten schools forming the strategy safari, provide an animal metaphor for each – the peacock for the cultural school, the lion to represent the power school, etc. Morgan (1997), who has done more per-haps than anyone to popularise a metaphorical approach to organisations, includes two 'life' metaphors in the eight he has developed – the organisation as brain and the organisation as organism. Elsewhere Morgan (1993) has developed the metaphor of the organisation as termite hill or spider plant. In an excellent case study of a knowledge-intensive firm (Wachtell), Starbuck summarises its characteristics with the twin metaphors of elephant and butterfly.[2] And at a more traditional level, what of the 'cash cows' and 'dogs' of the BCG Portfolio Matrix? It seems that we love animal images, and each of these individual metaphors has its use, as discussed in Chapter 6.

The relationship between the organisation and the environment at this level is largely opportunistic. It is accepted that the environment is of increasing con-cern, and that organisations can no longer ignore this. Welford's Stage 3, 'Accommodate', fits at this level: the organisation is beginning to adapt to change, with some proactive and responsive behaviours. Actions are no longer based entirely on complying with environmental legislation but the organis-ation begins to exhibit voluntary behaviour.

LEVEL 3: INTERACTIVE

De Geus has provided perhaps the most extended ecological metaphor of the organisation in his characterisation of the 'living company'. This does not link to a focus on ecological issues: 'When I say "environment" I do not use the word as an ecologist might, to refer to natural surroundings. Rather, I use it to mean the sum total of all forces that affect a company's actions' (1997: 26). His con-trast between machine and living characterisations is summarised in Table 9.3.

Vignette 9.2

Nature in Art Nouveau

It is no surprise that the richness of nature leads to multiple interpretations. Both nature and scientific thinking on the matter have been used in a variety of ways in management thinking: the same applies elsewhere. A good example is Art Nouveau.

There were many views on the meaning of nature within the Art Nouveau style, and not a little antagonism between them. In the various schools of thought it might stand for nationalism or cosmopolitanism; progress or reaction; eroticism or innocence; individuality or collectivity; conservatism or anarchism; science or mysticism; social movement or stasis. Underpinning all this variety, however, was one common meaning. Wherever it surfaced in Art Nouveau it signified modernity and in several instances it anticipated future modernisms. (Greenhalgh 2000: 55)

Note here the link with modernity: nature is not contrasted with the machine, but embraced within the movement. Thus Chicago architects drew in part on the Rationalist thought of Viollet-le-Duc, for whom 'the flora and fauna of the natural world provided a model for exhibiting the direct correlation between form and function, a correlation especially apt for expressing the modern reality of metallic cage construction' (Greenhalgh 2000: 323).

The contrasts illustrated in the quotation above derive in part from alternative readings of evolution. 'From the late Enlightenment onwards major thinkers, culminating with the work of Charles Darwin, changed the very nature of nature. Darwin provided the scientific framework which allowed for the full development of the theory of evolution. By 1890, the work of evolutionists all over Europe led to a new vision of nature which came to act powerfully on the cultural sphere, and not least upon the decorative arts' (Greenhalgh 2000: 35).

Evolutionary theory attracted those for whom 'survival of the fittest' held a clear political message, reinforcing the status quo. But it equally attracted those who drew a very different message about nature: 'Nature proceeds by continuity, connecting and linking together the different organs that make up a body or a tree; she draws one out of the other without violence or shock' (Van de Velde, quoted in 2000: 69).

Table 9.3 The organisation as machine or living being

A machine	A living being
Controllable by its operators	Not controllable in the same way
Created by someone outside	Creates its own processes
Fixed, static, unless somebody changes it	Evolves naturally
Only sense of identity is that given to it by its builders	Has its own sense of identity
Actions are reactions to goals and decisions made by management	Has its own goals and its own capacity for autonomous action
It will run down unless rebuilt	Is capable of regenerating itself
Its members are employees	Its members are human work communities
It learns only as the sum of the learning of its individual employees	It can learn as an entity

Source: Based on de Geus (1997: ix–x).

The argument for seeing the environment as important in its own right was neatly summarised by Boulding in his 1968 essay on the economics of Spaceship Earth. He compared cowboy and spaceship economics, arguing that we operated on the former basis, when the latter is our true position. In cowboy economics, best characterised in the old American West, resources are apparently limitless, free to be taken and then thrown away, confident in the knowledge the environment can absorb our waste. This view, as we have seen in Chapter 1, can be traced back at least as far as Francis Bacon.

By contrast, those living on a spaceship have limited and very exhaustible resources. As a result, they must ensure that all is wisely used, and then recycled – there can be no such thing as waste. This is perhaps best illustrated by considering a single natural resource: water. The World Commission on Water for the 21st Century, a United Nations-backed body, argues:

> huge investment in global water supplies is urgently needed to turn around a humanitarian crisis in which billions of people are forced to rely on unsafe water. The 45 to 50 billion pounds a year now spent on giving people safe water should leap to 115 billion pounds, with the private sector providing most of the investment. The current water crisis, in which one billion people do not have access to safe water and two billion go without adequate sanitation, will worsen and affect millions more, unless action is taken now. (http://www.world watercommission.org/)

The characterisation of complex adaptive systems introduced in Chapter 6 used the rich metaphor of the ecosystem. Within such a landscape it is the transitional zones that are often of particular interest, characterised by Raphael as 'the edges':

> Many of the most interesting things, say the biologists, happen on the Edges – on the interface between the woods and the field, the land and the sea. There living organisms encounter dynamic conditions that give rise to untold variety. Scientific studies of bird populations reveal that 'forest edge' species are generally more abundant than those which confine their territory to the interior of the forest. The inter-tidal zone, meanwhile, that thin ribbon which separates the land from the sea, supports a plurality of life uniquely adapted to both air and water.... Variety, perhaps, but there is tension as well. The flora of the meadows, as they approach the woodlands, finds themselves coping with increasingly unfavourable conditions: the sunlight they need might be lacking, and the soil no longer feels right. There is also the problem of competition with alien species of trees and shrubs. The Edges, in short, might abound with life, but each living form must fight for its own. (Raphael 1976: 5–6)

This resonates nicely with the 'boundary between order and chaos' considered in complexity theory, and seen as the area in which there is greatest variety and creativity. The role of competition is important, and it is worth revisiting a key characteristic of the complex adaptive system, the interplay between competition and cooperation.

For many years environmental lessons drawn by management theorists tended to limit themselves to the exploration of competition. In part this reflected the focus of ecology itself:

> Several recent articles have commented that mutualistic interactions are not covered in sufficient detail in modern ecology texts. This is a contrast to ecological textbooks of the 1920s–1940s where positive interactions were hypothesised to be important driving forces in communities. However, even in the ecological literature, the frequency of research articles on mutualism (14%) is much less than that for such other interaction types as competition (31%), predation (24%) or herbivory (30%). So textbooks may merely reflect the state of the ecological literature. This low level of representation could be because many mutualism

studies have been descriptive and have focused on particular adaptations or life-history characteristics of organisms and not on theory, whereas studies on other interactions focus on the interaction itself and the mechanisms involved. (Stiling 1996: 152)

However, the emergence of the 'network form' of organisation in the 1990s reversed this trend, although at times the 'tyranny of the Or' has surfaced, and debate has veered toward a picture of co-operation as non-conflictual. Thus a common metaphor when considering partnerships is that of marriage. Kanter (1996) identifies five stages of a partnership:

- **Courtship** where two companies meet, and find each other attractive
- **Engagement** where they draw up plans for their future together, and close the deal
- **Newly partnered companies** spending time together, they discover each other's differences, and varying opinions about how the relationship should operate
- **Bridging the differences** entails devising mechanisms for acceptance of each other's differences, and developing techniques for a lasting relationship
- **Old marrieds** whereby each company discovers that it has changed internally as a result of its collaboration in the ongoing relationship

Similarly Bergquist et al. suggest that:

A significant number of the people we interviewed considered partnership in ways similar to how many of us consider marriage. They may have been able to make a satisfactory living on their own, but they chose not to. They wanted to be in a partnership of commitment primarily because they enjoyed the experience and preferred the at-work life-style. In particular, they liked the experience of sharing not only risks and responsibilities but also ideas, goals, hopes and dreams. (1995: 61)

They continue:

Our associate drew an analogy ... to a pair of lovers who live together without a formal marriage license. While not bound together legally, their union is certainly as strong and deep as the most committed of marriages. As a result, it is not a partnership based primarily on business considerations (a partnership of function) but, in the interviewer's words, it is 'an alliance of the heart' (a partnership of commitment). (Bergquist et al. 1995: 62)

When working in the Pluralist arena such a stance may be possible, but in the Open arena this is rather less likely, and here the metaphor of 'partnership as organic mutualism' may be more appropriate, recognising that it is a process of both competition and cooperation. A five-stage process for this would be:

- **Initiate** Identify who you want and who you need in the collaboration; and why you want or need it
- **Negotiate** Consider relative power and interest, potential for agreement and value gain. Negotiate the contract.

- **Pact: contract and trust** Seek ways for creative collaboration, while maintaining your Black Box
- **Balance of power** Frequent reappraisal of relative positions, power, perspectives, objectives and outcome
- **End game** Get closer, renegotiate, reassess Black Box, move to positive sum, revert to zero sum, consider exit strategy

By way of illustration of the interlinking between cooperation and competition, the *Independent on Sunday* (27 July 1997) reported that four leading consumer goods companies – Unilever, Bass, Cadbury-Schweppes and Kimberly-Clark – together accounting for about 18 per cent of UK television advertising spending, and a large number of consumer goods on supermarket shelves, were considering a wide ranging cooperation to improve the terms they get when dealing with supermarkets, and when buying advertising airtime. This was beginning with a pilot programme to share market research and to explore joint marketing initiatives. A consultant was quoted as saying: 'It is impossible to detect any downside to this arrangement. It will lessen the influence of retailers in price negotiations and allow the companies to extract better terms from ITV and Channel 4 for airtime rates.' This comment reinforces an important point – this is not cooperation pure and simple, but cooperation intertwined with competition. Coevolution embraces both competition and cooperation.

Similar considerations apply in the airline industry. Airlines are required to compete with each other, but they also need to cooperate, and we have seen in recent years the emergence of several global alliances between companies that nevertheless continue to compete.

In the public sector 'partnership' has become the *sine qua non* of activity, stimulated by both carrot – it is a good thing to do – and stick – it is a prerequisite in many funding regimes, and becomes more and more necessary as traditional forms of expenditure are restricted. Indeed, partnership by necessity has become a familiar pattern in both public and public-private linkages. Here the marriage metaphor would become even more forced – are we talking about arranged marriages, or shotgun marriages? The ecological metaphor fits rather better: live forms need to develop some modus vivendi with the surrounding environment and other life forms, including parasitism (to be found also in the organisational sphere), mutualism and symbiosis.

Returning to Welford's ROAST scale, we are here at stage 4, 'Seize and preempt', where the organisation voluntarily seizes and pre-empts its actions with environmental concerns. It proactively engages in setting the agenda. It is responsive to the many external stakeholders. The latter phases would display the attributes of sustainable development. A number of firms aspire to this stage: one example is the Kao Corporation (see their website: http://www.kao/co.jp/e/corp_e/responsible/index.html).

LEVEL 4: INTEGRATIVE

At this level we have to be speculative: indeed the argument of this chapter is not that such a level currently exists in any organisation, but that it provides an interesting stance from which to consider an organisation and its possible futures. On Welford's ROAST scale we are here at stage 5, 'Transcend', where the organisation's environmental values, attitudes, beliefs and culture exhibit a total support for the environment. Such an organisation would proactively support and be responsive to all living things. It would act in a way which is fully consistent with sustainable development. The characteristics of such an organisation are developed in more detail in Table 9.4.

Welford (1995) notes that his scale can also be used to categorise the environmental attitudes of consumers. In Stage I consumers would purchase services or products without considering the environmental consequences. The sole criterion for purchase is to satisfy the needs of the consumer. No attention is paid to any environmental attributes of the purchase. Moving to Stage II, consumers become more observant of environmental activities and reluctantly comply with existing laws. However, they display negative attitudes towards environmental legislation as restricting personal choice. Purchasing behaviour reflects only enforced actions. Those customers at Stage III begin voluntarily to seek out products that are less damaging to the environment. They are accommodative to environmental concerns. Stage IV consumers will question the need for the product as a legitimate use of the world's resources. A decision to purchase a product or service must meet the buyer's personal criteria for minimum environmental impact, resource and energy use. The purchasing behaviour would exhibit strong environmental demands of the manufacturer, focusing on impacts over the total product life cycle and its respect for human-

Table 9.4 Environmental performance scale extremes

Resistant organisation	Transcendent organisation
Resists any green behaviour	Internalises sustainable development
Disregards green aspects in decisions	Green criteria become paramount in decision making
Willing to damage environment if beneficial to the organisation	No decision of the firm will upset the ecological relationships
Negative environmental values	Environmental values take on an ideology associated with sustainable development
Sees resources and nature for human profit and pleasure	Human beings are not above nature but with nature; all decisions must reflect
Resists any green intellectual or philosophical argument as trite views of extremists	the intrinsic values and interrelationships of other members of the biosphere

Source: Welford (1995).

ity and other living things. Finally, Stage V consumers have strong values for all living things in the biosphere. Therefore all production and consumption must show deep respect for others in the ecosystem. This translates to a reduced level of human consumption to ensure that the ecobalance is maintained.

For the nearest real-life example, we probably have to turn not to modern organisations, but to those rooted in non-Western traditions, and often under threat for that reason. An example would be the Native American cultures, briefly considered in Chapter 6.

To date much of the thinking which would inform level four remains frankly speculative and theoretical. Shrivastava contrasted the 'CASTRATED' environmental landscape with that of GREENING: Good Returns, Economics to Ethics, Nature's Independence and Nature's Goodness (it may be argued that the search for acronyms is stretching a little far at this point!). In more detail:

- Good Returns: Not just profits or economic wealth – also environmental impact and protection of human health and the natural environment.

- Economics to Ethics: Calls into question the very reason for the existence of business organisations. If the profit motive is not enough to justify their existence, then revered notions of efficiency, productivity, profitability and competitiveness become less meaningful. Includes concerns and responsibilities of all stakeholders.

- Nature's Independence: Nature has a moral right to exist independently of the welfare or economic interests of humans. Nature's Goodness: Nature has historically provided and can continue to provide to humans a basis for reasonable, even bountiful living (Shrivastava 1994: 718).

In a similar vein the Elmwood Institute (Callenbach et al. 1993) argued for a number of shifts in thinking, which can be seen to resonate well with the view of the organisation as complex adaptive system, and involving the recognition of the interconnectedness of problems. These are first a shift from objects to relationships: the shift from the perception of the world as a machine or resource to be used, to the world as a living system is a key characteristic of a new ecological paradigm. Second, a shift from parts to the whole: living systems comprise individual organisms, social systems and ecosystems, all of which are integrated. Third, they advocate a shift from domination to partnership: the shift from domination to partnership is also central to the ecological paradigm. In the business world this translates to a shift from competition to cooperation and from managerial hierarchy to participative arrangements. Fourth, a shift from structures to processes: systems thinking is process thinking and every structure is a manifestation of underlying processes. Fifth, a shift from individualism to integration. Finally, a shift from growth to sustainability.

> ## Vignette 9.3
>
> ### Native American philosophy
>
> Bohm draws a number of contrasts between current thinking and native American philosophy, designed to illustrate both the similarities and the differences. Four examples are:
>
> - Quantum theory stresses the irreducible link between observer and observed and the basic holism of all phenomena. Indigenous science also holds that there is no separation between individual and society, between matter and spirit, between each one of us and the whole of nature.
>
> - In modern physics the essential stuff of the universe cannot be reduced to billiard ball atoms, but exists as relationships and fluctuations at the boundary of what we call matter and energy. Indigenous science teaches that all that exists is an expression of relationships, alliances, and balances between what, for lack of better words, we could call energies, powers or spirits.
>
> - Several leading-edge thinkers in physics suggest that nature is not a collection of objects in interaction but is a flux of processes. The whole notion of flux and process is fundamental to the Indigenous sciences of Turtle Island. Algonkian-speaking peoples, such as the Cheyenne, Cree, Ojibwaj, Mic Maq, and Blackfoot, all share a strongly verb-based family of languages that reflects this direct experience.
>
> - Ecologists stress that we must attend to the basic interconnectedness of nature and to the sensitivity and complexity of natural systems. This has always been the approach of Indigenous peoples. The traditional Thanksgiving Address of the Iroquois people, for example, specifically acknowledges the wholeness that is inherent within all of life.
>
> Peat also comments that 'It is difficult to imagine an Indigenous scientist having written Darwin's *On the Origin of Species*. Its hypotheses about the survival of the fittest and progress through competition are essentially the values of Victorian politics, society, economics, industrial progress, checks, and balances projected onto the natural "world"' (Peat 1995: 118)
>
> By contrast, an Indigenous scientist would view nature as cooperative and operating through relationship and alliance. In a universe in which time turns in a circle, and in which the ceremonies of renewal are the continued obligations of The People, the emphasis is always upon balance and harmony as opposed to progress, advancement, and accumulation. Within such a world the whole idea of sickness and health must have a profoundly different meaning.

CONCLUSION

The purpose of this chapter is to suggest that the ecological metaphor is more powerful than many others which could be chosen for organisations, because it relates to a subject of pressing, though still underemphasised, concern.[3] We invite you to consider it in relation to your own organisation, and to your own value system. Each of the four levels we have outlined provides a different mind-set and a different landscape: which fits you, and how comfortable are you with this?

NOTES

1 For example: *'If the eye attempts to follow the flight of a gaudy butterfly, it is arrested by some strange tree or fruit; if watching an insect, one forgets it in the strange flower it is crawling over; if turning to admire the splendour of the scenery, the individual character of the foreground fixes the attention. The mind is a chaos of delight'* (in a letter home on his impressions of the Brazilian tropical rain forest).

2 Wachtell is an elephant, in the sense of the ancient Indian metaphor, with each person seeing it differently, with varying strengths and weaknesses depending on their viewpoint. It is a butterfly, in that it is an elegant, colourful creation that flits from one success to another, and almost no one will be surprised if Wachtell metamorphoses into something more ordinary. Wachtell flits because it opportunistically goes where the flowers look brightest.

3 In his article Gladwin (1999) notes that 'Most writers in the FT Mastering Strategy series have highlighted the economic and technological dimensions of corporate strategy, presenting their ideas as seemingly "value free". A few have examined social issues but virtually none have related the topic to the natural world.' In total there were more than 60 articles in the series, and only two others mentioned ecological concerns.

REFERENCES AND FURTHER READING

Beder, S. (1997) *Global Spin: The Corporate Assault on Environmentalism*, Dartington: Green Books.

Bergquist, W., J. Betwee and D. Meul (1995) *Building Strategic Relationships: How to Extend your Organization's Reach through Partnerships, Alliances, and Joint Ventures*, San Francisco: Jossey Bass.

Boulding, K. (1968) 'The Economics of Spaceship Earth', in H. Jarret (ed.) *Environmental Quality in a Growing Economy*, Baltimore: Johns Hopkins Press.

Briggs, J. (1992) *Fractals: The Patterns of Chaos*, London: Thames and Hudson.

Cairncross, F. (1995) *Green, Inc.: A Guide to Business and the Environment*, London: Earthscan Publications.

Callenbach, E., F. Capra and L. Goldman (1993) *Ecomanagement: The Elmwood Guide to Ecological Auditing Sustainable Business*, San Francisco: Berrett-Koehler.

Cannon, T. (1995) *Corporate Responsibility*, London: Pitman.

Clarke, T. and S. Clegg (1998) *Changing Paradigms*, London: HarperCollins Business.

Croker, K.J. (1999) 'Managing Risk before it Manages You', *Financial Times* (11 October).

De Geus, A. (1997) *The Living Company*, Cambridge, MA: Harvard Business School Press.

Elkington, J. (1989) *The Green Capitalists*, London: Victor Gollancz.

Gladwin, T.N. (1999) 'A Call for Sustainable Development', *Financial Times* (13 December).

Greenhalgh, P. (ed.) (2000) *Art Nouveau 1890–1914*, London: V&A Publications.

Haajer, M.A. (1995) *The Politics of Environmental Discourse*, Oxford: Clarendon Press.

Hawken, P., A.B. Lovins and L.H. Lovins (1999) *Natural Capitalism: the Next Industrial Revolution*, London: Earthscan Publications Ltd.

Held, D., A. McGrew, D. Goldblatt and J. Perraton (1999) *Global Transformations*, Cambridge: Polity Press.

Kanter, R.M. (1996) *World Class*, New York: Simon and Schuster.

Martell, L. (1994) *Ecology and Society: An Introduction*, Cambridge: Polity Press.

Mintzberg, H., B. Ahlstrand and J. Lampel (1998) *Strategy Safari*, Hemel Hempstead: Prentice Hall.

Morgan, G. (1993) *Imaginization*, Newbury Park, CA: Sage.

Morgan, G. (1997, 2nd edition) *Images of Organization*, Newbury Park, CA: Sage.

Oswick, C. and D. Grant (1996) *Organisation Development*, London: Pitman Publishing.

Peat, F.D. (1995) *Blackfoot Physics*, Fourth Estate.

Raphael, R. (1976) *Edges: Backcountry Lives in America Today on the Borderlands between Old Ways and the New*, New York: Knopf.

Schmidheiny, S. (1992) *Changing Course: A Global Perspective on Development and the Environment*, Cambridge, MA: MIT Press.

Shrivastava, P. (1994) 'CASTRATED Environment: GREENING Organisational Studies', *Organization Studies*, 15(5): 705–26.

Stead, W.E. and J.G. Stead (1992) *Management for a Small Planet: Strategic Decision Making and the Environment*, Newbury Park, CA: Sage.

Stiling, P. (1996) *Ecology: Theories and Applications*, London: Prentice Hall International.

Welford, R. (1995) *Environmental Strategy and Sustainable Development*, London: Routledge.

Welford, R. and R. Starkey (eds) (1996) *Business and the Environment*, London: Earthscan Publications.

Part 4

HOW DOES IT ALL HAPPEN?

Chapter 10

CHOICES IN CHANGE – CHANGE THROUGH THE STRATEGIC RECIPE AND CHANGE THROUGH UNDERSTANDING

The aims of this chapter are to:

1 Explore the idea that there are varieties of strategic recipe that underpin approaches to the management of change.

2 Discuss ways in which different forms of strategic recipe can be seen as both advantageous and problematic and discuss the sorts of approach to them that enable them to be successful as change interventions.

3 Develop an understanding of approaches to change that represent alternatives to the strategic recipe – can there be such an approach, or are all approaches some way or another a 'strategic recipe'?

4 Develop subtlety in the strategic recipe through the processes of organisational reflexivity.

INTRODUCTION

Earlier chapters have indicated that strategy-making is a complex process. Mintzberg and Lampel state that it is 'a combination of judgmental designing, intuitive visioning, and emergent learning; it is about transformation as well as perpetuation; it must involve individual cognition and social interaction, co-operative as well as conflictive; it has to include analyzing before and programming after as well as negotiating during, and all of this must be in response to what may be a demanding environment' (1999: 28). This rather metaphysical conceptualising of the process compares with the more pragmatic definition of strategic success in what are characterised by Ferlie, Ashburner, Fitzgerald and Pettigrew (1996) as 'high performance firms'. According to them the strategic approach prescribes 'environmental assessment . . . change leadership which can include people at every level . . . linking strategic and operational change . . . treating human resource management as a strategic concern . . . coherence in the management of change' (1996: 150) as the core ingredients for success. Contained within the definition is a meta-recipe, a comprehensive prescriptive listing, of what it is the strategist 'must do' in order to be successful. Different authors and managers, coming from different positions with regard to their understanding of the strategy process, suggest the enactment of the meta-recipe in different ways with different levels of belief or scepticism in the strategy process itself. The issue of the enactment of strategy as recipe is a major topic for this chapter.

In understanding strategic process different writers suggest that there are dominant approaches to undertaking it. Whether or not these dominant approaches are in the minds of academics writing about strategy or in the minds of the actors undertaking strategic process is, on occasion, questionable. In a spirit of scientific categorisation and labelling Mintzberg and Waters (1985) discussed eight forms of strategic process and suggested that the style of strategy making and implementation be closely related to the environment in which the organisation existed. More recently, Mintzberg and Lampel (1999) have suggested that they discern ten styles of strategy-making, such that there are common themes with the earlier formulation but also a degree of reformulation of the original model. In the more recent formulation Mintzberg and Lampel (1999) assert that strategy-making is becoming more eclectic in its intellectual resource. Decisions about the style of strategy-making or process to be adopted in organisations is related to such matters as the stage of development of the organisation, size of business, maturity or volatility of the production process and the perceived nature of the environment.

A somewhat different approach to taxonomy of approaches to strategy is to understand the strategic enterprise as having core dimensions. For example, Whittington (1993, 2001) suggests a two-dimensional model which looks at strategic process and outcomes. In relation to the issue of strategy making and strategy process it is suggested that in some organisations strategy is treated as a concrete phenomenon. At the other end of the axis are organisations in which strategy process is understood to be an emergent phenomenon so that when the strategy document is developed, it is understood to be a *post hoc* shaping of the world. The second dimension is that of anticipated outcomes from the strategic process. Thus, on the one hand, there are strategic processes that are overtly and clearly geared towards profit-maximising outcomes or, at the other end of the continuum, pluralistic, 'envisioning other possible outcomes as well as just [*sic*] profit' (Whittington 2001: 2).

The ways in which strategy-makers and change agents understand, sometimes explicitly and more often implicitly, these two axes constitute their strategic recipe. According to Wilson (1992), a 'strategic recipe' is a response to change which is based on a patterned response to the issues that are identified as being significant in the change process. Strategic recipes are essentially vague, numinous in their nature – 'no-one has ever seen or touched a strategy. Strategies . . . do not exist as tangible entities. They are abstract concepts, in the minds of people' (Mintzberg 1994: 240), although, as has been suggested, they may well be articulated through such concrete evidences as business plans and other strategic documents. There are two significant issues. One is that the strategic recipe followed by an organisation is the response that flows from 'generalised norms in the environment' (Wilson 1992: 84). In this sense the recipe adopted by the organisation is essentially imitative behaviour. At the same time there are organisations, within an industry or business milieu that may wish for rational or less rational reasons to go their own way in developing strategy, a desire for their organisation to be seen as unique (Mintzberg and Lampel 1999), or idiosyncratic. In this latter sense, as Wilson (1992) points out, organisations do not necessarily follow recipes in a slavish sort of way. He cites the work of Grinyer et al. (1987) in which it was demonstrated that there were a number of organisations that effectively managed change and avoided the adversity confronted by other organisations in the same sector, by moving outside the commonly accepted recipe for that industry. This is a theme to which we shall return in the chapter. However, for many organisations there is a relationship between the strategic recipe and the approach to change. There is a revealed orthodoxy. To cite Wilson: 'the extent to which changes conform to established patterns in the operating environment will determine greatly how change is hindered or facilitated and will also influence how changes are evaluated later on' (1992: 84).

The second, related form of strategic recipe is that which is based on the understandings of the approaches to strategy and change undertaken by what are understood to be the industry leaders, the exemplars. It might also be suggested that the prescriptions, recipes and nostrums promulgated by consultants, who characteristically elevate partial, local knowledge into the status of disinterested theory (Magala 1997), will also, if they gain the attention of strategists, form the bases of strategic recipes. As an aspect of the mindset, strategic recipes are underpinned by strategic imperatives. These are the 'unchallenged and taken for granted imperatives to action derived from the analysis of strategy' (Clark 2000: 251) which guide, at a behavioural level, the implementation of the strategy whether or not they are essentially correct or not correct in achieving the superordinate goals of the organisation. In other words strategic recipes and the strategic imperatives can be mistaken but still adhered to because they are not properly understood.

We have seen that organisations have different sorts of approach to strategy. Speaking rationally, choice of strategic recipe is in accord with such matters as estimates of the state of development of the organisation, its markets and means of production, and so on. In this view of the matter choice of strategic recipe has a degree of will and intent about it as managers make sense of the world. A somewhat different spin on the matter is that the choice of strategic recipe may lack this level of scientific rigour. In the rather less rational view, choice of strategic recipe is either a matter of imitation or evidence of idiosyncrasy, to think differently from the common herd. Whatever the case the notion of strategy as a means of developing the organisation is all-pervasive – such that 'no aspect of corporate life is indifferent to strategy' (Zalenik 1996: 245). However, given the pervasive nature of the strategy process there may well be other elements than the directly instrumental present in the development of the strategic recipe.

There may, for example, be an element of aesthetic appreciation, a perception of beauty (Strati 1999) in the recipe. This might, to take Whittington's (2001) model as an example, relate either to the 'scientific' rationalist or to the 'artful' crafting strategist. Both believe in the very reality of strategy such that there may be a perception of beauty in the elegance of the expression of the route towards profit-maximising or complex, pluralistic outcomes. The strategy document has an iconic status; it is, as form fits function, a thing of beauty and elegance in itself. On the other hand, there may well be aesthetic appreciation for those who believe that strategy is emergent. This is an aesthetic of excitement. The beauty of the strategy process lies in the expression of intuition, the 'gut feeling' as to what will work and what will not. In this case the end point is 'the imponderable and the inexhaustible' (Strati 1999: 130) so that the strategic recipe has, as its mantra, turbulence and constant reinvention. In this case the successful strategic recipe is one that avoids hysteria about the very idea of turbulence and the consequent temptation to plan to control it. The other element of the recipe is to achieve a deep understanding of the nature of the 'turbulence' in order to creatively craft a response to it (Mintzberg 1994).

In some respects the sense of the aesthetic, indeed the total Gestalt of the strategic recipe, emerges from the dominating basic assumptions of the strategists, whether they be rational-economic, social, based on concepts of self-actualisation or those which reflect 'a more variable, complex model of human nature' (Schein 1988: 52). The strategic recipe, crucially, represents an enactment of the mindset of the CEO and the Board and although it may well have elements of the rational response to the exigencies of the internal and external environments of the organisation, it also has elements of the affectual.

A MODEL FOR THE EXPLORATION OF STRATEGIC RECIPES

In capturing the essence of the different positions there is a close similarity between the different sorts of strategic recipe and the diagram introduced in Chapter 2 of different approaches to organisational culture. This is on the basis that culture and strategy are intertwined. Strategy may be seen as an expression of the culture and as a reinforcement of the strategist's understanding of culture as it gets enacted – unless there is a deliberate attempt to change the culture through the adoption of a different strategic recipe. In this sense, strategic recipes represent a discourse (Knights and Morgan 1991) which makes a claim to determine, overall, the sort of culture and the approaches to the formulation of strategy that is permissible within the organisation.

In Figure 10.1 there is an attempt to explore some of the ways in which strategic recipes are formulated and enacted.

Along the horizontal axis there is a continuum. At one end is a determination of overall strategy for the organisation that is highly centralised, in which there is a very clearly defined strategic apex from whence clearly directed strategies

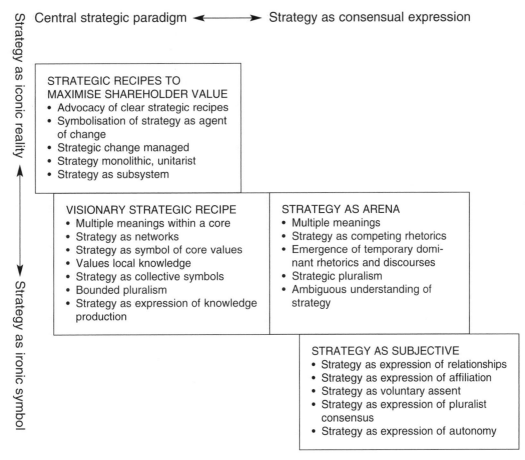

Figure 10.1 Strategic options

emanate. Moving to the right there is a situation in which strategy is consensual, a situation in which the membership itself creates, develops and sustains the strategy.

Along the vertical axis there is a depiction of the 'reality' of the strategy to members in terms of its substantiveness. Thus at the top of the axis the strategy is real in its documentation and real in the sense that its enactment pervades, one way or another, the lives of its members and indeed key external stakeholders. At the other end of the continuum the strategy is a thing of shadows; it is not a significant part of members' lives as document or discourse (although documentation may be produced in order to create the right impression for those stakeholders who may like to see such documentation). In this recipe strategy making is informal as opposed to the formality of strategy making at the other end of the continuum.

However, it is important to stress that within each of the 'boxes' there is also a continuum, that within them there may be different approaches to the strategic recipe. What we have tried to do in the different models is to understand the recipe as an actor within the recipe might understand it – as if that recipe were real to that strategist. Inevitably (we cannot do other) there may be moments of scepticism but overall we have presented the recipes as if they were believable, sustainable models of being in the world.

Strategic recipes geared to maximising shareholder and corporate value

Vignette 10.1 Linking the customer and shareholder value

Heinz Continues Global Growth in 2000

Innovation and Aggressive Marketing Drive Record Sales and Earnings

Fiscal 2000 was another strong year for Heinz, resulting from a stronger focus on market-oriented innovation and top-line growth in core businesses ... This intensive consumer focus is spurred, as ever, by our single-minded dedication to increasing shareholder value ...

Our goal for Fiscal 2001 and beyond is to generate consumer excitement, enjoyment and convenience. ...

A consistent growth rate, combined with excellent management and growing global brands, makes Heinz an attractive investment and a consumer favourite – anytime, any-place, anywhere.

(Excerpt from statement to shareholders of H.J. Heinz Company for fiscal year ended 3 May 2000. Cited with permission H.J. Heinz Company Limited.)

An underpinning assumption within this model of strategy is that the corporate approach is dominated in its direction by the concept of the maximisation of shareholder value (as in Friedman 1970). This is legitimated by the very conditions of a capitalist, free market driven, economy (Friedman 1970) as an approach to the conduct of strategy in private sector business and industry, and by the 'shadow' of shareholder value in public sector organisations.

In the case of the latter the 'virtual shareholder' is characteristically the government which claims to drive organisations within its control by strategies which emphasise 'best value' or maximising value for money (see, for example, McAuley, Lohen and Duberley 2000; Johnson and Scholes 2000). Overall, in public sector organisations, the 'concept of strategy should be understood as referring ... to a set of expressly political purposes which themselves reflect public aspirations as revealed by a process of public debate' (Pollitt 1993). In order to achieve this, government agencies place great emphasis on processes of control and accountability in order to achieve strategic purpose.

The claims of shareholder value as pre-eminent strategic value are vigorously contested (e.g. among many authors, in the private sector by Mintzberg (1984) and, in the public sector by Pollitt (1993), Exworthy and Halford (1999)). For the strategist working within this model, strategy is the very lynchpin by which shareholder value is enacted; the documents, which express the strategy, have iconic status. They are the rational means by which the essentially non-rational ends of shareholder value are achieved. They express the very essence of organisational aspiration. In this sense there is high strategic agency (Clegg 1998) such that the strategy determines other aspects of organisational life such as design, employment practices, the general cultural paradigm, organisational systems, and so on. The ethics of shareholder value are firmly located in understandings of capitalism and the philosophical presuppositions that underpin utilitarianism (Mintzberg 1984; McAuley 1996) with an emphasis on strategies that are based on ends, in terms of maximising shareholder value, rather than means (Smith 1998). In this sense issues such as investment and employment strategy in organisations 'become compelling as investors *demand* that corporations consistently deliver shareholder value *regardless of their long term strategy* for deploying human and financial capital' (Boquist, Milbourn and Thakor 1998: 59; our emphasis). Central to the paradigm is an understanding that 'every company with a share quote knows that it is vulnerable to take-over if it neglects to make the share price the absolute focus of its efforts' (Hutton 2000: 28). Within this paradigm 'an explicit and relentless focus on shareholder value growth as the objective of corporate strategy' (Wise 1999: 18) may be presented as a significant driver for radical organisational change. Its achievement calls for 'a rare combination of commitment and rigorous application (with) a management philosophy of long-term positive returns, based on a transparency of information about the company' (Dore 1999). This may involve such measures as the development of a clear view as to the nature of shareholder value and how to maximise it within the organisation. Implementation of the recipe calls for the development of internal measures of performance and the establishment of bottom up, non-centralised strategies with detailed implementation targets (McTaggart and Gillis 1998). From the point of view of critics of this strategic mindset, 'shareholder pressures are experienced by employees, including managers, as work intensification and increased job insecurity' (Alvesson and Willmott 1996: 36). As we shall see also, the relationship between the strategy, the organisation and shareholders need not always be of this nature.

In his study of transformation at Coca-Cola, Wise shows a powerful connection 'between the various business design elements (and) also between its business design and the levers of shareholder value creation' (1999: 18). He suggests that this was achieved through a strategy that emphasised the creation of high-margin, premium business, asset efficiency and through 'enhanced earnings predictability through its improved ability to manage the value chain' (Wise 1999: 19). This emphasis on the significance of an accountancy-based approach to the maximisation of shareholder value (Rappaport 1981) may be illustrated by the development of techniques such as Discounted Cash Flow Analysis which continues to be 'the most widely used investment appraisal technique' (Johnson and Scholes 1999: 372). In the relentless pursuit of shareholder value there is an estimation of the future cash flows to be associated with each of the strategies to be pursued by the organisation. This process allows 'assessment of the economic value to shareholders of alternative strategies at both the business unit and corporate levels' (Rappaport 1981: 139). It is claimed that this methodology enables estimation of incremental development of sales, a clear understanding of acceptable rates of return over a five-year forecasting period and a clear view of strategic alternatives (Rappaport 1981). There is an emphasis on what is 'real' (that is, to say, cash rather than vision), on methodologies that are strictly rational (that is, in accord with the rules of accountancy and economics rather than appeals to such numinous matters as common purpose or mission) and are amenable to techniques (that is, the processes are apparently scientific and transparent as opposed to artful). Concepts of vision and mission are used in this strategic recipe as techniques that will facilitate a sense of binding loyalty to the organisation both from customers and from employees.

Within the concept of the strategies that focus on shareholder value as presented in this model two quite contrasted approaches to strategy may be discerned which may be claimed to facilitate the change process. The first of these is one that emphasises classical order and unity within the organisation. The second is one which is more geared towards interest in the external environment but with an enduring view that the environment is to be controlled through the organisation. The first approach is characterised by Whittington (2001) as the classical approach. It is geared to the development of strategies to achieve corporate unity in the pursuit of shareholder value. Overall, within this perspective there is a view of the future that it is amenable to control – for if it were not, then shareholders would lose faith and there would be replacement in the Board. It is pervaded, Whittington suggests, by a view that the future can be looked at in terms of rational inputs leading to rational outputs and that management can take a detached view of the future. In this the role of leadership is critical from the practical perspective of 'steering the boat'. There is, within this view, and to paraphrase Mintzberg and Lampel (1999), emphasis on issues of design (the achievement of fit between the organisation and its environment), formal planning (cerebral, with an emphasis on the creation of order) and analysis (the development of very formal 'scientific' analysis of the industry or business).

Overall there is a view that the future can be managed in a sequential and formal manner as may be seen by the use of methodologies such as Discounted Cash Flow and by the use of methodologies such as Organisation Development to develop a gradualist view of change. Johnson and Scholes suggest that:

> Such gradual change makes a lot of sense. Incremental change might therefore be seen as an adaptive process to a continually changing environment: and in this sense it corresponds to ... the 'fit' concept of strategic change. There are, however dangers. Environmental change may not always be gradual enough for incremental change to keep pace.... There is

another danger: that organisations become merely reactive to their environment and fail to question or challenge ... or to innovate and create new opportunities. (1999: 47)

In undertaking the change process there is a strong adherence to the principles of multiple unfreezing, movement and refreezing with an assumption that there can be an end-point to the change process which is profit maximisation. This process is undertaken, within this paradigm, with a degree of caution. Thus Boquist, Milbourn and Thakor (1998) suggest, quite prescriptively, that a company 'must first identify a *status quo* strategy and its performance to maximise shareholder value. It [*and notice the degree of reification characteristic of the classical stance*] must ask what kinds of investment have enabled the strategy to be successful. The company can then understand the effective parts of the strategy and the amount of risk within which it must operate' (1998: 66).

In this sense there can be some tolerance of short-term decline as long as there is the promise of recovery. For example, when the retailer Marks & Spencer reduced its dividend for the first time in its history, a company 'insider' said: 'There's not going to be a great argument. ... The argument for cutting is pure logic – that M&S has been paying out more than it has earned for some time now, and there comes a point when you have to do a lot of investment. *It's an opportunity to say the worst is behind M&S.*' (Hughes 2000: 6) There is also an assumption that the level of strategic analysis can make the crucial issues of strategy and change explicit and that there need be no hidden agendas for these would not accord with the overall desire for strategic transparency. In this light Boquist, Milbourn and Thakor (1998) develop their concept of capital budgeting 'with the familiar objective of maximising shareholder wealth' (1998: 66). In their discussion of the model they stress, *inter alia*, the need for constant evaluation of the alignment between capital budgeting and the strategy with a clear evaluation strategy to 'separate winners from losers; the effectiveness with which a chosen project helps execute the strategy is the measure of success' (1998: 66).

Within this there is an assumption that the agenda for change will be universal, for the entire organisation. As a consequence, resistance to change is essentially a non-rational response to the situation with an emphasis on resistance being caused by issues such as loss of position, loss of income and other instrumental issues. In this sense, resistance is the mirror image of the utilitarianism of the overall organisational strategic paradigm. The focus of change tends to be through internal processes (Whittington 2001) and by the use of formal documentation such as business planning with traditionally an emphasis on quantitative measures. Johnson and Scholes write:

The manager faced with managing change needs to consider carefully the extent to which various components of change agency are in place or need to be developed ... [T]hese components include ... *clarity of direction* or *vision* which can be communicated clearly to others ... the importance of *context*. ... The successful change agent ... is someone who can perceive the nature of required change and the opportunities for change and turn these into triggers for change ... [The change agent will] employ an appropriate *style* of managing change

> ... [possess] the ability to use the political and symbolic processes that provide the levers and mechanisms for change. (1994: 411)

Within the shareholder value corporate model there is also a rather more dynamic model of strategic recipe and change which contrasts interestingly with the classical model. If the classical model suits what the strategy makers and change agents consider to be a *relatively* stable environment, then the evolutionist model is more suited to the less stable environment. Whittington (2001) suggests that upholders of this recipe tend to focus on the external environment as markets with a view that the environment is too volatile to anticipate and pre-empt entirely. Characteristically, however, there will be strenuous attempts, through the processes of strategic control, to protect the profit stream through maintenance of the brand, through product development approaches that align to emergent markets, control of the value chain and by being understood to be *the* industry defining company (Wise 1999). Within this recipe there is an emphasis on leadership and vision as technique in the entrepreneurial organisation (Mintzberg and Lampel 1999). These leaders (so the recipe has it) raid and dive, are fiercely competitive. However, they may be doing this rather more as symbol than as actuality. If they go too far they will run the danger of not meeting shareholder expectation; they may be perceived as 'too risky'. The organisation changes form (and personnel) as key members see the market changing. As with the more classical version of this recipe, the notion of vision is as technique rather than as core commitment. There is also, Whittington (2001) suggests, scepticism with regard to an overemphasis on rationality in decision-making with more of a role for intuition in the strategic recipe. This accords with the view expressed, on the basis of studies of organisations in different market environments, that 'intuition needs to be used cautiously and less often (perhaps, in combination with rational analysis) in a stable and moderately unstable environment, but more often in a highly unstable context' (Khatri and Ng 2000: 78). Thus it might be suggested that when organisations move from this mode of operation back into a more stable recipe intuition will be the less valued as a more ordered bureaucratisation of the organisation takes over. This process of movement and transition may be explored as the negotiated form of strategic recipe, which is discussed below.

Thus although there may be a rhetoric of constant change and turbulence, strategists with an eye to shareholder value will have a clear understanding, unless they are trapped in the rhetoric, that constant change is expensive both psychologically and in the use of resources. Change is gauged in terms of the capacity to adapt to rapidly changing markets and ability to adopt strategies that will dampen down shareholder volatility. It is likely that organisations that are in the business of maximisation of shareholder value might move between the rather more discontinuous evolutionary approach and the rather more stable classical approach although the periods of relative stability may be of fairly short duration. They take a Contingency approach (Mintzberg and Lampel 1999). Thus Wise comments of Coca-Cola that 'strategy is not based on a static snapshot of the firm's capabilities but on a constantly evolving business environment ... Coke, having successfully adopted and implemented its 'manage-the-value-chain' design must now redesign itself again as it faces a revitalized Pepsi and global market turbulence ... The best players ... are prepared to reinvent their business design *every few years*' (Wise 1999: 19; emphasis added).

It might, however, be appropriate to remember that all the fields in the model represent continua. At the top left (if you will) of the model are the most extreme positions taken by those adherents to shareholder value. At the bottom right is a position in which senior management, whilst still attentive to the significance of profit and strategic approaches to its achievement, do so in rather a more subversive, indirect manner. Thus the Chief Executive Officer of Nestlé, Peter Brabeck, commented that what he characterises as the vogue for shareholder value promotes short-termism at the expense of sound planning and asserts that 'you decide what to do with your business and then comes the shareholder value' (Koenig 1999: 1). He is, according to his account, liberated to enter into arenas of activity that the careful techniques of conventional shareholder-driven strategies would forbid. He cites, for example, the need to create a very clear understanding of the nature of emerging markets and the possibilities of creating relationships within them. Part of this strategy is to create alliances such that what he calls radical governments (that is, governments that are not highly aligned to capitalist perspectives) end up 'thinking it is better to work with us than against us'. This is a belief that a successful strategy is about sustaining the presence in emergent markets when the more cautious flee. He also expresses a belief in sustaining the debates about the nature of the business and its relationship with its markets with intellectual rigour and with candour in the exploration of issues. In this sense Brabeck (1999) takes us close to the subjectivist view of strategy which will be discussed later in this chapter. The maximisation of shareholder value, similarly, is subordinated to a different concept of organisation purpose in Hewlett Packard. A former Chief Executive commented to Collins and Porras that 'maximising shareholder wealth has always been way down the list. Yes profit is at the cornerstone of what we do ... but it has never been the *point* in and of itself. ... If we provide real satisfaction to real customers – we will be profitable' (Collins and Porras 2000: 57).

An alternative to the transcendence of shareholder value is expressed by Hammer. He eschews what he characterises as the cult of shareholder value in favour of customer value. He suggests that gearing organisations towards the idea of shareholder value was a useful corrective to the abuses of management power that became transcendent in the 1960s and the 1970s. Ultimately, however, 'satisfying shareholders is something that needs to be done, but it is not the reason a company exists. ... Creating shareholder value yields nothing but questions' (Hammer 1996: 100). He goes on to suggest that creating shareholder value is demotivating whereas 'creating customer value – being of service to one's fellow man – enriches one's spirit' (Hammer 1996: 101).

There is a paradox in this. This notion of customer service is not altruistic; it represents an exchange between the consumer and the organisation. Customer value comes at a price. In a more general sense, it is suggested that emphasis on the customer and the consumer 'encourages, and is encouraged by, economic rationales for behavior. Such rationales defend the elites within organizations (namely management, policy makers, owners ...) against the anxieties attendant upon the uncertainties and changes occurring in a world that is increasingly dominated by global markets. ... Organizations have rediscovered the "customer" and instituted a producer/customer pair' (Long 1999: 724). Furthermore, if the findings from the study undertaken by Knights and McCabe in a major financial sector organisation are capable of generalisation, the concept of customer value may be seen as a mantra capable of reinterpretation. Thus in their study, although there were claims that Business Process Re-engineering was concerned with the primacy of the customer, it was, in the event, financially driven. They point out that in the tendency to centralise, customer–staff interactions, as an aspect of process design, 'BPR would constitute a move away from the traditional customer ethos, toward one where bottom-line concerns predominate' (Knights and McCabe 1998: 791). In a more general sense Long suggests that the focus on the customer 'defends all organizational members from anxieties surrounding the loss of past institutional values ...' (1999: 724).

THE STRONG CULTURE RECIPE: STRATEGIC RECIPES IN THE MISSION-DRIVEN LEARNING ORGANISATION

In capitalist societies shareholders are important. The issue for organisational members is the extent to which they become the dominant symbol as to purpose, as in the previous section, or whether there is an attempt to reconcile shareholder value with other criteria for organisational survival and success. De Geus (1997) has explored European business organisations that have achieved considerable longevity and has proposed a number of modest hypotheses that might account for their survival over, in some cases, hundreds of years. These very issues will, of course, be of particular appeal to those shareholders who are prepared to take the long view, and who are comfortable with the values embodied in the sort of organisation discussed by De Geus and others in this tradition. It is, for example, the extent to which shareholder values are congruent with the idea that strategy formation can be seen as focusing, as in the Cultural School, on 'common interest and integration – strategy formation as a social process rooted in culture' (Mintzberg and Lampel 1999: 23). At the same time there is, within this typology, a view that strategy is concerned with learning such that 'strategies are emergent, strategists can be found throughout the organization, and so called formulation and implementation intertwine' (Mintzberg and Lampel 1999: 23). However, as we shall see, lying within this picture of emergence and culture there may well be recipes that are just as prescriptive as those in the more explicitly shareholder orientated view of strategy.

De Geus suggests that for these companies the appropriate measure of corporate success would be corporate longevity. The organisation is designed to stay in the world as a source of influence and integrity. For these organisations profits are the oxygen for survival, but not the goal. To help them in this process they tend to be very conservative in financial matters; they regard money in the 'pocket' as being better than money elsewhere. This maximises flexibility and reduces dependency on shareholders. In the development of these organisations there are, he suggests, three key elements. The first of these is clear steering and control from senior management. This is achieved by ensuring that the corporate leaders are in the world and that they are clearly associated with the society in which they live. They have a high awareness of the world because they are participants in it. The second criterion is that they are deeply aware of the ways in which the community of which they are a part shapes itself and so are enabled to develop the sort of culture within the organisation that mirrors that of the environment. This means that the company shows a clear sense of cohesion and identity; there is a good understanding of what the company stands for and is about so that its members are 'happy' to be linked with the organisational values. This leads to the third element, which is that there is a strong ability to create the preconditions within the organisations for identifying changes in environment. There would be, within the strategic recipe, an attitude towards turbulence that desires to manage members' understanding of the nature of the turbulence. This understanding enables members to discomfort competitors through the ability of the organisation to understand what is *really* going on (Mintzberg 1994).

If the organisation is looking to issues of long-term survival there is less need for the clarity of strategy making demanded in the shareholder value-driven recipe. Indeed, in the context of organisations studied by Collins and Porras in the United States which had a strong survival drive (in their case over 50 years) they found that what they called visionary companies 'make some of their best moves by trial and error, and – quite literally – accident. What looks *in retrospect* like brilliant foresight and planning was often the result of "let's just try a lot of stuff and keep what works". ... We found the concepts of Charles Darwin's *Origin of Species* to be more helpful for replicating the success of certain visionary companies than any textbook on corporate strategic planning' (2000: 9). In the development of what may be characterised as a processual (Whittington 2001) view of strategy, Hamel and Prahalad discuss the need to ask 'new' strategy questions. They pose these issues as prescriptions: 'who do we want to be as a corporation in ten years time, how can we reshape this industry to our advantage, what new functionalities do we want to create for our customers and what new core competencies should we be building'. To accomplish this there is a need to rely 'on the creativity of hundreds of managers and not just on the wisdom of a few planners' (1994: 282). This emphasis on corporate collaboration means that resistance to the strategy is perceived by the strategist to come from alienation from the strong sense of identification with the common organisational purpose. The strategist may perceive in resisting members a sense of 'disengagement [which] is a psychological removal from the effects of change. [D]isidentification ... involves the person's feeling victimized and threatened by change ... Disenchantment is another reaction to change in which the employee [*and note that it is employee rather than manager*] expresses anger over the loss of the past' (Weiss 1996: 392).

At the same time the strategic recipe and the change process are claimed to be a product of learning and understanding from within the organisation. De Geus suggests that in these organisations the strategic recipe invites a notion that change comes from the margins; structurally (if not culturally) these organisations operate very successfully in a decentralised manner. They 'stimulate evolutionary progress toward desired ends within the context of a core ideology – a process we call purposeful evolution' (Collins and Porras 1996: 149). Overall the strategic recipe claims engagement with double loop learning (Argyris 1990), with the ability to change the rules of the game through transformation of the organisation, redrawing industry boundaries, or create entirely new industries but retaining the integrity of the core values of the organisation itself. Critical here is a view that the strategic process concentrates on development of skills and capabilities. Through this crafted process, the recipe lays claim to 'the development of capabilities to develop the foresight to pre-empt other organisations through the processes of global pre-emption' (Hamel and Prahalad 1994: 23). In this sense the strategy is crafted to form a '*strategic architecture* ... concerned with creating *stretch goals* that challenge employees to accomplish the seemingly impossible. ... Strategy is the quest to overcome resource constraints through a creative and unending pursuit of better resource leverage' (Hamel and Prahalad 1994: 23). In their catechism of core characteristics of the strategic architecture they suggest that strategic direction is underpinned by the desire of the organisation to be not merely competitive in the normally accepted sense but to 'shape the structure of future industries' (Hamel and Prahalad 1994: 23).

It may be, however, that within all this magnificent prescription the strategic architecture in this sort of organisation, with its emphasis on capability and learning, has within it some rather more reflective moments. A core issue for organisations within this configuration is that of identity – vision, sense of survival, the development of capability are all dependent on the strong culture and an unwavering sense of the organisation 'being' in itself and in the world. In such an environment there may well be considerable power, in the development of the strategic recipe, of 'retrospective reframings'– 'new interpretations of old actions [which] bubble up in ongoing events' (Weick 1995: 78).

THE NEGOTIATED ARENA: THE STRATEGIC RECIPE AS AN OUTCOME OF MANOEUVRES IN THE DARK

Mintzberg is of the opinion that this strategic recipe is a manifestation of organisations which are in very uncertain environments, where there is a need for innovation and where the formation of strategy 'is not formulated consciously in one place so much as formed implicitly by the specific actions taken in many places' (1989: 210). In this organisation top managers 'must spend a good deal of their time in the battles that ensue over strategic choices and in handling the many other disturbances that arise ...' (Mintzberg 1989: 210). Whittington (2001) suggests that the focus of the strategy making, within this quadrant, tends to be on internal arrangements with a conscious attempt to understand the political issues. There is an attempt to develop understanding amongst members of the core issues of vision and mission from which the strategy flows. However, because the key organisational processes are concerned with a 'combination of political bargaining and bounded rationality' (Whittington 2001: 22) so the approach to change will tend to be cautious and incremental. There is also within the recipe the possibility of a degree of non-rationality; no one group of people can possibly see the 'whole truth' of organisational strategy. However negotiation can take place for reasons other than these.

There is the possibility, in any organisation with any dominant strategic recipe, for political disturbance to take place because of an emotional commitment to the essential rightness of the strategic approach to be advocated and an affectual distaste for those that are contested. Strategic position may be seen to be lodged in the sense of identity of the individual or the group. This dynamic may be illustrated through the example of the transformational leader. Mintzberg and Lampel suggest that 'the entrepreneurial school [of strategy] centred the process on the chief executive ... [This tradition] rooted that process in the mysteries of intuition' (Mintzberg and Lampel 1999: 22). The political processes that underpin the transformational leader are captured by the suggestion that 'the initiation of strategic change can be viewed as a process whereby the Chief Executive Officer makes sense of an altered version of the organization and engages in cycles of negotiated social construction activities to influence stakeholders and constituents to accept that vision' (Gioia and Chittipeddi 1991: 434). In relation to the emotional aspects of this work, it is suggested, with particular reference to the transformational leader, that 'self-awareness may provide individuals with greater perceived individual control over interpersonal events and consequences in their life ... that transformational leaders who are self-aware possess high levels of self-confidence and self-efficacy, and provide orientation for others' (Sosik and Megerian 1999: 381).

There is, however, a paradox in that the transforming energy required of the transformational leader sits uneasily with the development of high levels of self-awareness. Thus although the ideal may well be that the transformational leader possesses a high level of emotional intelligence, for mundane purposes the practice of the role may require a presentation of self that emphasises certainty and alignment with the vision. There is, at its heart, profound 'ambiguity and tension in the way in which hero entrepreneurs and new leaders are being advocated' (Buchanan and Badham 1999: 146) by those management theorists and gurus with an interest in this strategic recipe. In this situation the balance in the relationship between the transformational chief executive and other stakeholders 'is particularly vulnerable to the volatility of power. . . . The judicious use of power is crucial to creating common goals and giving meaning to organizational life, but failure to recognize the dual nature of power . . . can affect one's ability to stay in contact with reality [*Whatever that is*]. When the sense of balance is lost, political gamesmanship may usurp the focus on organizational effectiveness' (De Vries 1993: 180). At a political level, however, transformational leaders inevitably have their sell-by date. It may be that the transforming vision is no longer attractive at an emotional level, or it may become corrupted in its own hubris (De Vries 1993). At a more practical level it may be felt that the vision is no longer appropriate to emergent 'reality' (Johnson and Scholes 1999). The dominating, imperialising discourse (Pritchard and Willmott 1997) held by the transformational leader and his/her true believers no longer holds. It becomes contested as other discourses and rhetorics vie for attention.

This issue is not, however, restricted to transformational leaders. The emergence of power blocs within the boardroom – 'a more or less precarious set of implicit or acknowledged alliances that are vulnerable to implosion or fragmentation precisely because their components are frequently heterogeneous' discourse (Pritchard and Willmott 1997: 291) – is always possible whenever the current strategic recipe becomes, for whatever reason, controversial. This situation is rendered even more interestingly complex in the sense that, to paraphrase Pritchard and Willmott, whilst the Board is attempting to capture the means of strategy, employees will work during this period of disruption to attempt to capture the means of production, to 'secure control over their immediate social conditions of everyday life' (1997: 291). Within the strategic apex there may be, in anthropological terms, rebellion or revolution. That is, in the case of the former, there may be the maintenance of broadly the same strategic recipe but enacted by different characters. In the case of the latter, the emergent power bloc displaces not only the *dramatis personae* of the current power bloc but also brings to bear a new strategic recipe.

STRATEGY AS AN EXPRESSION OF SUBJECTIVE EXPERIENCE: THE UNANSWERED QUESTION

We would suggest – and the title of the section respects the ambivalence – that this form of strategic recipe is, in organisational terms, one that is problematic although possible. It is a recipe that invites 'high discretionary strategic agency' (Clegg 1998: 40) such that strategy is developed through 'the disciplined discretion of the agency of empowered authorities' (Clegg 1998: 40). Clegg suggests that this mode of conduct is akin to the idea of the professional organisation as initially advocated by Weber. However, even for Weber, the image of the university as a truly collegial atmosphere had already become mythic. He suggests – and it was 1918 when this was written:

Of late we can observe distinctly that the German universities in the broad fields of science develop in the direction of the American system. The large institutes of medicine or natural science are 'state capitalist' enterprises, which cannot be managed without very considerable funds. Here we encounter the same condition that is found wherever capitalist enterprise comes into operation: the 'separation of the worker from his means of production'. The worker [*i.e. the lecturer*] ... is just as dependent upon the head of the institute as is the employee in the factory upon the management. For, subjectively and in good faith, the director believes that this institute is 'his' and he manages his affairs. (Gerth and Mills 1948: 131)

Since that was written there has been ambivalence about the nature of management and strategy-making in the professional organisation. In his discussion of the matter Mintzberg suggests that 'many strategic issues come under the direct control of individual professionals while others ... require the participation of a variety of people in a complex, collective process' (1989: 183). In this sense, he suggests, the professional organisation is 'democratic, disseminating its power directly to its workers (at least those lucky enough to be professional). And it provides them with extensive autonomy, freeing them even from the need to co-ordinate closely with their colleagues' (1989: 189). He points out that these features have advantages and disadvantages. On the one hand, the environment is very motivating because of the freedom it gives; on the other hand, it is akin to herding cats for the work cannot be controlled and there 'is no way to correct deficiencies that professionals choose to overlook' (1989: 189). These issues of, on the one hand, tight control by the directorate of the sort suggested by Weber (particularly in a political milieu in which there is a desire for greater strategic control), and on the other, the relatively autonomous strategy-making suggested by Mintzberg, are enacted in very different ways in different professional organisations (e.g. McAuley, Duberley and Cohen 2000; Exworthy and Halford 1999; Pritchard and Willmott 1997 among many others).

If, however, we characterise the professional organisation as engaged in a search for autonomy for its members there would be a general view that the strategic recipe points towards an approach that is 'less dependent on detailed plans and projections than on reaching an understanding of the complexity of the issues concerned and identifying the range of available options' (Burnes 1996: 188). There is an emphasis on the idea of crafting an approach to change, but this time in a responsive way as opposed to the neat designs of the processual approach (Whittington 2001). Certainly within the more romantic view there is an emphasis on understanding the local ecology of the organisation in relation to the global. High value is placed on 'local knowledge', an attempt to reach into and respect the understandings of every member of the organisation about what works and does not work. For this reason 'resistance' to the outcomes from the strategic process would be regarded as a source of energy, to be respected and taken on board (Nevis 1987). In this sense the strategic recipe is one that involves constant cycles of involvement, moving in and moving out so that strategy is constantly evolving and shifting as different communities of interest create and develop it. The very tension between control and autonomy is part and parcel of the dynamic tension that is part of the strategic mix.

This view of the strategic recipe has interesting coincidences with what Whittington (2001) has characterised as the systemic view of strategy. This view takes a much wider view of the nature of the organisation and its strategy and Whittington tends to use the concept as academics and theorists have developed it, not as if it were a recipe to be adopted within organisations. In this view the strategic recipe is deeply rooted in the society in which it is located. As Whittington suggests this means that the strategy can be driven from very diverse roots – from in some societies, profit maximisation, to, in others, quite altruistic socially driven strategies. It may even be that the strategic recipe is to not value the idea of strategy at all, at least as practised in Western societies (Whittington 2001).

This strategic recipe invites an understanding of the processes of change, that is through understanding social aspects so that organisational change is aligned with social change. The approach to change may therefore start with a vision and complete uncertainty as to how to fulfil it, but the route to fulfilment comes as the visionholders come into contact with stakeholders. For example, banks and other financiers may want to see the expression of a classical strategic route – in which case the visionaries will proceed in that way for that audience. This catholicity of approach may be seen to 'expose and disrupt the taken-for-granted assumptions that underpin ostensibly neutral management practices' (Smith and Johnson 1996: 274). This demystification of management and conventional strategic recipes potentially equalises organisational members and other stakeholders although it might be claimed that management would continue to have a special leverage role. In this light it is suggested:

> Modern societies are not market economies; they are organisational economies in which companies are the chief actors in creating value and advancing economic progress. The growth of firms and therefore economies is predominantly dependent on the quality of their management. The foundations of a firm's activity is a new 'moral contract' with employees and society, replacing paternalistic exploitation and value appropriation with employability and value creation in a relationship of shared destiny. (Ghoshal, Bartlett and Moran 1999: 9)

It is worth noting, however, that this prescription is one that is firmly located (although the authors do not say so) in Anglophone societies. Sievers (1994) shows that habits of collective organisation have been the common route within many European organisations over a long period of time and that the dislocation between work and meaning is, perhaps, something of an Anglo-American phenomenon that has tended to have colonising force. In a systemic sense there may well be a transition, strategically speaking, from the rampant capitalism of the 1980s to less assertive forms of capitalism in the 1990s. One of the insights from Habermas on this issue comes from his discussion of the ecological damage that late capitalist organisations commit. He writes that 'Capitalist societies cannot follow imperatives of growth limitation without abandoning their principle of organization; a shift from unplanned, nature like capitalist growth to qualitative growth would require that production be planned in terms of *use values*' (1976: 42) – even though this may conflict with the creation of shareholder value (Reinhardt 1998). These paradoxes of late capitalism, poised between the exigencies of discourses of shareholder value and the rhetoric of care for the environment, finds echoes in some strategic writing of the present period.

CONCLUSION: STRATEGIC RECIPES AND THE DEVELOPMENT OF HABITS OF REFLEXIVITY

What has been attempted in this chapter is to explore the idea of the strategic recipe as if it were an aspect of the mindset of those with responsibility for undertaking strategy. That is, we have treated the recipe as if it were real. We have shown that the four positions are sustainable in terms of the conduct of the enterprise. They all have their strengths; they all have their limitations. It is possible, for all these recipes, that there are discrepancies between what Argyris (1990) has characterised as the espoused theory and the theory in use. Horkheimer (1937: 220) argued that there could be a profound separation between the practical application of conceptual system from the theoretical underpinning to the concept itself. This leads, he asserted, to failure to distinguish between the value system that underpins the theory and the theory itself. This leads to a failure to understand the implications of the transition between knowledge and action and a protection of the theorist. This tension may be illustrated by reference to natural science itself. Ruse (1999), for example, has shown that scientists from Darwin onwards, in the development of their magnificent theorising, have worked in accord with the strictest ideals of scientific method (themselves, of course, social constructs) and also by the underpinnings of the society in which they live at the time. What he shows is that different theorists are influenced by one rather than the other to very different degrees and that this has a profound influence on their work.

Of course, the extent to which the development of any strategic recipe is underpinned by scientific theory is itself questionable. Writers such as MacIntyre (1981) suggest that much management theorising (including writing on strategy) is a moral fiction, that these theories are incapable of developing predictable, law-like generalisations. Much of the material about the need to undertake dramatic paradigm shifts and to adopt strategic recipes comes from 'management gurus', charismatic consultancies and academics whose methodologies present an 'only way forward' approach to organisational problems. In this light, Huczynski (1993) discusses the way these folk-heroes work on beleaguered managers. He suggests that their claims 'to create order out of disorder' and the provision to managers 'with new systems of coherence and continuity' (Huczynski 1993: 198) can provide managers with delusions of grandeur. If managers take these recipes seriously they are liable, however, to run into problems.

The first is the imposition on organisational members of recipes that are frequently short-termist where the underlying issues are not. The second issue is that adherence to recipe leads to an idealisation of the change management process, and an idealisation of the 'heroic' manager's role. The third issue, particularly within Anglophone societies, is the tendency to turn theories or ideals into simple techniques that can be used instrumentally to create short-term strategies. These are the practicalities of pragmatic thought and action.

Ultimately, what matters is the way in which the strategists understand their recipes. Habermas discusses the distinction between reflexive and non-reflexive thought. He distinguishes between practical learning and theoretical learning. When we are learning non-reflexively we do not raise to the level of consciousness the core issues that lie behind the theory or the practical action – they are 'taken for granted'. Thus when the strategist accepts the recipe as both practical action and theory without exploration of the background features, the meaning-structure in which it is located, then he/she is thinking non-reflexively. On the other hand, reflexive learning takes place 'through discourses in which we thematize practical validity claims that have become problematic or have been rendered problematic through institutionalised doubt' (Habermas 1976: 15). In other words, reflexive thinking can take place when there is a precondition that members can see the issues which confront them as problematic, worthy of thought and understanding. He suggests that the level of learning that could occur within the organisation is dependent on 'the differentiation between theoretical and practical questions and the transition from non-reflexive (pre-scientific) to reflexive learning' (Habermas 1976: 15).

As Weick (1998) has pointed out, within the practices of reflexive thought there is considerable breadth from the most radical reformulation and redevelopment of thought to an essentially uncritical introspection. He also points to the ways in which reflexive thinking can produce negative effects when reflexive thought is undertaken without reflection on its consequences. He points to the particular issue that could afflict the strategist – paralysis through analysis. However, despite these reservations it is suggested that in the development of organisations:

> Learning depends upon the surfacing of difference and subsequent reintegration of conflicting views of the nature of self in the healing of the divisions that may thus arise. If skilfully managed, the outcome is a self-reflexive and wise organization, secure in its ability to understand and accept its limits and to negotiate identity change as part of its ongoing strategic development. (Brown and Starkey 2000: 114)

It is a process of understanding that 'lying behind all strategies are assumptions, which often remain implicit and untested. Frequently these assumptions have internal contradictions. When they do the strategy also has internal contradictions, which will prove to make it difficult or impossible to implement' (Senge 1990: 316). These contradictions, Senge suggests, can be explored by managers through what he terms 'microworlds'. These claim to 'enable managers and management teams to begin "learning through doing" about their most important systemic issues. . . . It becomes possible to experiment and learn when the consequences of our decisions are in the future and in distant parts of the organization' (Senge 1990: 314). Their emphasis on knowledge and understanding that concerns both the intellectual and emotional aspects of organisation as habits of reflexive thought is a useful corrective to unreflexive thought. This includes the adoption of recipes or reinforcing technologies because they are just the way things get done in the business or because this is the latest prescription that has appeared in the crowded marketplace of post-millennial ideas as to how to run the organisation.

REFERENCES

Alvesson, M. and H. Willmott (1996) *Making Sense of Management: a Critical Introduction*, London: Sage.

Argyris, C. (1990) *Overcoming Organizational Defenses*, New York: Allyn and Bacon.

Belmiro, T.R., P. Gardiner and J.E.L. Simmons (1997) 'Business Process Re-engineering – A Discredited Vocabulary?', *International Journal of Information Management*, 17(1): 21–33.

Boquist, J.A., T.T. Milbourn and A.V. Thakor (1998) 'How Do You Win the Capital Allocation Game?', *Sloan Management Review*, 39(2): 59–71.

Brown, A.D. and K. Starkey (2000) 'Organizational Identity and Learning: A Psychodynamic Perspective', *Academy of Management Review*, 25(1): 102–20.

Buchanan, D. and R. Badham (1999) *Power, Politics and Organizational Change: Winning the Turf Game*, London: Sage.

Burnes, R. (1996) *Managing Change: A Strategic Approach to Organisational Dynamics*, London: Pitman.

Clark, P. (2000) *Organisations in Action: Competition between Contexts*, London: Routledge.

Clegg, S. (1998) 'Foucault, Power and Organizations', in A. McKinlay and K. Starkey, *Foucault, Management and Organization Theory: From Panopticon to Technologies of Self*, London: Sage.

Collins, J.C. and J.I. Porras (1996) *Built to Last: Successful Habits of Visionary Companies*, London: Century Business.

Collins, J.C. and J.I. Porras (2000, 2nd edition) *Built to Last: Successful Habits of Visionary Companies*, London: Random House.

De Geus, A. (1997) *The Living Company: Habits for Survival in a Turbulent Business Environment*, Boston, MA: Harvard Business School.

De Vries, M.F.R. (1993) *Leaders, Fools and Impostors: Essays on the Psychology of Leadership*, San Francisco: Jossey Bass.

Dore, L. (1999) 'How Financial Institutions Can Maximise Shareholder Value', *Financial World*, (November): 19–51.

Exworthy, M. and S. Halford (eds) (1999) *Professionals and the New Managerialism in the Public Sector*, Buckingham: Open University Press.

Ferlie, E., L. Ashburner, L. Fitzgerald and A. Pettigrew (1996) *The New Public Management in Action*, Oxford: Oxford University Press.

Friedman, M. (1970) 'A Friedman Doctrine: the Social Responsibility of Business is to Increase its Profits', *The New York Times Magazine* (13 September).

Gerth, H.H. and C. Wright Mills (1948) *From Max Weber: Essays in Sociology*, London: Routledge and Kegan Paul.

Ghoshal, S., C.A. Bartlett and P. Moran (1999) 'A New Manifesto for Management', *Sloan Management Review*, 40(3): 9–20.

Gioia, D.A. and K. Chittipeddi (1991) 'Sensemaking and Sensegiving in Strategic Change Initiation', *Strategic Management Change Journal*, 12: 433–88.

Grinyer, P.H., D. Mayes and P. McKiernan (1987) *Sharpbenders: The Secrets of Unleashing Corporate Potential*, Oxford: Basil Blackwell.

Habermas, J. (1976) *Legitimation Crisis*, London: Heinemann.

Hamel, G. and C.K. Prahalad (1994) *Competing for the Future*, Cambridge, MA: Harvard Business School.

Hammer, M. (1996) *Beyond Reengineering: How the Process-centred Organization is Changing Our Work and Our Lives*, London: HarperCollins Business.

Horkheimer, M. (1937) 'Traditional and Critical Theory', in P. Connerton (ed.) (1976) *Critical Theory: Selected Readings*, Harmondsworth: Penguin.

Huczynski, A.A. (1993) *Management Gurus: What Makes Them and How to Become One*, London: Routledge.

Hughes, C. (2000) 'Vandevelde Set to Make First Ever Dividend Cut in History of Marks', *Independent* (15 May).

Hutton, W. (2000) 'Sold out to the Highest Bidder', *The Observer* (18 June).

Johnson, G. and K. Scholes (1994, 4th edition) *Exploring Corporate Strategy: Text and Cases*, London: Prentice Hall.

Johnson, G. and K. Scholes (1999, 5th edition) *Exploring Corporate Strategy: Text and Cases*, London: Prentice Hall Europe.

Johnson, G. and K. Scholes (eds) (2000) *Exploring Public Sector Strategy*, London: Prentice Hall.

Khatri, N. and H.A. Ng (2000) 'The Role of Intuition in Strategic Decision Making', *Human Relations*, 53(1): 57–86.

Knights, D. and D. McCabe (1998) 'Where "Life is but a Dream": Obliterating Politics through Business Process Reengineering?', *Human Relations*, 51(6): 761–99.

Knights, D. and G. Morgan (1991) 'Corporate Strategy, Organizations and Subjectivity: A Critique', *Organisation Studies*, 12(2): 251–73.

Koenig, P. (1999) 'Mr Nestlé gets angry: Profile: Peter Brabeck', *Independent on Sunday (Business Section)*, 9 May.

Long, S. (1999) 'The Tyranny of the Customer and the Cost of Consumerism: An Analysis Using Systems and Psychodynamic Approaches to Groups and Society', *Human Relations*, 52(6): 723–45.

MacIntyre, A. (1981) *After Virtue: A Study in Moral Theory*, London: Duckworth.

Magala, S.J. (1997) 'The Making and Unmaking of Sense', *Organisation Studies*, 18(2): 317–38.

McAuley, J. (1996) 'Ethical Issues in the Management of Change', in K. Smith and P. Johnson (eds) *Business Ethics and Business Behaviour*, London: Thomson Business Press.

McAuley, J., L. Cohen and J. Duberley (2000) 'The Meaning Professionals Give to Management . . . and Strategy', *Human Relations*, 53(1): 87–116.

McKersie, R.B. and R.E. Walton (1991) 'Organizational Change', in M.S. Scott Morton, *The Corporation of the 1990's: Information Technology and Organizational Transformation*, New York: Oxford University Press.

McTaggart, J. and S. Gillis (1998) 'Setting Targets to Maximise Shareholder Value', *Strategy and Leadership*, 26(2): 18–22.

Mintzberg, H. (1984) 'Who should control the organization?', *California Management Review*, (Autumn): 90–115.

Mintzberg, H. (1989) *Mintzberg on Management: Inside the Strange World of Organizations*, New York: Free Press.

Mintzberg, H. (1994) *The Rise and Fall of Strategic Planning*, Englewood Cliffs, NJ: Prentice Hall.

Mintzberg, H. and J. Lampel (1999) 'Reflecting on the strategy process', *Sloan Management Review*, 40(3): 21–30.

Mintzberg, H. and J.A. Waters (1985) 'Of Strategies, Deliberate and Emergent', *Strategic Management Journal*, 6: 257–72.

Nevis, E.C. (1987) *Organizational Consulting: A Gestalt Approach*, New York: Gardner Press.

Pollitt, C. (1993, 2nd edition) *Managerialism and the Public Services*, Oxford: Basil Blackwell.

Pritchard, C. and H. Willmott (1997) 'Just How Managed is the McUniversity?', *Organisation Studies*, 18(2): 287–316.

Rappaport, A. (1981) 'Selecting Strategies that Create Shareholder Value', *Harvard Business Review*, 59(3): 139–50.

Reinhardt, F.L. (1998) 'Environmental Product Differentiation: Implications for Corporate Strategy', *California Management Review*, 40(4): 43–73.

Ruse, M. (1999) *Mystery of Mysteries: Is Evolution a Social Construct?*, Cambridge, MA: Harvard University Press.

Schein, E.H. (1988, 2nd edition) *Organizational Psychology*, Englewood Cliffs, NJ: Prentice Hall.

Senge, P.M. (1990) *The Fifth Discipline: The Art and Practice of the Learning Organization*, London: Century Business.

Sievers, B. (1994) *Work, Death, and Life Itself: Essays on Management and Organization*, Berlin: Walter de Gruyter.

Smith, B. (1998) 'Ethics of Du Pont's CFC Strategy 1975–1995', *Journal of Business Ethics*, 17(5): 557–68.

Smith, K. and P. Johnson (1996) 'Conclusions: Accounting for the Field of Business Ethics', in K. Smith and P. Johnson (eds) *Business Ethics and Business Behaviour*, London: Thomson Business Press.

Sosik, J.J. and L.E. Megerian (1999) 'Understanding Leader Emotional Intelligence and Performance: The Role of Self–Other Agreement in Transformational Leadership Perceptions', *Group and Organization Management*, 24(3): 367–90.

Strati, A. (1999) *Organization and Aesthetics*, London: Sage.

Weick, K.E. (1995) *Sensemaking in Organizations*, Thousand Oaks, CA: Sage.

Weick, K.E. (1999) 'Theory Construction as Disciplined Reflexivity: Trade-offs in the 90's', *Academy of Management*, 24(4): 779–88.

Weiss, J.W. (1996) *Organizational Behaviour and Change: Managing Diversity, Cross-cultural Dynamics and Ethics*, St. Paul, MN: West Publishing.

Whittington, R. (2001, 2nd edition) *What is Strategy and Does it Matter?*, London: Thomson Learning.

Wilson, D.C. (1992) *A Strategy of Change: Concepts and Controversies in the Management of Change*, London: Routledge.

Wise, R. (1999) 'Why Things Go Better at Coke', *The Journal of Business Strategy*, 20(1): 15–19.

Zalenik, A. (1996) 'Managers and Leaders: Are They Different?', in J. Champy and N. Nohria, *Fast Forward: The Best Ideas on Managing Business Change*, Cambridge, MA: Harvard Business School.

Chapter 11

ACTION RESEARCH AND WHOLE SYSTEMS EVENTS: TWO CHANGE METHODOLOGIES WITH PROMISE

The aims of this chapter are to:

1 Introduce two forms of intervention in organisation(s), Action Research and Whole Systems Events, and explore their history and development.

2 Outline the practical nature of these forms of intervention, focusing on approaches consistent with the argument of the book.

3 Explore the strengths and weaknesses of these methodologies.

4 Provide practical illustrations of their use.

5 Link these methodologies to the wider argument of the book.

INTRODUCTION

The literature on Action Research is already voluminous, while that on Whole Systems Events is growing rapidly. It would be pointless to seek a neat summary of this material. The intention is to explore their relationship to the arguments of this book and in particular to draw out the different ways in which these methods have been developed and used, and review the extent to which it is possible to put Critical Theory's democratic ideals into practice.

Action Research has developed from a number of scientific and social sources, and has become prominent as a method in education, in industry and in community development (the latter in both urban and rural settings). The lineage of Action Research stretches back at least to Kurt Lewin and his work in Group Dynamics; some would argue that it goes much further (see McKernan 1991). Frideres (1992: 3–4) asserts that the concept of participatory research emerged in the 1970s from development work in low-income countries and mentions in particular the work of Fals-Borda, which we consider below. Despite the clouded origins of action research, Lewin, in the mid-1940s, constructed a theory of Action Research, which described it as 'proceeding in a spiral of steps, each of which is composed of planning, action and the evaluation of the result of action' (Kemmis and McTaggert 1990: 8). Lewin argued that in order to 'understand and change certain social practices, social scientists have to include practitioners from the real social world in all phases of inquiry' (McKernan 1991:

10). This construction of Action Research theory by Lewin made Action Research a method of acceptable inquiry (McKernan 1991: 9).

There appear to have been six movements which have made a particular impact on Action Research, reflecting the variety of fields within which it has been pursued. The first was the Science in Education Movement of the nineteenth and early twentieth centuries. The second was the experimentalist and progressive educational work, especially of John Dewey, who applied the inductive scientific method of problem-solving as a logic for the solution of problems in such fields as aesthetics, philosophy, psychology and education (McKernan 1996).

The third movement was group dynamics in social psychology and human relations training. McKernan sees this as a 'full circle ' in research on social problems, from the qualitative social inquiry in the nineteenth century into problems of poverty, housing and urban life, to the social science response to the impact in the 1940s of war, problems of intergroup relations, social reconstruction, prejudice and various other social issues. Out of this need to understand and solve social problems, practitioner enquiry was again rediscovered and action research was seen as a credible response.

In the mid-1940s, Lewin discussed Action Research as a form of experimental inquiry based on the study of groups experiencing problems. Lewin argued that social problems should serve as the locus of social science research. Basic to his model is a view of research composed of action cycles (Lewin 1946 and 1947). This is illustrated in Figure 11.1, which, however, adds an important element that prefigures later discussion: ideological perspective. Lewin was interested above all in group dynamics and the concept of action in group settings.

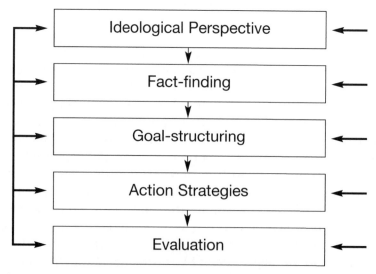

Figure 11.1   Cyclical processes in action
Source: Lewin, adapted by Cassell, Darwin and Fitter in Cassell and Fitter (1992)

Lewin's contribution is important because, although not the first to use and write about Action Research, he did construct an elaborate theory and made Action Research a 'respectable' enquiry for social scientists. Lewin believed that science should have this social help function: 'research that produces nothing but books will not suffice' (Lewin, 1948: 203).

Action Research was also used in the study of industry and developed a committed following in the US at the Massachusetts Institute of Technology and its Research Center for Group Dynamics, and through links with the Tavistock Institute of Human Relations in London. McKernan (1996) points to arguments that Action Research as promoted by the Tavistock approach paved the way for the 'external intervention' style of collaborative Action Research currently enjoying widespread usage; a style that highlights the concerns of the target group rather than the professional researchers. Lewin argued that, in order to understand and change certain social practices, social scientists have to include practitioners from the real social world in all phases of inquiry, and both critical and participatory action research, as we shall see, develop the implications of this.

The fourth movement was the postwar Reconstructionist Curriculum Development Activity. Action Research in education was used as a general strategy for designing curricula and attacking complex problems, such as intergroup relations and prejudice through large curriculum development projects (McKernan 1991).

The fifth movement shifted the focus from education to community development and again to social problems. In America the War on Poverty in the 1960s adopted an Action Research Approach. The subsequent impact of this in Britain – for example, through the National Community Development Project in the 1970s – brought the wider use of Action Research in tackling social problems.

The final movement has come through new linkages with other streams of idea. In the educational field Critical Theory has had a significant impact, while in community and industrial settings experience in Scandinavia and South America has enriched the development of both thinking and practice. The common core has been the desire to make those affected by Action Research much more substantial partners in the exercise.

ACTION RESEARCH: WHAT IS IT?

McKernan has brought together several definitions of Action Research. From these he suggests the following as a 'minimal definition of action research'. This minimal definition stresses two essential points: first, action research is rigorous, systematic inquiry through scientific procedures; and second, participants have critical-reflective ownership of the process and the results:

> Action research is the reflective process whereby in a given problem area, where one wishes to improve practice or personal understanding, inquiry is carried out by the practitioner – first, to clearly define the problem; secondly, to specify a plan of action – including the test-

ing of hypotheses by application of action to the problem. Evaluation is then undertaken to monitor and establish the effectiveness of the action taken. Finally, participants reflect upon, explain developments, and communicate these results to the community of action researchers. Action research is systematic self-reflective scientific inquiry by practitioners to improve practice. (1996: 4–5)

Action Research has been identified by Gill and Johnson as 'a valuable variant of the quasi-experimental approach' (1991: 57); they contrast the approach with

Table 11.1 Action research compared

Stages	'Pure' research	Consultancy	Action Research	Action Learning
Entry	Researcher presents problem and defines goals	Client presents problem and defines goals	Client or researcher presents problem. Mutually agreed goals	Common problems defined by learning set
Contracting	Researcher controls as expert. Keeps client happy. Minimal contracting	Business contract. Consultant controls client	Business and psychological contracting. Mutual control	Mutual learning contract. Learning set created
Diagnosis	Researcher carries out expert diagnosis. Client provides data	Consultant diagnosis. Often minimal. Sells package	Joint diagnosis. Client data/ researchers' concepts	Joint diagnosis. Participatory action research. People develop personal insights and theories
Action	Report often designed to impress client with how much researcher has learnt and how competent s/he is. Published	Consultant prescribes action. Not published	Feedback. Dissonance. Joint action plan. Client action with support. Published	Action and learning inseparable. Learning by doing.
Evaluation	Rarely undertaken	Rarely undertaken by neutrals	New problems emerge. Recycles. Generalisations emerge	Outcomes tested in real world or real responsibility by real people. Generalisable insights, strategies and tactics. Resonance
Withdrawal	Client dependent	Client dependent	Client self-supporting	Client self-supporting

Extended from Gill and Johnson (1991).

'pure' research, and with consultancy. This can be extended to provide a comparison also with action learning, using ideas drawn from Revans and Morgan, whose work will be considered later. This is done in Table 11.1.

This immediately identifies the more active role of the 'client' (although we shall later recognise that in practice there is a much wider range of possible levels of involvement than is suggested here). It also sets action research apart from the classical experimental approach, replete with 'ceteris paribus' clauses. Instead we have an iterative method in which research feeds back into further action (see Figure 11.2).

Two points may be made about this. First, the cycle shown in Figure 11.2 bears a striking resemblance to the cycle of strategy, sometimes styled the 'Strategy IDEA':

Investigate = Observe

Decide = Reflect

Enable = Plan

Act = Act

Second, the timing of cycles can vary. Some Action Research projects have long cycles in which the action and research phases are relatively distinct; others interweave the two very closely.

Figure 11.2 The 'moments' of Action Research

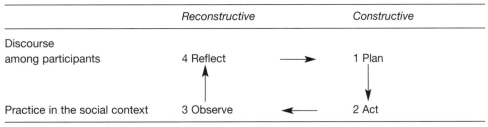

	Reconstructive	Constructive
Discourse among participants	4 Reflect	1 Plan
Practice in the social context	3 Observe	2 Act

Source: Carr and Kemmis (1986: 186)

Action Research has been more popular in the fields of education and community work than it has in relation to organisations. Thus Maruyama (1996: 93) identifies four factors in the field of education which transformed Action Research from a set of approaches driven by university researchers to research initiated and conducted by practitioners. The first has been consideration of power and status issues; the second a response to what are seen as egocentric and ethnocentric perspectives of researchers; the third factor has been a grass-roots orientation that argues that those best able to change a situation are those involved in it and who understand it best. Finally, there have been arguments that the best way to get individuals in applied settings to commit themselves to change is to make them the initiators of the change.

Action Research merits greater consideration in organisational activity than has to date been the case. This is not least because the above factors can easily be translated into change management, where there has been a growing focus on the need to involve practitioners, to obtain commitment through participation, and to address issues of power.

TYPES OF ACTION RESEARCH

Thus far we have considered Action Research in broad terms: it is now appropriate to recognise the differences which exist, as hinted earlier. A number of authors have identified three major approaches to action research: scientific-technical or positivist; practical-deliberative, mutual collaborative or interpretivist; critical-emancipatory or enhancement. This distinction has its inspiration in the work of Habermas, discussed in Chapter 5. As we saw there, Habermas identified three knowledge constitutive interests. These three categories are summarised in Table 11.2. The types of action research that flow from each will now be explored in turn.

The technical interest: Scientific-technical or positivist action research

Early advocates of action research such as Lippitt and Radke in 1946, Lewin in 1947, Corey in 1953, and Taba and Noel in 1957 put forward a scientific method of problem solving (McKernan 1991). The underlying goal of the researcher in this approach is to test a particular intervention based on a pre-specified theoretical framework, the nature of the collaboration between the researcher and the practitioner is technical and facilitatory. The researcher identifies the problem and a specific intervention, then the practitioner is involved and they agree to

Table 11.2 The categories of enquiry

Interest	Knowledge	Medium	Science	Fundamental Interest
Technical	Instrumental (causal explanation)	Work	Empirical-analytic or natural sciences	Controlling the environment through rule-following action based upon empirically grounded laws
Practical	Practical (understanding)	Language	Hermeneutic or 'interpretive' sciences	Understanding the environment through interaction based upon a consensual interpretation of meaning
Emancipatory	Emancipatory (reflection)	Power	Critical sciences	Emancipation and empowerment to engage in autonomous action arising out of authentic, critical insights into the social construction of human society

Source: Based on Carr and Kemmis (1986) and Grundy (1987).

facilitate with the implementation of the intervention (Holter and Schwartz-Barcott 1993: 301). The communication flow within this type of research is primarily between the facilitator and the group, so that the ideas may be communicated to the group (Grundy 1982: 360).

A project guided by technical action research has the following characteristics: the project is instigated by a particular person or group of people who, because of their greater experience or qualifications, are regarded as experts or authority figures. Technical action research promotes more efficient and effective practice. It is product-directed, but promotes personal participation by practitioners in the process of improvement. This approach to Action Research results in the accumulation of predictive knowledge, the major thrust is on validation and refinement of existing theories and is essentially deductive (Holter et al. 1993).

This approach has kept closest to the legacy of Lewin. Carr and Kemmis argue that Lewin presaged three important characteristics of modern Action Research: its participatory character, its democratic impulse and its simultaneous contribution to social science and social change. However, they believe that in each of these three areas contemporary action researchers would take exception to Lewin's approach.

First, they would regard group decision-making as important as a matter of principle, rather than as a matter of technique; that is, not merely as an effective means of facilitating and maintaining social change but also as essential for authentic commitment to social action. Second, contemporary exponents of action research would object to the notion that participants should, or could, be 'led' to more democratic forms of life through action research. Action Research should not be seen as a recipe or technique for bringing about democracy. Rather, it is an embodiment of democratic principles in research. It allows participants to influence, if not determine, the conditions of their own lives and work, and collaboratively to develop critiques of social conditions which sustain dependence, inequality or exploitation.

Third, contemporary action researchers would object to the language in which Lewin describes the theoretical aims and methods of social science ('developing deeper insights into the laws that govern social life through mathematical and conceptual analysis and laboratory and field experiments'). This language would now be described as positivistic and incompatible with the aims and methods of any adequate social or educational science (Carr and Kemmis 1986: 164).

The practical interest: practical-deliberative, mutual collaborative or interpretivist action research

In this type of Action Research project the researcher and the practitioners come together to identify potential problems, their underlying causes and possible interventions (Holter et al. 1993: 301). The problem is defined after dialogue with the researcher and the practitioner and a mutual understanding is reached. 'Practical action research seeks to improve practice through the application of the personal wisdom of the participants' (Grundy 1982: 357). This design of

Action Research allows for a more flexible approach, not available in the positivist paradigm.

McKernan (1991: 20) feels that the practical model of Action Research trades off some measurement and control for human interpretation, interactive communication, deliberation, negotiation and detailed description. 'The goal of practical action researchers is understanding practice and solving immediate problems' (McKernan 1991: 20). The practitioners involved in the mutual collaborative approach to Action Research gain a new understanding of their practice; the changes implemented tend to have a more lasting character. However, the changes tend to be connected to the individuals directly involved in the change process, and therefore the interventions tend to be short lived when these individuals leave the system or there is an influx of new people (Holter et al. 1993: 301).

This mode of Action Research is primarily concerned with understanding what occurred, and the meaning ascribed to this by those involved. It therefore moves beyond the technical approach in recognising multiple perspectives, but the change focus is muted, and rests primarily at the individual level. For a wider vision of change, at the collective level, we must turn to the third approach.

The emancipatory interest: critical-emancipatory or enhancement Action Research

Emancipatory Action Research 'promotes emancipatory praxis in the participating practitioners; that is, it promotes a critical consciousness which exhibits itself in political as well as practical action to promote change' (Grundy 1987: 154). There are two goals for the researcher using this approach. One is to increase the closeness between the actual problems encountered by practitioners in a specific setting and the theory used to explain and resolve the problem. The second goal, which goes beyond the other two approaches, is to assist practitioners in identifying and making explicit fundamental problems by raising their collective consciousness.

Habermas has been an important influence on this approach, which does not begin with theory and end with practice, but is informed by theory. Often it is confrontation with the theory that provides the initiative to undertake the practice (Grundy 1982: 358). The dynamic relationship between theory and practice in emancipatory Action Research entails the expansion of both theory and practice during the project.

When a person reflects on theory in the light of praxis or practical judgement, the form of knowledge that results is personal or tacit knowledge. This tacit knowledge can be acquired through the process of reflection. The interaction of theory and practical judgement through the process of reflection, with the input from critical intent leads to critical theorems (Grundy 1982: 359). The second function, which Habermas distinguishes in the mediation of theory and practice, is the organisation of the process of enlightenment. Critical theorems are applied and tested in a unique manner by the initiation of processes of reflection carried out within certain groups towards which these processes have been directed. These group processes of reflection will give rise to enlightenment in the form of authentic insights (Habermas 1972, cited in Grundy 1982: 360). The facilitator must not attempt to direct the outcome of the deliberative process by attempting to thrust enlightenment on the participants, but must allow symmetrical communication to occur from which enlightenment will flow (Grundy 1982: 360).

The third function that Habermas distinguishes is the organisation of action. The organisation of enlightenment has its focus upon the past while the organisation of action is future orientated (Grundy 1982: 361). The form of strategic action resulting from enlightenment is a form of praxis. 'Whereas action which resulted from phronesis was also a form of praxis, the development of "critical theorems" and the process of enlightenment result in the true praxis for it is action which is freed from the dominating constraints of the environment' (Grundy 1982: 361).

Carr and Kemmis provide a definition of Action Research rooted in critical-emancipatory terms: 'Action research is simply a form of self-reflective enquiry undertaken by participants in social situations in order to improve the rationality and justice of their own practices, their understanding of these practices, and the situations in which the practices are carried out' (1986: 162). They develop this by arguing that there are three minimal requirements for Action Research. These requirements incorporate the goals of improvement and involvement which characterise any action research project. The conditions, which are set out there as individually necessary and jointly sufficient for action research to exist, are:

- The project takes as its subject-matter a social practice, regarding it as a form of strategic action susceptible of improvement.
- The project proceeds through a spiral of cycles of planning, acting, observing and reflecting, with each of these activities being systematically and self-critically implemented and interrelated.
- The project involves those responsible for the practice in each of the moments of the activity, widening participation in the project gradually to include others affected by the practice, and maintaining collaborative control of the process.

(Carr and Kemmis 1986: 165–6)

They relate this to five requirements for a coherent educational science which, they have previously suggested, can be satisfied by Habermas's notion of a critical social science. We can generalise these as follows:

- Theory must reject positivist notions of rationality, objectivity and truth.
- Theory must accept the need to employ the interpretive categories of participants.
- Theory must provide ways of distinguishing ideologically distorted interpret-

Table 11.3 Types of Action Research

	Technical/Experimental	Mutual-Collaboration	Critical/Emancipatory
Philosophical base	Cartesian–Newtonian	Historical–hermeneutic	Critical Sciences
Arenas of power	Unitary, Control	Pluralist	Control (by those not in control) Open
The nature of reality	Measurable, Reductive	Multiple, constructed, holistic	Multiple and constructed, rooted in social, economic, and political
Problem focus	Defined in advance. Relevant to social science/management interests, or most powerful group. Success defined in their terms.	Interpreted in situation by participant experience. Different interpretations of success	Emergent from members' experience and negotiated in the situation based on values. Competing definitions of success.
Relationship between the knower and known	Separate	Interrelated	Interrelated, embedded in society
Focus of collaboration theory	Technical validation, deduction	Mutual understanding, new theory, inductive	Mutual emancipation, validation, new theory, inductive, deductive
The nature of understanding	Cause–effect	Interpretive	Interpretive within socio-political framework
Purpose of research	Discovery of laws underlying reality	Understand what occurs and the meaning people make of phenomena	Understand, challenge, and change to greater equity
Educative base	Education based on identifying causal relationship and/or overcoming resistance to change	Reflective practice	Consciousness raising and empowerment
Individuals in groups	Researcher/Manager formed. Closed group with fixed/selected membership	Practitioner formed. Negotiated boundaries with shifting membership	Natural or negotiated boundaries with fluid membership
Change intervention	Top-down to test/ generate theory. Problem to be solved in terms of research/ management aims	Predefined, Process led. Problem to be resolved in the interests of research based practice	Problem to be explored as part of process of change, developing an understanding of meanings of issues in terms of problem and solution

Table 11.3 *continued*

	Technical/Experimental	*Mutual-Collaboration*	*Critical/Emancipatory*
Cyclic processes	Identifies causal processes that can be generalised	Identifies causal processes that are specific to problem and/or can be generalised	Recognises multiple influences on change
Research relationship	Action and research distinct, with differentiated roles	Action and research merged	Action and research integrated, with shared roles

Source: developed from Grundy (1987) and Hart and Bond (1995).

ations from those that are not. It must also provide some view of how any distorted self-understanding is to be overcome.

- Theory must be concerned to identify and expose those aspects of the existing social order which frustrate the pursuit of rational goals and must be able to offer theoretical accounts which make participants aware of how they may be eliminated or overcome.

- Theory must be practical, in the sense that the question of its status will be determined by the ways in which it relates to practice.

The approach to Action Research that emerges from these considerations is illustrated in Table 11.3, which is based on work by Grundy (who collaborated with Carr and Kemmis in exploring the implications for Action Research of the criteria above), and by Hart and Bond. This critical emancipatory approach, as we have seen, has developed primarily in the field of education. At the same time in the fields of economic development and community development (in large part in Scandinavia and Latin America) Participatory Action Research (PAR) has emerged as an important strand. The two have much in common.

We can see this by considering Maguire's (1987) analysis of PAR. She identifies three types of change sought in participatory research: the development of critical consciousness of both researcher and participants; the improvement of the lives of those involved in the research process; and the transformation of fundamental societal structures and relationships. She links the emergence of participatory research to three trends:

1 radical and reformist reconceptualisations of international economic development assistance;

2 the reframing of adult education as an empowering alternative to traditional educational approaches;

3 an ongoing debate within the social sciences, challenging the dominant social science paradigm.

Fals-Borda and Rahman (1991) comment that PAR does not exclude 'orthodox' methods such as interviews, surveys and observation, but what is critical to the approach is that it includes four techniques: collective research, critical recovery of history, valuing and applying folk culture, and the production and diffusion of new knowledge.

As will be apparent, these relate to the full involvement of participants, and the legitimacy accorded to their viewpoint. This can be expanded through the work of Gustavsen (quoted in Elden and Levin 1991), who builds partly on Habermas to postulate nine criteria for evaluating the degree of democracy in a dialogue in PAR aimed at democratising work:

- The dialogue is a process of exchange: points and arguments move to and fro between the participants.
- All concerned must have the possibility to participate.
- Possibilities for participation are, however, not enough: everybody should also be active in the discourse.
- As a point of departure, all participants are equal.
- Work experience is the foundation for participation.
- At least some of the experience which each participant has when he or she enters the dialogue must be considered legitimate.
- It must be possible for everybody to develop an understanding of the issue at stake.
- All arguments which pertain to issues under discussion are – as a point of departure – legitimate.
- The dialogue must continuously produce agreements which can provide a platform for investigation and practical action.

There is little distinction to be made between PAR and Critical Action Research. While they have arisen in different areas of inquiry, the literature on each cites common sources, while the aims and aspiration of each are the same. Thus Deshler and Ewert (1995), like a number of writers on PAR, cite similar movements to those identified earlier in this paper. They also identify as major assumptions of PAR the following, all of which apply equally to critical action research:

- Common values, including the democratisation of knowledge production and use; ethical fairness in the benefits of the knowledge generation process; an ecological stance toward society and nature; appreciation of the capacity of humans to reflect, learn, and change; and a commitment to non-violent social change. The community's interests are identified and defined as a starting point rather than beginning with the interests of external researchers.
- Commitment to action.
- Active involvement by participants.
- The external researcher's role as with and alongside the community, not outside as an objective observer or external consultant.

- The research process allows and encourages the community to learn about research methods and knowledge generation.
- The research process allows for flexibility or change in research methods and focus, as necessary.
- Research outcomes are intended to benefit the community.
- Differences between researchers and community participants regarding research processes, interpretation of results, ownership of research products, or dissemination of results are to be acknowledged, negotiated at the outset, or resolved through a fair and open process.

It is therefore fair to see these two streams of thinking as mutually enriching.

The three approaches compared

It is not in the methodologies that the three modes of action research differ, but rather in the underlying assumptions and world views of the participants that cause the variations in the application of the methodology (Grundy 1982: 363).

> The differences in the relationship between the participants and the source and scope of the guiding 'idea' can be traced to a question of power. In technical action research it is the 'idea' which is the source of power for action and since the 'idea' often resides with the facilitator, it is the facilitator who controls power in the project. In practical action research power is shared between a group of equal participants, but the emphasis is upon individual power for action. Power in emancipatory action research resides wholly within the group, not with the facilitator and not with the individuals within the group. It is often the change in power relationships within a group that causes a shift from one mode to another. (Grundy 1982: 363)

Action Research does not follow the strict experimental scientific method espoused within the Cartesian–Newtonian Synthesis. However, it is a very appropriate method to conditions of uncertainty and change, particularly when action and research are fully integrated. Nevertheless, guidelines by which to assess the research aspects of Action Research are of value, and Eden and Huxham (1996a and b) have usefully provided fifteen, which may be summarised as follows:

- An integral involvement by the researcher in an intent to change the organisation.
- Implications beyond those required for action or generation of knowledge in the domain of the project.
- Valuing theory, with theory elaboration and development as an explicit concern of the research process.
- The basis for the design of tools, techniques, models and method must be explicit and shown to be related to the theories which inform the design and which, in turn, are supported or developed.
- A system of emergence in which theory building will be incremental.

- Recognition that description will be prescription, even if implicitly.

- A high degree of method and orderliness in reflecting about, and holding on to, the emerging research data and the emergent theoretical outcomes of each episode or cycle of involvement in the organisation.

- The process of exploration of the data – rather than collection of the data – in the detecting of emergent theories, must be either replicable, or, at least, capable of being explained to others.

- A series of interconnected cycles, where writing about research outcomes at the latter stages is an important aspect of theory exploration and development, combining the processes of explicating pre-understanding and methodological reflection to explore and develop theory formally.

- The reflection and data collection process – and hence the emergent theories – are most valuably focused on the aspects that cannot be captured easily by other approaches.

- Opportunities for triangulation should be exploited fully and reported.

- The history and context for the intervention must be taken as critical to the interpretation of the likely range of validity and applicability of the results.

- Theory development which is of general value should be disseminated in such a way as to be of interest to an audience wider than those integrally involved with the action and/or research.

ACTION LEARNING

We turn now to Action Learning, which has different parentage to Action Research: the founding father is generally agreed to be Revans. Yet there is much in common. Thus the cycle of Action Learning has been developed by Pedler et al. (1996), based on Kolb's cycle of experiential learning, and involving four interlinking elements:

1 **Experience**: Observing and reflecting on the consequences of action in a situation.

2 **Understanding**: Forming or reforming understanding of situation as a result of experience.

3 **Planning**: Planning actions to influence the situation based on newly formed or reformed understanding.

4 **Action**: Acting or trying out the plan in the situation.

We can now extend and complete the developing comparison with the Strategy IDEA, as shown in Figure 11.3. As will be evident, this does not constitute isomorphism: in most cases, each of the four perspectives on each of the four 'moments' says something different. But again we have a 'pattern that connects', as these differences enrich the overall picture.

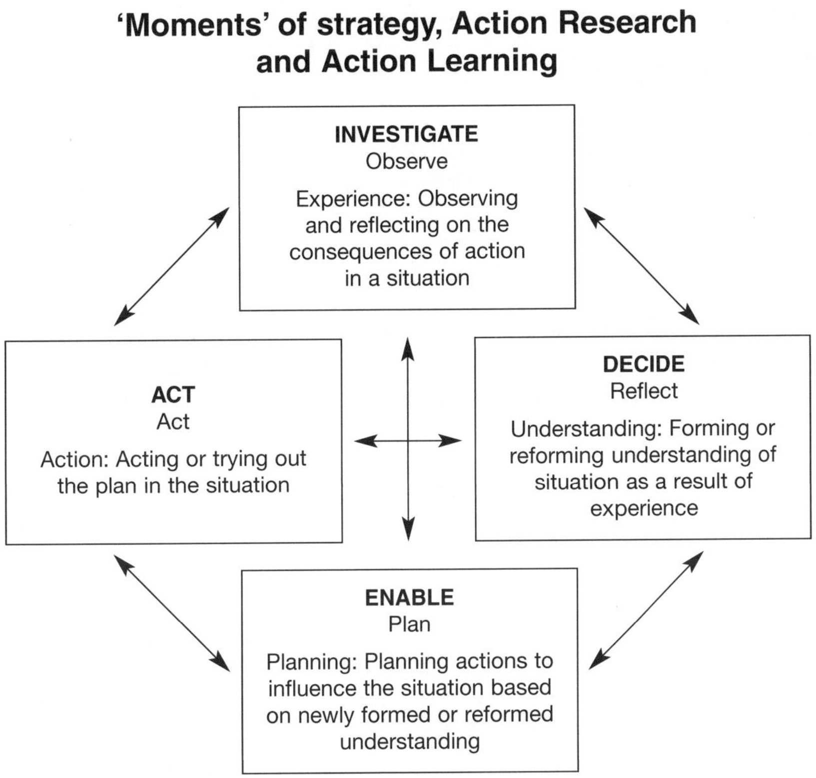

'Moments' of strategy, Action Research and Action Learning

INVESTIGATE
Observe

Experience: Observing and reflecting on the consequences of action in a situation

ACT
Act

Action: Acting or trying out the plan in the situation

DECIDE
Reflect

Understanding: Forming or reforming understanding of situation as a result of experience

ENABLE
Plan

Planning: Planning actions to influence the situation based on newly formed or reformed understanding

Figure 11.3 The Strategy IDEA, Action Research and Action Learning

Action Learning has been much more popular than Action Research in management circles, and the link with the fashionable idea of the 'learning organisation' does much to explain this. As with Action Research, several approaches have been identified. Alvesson and Willmott (1996) have built upon earlier work by McLaughlin and Thorpe to produce the characterisation of Critical Action Learning given in Table 11.4. However, this typology appears much rarer in discussions of Action Learning than it does when Action Research is considered. Books advocating Action Learning to organisations present only one approach, akin to the middle column of Table 11.4 (see, for example, Pedler et al. 1996; McGill and Beaty 1995). In keeping with this consensual bias, they also tend to underplay power in the organisation.

The relationship between Action Research and Action Learning is not often discussed. One exception is Morgan and Ramirez (1983). They link action learning to self-organisation, and seeing the former as holographic in that it simultaneously attempts to combine within itself a number of dimensions that are often regarded as separate – including theory and practice, subject and object, knowledge and action. They identify minimum critical conditions for action learning: it strives to be democratic and heterarchical, pluralistic, proactive and

Table 11.4   Approaches to management education

	Traditional management education	Action Learning	Critical Action Learning
Worldview	The world is something to learn about	The world is somewhere to act and change	The world is somewhere to act and change
	Self-development is somewhat important	Self-development is very important	Self-development and social development are interdependent
	Some notion of correct management practice, established by research, defines the curriculum	Curriculum defined by the manager or organisation	The interdependence of beings means that no individual or group can gain monopoly control of the curricula
	Managers should learn theories or models derived from research	Managers should be facilitated by a tutor to solve problems	Managers are potentially receptive to, and can be facilitated by, the concerns of other groups, in addition to individual tutors, when identifying and addressing problems
Modus operandi	Experts decide on what should be learnt, when and how much	Experts are viewed with caution	Received wisdom, including that of Experts, is subject to critical scrutiny through a fusion of reflection and insights drawn from critical social theory
	Models, concepts, ideas are provided to offer tools for thinking and action	Models, concepts, ideas are developed in response to problems	Models, concepts and ideas are developed through an interplay of reflection upon practice and an application of ideas drawn from critical traditions

Adapted from McLaughlin and Thorpe (1993), by Alvesson and Willmott (1996).

empowering. It should link individual and social transformation, and integrate different kinds and levels of understanding. It should create conditions that are always evolving and open-ended, and demonstrate its worth in terms of the capacities it creates for intelligent action rather than in terms of its contribution to formal knowledge. They suggest a number of approaches and techniques relevant to the design of action-learning projects, including Revans' approach, the techniques of Action Research, and search conference methodology.

McLaughlin and Thorpe (1993) see Action Learning as a derivation of Action Research, while McGill and Beaty (1995) recognise that they are based on the same learning cycle, but see Action Research as a method which seeks to question the traditional research paradigms copied from the natural sciences. On this basis, action researchers reject experimental design with its control groups and the external impartial scientific observer in favour of bringing research and the application of findings from research into one process. Thus for McGill and Beaty the action researcher is committed to learning from investigation, to making decisions about necessary change, and to applying these and then evaluating the consequences. The researcher is usually an active participant within the application as well as in the investigative and evaluation phases.

They view Action Learning as a more general approach to learning, in which research is not the primary aim and the project may not involve any formal research at all. The individual is undertaking learning through the process of reflection in the set and therefore the process is essentially a group process. Thus Action Learning may involve some research in the action phase, but it is not essentially a research-oriented venture. They suggest that the research undertaken in AL 'may use techniques quite different from those advocated by action research', although it is difficult to envisage such techniques, since Action Research is not restrictive in its approach (arguably even strict experimental techniques could be employed within a wider canvas).

McGill and Beaty conclude that an action researcher could use an Action Learning set to help learn from the action research project but does not necessarily do so. There are therefore many action researchers who do not have action learning sets and there are many action learning sets that do not use action research. Nevertheless, they see action learning and action research as sharing the same learning cycle, and sharing many of the same values.

There is undoubtedly a distinction: Action Research projects are often not Action Learning projects, and many of the Action Learning projects described in the literature have little in the way of a research component. Even so, there is an advantage in considering the two together, and indeed seeking some integration. The requirement of Action Research for output aimed at a wider audience helps to prevent an inward-looking focus. The danger of the latter has been identified by Weick: 'Continuous updating of what is known within the firm, coupled with continuous monitoring to determine if updating is necessary, is expensive, not to mention susceptible to political manipulation. Consequently, assessment is short-circuited, learning is superstitious and misleading, and what appears to be knowledge creation in fact becomes the enlargement of ignorance' (1996: 310).

McGill and Beaty argue that Action Learning is for the people within it. 'The focus of the action learning process is on individually based learning from action, which leads to development for the individual, and for their organisation, through the project' (1995: 27). They qualify this by arguing that work through Action Learning sets can have influence beyond the people immediately involved: it should have an effect, for example, on those who work closely with the set members and who will surely notice the difference in their demeanour and their ability to get things done. They suggest that Action Learning sets involve many people in an organisation, then the organisation itself may change. This in itself, however, may not address the concern expressed above. More generally, the external focus required of Action Research can be an antidote to the dangers of the Icarus Paradox (Miller 1990).

At the same time, the Action Learning process can ensure that Action Research remains intimately tied to the needs of the individuals involved, and retains its necessary action focus. Support for this argument for integration comes also from the work of Morgan, who speaks of 'action-learning approaches to research ... as a research methodology, "action learning" is closely linked with what others describe as "action research" and "action science"' (1993: 296–7).

WHOLE SYSTEMS EVENTS

Whole Systems Events (WSE) have been developed to address what are seen as issues of growing concern to present-day organisations. These include the need for constant internal change in response to external pressures; the need to reappraise purpose and direction; the need to involve people in the development and implementation of strategy, and thereby gain their commitment and ownership of activity. While a variety of interventions have been developed, they are based on certain common characteristics, including participation, information-sharing, finding common ground, developing action plans, and implementing rapid change in organisational processes.

The roots of WSE can be found in the Organisational Development field, in particular the work of Emery, Trist, the Tavistock Institute, and coal miners in South Yorkshire. In some cases a WSE can involve meetings without agendas, no limit on participants and no real guest list. At the other extreme, there are settings that involve intensive preparation, agendas, exercises and lots of up-front planning. Some can be used for everything from visioning to designing a new organisation, whereas others might tackle only one aspect of a production problem. And some have limits on how many people can or should participate; other approaches may involve thousands of people in a single event. In this chapter we consider and interlink two of these: Future Search Conferences and Technology of Participation.

Future Search Conferences

Future Search Conferences are intended to 'excite, engage, produce new insights, and build a sense of common values and purpose. They have been especially attractive to organisations faced with significant change: markets, mergers, reorganisations, new technologies, new leadership, the wish for a coherent culture and corporate philosophy.' (Weisbord 1987: 285)

Weisbord, the main inspiration for this particular form of WSE, has described it as

the purest example of action research that we know. We do not strive to reduce comp[l
to a few manageable issues, to resolve disagreements, or to solve long-standing pro[l
We do not give people a management model for organizing their diverse percept[l
Instead, participants engage in a series of open dialogues on where they've been, where they
are, and what they want to work toward. (Weisbord and Janoff 1995: 71)

Two sources of inspiration are identified: one is the work of Schindler-Rainman and Lippitt in large-scale community futures conferences; the other the work of Trist and Emery in developing the Search Conference (discussed in Weisbord et al. 1992). 'Both sets have a common ancestor who is also ours – Kurt Lewin. His field theory and action research underlie their work as well as our own' (Weisbord and Janoff 1996: 72).

They are based on three assumptions:

1 Change is so rapid that we need more, not less, face-to-face discussion to make intelligent strategic decisions.

2 Successful strategies – for quality goods and services, lower costs, more satisfying ways of working – come from envisioning preferred futures.

3 People will commit to plans they have helped to develop.

This is an immediate challenge to a central aspect of hierarchical organisations: they 'positively discourage subordinate intervention in superordinate decision making' (Grint 1995: 83). Weisbord and his colleagues (1992) have identified nine things that Future Search Conferences can achieve:

1 Encourage collective learning about the external environment, the 'system' of the problem or concern and its history.

2 Stimulate creative thinking and visioning by participants.

3 Acknowledge and respect all views or beliefs regardless of background or expertise level of their holder.

4 Build a shared terrain of ideas and values.

5 Increase cooperation and mutual support.

6 Build commitment to, and a sense of responsibility for, action on the issue.

7 Produce a concrete and precise statement of goals, strategies and actions.

8 Lead to the prompt follow-up action.

9 Be time-efficient.

Minimum critical specifications

The typical Future Search Conference brings together 30–60 people for 2–3 days. Together they do a series of structured tasks, looking at the organisation's past, present and preferred future. Tasks are cumulative. Each session builds on previous ones. The last event involves everybody in action planning for the future. There are a number of minimum requirements, linking to core values:

1 Get the whole system in the room, the broadest temporary planning community feasible for the task at hand. This means maximum variety and diversity of interdependent people. Invite a much broader cross section of stakeholders than is usual. Include widely diverse people who affect each other but rarely or never meet. (Core value: Diversity should be appreciated and valued.)

2 Ask people to be task-focused and to self-manage as much of their work as they are ready, willing and able to do. That means reducing dependency, conflict and task avoidance. Have them self-manage tasks of discovery, dialogue, learning and planning. (Core values: People want opportunities to engage their heads and hearts as well as hands. They want to and are able to join the creative processes of organisation rather than that being the sole domain of the organisation's elite. Given the chance, people are much more likely to cooperate than fight. The consultant's task is to structure opportunities to cooperate.)

3 Have the whole conference community look at itself in a global context, and explore the entire open system – events, trends, relations, within and between the wider world and the focal institution/issue, in the past, present and future. That means the broadest feasible data base and common ideals before zeroing in on what to do about the issue being searched. (Core values: We believe the real world is knowable to ordinary people and their knowledge can be collectively and meaningfully organised. In fact, ordinary people are an extraordinary source of information about the real world. Thus, we believe people can create their own future.)

4 All participants need to agree and act upon a number of ground rules:
  – This is not a problem-solving conference. It is an exercise in learning, awareness, understanding and mutual support. (Core value: The process should empower people to feel more knowledgeable about and in control of the future.)
  – Every idea and comment is valid. People need not agree. (Core value: Egalitarian participation. Everyone is equal.)
  – It is a task-focused meeting. Every task has output, and all output is recorded and discussed.
  – We stick to time, and groups are responsible for completing tasks on schedule.
  – The consultants manage time and structure tasks. Participants generate and analyse information, derive meanings, propose action steps, take responsibility for output.

Some immediate words of caution are appropriate. Weisbord and Janoff (1996) identify three things that cannot be done with a Future Search Conference. It cannot compensate for weak leadership; it will not work with sceptics or people paralysed by worry about losing control, and it will not reconcile intractable value differences.

These reservations are reinforced by Jacobs (1994) in his discussion of Real Time Strategic Change, a methodology which shares the assumptions outlined above, but uses slightly different techniques, some of which are incorporated into the template considered below. He suggests that the approach would be inappropriate where minor or incremental changes are the goal. A second case would be if an organisation's leaders were not fully committed to creating 'an empowered, interdependent, organisation-wide team'. Third, it is unlikely to work if the necessary commitment cannot be secured from other key stakeholders. Finally, it is pointless when an organisation's leaders do not commit the required resources up front.

Technology of participation

This approach involves five stages, following identification of the Focus Question, around which the whole event is centred (Spencer 1989). These stages are explained in the next section.

A particular process is involved. At each stage, people begin work as individuals, identifying their answers to the question. These are then shared in the group (like all these approaches, people are sitting in groups of 6–10 around tables), and each table is asked to identify about six responses. These are written on cards, which are collected, using a variety of techniques, by the facilitators, who place them on a wall, clustered according to common themes. Each cluster is then named, and these named clusters (typically 6–8) form the basis of the next stage.

This interplay between individual and group activity is an important feature of the process. Its efficacy is supported by evidence from other team activities. Thus Hosking and Morley (1991: 183) bring together research findings which suggest that creative work is best achieved where individuals generate ideas alone before joining decision-making groups. They claim this is preferable to working just in 'brainstorming' groups, which research shows to be outperformed by 'nominal' groups (formed by taking the output from a number of individuals working alone and combining it to form a single product).

AN INTEGRATED APPROACH

The 'template' now to be described is flexible, allowing a unique variation for each organisation, depending on their nature and the specific requirements of the task. It is centred on the Technology of Participation model, but with a number of adaptations, drawing from Future Search conferences and from Real-Time Strategic Change.

The template is summarised in Figure 11.4. This adds three stages to the ToP model – 'Review the Past', 'Consider the Present' and Action/Review (this final stage is not strictly part of the event, but it is essential that action is followed through, and this is therefore incorporated into the model). This figure also illustrates the relationship between WSE and the Strategy IDEA.

A preparation stage, involving some of the key internal people, is a valuable first step. This serves several purposes:

- It clarifies what the organisation wants from the work.
- It engages these people directly in its design.
- It allows discussion of the role of these people during the event. As these tend to be the most powerful and influential members of the 'community of concern', they can be briefed on the need to act as enablers at their tables during the event, and to help avoid the situation where a few dominate the discussions. Thus their influence should be on the process rather than the product, where they are to engage as equal partners.
- It offers the opportunity to discuss with them their responsibility after the event in seeing through the programme of activity generated.

All participants can be encouraged to do some preparatory work:

- Thinking through the present position and how it could have been better.

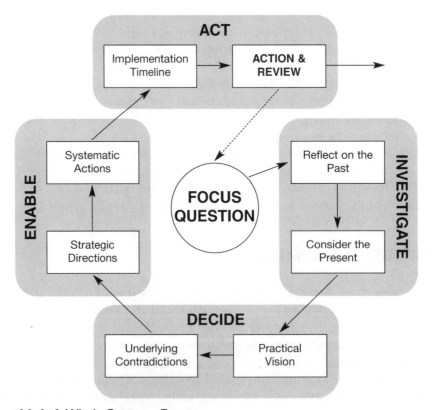

Figure 11.4 A Whole Systems Event

- Talking with colleagues and friends about the present and future.
- Bring articles from papers, or other things illustrating something that will influence their future situation.
- Prepare material using conventional strategic tools, such as PEST, five force analysis and stakeholder mapping. This material can then be the basis of the initial discussion at the preparation meeting, which might use a technique such as ColourFlow Dialogue to guide its progress.

The outcome of this preparation stage needs to include clarity on the Focus Question, and on the ways in which it will be tackled in the main event. Background material generated at this stage can be circulated to help give all participants in the main event some shared information – especially useful for external stakeholders, who might otherwise feel at a disadvantage in the discussions. An alternative approach, drawing from the WSE 'real time strategic change', involves the preparation in advance of strategic proposals, perhaps through an initial event, which are then tested at the full event.

The full model is as follows (stages 3–7 are those used in ToP):

1 **Reviewing the past**: The purpose here is to help develop a shared understanding between participants, and to give them the opportunity to reflect on what has brought themselves and the organisation(s) to this point. They might identify significant events, milestones, highlights or activities they recall during each time period. These can be transferred to the appropriate sheets on the wall. Each group then analyses one theme across the whole time period, looking for patterns and meanings. Examine the collective past from three (or four) perspectives: Individual, (Group), Organisation, Society.

2 **Considering the present**: Here participants can provide both an external and an internal perspective. The former will include events, trends and developments shaping the future now, and might involve STEEP Investigation (Social, Technological, Economic, Environmental, Political) and Stakeholder Investigation. The internal perspective can be developed through 'Prouds and Sorries': Participants are invited to generate at each table a list of these, which are then stuck to the wall.[1] They are invited to read these and 'vote' for the ones generated by other tables with which they particularly agree (or disagree).[2] Again, this process has an additional purpose – by encouraging people to move around, they are breaking away from the pattern of sitting for long periods in a formal meeting – especially important in local government circles, where such formalities are deeply entrenched. It can also be useful to investigate the organisation's culture, the use of power and influence, its current structure, and the current and potential resources, competencies and capabilities. If the questionnaires have been used in the preparatory stage then the results can be shared and discussed – the different perspectives about, for example, the nature and expectations of key stakeholders can be very revealing.

3 **Mapping out the practical vision**: What will our organisation look like five years from now?

4 **Analysing the underlying contradictions**: What stands in the way of the realisation of our vision?

5 **Setting the strategic directions**: What arenas of activity will resolve the contradiction and release the practical vision to come into being?

6 **Designing the systematic actions**: What specific actions will implement the Strategic Directions?

7 **Drawing up the implementation timeline**: What steps are required to implement this action? How will they get done? Where? By whom? By when?

8 **Action and review**: A regular review process is required to ensure that the momentum generated by the event is not lost.

The next stages follow the pattern of ToP, with ideas being generated by each table, brought together in a plenary discussion, and common themes identified. Gradually, the focus shifts from generation of ideas to generation of action, and final stages become increasingly practical, with detailed listings of activity over the coming year (the usual time frame). Depending on the participants, a light-hearted conclusion may be appropriate; if not, some other form of closure is important which recognises what people have achieved, but reinforces the point that this is by no means the end of the story.

Physical location and logistics are important factors in the Conference. Practitioners emphasise the value of a light and airy room. Traditionally, when people at a large event break into smaller groups, each goes to a different room. Here they stay together, working at tables in the one room. This creates a 'buzz' as well as a feeling that all are working together on a common project.

Table membership needs careful consideration. Each participant is given his or her own 'route map' for the event, indicating which table they will be at for each session. In Weisbord's ideal model, there are eight groups of stakeholders each with eight members. In some sessions stakeholders sit together, while for others they are distributed across all the tables. Such perfect numbering is rarely achievable, but 'clusters' of people with some communality (such as the management team, or the sales team, or in local authorities the Councillors) should be given route maps so that they spend much of their time apart from each other, working with other people at their table.

An important consideration in encouraging people to try this approach is to identify and address some of their concerns. Box 11.1 was designed to help in this and has been used with groups in the preparation of events, not least to encourage them to 'let go', and accept that the outcome of such events cannot be predicted in advance. 'Trusting the process' is required from participants in whole systems events. As Jacobs (1994) argues, many people in organisations are accustomed to a certain level of personal control over their work and the results they achieve. Predictability, certainty and having everything go according to

Box 11.1

Is It Safe?!

Engaging in a Whole Systems Event means taking risks. There isn't the safety of the conventional meetings, with its rules and procedures, or of the conventional conference with its speakers and breaks (when, people often say, most of the real value is found). It is worth reviewing a few of the likely objectives, with comments from people who have run Whole Systems Events. The spirit of the approach is well summarised in the comment of Alan Davies, who has managed 100 search conferences, many of which, he says, 'failed to meet their primary organisational objectives ... but had one consolation in that they have been rich learning experiences for all involved.'

- *We have done it all before.* It is unlikely that anything has been done in this form before. Furthermore, the initial stage of a Whole Systems Event, reviewing the past, allows those who have been in the organisation some time to review what has and hasn't happened or worked before. It gives those who arrived more recently the chance to learn from this and avoid re-inventing the square wheel.
- *We have no experience of this.* Rather more likely! But there is a rich experience and expertise that every organisation does have, and if anything the problem is more about unlearning than learning.
- *There are too many constraints on our future.* One of the purposes of strategic thinking is to understand constraints, and seek to maximise opportunities given that understanding. The process incorporates the chance to do this. This attitude is also negative: undoubtedly constraints are great, but if potential capabilities are not also great then what is the organisation doing here? 'Some aspects of a desirable future were beyond the powers of those attending. But other goals could be achieved by people operating in collaboration with a clearer sense of their mutual objectives.' (Schwass)
- *It is no good forcing people to take part.* Just so: participation should be entirely voluntary, involving people who want to try something new. If it works, then subsequent activity will hopefully bring on board others –the process should be non-exclusive and non-hierarchical throughout.
- *It won't work if key people are missing.* This will undoubtedly diminish the value of the event, although it does not negate it. The important thing is to **do something**, and to ensure that this harnesses the abilities of all.
- *Nothing will come out of it.* The worst that can happen is that a group of people with a common commitment and concern spend some time together learning from each other, and go away with a better appreciation

317

of the issues. This assumes nothing is achieved in terms of follow-up action. That in itself would say a great deal about the organisation. However, one of the principles of complexity theory is that new ideas and practices emerge from the maelstrom. 'Whatever their long term outcomes, search conferences tend to create intense environments for learning and socialising. People with common interests, but often widely differing perspectives, explore the concerns that they share, and appreciate more clearly those they do not. They also come to discover jointly the areas that are not normally considered – particularly as these relate to the future. All of this promotes scepticism and uncertainty, questioning and discovery, excitement and disagreement, and hope and disillusionment too' (Morley and Trist).

• *There will be plenty of talk, but little commitment to action.* This indeed would be disappointing. But concerns about the 'implementation gap' are common in many organisations. The event gives the chance to explore why it happens. 'The discovery of a shared vision and the number of volunteers for action task groups exceeded many peoples' expectations. It created an atmosphere of hope and encouragement at the close of the conference. Anecdotal feedback afterwards indicated that there is considerable energy to carry this spirit forward' (Rehm, Schweitz and Granata).

Source: from Weisbord et al. (1992).

plan becomes a goal, even if an unconscious one. Control is exercised by deciding who is going to do what in the plan, and then monitoring things to make sure that they happen in the prescribed manner.

In place of control by a few, whole systems events value participation and involvement of many: they assume that participation begets participation (Grint 1995). This implies the building of a common understanding throughout an organisation by free and open sharing of strategic information, as well as allowing decisions to be made by those most affected. There is no place in this formula for establishing and reinforcing a small group's privilege and power. Controlling information and making decisions for others runs counter to the basic premises of these approaches. In fact, it most often leads not only to uninformed decisions being made, but also to people who lack motivation and a belief that they can make a difference in their organisational lives.

Table 11.5 reflects further on these considerations by characterising WSEs as Complex Adaptive Systems. WSEs can also be seen as open arenas, in which provisional agreement is sought at several points in the process, leading to an overall outcome that is actionable. The process is designed to facilitate the

Table 11.5 Whole Systems Events as complex adaptive systems

Complex Adaptive Systems	Whole Systems Event
A network of many 'agents'	WSE seeks to 'get the whole system in the room, the broadest temporary planning community feasible for the task at hand'.
'Adaptively intelligent'	Learning is central to WSE, and as noted even events that failed to meet their primary organisational objectives proved to be rich learning experiences for all involved.
Control dispersed	There should be egalitarian participation, in which everyone is equal and is valued.
Competition and cooperation	This is recognised in two core values. First, that 'given the chance, people are much more likely to cooperate than fight'. Second, that 'diversity should be appreciated and valued'. The process is such that competition between ideas is encouraged, and different views are raised. Attempts to create a total consensus are likely to result in 'lowest common denominator' results, of doubtful value. But agreement is possible, while recognising dissent: 'Competition can produce a very strong incentive for co-operation'.
Coevolution, emergence and self-organisation	It is impossible to say in advance what ideas will emerge, and what the outcome will be. Within the overall structure there is considerable scope for self-organisation: indeed, if groupings did not self-organise, the event would fail.
Many levels of organisation	The process deliberately operates at individual, group and plenary levels, and moves between these a number of times, with each level serving as the building block for a higher level.
Constant revision and rearrangement	The structure is such that groupings are rearranged a number of times, to encourage cross-fertilisation of ideas.
Anticipates the future	An important element of the process is 'Mapping out the Practical Vision: What will our organisation look like five years from now'.
Always unfolding	The process itself is dynamic. By the end there is an action programme, but this does not mark an equilibrium: it is a stage in an unfolding process. As has been clear from the case studies, WSE need to be seen as part of a wider process.
Between order and disorder	This is critical to WSE. The structure is intended to provide order – but what happens within that is unpredictable. This inevitably creates some discomfort, leading to the 'Rollercoaster' effect.
Interaction with the environment	Advance preparation can provide many thoughts on the organisation and its interaction with the environment. But also important is the premise that 'ordinary people are an extraordinary source of information'. A further advantage of the process is that bringing people together from diverse backgrounds and interests can lead to recognition that there are multiple perspectives on issues, involving different schemata, and that both the organisation and the environment are enacted. Finally, the structure of the event, with a variety of stakeholders involved, emphasises the fuzzy boundaries of the organisation(s).

application of Creative Intelligence, with people encouraged to look for ways to develop collaborative working which will move them toward their envisioned future.

We can also relate WSEs to the principles outlined in Chapter 7.

Recognise fuzzy boundaries: WSE allows for fuzzy boundaries – indeed the 'whole world' brought together in the room can be seen as a fuzzy set in relation to the organising body. Each participant is there because s/he has an interest in that organisation, but the degree of interest varies.

Keep thinking and action in dynamic tension: We can see that the flow of a search conference begins and ends in action. The past/present phases focus on what the organisation is or has been doing; the final phases focus on action planning for the future. In between come phases where thinking about the future is dominant, but overall there is a continuous interplay between the two – and crucially, they are not seen as being done by separate groups of people.

Value Process, and Put Trust in Process: Valuing process is a consideration uppermost in the minds of those organising search conferences (see, for example, Weisbord and Janoff 1995; Wheatley 1992). Trust in self-organisation could be seen as a matter of belief, but the tenets of complexity theory and autopoiesis allow us to make a stronger claim – that this is an identifiable tendency which can emerge in many situations. We have found through experience that this is also easy to suppress, often out of fear that we will 'lose control'. There is a strong temptation to go for 'tried and trusted' techniques – which often means perpetuating customs and practices that reinforce 'theory-in-use'.

Search conferences, by contrast, use techniques that deliberately disrupt custom and practice. They are therefore risky, and the facilitator in particular has to trust the process and resist the temptation to fall back on a 'safer' option. Here again we have a paradox: the free-flowing movement and opportunities that search conferencing offers have to be protected by a 'process guardian' who imposes a particular structure to allow this.[3]

Allow for and encourage proactive emergence: 'Proactive emergence' features strongly in search conferencing: indeed the whole ToP approach adopted in several of these studies is only possible through emergence. At each stage the plenary group identify common themes from the work just done which become the basis of the next stage: these common themes cannot be predicted in advance.

Facilitate learning: And alongside this comes learning. The output from a search conference can be considerable, even where preparatory work was not done. The participants learning from each other, and integrating their experience, knowledge, ideas and aspirations achieve this output.

Accept (indeed embrace) the absence of certainty and foundations: Finally, WSE accepts – indeed is premised on – uncertainty and the lack of foundations. It is impossible to say at the outset what will be achieved, and practitioners have identified the uncertainty involved, even to the point where the WSE fails to achieve its initial goals, but nevertheless provides rich learning in the process.

DRAMA THEORY

In this chapter we have focused on two methodologies which reflect the above values and philosophy. There are others, including dialogue (outlined in Chapter 7), appreciative inquiry and drama theory. Recently there has been work linking the latter with whole systems events, and this is summarised in Box 11.2.

Box 11.2

Drama theory and immersive drama

Analytical drama theory (Bryant 1997; Howard 1998), a generalisation of game theory, provides the theoretical base to the practical approach of immersive drama. One of the strong conclusions of drama theory is that there are six (and only six) key dilemmas that can occur for characters caught up in any confrontation:

- I benefit by reneging from my solution – so why should you think I would implement it?
- You benefit by reneging from our mutual solution – so why should I trust you?
- I'd rather not carry out my threat – so how can I use it to pressure you?
- You'd rather carry out your threat than take my solution – so how can I deter you?
- I'd rather adopt your solution than carry out my threat – so how can I persuade you to my view?
- I'd rather adopt your solution than implement my own – so how can I attract you to my solution?

Characters engaged in an immersive drama will inevitably encounter some of these dilemmas and their success in handling them will shape the outcome of the situation. Indeed it can be argued that the proficient handling of dilemmas is the cornerstone of effective interaction.

Immersive drama is delivered through an intensive workshop experience in which participants take on specific roles in a fully described setting. The aim is to provide both cognitive and affective personal insights for those involved, as well as drawing out systemic features in a non-destructive manner. Dramas are created in a bespoke manner for specific situations and requirements, and this demands a period of applied research usually involving interviews with key players in the situation to be represented.

The creation of an effective immersive drama involves identification and inclusion of key issues – 'bones of contention' – between the principal 'characters' involved in a situation. It is these issues that become the main arenas for collaboration and conflict as the drama unfolds. Characters will have or will be given (explicitly or implicitly) a particular stance on each issue and this provides the base from which they interact with others. Changing stance demands that a character can convince or persuade others that it has done so. Resolving issues requires that characters invent and settle upon solutions (reluctantly or enthusiastically) from which no one feels under any pressure to abscond: in turn this may mean modifying intentions, changing priorities or conceding claims. All interactions in an immersive drama are free form – participants can work with others as and when is mutually agreeable – subject only to the overriding requirement of dramatic conviction.

CONCLUSION

Overall, WSE offers a viable approach to change management. While it uses many tools and techniques drawn from conventional strategic management, it differs in certain critical respects. First, it is not 'top down' in the way that so much strategic planning is; nor is it simply consultative in the way that logical incrementalism can be. The methods used are deliberately chosen as ones that can be rapidly assimilated and implemented – there is no requirement here to first attend a course in strategy. In this way participation from a wide range of people is possible – indeed, the democratic ideals drawing from critical theory as described in Chapter 5 are only too evident, even if their full realisation is always going to be problematic.

Second, the link between thinking and doing is emphasised throughout, and this is reinforced in WSE by the compressed timescale uses, as compared with other approaches to strategic management.

Third, as far as possible existing power structures are 'suspended'. There are, of course, limitations to this, particularly where the event occurs within a wider Control arena. But effective facilitation (including the cooption of the most powerful in the organisation into collaborative facilitating roles) can help to create a complex adaptive system.

Fourth, there is the challenge to control. In WSE the structure provides an order within which there is chaos: what happens within the process, and what the final outcome will be, are neither controlled nor predicted. Increasing confidence in the process, and in the Worldview and Management Mindset associated with it in this thesis, have made it possible to change this balance, reducing the level of control (see Vignette 11.1).

Vignette 11.1

Freeing the system

Two WSEs facilitated by one of the authors illustrate this theme. Each involved the major players in a local authority, and were concerned with developing the overall strategy of each organisation. In one, the latter changed the overall structure prepared (by the author, in conjunction with the client) at a very late stage, so that the author was only aware of this minutes before the event began. It proved possible to improvise, drawing on several of the approaches and tools considered here, and even to shift more toward Conferencing methods as the event unfolded. For example, the event began with all (30) participants in serried ranks along a formal table; it ended with people in a plenary scattered around several small round tables.

In the second, the author was asked to facilitate at a very late stage (the original intention had been to do without a facilitator). The Council leader commented afterward that he had been very pleased with the productivity of the event, not least because he had had very little time to prepare and think about what he wanted from the event, and had been concerned about this 'lack of control' (his words). An explanation of the philosophy underlying the approach adopted came therefore as something of a surprise. Again, the event involved improvisation to take account of the developing pattern.

NOTES

1 This emphasis on the use of walls is worth noting. Over the period of the conference, output builds up around the walls of the room, providing a visible demonstration of what is being achieved, as well as making it easy for people to see what has been said. This material is usually written up afterwards and provided to all participants.

2 This voting is done by putting coloured stars or dots on the statements.

3 It should be noted that there are some forms of WSE, such as Open Space, where no such structure is offered. These have not been used as part of the work for this thesis, and therefore no comment is offered on their efficacy.

REFERENCES

Alvesson, M. and H. Willmott (1996) *Making Sense of Management*, London: Sage.
Bryant, J. (1997) 'All the World's a Stage: Using Drama Theory to Resolve Confrontations', *OR Insight*, 10(4): 14–21.

Carr, W. and S. Kemmis (1986) *Becoming Critical*, Lewes: Falmer Press.

Cassell, C. and M. Fitter (1992) 'Responding to a Changing Environment', in D.M. Hosking and N. Anderson (eds) *Organizational Change and Innovation*, London: Routledge.

Clegg, S.R., C. Hardy and W.R. Nord (1996) *Handbook of Organization Studies*, London: Sage.

Deshler, D. and M. Ewert (1995) *Participatory Action Research: Traditions and Major Assumptions*, Cornell University (posted on Internet: http://www.parnet.org/tools/tools_1.cfm).

Eden, C. and C. Huxham (1996a) 'Action Research for Management', *British Journal of Management*, 7: 75–86.

Eden, C. and C. Huxham (1996b) 'Action Research for the Study of Organizations', in S.R. Clegg, C. Hardy and W.R. Nord, *Handbook of Organization Studies*, London: Sage.

Elden, M. and M. Levin (1991) 'Cogenerative Learning', in W.F. Whyte (ed.) *Participatory Action Research*, London: Sage.

Fals-Borda, O. and M.A. Rahman (eds) (1991) *Action and Knowledge: Breaking the Monopoly with Participatory Action*, London: Research Intermediate Technology Publications.

Frideres, J.S. (1992) 'Participatory Research: An Illusionary Perspective', in J.S. Frideres (ed.) *A World of Communities: Participatory Research Perspectives*, York, Ontario: Caputus University Publications.

Gill, J. and P. Johnson (1991) *Research Methods for Managers*, London: Paul Chapman.

Grint, K. (1995) *Management: A Sociological Introduction*, Cambridge: Polity Press.

Grundy, S. (1982) *Three Modes of Action Research*, cited in Kemmis and McTaggert (1990).

Grundy, S. (1987) *Curriculum: Product or Praxis*, Lewes: Falmer Press.

Habermas, J. (1968, published in English 1972) *Knowledge and Human Interests*, London: Heinemann.

Habermas, J. (1974) *Theory and Practice*, London: Heinemann.

Hamel, G. (1996) 'Strategy as Revolution', *Harvard Business Review* (July).

Härnsten, G. (1994) *The Research Circle – Building Knowledge on Equal Terms,* Stockholm: Swedish Trade Union Confederation.

Hart, E. and M. Bond (1995) *Action Research for Health and Social Care: A Guide to Practice*, Buckingham: Open University Press.

Holter, I.M. and D. Schwartz-Barcott (1993) 'Action Research: What is it? How Has it Been Used and How can it be Used in Nursing?', *Journal of Advanced Nursing*, 128: 298–304.

Hosking, D.-M. and I.E. Morley (1991) *A Sociology of Organizing*, London: Prentice Hall/Harvester Wheatsheaf.

Howard, N. (1999) *Confrontation Analysis: How to Win Operations Other than War*, Vienna: CCRP.

Hyman, J. and B. Mason (1995) *Managing Employee Involvement and Participation*, London: Sage.

Jacobs, R.W. (1994) *Real Time Strategic Change*, San Francisco: Berrett-Koehler.

Kakabadse, A. and C. Parker (eds) (1984) *Power, Politics and Organizations*, Chichester: John Wiley and Sons.

Kemmis, S. and R. McTaggert (1990) *The Action Research Planner*, Geelong: Deakin University Press.

Lewin, K. (1946) 'Action Research and Minority Problems', *Journal of Social Issues*, 2.

Lewin, K. (1947) 'Frontiers in Group Dynamics', *Human Relations*, 1.

Maguire, P. (1987) *Doing Participatory Research: A Feminist Approach*, Amherst, MA: Center for International Education.

Maruyama, G. (1996) 'Application and Transformation of Action Research', *Educational Research and Practice Systems Practice*, 9(1).

McCutcheon, G. and B. Jurg (1990) 'Alternative Perspectives on Action Research', *Theory into Practice*, 24(3) (Summer).

McGill, I. and L. Beaty (1995) *Action Learning*, London: Kogan Page.

McKernan, J. (1988) 'The Countenance of Curriculum Action Research: Traditional, Collaborative and Critical-Emancipatory Conceptions', *Journal of Curriculum and Supervision*, 3(34) (Spring): 173–200.

McKernan, J. (1991) *Curriculum Action Research. A Handbook of Methods and Resources for the Reflective Practitioner*, London: Kogan Page.

McKernan, J. (1996) *Curriculum Action Research*, London: Kogan Page.

McLaughlin, H. and R. Thorpe (1993) 'Action Learning – A Paradigm in Emergence', *British Journal of Management*, 4(1): 19–27.

McNiff, J., P. Lomax and J. Whitehead (1996) *You and Your Action Research Project*, London: Routledge.

McTaggert, R. (1992) *Action Research: Issues in Theory and Practice*. Keynote address to the Methodological Issues in Qualitative Health Research Conference, 27 November, Deakin University, Geelong.

Miller, D. (1990) *The Icarus Paradox*, New York: Harper Business.

Morgan, G. (1993) *Imaginization*, London: Sage.

Morgan, G. and R. Ramirez (1983) 'Action Learning: A Holographic Metaphor for Guiding Social Change', *Human Relations*, 37(1): 1–28.

Pedler, M. (ed.) (1991) *What is Action Learning?*, Aldershot: Gower.

Pedler, M., J. Burgoyne and T. Boydell (1996) *The Learning Company*, Maidenhead: McGraw-Hill.

Rapaport, R.N. (1970) 'Three Dilemmas in Action Research', *Human Relations*, 23(6): 499.

Revans, R.W. (1980) *Action Learning*, Blond & Briggs.

Revans, R.W. (1982) *The Origins and Growth of Action Learning*, Bromley: Chartwell-Bratt.

Revans, R.W. (1983) *The ABC of Action Learning*, Bromley: Chartwell-Bratt.

Schindler-Rainman, E. and R. Lippitt (1989) *Building the Community: Mobilizing Citizens for Action*, Irvine: University of California.

Spencer, L. (1989) *Winning through Participation*, Kendall Hunt.

Weick, K. (1996) 'Drop Your Tools: An Allegory for Organizational Studies', *Administrative Science Quarterly*, 41.

Weisbord, M.R. (1987) *Productive Workplaces*, San Francisco: Jossey Bass.

Weisbord, M.R. and S. Janoff (1995) *Future Search: An Action Guide*, San Francisco: Berrett-Koehler.

Weisbord, M.R. and S. Janoff (1996) 'Future Search: Finding Common Ground', *Organizations and Communities Systems Practice*, 9(1).

Weisbord, M.R. et al. (1992) *Discovering Common Ground*, San Francisco: Berrett-Koehler.

Wheatley, M. (1992) *Leadership and the New Science*, San Francisco: Berrett-Koehler.

Chapter 12

CONCLUSIONS: REFLECTING THE REFLEXIVE

Three colleagues have written this book. Over a number of years we have taught, learnt and worked together, and through these experiences have had the opportunity to compare our thinking and practice. We recognised that we agreed on many aspects of our approach to change in organisations, while disagreeing on a few. We have sought to reflect both in this book. Each chapter has been written by one of the authors, although the detail of each has been the subject of extensive discussion between us. It was our view that this fitted well with the spirit of our overall approach, in which nothing is privileged and there is no question of finding some indisputable ultimate truth. Everything we say can, and no doubt will, be disputed. In this final chapter we draw together some of the common strands, while also identifying and reflecting on some of the concerns and interests that have motivated our work.

One persistent theme which has emerged during the writing of this book has been the need for reflexivity on the part of both management researchers and practitioners during their engagements with organisations and change-management processes. However, some caution is advisable here because what is meant by reflexivity, and indeed whether or not it is considered possible in the first place, varies according to the different approaches to change considered in this book.

Generally, reflexivity is concerned with the relationship between any observer and the objects of observation. Whether one is a management researcher or a practitioner it is about thinking about our own thinking, by noticing and evaluating how our pre-understandings influence the way we engage with our topics of interest and impact upon what we find. It follows that the *a priori* beliefs of the observer must be as much open to critical scrutiny as what is conventionally defined as empirical evidence. Thus calls for reflexivity imply that it is possible for management researchers and practitioners to autonomously and rationally reflect upon different aspects of ways in which s/he engages with various organisational phenomena.

Of course, here we must not underestimate the resistance to any form of reflexivity which abounds amongst management academics and practitioners. This resistance derives from the technicist predilections which have been widely noted to hold sway in these groups (see, for example, Whitley 1984; Reed and Antony 1992; Grey and Mitev 1995). These predilections envisage management and the processes of change as socially, morally and politically neutral – as merely technical activities which ought to be discharged by those members who have acquired through their education and experience the requisite superior knowledge and expertise. Such an understanding of management and change processes in organisations as morally and politically unproblematic can be sustained only by the usually tacit appropriation of the Cartesian–Newtonian synthesis discussed in Chapter 1 – where observers can, in principle, passively register the facts that constitute a cognitively accessible objective reality. As we noted in Chapter 4, unchallenged claims to an objective analysis of how things 'really are' are important for the preservation of management prerogative – the lynchpin of management power.

So, although the position is not unproblematic, in the last twenty years or so there have been numerous calls for more reflexivity in conducting management research and practice. For instance, with regard to the latter, Morgan (1986, 1993) has advocated the reflexive interrogation of the metaphors practitioners use to constitute organisations and members as objects of investigation as a means of management development. Indeed, according to Morgan there is much to gain here for 'metaphorical images can provide powerful tools for helping people look at themselves and their situations in new ways and, as a result, see and act in the world somewhat differently' (1993: 291).

Chapter 9 provided an extended example of one metaphor – the ecological – in order to examine the many different ways in which such an approach can be used. This metaphor was chosen both because it is rich and varied, and because it is one which, as the debates on environmental change and the ethics of business develop, may be expected to gain increasing prominence. As we saw, its use can vary from a realist stance to one of social constructivism.

As Morgan (1993) observes, the dynamic tension created between existing and potential understandings by such 'imaginization' resonates with Schon's (1983) study, which found that managers do sometimes conduct what he calls 'reflection-in-action' as an everyday activity.

However, as Morgan (1993) implies, reflexivity can go much further than Schon's 'reflective conversations'. Much here depends on the underlying epistemological commitments being deployed – and Morgan is clearly deploying social constructivist commitments. As we demonstrated in Chapter 5, social constructivist concerns with reflexivity derive from Kant's undermining of empiricism through his argument that our minds were not passive receivers of sense data emanating from a cognitively accessible external reality. Instead we endow the world with meaning (and not vice versa as the empiricists claimed). Although the categories, concepts and meanings we use seem to originate in what we take to be the external world, Kant claimed that they naturally derive from our *a priori* cognitive structures. Hence for Kant all we can have is knowledge of how the world appears in our consciousness via the filtration and order imposed by our *a priori* mental forms – which are themselves independent of reality itself. Through rational reflection we can know what the *a priori* grounds of experience are and understand how we organise our sensory inputs.

In Chapter 10 there was an exploration of four approaches, metaphors if you will, of strategy. The interesting issue there was the extent to which actors occupying those four positions could look at the stance they take in relation to strategy as metaphor – or is that strategic stance real as phenomenon and real in its consequences? Whittington clearly has a special place in his heart for what he terms the systemic approach to strategy (which we placed, in our model, as an aspect of strategy as expression of subjective experience). He suggests that the systemic perspective 'arms managers with sardonic self awareness. ... Sociologically sensitive and just a little bit cynical, the Systemic manager ... secures her advance by drawing on a much more catholic range of social resources, and manipulates them with far greater sophistication' (2001: 119) than do strategists from other positions. We would suggest, however, that all the strategic positions are amenable to this quality of self-awareness (although maybe not sardonic), to epistemic reflexivity.

Debates about epistemic reflexivity have usually focused upon social science research even though their implications are of equal relevance to natural scientists and, of course, management practitioners (see Bourdieu 1990; Pollner 1991; Steier 1991; Beck 1992; Sandywell 1996; Holland 1999). Epistemic reflexivity entails the researcher attempting to think about his/her own thinking by excavating, articulating, evaluating and in some cases transforming the *a priori* assumptions s/he deploys in structuring research activities as well as in apprehending and interpreting what is observed. Here, the implication is that researchers must hold their own 'research structures and logics as themselves researchable and not immutable, and by examining how we are part of our own data, our research becomes a reciprocal process' (Steier, 1991: 7).

This has been an issue of particular moment for the author of Chapter 2. In 1980 I completed my doctoral thesis on culture in organisations. The literature search revealed little on the topic of culture as organisational phenomenon although there were hints that such a phenomenon might be found. In 1982 Deal and Kennedy produced what was probably the first popular text on this matter. A paradigm was born. What they did that was so appealing to managers (and many teachers in Higher Education) was that they took culture as a 'real' phenomenon. So did I in my doctoral thesis, and in the years which followed so I did as the author of Chapter 2. Throughout my academic and consultancy career I have 'seen' its thereness. Organisation culture has been a topic for analysis. However, as manager and member of the academic community – a sometimes herding and sometimes herded cat – I have felt, lived, experienced its ambiguity, the uncertainty of culture. The idea of managing the culture seems enormously challenging or even chimera.

As I developed Chapter 2 there was a reflexive moment. This was the opportunity to synthesise my research, academic perspective and my understanding of the world as I experience it. It was this dawning realisation that the theory of research that was part and parcel of my understanding of the world was not the same as the one that was experienced as part of daily life. There was a separation. The outcome of this realisation was also an understanding that as a researcher I can legitimately hold the theory of culture that I do, but also have a deep understanding that that theory needs to be constantly tested out. We can hold in our minds a practical metaphor of culture as theory that enables us to gain some sense of order. However, at the same time we can understand and feel that ambiguity and uncertainty pervade the theory itself. As manager this helps us to realise that although I might try to 'manage' culture the outcome may well end up in a very different place from that initially envisaged. The principle of reciprocity applies, then, for both researchers and for managers in the sense that the data I collect as researcher and the actions I make as manager are themselves open to self-scrutiny, to the reflexive process.

Bourdieu (1990) attempts to cast some light on how what we have called epistemic reflexivity might be accomplished. He argues that any science is embedded in, and conditioned by, an underlying socially derived collective unconsciousness that conditions what is taken to be warranted knowledge. For Bourdieu epistemic reflexivity entails systematic reflection by the social scientist aimed at making the unconscious conscious and the tacit explicit so as to reveal how his/her social location, or 'habitus', forms a sub-text of research which conditions any account – an analysis of analysis. This must entail some form of metatheoretical examination of the presuppositions which researchers have internalised and will inevitably deploy in understanding any organisational experiences. It follows that management research cannot be carried out in an intellectual space that is autonomous from the researcher's own biography. Indeed, it would seem that epistemic reflexivity must relate to how a researcher's own biography affects the forms and outcomes of research (Ashmore 1989) as well as entailing acceptance of the conviction that there will always be more than one valid account of any research.

By way of modest example. The authors of the chapters in this book (or indeed any book) are the outcomes of our emotional, psychological, social, intellectual biographies. These have influenced the way in which we have researched, lived our lives, written the chapters. But at the same time they have not done such that it invalidates our work as mere expressions of subjective impressions. Ruse (1999) has explored the relationship between culture and science with particular reference to the relationship between the development of evolutionary theory and the culture in which different theorists were located. What he found was that whilst some theorists' work was permeated to the point of pollution by the immediate cultural milieu in which they live, others could legitimately claim to have produced science that is relatively free of cultural accretions. He suggests that 'it is true that science is special, and this is because of its standards. ... But it is also true that science is not special, and this is because of culture' (1999: 255). Ultimately, what Ruse is suggesting is that we can differentiate between good science and 'poor quality theories or discourses – pseudo or quasi-sciences'. These latter do not 'tell us' about the reality of 'reality versus illusion: Macbeth's dagger right there in the room' (1999: 255). Whereas the former illuminate reality.

The author of Chapter 3 – mindsets and paradigms – has through training and work as researcher some claim to an understanding of the standards of research.

However, at the emotional core of the mindset, I have an understanding of the world that wants it to be a good place, a world in which I want to love and be loved. When I read that those with a high need for affiliation 'are typified ... 1) by a strong desire for approval and reassurance from others: 2) a tendency to conform to the wishes and norms of others when pressurised by people whose friendship they value, and 3) a sincere interest in the feelings of others' (Steers 1987: 62) I felt at home. That emotional core is part of my biography – this biography has shaped the desire for affiliation as the desire for affiliation has permeated one way or another, the biography. This influences the way in which I approach research, management, and membership of the organisation. In research interests, I would claim, modestly, to be a Kuhnian in his search for reality (preferring Kuhnian coherence over Popperian correspondence), my research interest in the qualitative over the quantitative, my preference for the hermeneutic paradigm over the 'natural science' paradigm, and so on. As manager I would claim that the human aspects of management are transcendent; I am averse to talk of the 'bottom line'.

However, as I developed Chapter 3 there was a growing awareness of mindsets other than my own – and a growing awareness of the strengths and limitations of my own. In this sense the author becomes novelist, immersing the self in the reality of others, suspending moral judgement the while. And as manager? Perhaps a dawning realisation is the need to be able to understand those other mindsets in a way that does not overwhelm the self but is still open to the contrary view. But, of course, this gentle liberal humanist view of the matter reinforces rather than challenges biography. As author I have confronted my own common sense – but as to change there is resistance.

For another of the authors this intellectual biography began in practice. An education in philosophy and mathematical logic led me to an initial approach to management that fell very neatly into the concept of the 'rational manager'. It was through hard experience that I discovered the limitations of this approach. The most graphic example of this occurred when a crisis arose in the organisation for which I then worked, one which threatened its future existence. Three of us spent several months identifying a rational solution to this, and prepared a detailed paper setting these out, then sitting back to await the plaudits. Instead a large number of brown bricks fell on our heads: we were accused of attempting to destroy the whole ethos of the organisation, fatally damaging its experimental and innovative nature, when our objective had been to retain this. We had completely failed to think through the cultural and political implications of what we were doing. We had focused entirely on the 'public performance', and failed to consider the 'backstage activity'. As a result it took over a year to get the proposals implemented, when a more sensitive approach might have delivered results more quickly – and given us much less aggravation! As someone trained and rooted in mathematical logic, this was an important lesson in *realpolitik*, akin to the lesson cited by Kissinger: 'Before I served as a consultant to Kennedy, I had believed, like most academics, that the process of decision-making was largely intellectual and all one had to do was to walk into the President's office and convince him of the correctness of one's views. This perspective I soon realised is as dangerously immature as it is widely held' (cited in Pfeffer 1992: 36–7).

This chastening experience was one of a number of events that brought home the limitations of 'rational management'. Subsequent experience made me question the rational approach to strategy. Working with consultants, I discovered their penchant for a neat rational, linear approach, which commenced with a *tabula rasa*, showing scant attention to the cultural and political dimensions. The schemata they provided looked impressive – I was subsequently to find them in many strategy textbooks. But they bore little relationship to strategy development as I had experienced it.

These concerns could have led no further than an appreciation of the importance of 'backstage' activity – in particular, the need to understand and work with the 'softer' dimensions identified in the textbooks, including power, leadership style and culture. But it seemed worth revisiting logic and the philosophy of science to consider how they might inform a richer approach to organisational work. This exploration involved three interconnecting realms of thinking. The first was that of philosophy, logic, epistemology, ontology and scientific method. Here the implications of complexity theory and fuzzy logic, explored in Chapter 7, were important. The second was theory itself – developing an understanding of management and organisational dynamics. The third was the practice of management and strategy.

An important aspect of this exploration, also developed in Chapter 7, was the rejection of any notion of foundations, instead viewing theory and practice as a pattern that connects. As we saw, the view of groundlessness expressed there extends to both object and subject, leading to a form of reflexivity in which both are under constant scrutiny, and neither is privileged. It will come as no surprise that a literature is slowly developing considering the relationship between this epistemology and postmodernism (see, for example, Magliola 1984).

Fay (1987) has pointed out that because epistemic reflexivity insists that researchers must confront and question the taken-for-granted assumptions that traditionally inform our knowledge claims and ultimately give meaning to our lives, resistance to epistemic reflexivity is only to be expected. Moreover, because epistemic reflexivity entails a denial of any neutral vantage point it forestalls any proclamation of immunity from the effects of the researcher's own biography and hence any claim to objectivity is undermined. This proposition – which will be opposed by those whose vested interests rely on maintenance of a claim to privileged knowledge and expertise (a claim which we noted in Chapter 8) – was pivotal to bureaucratic organisational designs where knowledge is assumed to be hierarchically ordered. However another, more fundamental, challenge to epistemic reflexivity can arise amongst those whom we have described in Chapter 6 as postmodernists.

Postmodernism problematises reflexivity in two quite different ways, both of which are driven by the same relativistic tendencies. For instance, decentring the subject would seem to imply that the possibility to reflect rationally on and develop self-knowledge by interrogating one's own assumptions is impossible since people can neither possess such agency and independent volition nor can they autonomously choose their discursive communities. In this vein Linstead (1994) doubts whether reflexivity can take the form of self-knowledge located in purging the biases and worldviews of researchers from their research. Moreover even foregrounding 'the researcher in research' (Linstead 1994: 1325) is tenuous since it is unlikely that researchers can access and understand their constitutive assumptions which are 'struggling and emerging and hence being realised from day to day' (Linstead 1994: 1326). Instead, Linstead's postmodern ontological and epistemological commitments seem to lead him (e.g. 1993) to advocate an alternative form of reflexivity located in an unending spiral of deconstructive unsettling where there can be no 'fixed' truth nor 'final' outcome.

Hence some postmodernists are often keen to demonstrate other implications of their relativism by arguing that reflexivity must be an endless process where the meanings that have been attached to experience may be reformulated to create what amount to rereadings and rewritings of the 'text'. Since no text should ever be left settled, the implication is that postmodernists must continuously deconstruct their own reflexive deconstructions of themselves.

Ashmore (1989) and Woolgar (1988a and b) advocate the use of what they call 'hyper-reflexivity', the 'deconstruction of deconstruction' and the development of 'new literary forms'. Released 'from the constraints of representational realism' (Ashmore 1989: xxix), their project abandons the conventional mode of writing exemplified by the authoritative monologue of a single official writer. Instead, a number of voices appear, disappear and reappear throughout the self-referential text, interrupting and disrupting each other where any 'author' is debated by 'meta-authors', who in turn are debated by their own 'meta-authors', and so on, in a potentially endless spiral of introspective, reflexive and deconstructive iterations.

So, for some postmodernists if there can be no external independent ontological referent, reflexivity becomes an autopoietic (i.e. self-generating) process (see Delanty 1997), within a recursively closed cognitive system. While embracing postmodernism's subjectivist epistemology, other commentators eschew a subjectivist ontology precisely because of the relativistic problems it creates (see Kilduff and Mehra 1997; Parker 1993). Here the implication is that reflexivity involves a hermeneutic relationship with an ontologically prior reality and a commitment to societal change through the transformation of knowledge. This Kantian combination of social constructivism and ontological realism is illustrated by Latour's (1988) critique of postmodernist hyper-reflexivity. He argues for 'infra-reflexivity', which is of the 'world not the word' and therefore entails a 'multiplicity of genres ... not ... the tedious presence of "reflexive loops"': genres which appertain to different interpretations of a world 'still unknown and despised' (Latour 1988: 73). Elsewhere Beck (1996: 7) describes this position as 'reflexive realism'. Reality, social construction and the interpreter interact so that the researcher has to be committed to investigation of how 'self evidence is produced, how questions are curtailed, how alternative interpretations are shut up in black boxes and so on'. By bringing postmodernism back from a relativistic abyss, Beck argues for the discursive democratisation of social science through public critique. This is an orientation which both radicalises and lends force to those who engage in more participative research where participants are those who are usually excluded from, and objectivised by, the research process (e.g. Fryer and Feather 1994; Reason and Rowan 1981).

Two methodologies were discussed in Chapter 11, which illustrate the possibilities of engaging in this form of research. These are two of a growing number of approaches that attempt to reflect the desire for a more radical and democratic stance on organisational and management practice. Others include Dialogue (reviewed in Chapter 7), Appreciative Inquiry and Drama Theory (also outlined briefly in Chapter 11). It should be stressed that of these, only Participatory Action Research can be seen to have incorporated from the outset some of the concerns discussed in earlier chapters. Nevertheless each can be enriched and developed further by looking at these interrelationships – at the pattern that connects – and this is evident in later work on each. All, for example, benefit from considering the implications of complexity theory. These methodologies embrace (explicitly or otherwise) a reflexive approach. Thus they recognise that the processes of change are not neutral, and that 'knowledge' is a social construction.

The role of the facilitator becomes an interesting one here. The goal is sometimes expressed as: 'you (the participants) will be responsible for the content, I (the facilitator) will be responsible for the process'. In practice, no such neat division occurs. Take drama theory. The content is inevitably strongly influenced by the setting prepared for the immersive drama. As the drama unfolds, the participants interrelate with this and each other to construct a new picture which, through the linkage with whole systems approaches outlined in Chapter 11, offers them the opportunity to reflect on their experience and thus inform their thinking and future practice. Again, any notion of a crisp distinction between the objective and the subjective and between theory and practice is challenged by mutual construction and interaction.

Before we leave this discussion of the postmodern view of reflexivity, the third of the authors would like to enter a note. We mentioned at the outset of this chapter that between the three of us there were sources of lively and interesting tension that have been bubbling around as we developed our work as colleagues and as co-authors. The author of the framework and main argument of Chapter 6 takes a view of postmodernism that attends to it as philosophy. The third of the authors understands this view, but is also much more determinedly realist about the matter. As I mentioned in Chapter 8 (for I am the realist) I see the origins of the modernist/postmodernist debate as coming from architecture and the arts. This contrast between what is essentially a philosophical take on post-modernism and the realist gaze came early in the development of the concept. Thus at about the same time that the writers in Reed and Hughes (1992) tend towards the philosophical, Clegg (1990) tends towards the realist. For the reflexive realist there are interesting issues. I was undertaking a seminar with our students on the Doctorate in Business Administration (all of them senior managers in the public and private sectors). We were discussing the depiction of modernism and postmodernism as discussed in Chapter 8. We started with the 'normal' managerial supposition that matters of structure – postmodern or modernist – are the prerogatives of management. Then we began to realise that in any organisation choices as to where to go for a modernist or a postmodernist design are a situational matter. Then we realised that what might well be important in achieving the maximal design features might be the local knowledge of the organisational members themselves. From that came a realisation that a more democratic approach to the ways in which members shape their organisational experience might be more satisfying for the members and be more useful for the organisation itself. Of course, this has implications for the manager. Stacey, on the concept of self-organisation, suggests that 'in organisational terms, the top executives have more power than others'. If, however, the members are able to respond to the communications and instructions from senior management 'according to their own local capacities, and their responses had some effect on the CEO, leading to further responses from the CEO, then this would be self organisation' (Stacey 2000: 335). The extent to which this interplay takes place would be an indicator of the relative democratisation of the design processes.

As we saw in Chapter 5, it is in Critical Theory that such a democratic mandate is most fully expressed. Here, due to their socio-rationalism, critical theorists will emphasise the role of epistemic reflexivity in enabling the construction of new interpretations and the achievement of consensus that engenders new forms of practice located in new versions of reality. It follows that knowing selection of one knowledge system as opposed to an alternative becomes an overt question of ethical priority which undermines the instrumental rationality critical theorists see to be prevalent in organisations.

Therefore epistemic reflexivity is seen as a resource which helps management researchers and practitioners recognise their own creative inputs and exposes the ethical priorities which construct what we know about management. This coincides with what Holland describes as the highest level of reflexive analysis, which is 'a method of evaluating existing systems of knowledge, tied in as they are to sectional interests and constellations of power. It invites re-entry into the epistemological and sectional complexities of our human condition to intervene, "knowingly" according to our ethical priorities' (1999: 476).

This self-comprehension demands a genealogy of their own discursive practices by management researchers and practitioners reflexively including themselves in any analysis so as to engender a consciousness of their own history, philosophy, aims, ethical priorities and practical implications. This issue pervades many of the chapters of this book. For example, we discussed in Chapter 8 the ways in which core issues of organisational design are pervaded by moral presuppositions, from a particular epoch, that underpinned management action during that particular period. The overriding reflexive concern is with how alternative modes of apprehending the world, constituted by those interests currently excluded by the engagements of much management theory and practice, might be democratically socially constructed. They can thereby fulfil an emancipatory potential by becoming the basis for socially transformative action (Friere 1972a and b).

So a key issue for critical theorists is that epistemic reflexivity reframes the management researcher's self-knowledge but does not lead to a 'better' and more 'accurate' account (see Melucci 1996). Rather by engendering the possibility of conscious variation of our constitutive assumptions epistemic reflexivity can denaturalise hegemonic accounts and can reclaim alternative accounts of the 'same' phenomena: 'transformative' redefinitions which thereby become available to transformative interventions (Alvesson 1996; Alvesson and Deetz 2000). It follows that our knowing selection of one knowledge system as opposed to an alternative becomes a question of ethical priority.

REFERENCES

Alvesson, M. (1996) *Communication, Power and Organization*, Berlin and New York: Walter de Gruyter.

Alvesson, M. and Deetz, S. (2000) *Doing Critical Management Research*, London: Sage.

Ashmore, M. (1989) *The Reflexive Thesis: Wrighting the Sociology of Scientific Knowledge*, Chicago: University of Chicago Press.

Beck, U. (1992) *The Risk Society: Towards a New Modernity*, Cambridge: Polity Press.

Beck, U. (1996) 'World Risk Society as Cosmopolitan Society? Ecological Questions in a Framework of Manufactured Uncertainties', *Theory Culture and Society*, 13(4): 1–32.

Bourdieu, P. (1990) *The Logic of Practice*, Cambridge: Polity Press.

Clegg, S.R. (1990) *Modern Organizations: Organization Studies in the Postmodern World*, London: Sage.

Deal, T.E. and A.A. Kennedy (1982) *Corporate Cultures. The Rites and Rituals of Corporate Life*, Reading, MA: Addison Wesley.

Delantey, G. (1997) *Social Science: Beyond Constructivism and Realism*, Buckingham: Open University Press.

Fay, B. (1987) *Critical Social Science*, Cambridge: Polity Press.

Friere, P. (1972a) *Pedagogy of the Oppressed*, Harmondsworth: Penguin.

Friere, P. (1972b) *Cultural Action for Freedom*, Harmondsworth: Penguin.

Fryer, D. and N.T. Feather (1994) 'Intervention Techniques', in C.M. Cassell and G. Symon (eds) *Qualitative Methods in Organizational Research: A Practical Guide*, London: Sage.

Grey, C. and N. Mitev (1995) 'Management Education: A Polemic', *Management Learning*, 26(1): 73–90.

Holland, R. (1999) 'Reflexivity', *Human Relations*, 52(4): 463–83.

Kilduff, M. and A. Mehra (1997) 'Postmodernism and Organizational Research', *Academy of Management Review*, 22(2): 453–81.

Latour, B. (1988) 'The Politics of Explanation: An Alternative', in S. Woolgar (ed.) *Knowledge and Reflexivity: New Frontiers in the Sociology of Knowledge*, London: Sage.

Linstead, S. (1993) 'Deconstruction in the Study of Organizations', in J. Hassard and M. Parker (eds) *Postmodernism and Organizations*, London: Sage.

Linstead, S. (1994) 'Objectivity, Reflexivity and Fiction: Inhumanity and the Science of the Social', *Human Relations*, 47: 1321–45.

Magliola, R. (1984) *Derrida on the Mend*, West Lafayette: Purdue University Press.

McAuley, M.J. (1980) 'The Analysis of "Culture" in Organisational Settings: Methodological and Substantive Problems in the Location of Shared Knowledge'. Unpublished thesis, University of Manchester.

Melucci, A. (1996) *Challenging Codes: Collective Action for the Information Age*, Cambridge: Cambridge University Press.

Morgan, G. (1986) *Images of Organization*, London: Sage.

Morgan, G. (1993) *Imaginization*, London: Sage.

Parker, M. (1993) 'Life after Jean-François', in J. Hassard and M. Parker (eds) *Postmodernism and Organizations*, London: Sage.

Pfeffer, J. (1992) *Managing with Power*, Boston, MA: Harvard Business School Press.

Pollner, M. (1991) 'Left of Ethnomethodology: The Rise and Decline of Radical Reflexivity', *American Sociological Review*, 56: 370–80.

Reason, P. and J. Rowan (1981) *Human Inquiry: A Sourcebook of New Paradigm Research*, Chichester: John Wiley.

Reed, M. and P.D. Anthony (1992) 'Professionalizing Management and Managing Professionalization: British Management in the 1980s', *Journal of Management Studies*, 29(5): 591–613.

Reed, M. and M. Hughes (1992) *Rethinking Organization: New Directions in Organizational Theory and Analysis*, London: Sage.

Ruse, M. (1999) *Mystery of Mysteries: Is Evolution a Social Construct?*, Cambridge, MA: Harvard University Press.

Sandywell, B. (1996) *Reflexivity and the Crisis of Western Reason: Logological Investigations, volume 1*, London: Routledge.

Schon, D.A. (1983) *The Reflexive Practitioner: How Professionals Think in Action*, London: Temple Smith.

Stacey, R.D. (2000, 2nd edition) *Strategic Management and Organisational Dynamics: The Challenge of Complexity*, Harlow: Financial Times/Prentice Hall.

Steers, R.M. (1987) 'Murray's Manifest Needs Theory', in R.M. Steers and L.W. Porter, *Motivation and Work Behavior* (4th edition), New York: McGraw-Hill.

Steier, F. (1991) *Research and Reflexivity*, London: Sage.

Whitley, R.D. (1984) 'The Scientific Status of Management Research as a Practically Orientated Social Science', *Journal of Management Studies*, 21(4): 369–90.

Whittington, R. (2001, 2nd edition) *What is Strategy – and Does it Matter?*, London: Thomson Learning.

Woolgar, S. (1988a) *Science: the Very Idea*, Chichester: Ellis Horwood.

Woolgar, S. (1988b) *Knowledge and Reflexivity: New Frontiers in the Sociology of Knowledge*, London: Sage.

Index